Designing Social Research

The Logic of Anticipation

Second Edition

Norman Blaikie

polity

Copyright © Norman Blaikie 2010

The right of Norman Blaikie to be identified as Author of this Work has been asserted in accordance with the UK Copyright, Designs and Patents Act 1988.

First edition published in 2000 by Polity Press
Published in 2009 by Polity Press
Reprinted 2010 (three times), 2011

Polity Press
65 Bridge Street
Cambridge CB2 1UR, UK

Polity Press
350 Main Street
Malden, MA 02148, USA

ISBN-13: 978-0-7456-4337-3
ISBN-13: 978-0-7456-4338-0(pb)

A catalogue record for this book is available from the British Library.

Typeset in 10 on 12 pt Sabon
by Servis Filmsetting Ltd, Stockport, Cheshire
Printed and bound by MPG Books Group, UK

The publisher has used its best endeavours to ensure that the URLs for external websites referred to in this book are correct and active at the time of going to press. However, the publisher has no responsibility for the websites and can make no guarantee that a site will remain live or that the content is or will remain appropriate.

Every effort has been made to trace all copyright holders, but if any have been inadvertently overlooked the publishers will be pleased to include any necessary credits in any subsequent reprint or edition.

For further information on Polity, visit our website: www.politybooks.com

Contents

Detailed Contents

List of Figures and Tables

Figures

Tables

Acknowledgements

I am extremely grateful to the hundreds of students who have taken my post-graduate research methods/methodology courses and workshops over the past twenty-five years. In the early days it was their struggles, uncertainties, excitement and feedback that helped me sharpen my own thinking and practices. Dealing with these led me to set out on the task of writing the first edition of this book over ten years ago. I am also indebted to a number of colleagues and friends, too numerous to mention here, who made suggestions and offered constructive comments on drafts of the first edition. Anonymous reviewers of both editions also made useful inputs leading to significant improvements. That I was unable (or unwilling) to accept all their ideas may be due to some stubbornness on my part, and certainly to the diversity in their comments. For this second edition, I am indebted to the folk at Polity Press, Emma Longstaff and Jonathan Skerrett, who saw the need for a second edition, twisted my arm to do it, and provided encouragement and support throughout the process. Their colleague, Clare Ansell, guided the production process efficiently and humanely, and Susan Beer brought some order and consistent style to my manuscript. Finally, I am profoundly grateful to Catherine who has both supported and tolerated me spending a large chunk of what is supposed to be our retirement on this time-consuming task.

The author and publishers are grateful to the following for permission to use copyright material:

Sage Publications for figure 5.2, from M. Waters, *Modern Sociological Theory,* London, 1994.

Introduction

It is a nuisance, but God has chosen to give the easy problems to the physicists.

(Lave and March 1975)

Purpose of the Book

Social research has three main phases: planning, execution and reporting. In some kinds of research, these three phases are discrete and follow this sequence. In other research, the three phases may blend into each other. This book is about the first phase, the designing of social research, not about the details of how to do it. Of course, the planning has to anticipate how the research will be done, and detailed knowledge of research methods is necessary at the planning stage in order to make good decisions.

Planning is vital in any kind of social research. Failure to plan is to run the risk of losing control of the project and failing to complete it successfully. The fact that some kinds of research require decisions to be made as the research proceeds is no excuse for avoiding careful planning at the outset. However, some preliminary or exploratory research may be needed to provide information for research design decisions.

A discussion of the core elements of a research design, and the connections between them, may look very much like the steps involved in doing social research. However, it is important to recognize the difference between the planning process, the execution of the research and the reconstruction of this process at the reporting phase. Kaplan (1964) has referred to the difference between 'logic in use' and 'reconstructed logic', between how research is done and how it is made to appear to have been done. The latter frequently converts a somewhat messy process into an apparently ordered and controlled one. This is particularly true of field research or ethnography.

> In the research worker's mind little did happen the way it is put down on paper, in terms of substance and sequence. What was ultimately assembled and ascertained got

caught in the familiar bouts of rationalizations that straighten out a zig-zag approach and turn the entire study into a well-organized logical design with a beginning and a rounded-off ending. (Hutheesing 1990: 10)

I wish to add the 'logic of anticipation' to Kaplan's two categories, i.e. the process of planning how the research will be conducted. Of course, it is always possible that the logic of anticipation cannot be followed in its entirety; changes may be required as unanticipated obstacles are encountered and the researcher's understanding of the phenomenon increases. I suspect that many researchers write up their projects to make them look as if they began with an anticipated logic when, perhaps, there was none, or it was poorly formulated.

From my observations of academics and postgraduate students over many years, a common approach to social research is to just muddle through. It is rare to encounter a fully developed research design that has been prepared before serious research begins. Novice researchers may be unaware of the dangers in not planning thoroughly, and, without appropriate guidance, may end up with very precarious, sometimes disastrous, outcomes. It is hard enough to do good social research without building in limitations due to poor planning. Hakim (2000: 2) has argued that while individual researchers may be able to muddle through, 'large-scale studies, contract research for central government and other organizations, studies involving multi-disciplinary teams, and research programmes that involve a range of studies concerned with a central topic or set of issues' require highly visible designs at the beginning. I can agree with the latter but not with the former. Individual researchers also need to plan their research carefully.

This book is more than a review of the literature in the field of social research, and research design in particular. It presents a point of view on how and why research designs should be prepared and the key elements that need to be included. It argues that social research should address research questions and that these questions are answered by selecting one or more logics of enquiry (research strategies). It also stresses that as researchers cannot avoid adopting certain ontological and epistemological assumptions, it is important that these be made explicit, not only to help the researcher be consistent in the research design decisions, but also to assist consumers of the research to understand and interpret the findings. Only after the problem, research question(s), strategy or strategies and the assumptions are stated should the choice of methods of data collection and analysis be considered.

While many of the research design elements discussed in this book may be dealt with in general textbooks on social research methods, their treatment is usually rather superficial. The concern of these texts is usually to introduce undergraduate students to the techniques of collecting and analysing data. While knowledge of these techniques is necessary, choices from among them have to relate to more fundamental aspects of research, particularly the research questions that are to be answered and the research strategies that will be used to answer them.

This book should be read alongside my *Approaches to Social Enquiry* (2007), which deals with the philosophy of social research. Topics that are common to the two books are dealt with only briefly here.

The Audiences

I have written this book primarily for social science postgraduate students who are setting out on an empirical research project for a thesis or dissertation. By 'an empirical research project' I mean research that attempts to produce answers to research questions by collecting and/or analysing empirical data related to some aspects of social life. The book is not intended for students who are undertaking purely theoretical theses, i.e. those that involve the review, critique or integration of existing theory, or projects that rely entirely on existing literature as a resource. However, parts of it may be useful to students who are undertaking historical studies, although this will depend on the particular style of historical research.

The target audience includes students in disciplines such as sociology, anthropology, social psychology and political science, and interdisciplinary fields such as social work, social geography, educational studies, communications, nursing studies, planning, business studies, management and development studies. While I hope that economics and psychology students will also find it useful, I am very aware that coming from my background in sociology, with its own peculiar range of approaches to social research, I may be meeting these latter two disciplines at a limited number of points. Nevertheless, my hope is that the book might help to broaden the view of research normally adopted in these disciplines.

The book is also intended for academics, particularly those who are new to the role of postgraduate research supervision. It is not intended as a guide to that role but as a framework for assisting students to prepare a research design and/or a research proposal. It will also be useful for academics who involve their undergraduate students in individual and group research projects.

What I have to offer is the result of my own peculiar experiences in teaching courses in research methodology to postgraduate students; in teaching research methods, statistics, and the philosophy of social science to undergraduate students; in supervising the research of many postgraduate students and groups of undergraduate students; and in undertaking my own research. In the early days, these postgraduate students and I struggled to formulate research designs and proposals with limited help from available textbooks.

The process of formulating a research design is probably the most difficult part of social research. Over the years, I have developed ways of helping students through this process. This book is an attempt to explicate these strategies and techniques.

There are no doubt many ways in which this task can be undertaken. Some versions will be related to the discipline-based views within which the research is occurring, while others will relate to a particular individual's preferences or views of research. It is not possible to write a book that will satisfy the preferences of all social researchers; the field is too diverse and many of the differences may be irreconcilable. While I have set out to challenge some of the positions that I regard as being unsatisfactory, I have also tried to be eclectic enough to satisfy a range of social research styles. However, my prejudices will no doubt show from time to time.

I used the first edition of this book extensively in courses and workshops with students from a wide variety of disciplines and from a number of countries. This has given it a very good testing. In addition to my experience in using it, I have had very favourable reports from many other lecturers about its value for their students. The general consensus is that it requires only minor changes and updating.

Writing the Book

Except for a brief period in the United States, my academic career has been pursued away from the main centres of social science activity. It began and has been conducted mainly on the furthermost fringes of the southern hemisphere, in the South Island of New Zealand and the southernmost tip of the Australian continent. There have been both advantages and disadvantages in occupying this marginal position. While work on the book began in this remote region of the world, the bulk of the writing of the first edition was done on the tropical island of Penang in South-East Asia. It was stimulated initially by problems encountered in teaching a compulsory postgraduate research methods/methodology course at the then Royal Melbourne Institute of Technology, now RMIT University. Students setting out on research for a master's or PhD degree by social research, for either a major or minor thesis/dissertation, were required to take this course. A few of these students came from social science disciplines such as sociology and political science. However, most came from disciplines and programmes such as psychology, social work, communications, history, planning, economics, accountancy and management, and even engineering, industrial design, information systems, computer science, and the fine arts. The only thing they shared in common was that their research topic required them to undertake some kind of *social* research. They were mostly older students who were returning to study on a part-time basis. Many had little idea, or had very confused views, about how social research is conducted, let alone how to design a research project. They also had little or no understanding of or exposure to social theory and issues in the philosophy of social science.

In the brief span of a semester, my task was to prepare these students to undertake a social research project. This has involved:

- introducing them to logics of social enquiry;
- providing them with some acquaintance with the role of social theory in research;
- providing them with a critical understanding of the range of major research methods; and
- helping them prepare a research design.

My *Approaches to Social Enquiry* (Blaikie 1993a) was written to satisfy the first two of these requirements; a second edition is now available (Blaikie 2007). There is no shortage of books that cover the third requirement. This book is intended to cover the fourth requirement.

From 1996 to 2001 I had the opportunity to teach a similar course, twice a year, to masters by research students in the social sciences and masters of public administration students, at the Universiti Sains (University of Science) Malaysia. I discovered that their needs and concerns were almost identical to those of students in Melbourne. Again, their academic backgrounds were diverse and many were older students. Most had no experience in doing social research and most had no idea of how to go about designing a research project. They provided me with the opportunity to try out the chapters of the first edition in lecture format, and their responses and feedback had a big impact on the its content and structure. Since resigning from my position, I have returned to this university on two occasions to run workshops with postgraduate students in the social sciences and many other disciplines and programmes. These experiences have led to further refinements.

While the structure and content of the book have been influenced considerably by teaching these courses, it has also emerged from supervising postgraduate students over many years, from twice being a postgraduate research student myself, and, subsequently, from my own experience in conducting research. All this has produced some firm convictions, including:

- the need to design social research in detail;
- the fundamental importance of research questions to provide focus and direction;
- the need to be clear about the differences in the research strategies (logics of enquiry) available in the social sciences, and to know how and when to use them;
- being aware of different ontological and epistemological assumptions behind these research strategies and how these impinge on research practice and outcomes;
- being very clear on what is involved in sampling;
- avoiding the misuse of tests of significance;
- knowing how case studies can be used;
- understanding the relationship between quantitative and qualitative methods; and
- being aware of the legitimate ways in which research strategies and methods can be combined.

This is a somewhat idiosyncratic list, and my views on these points might also be regarded by some in the same way. I make no apology for this. I can only hope that the positions I have adopted will either ring bells with some readers, or stimulate others to re-evaluate their taken-for-granted positions.

Two underlying principles have been used in writing the book. The first is to introduce the reader to new ideas and activities in stages, with each successive encounter taking the idea further. The second principle is to revisit an idea or activity from different points of view, or from the points of view of different themes. The decision to adopt these principles was based on my experience in teaching this material. I also believe that it is good pedagogy. Therefore, if you experience repetition as you work your way through the book, you will know that it is intentional.

Structure of the Book

The book reviews and elaborates the main elements that need to be addressed in preparing a research design. It focuses on the critical decisions on each element and the options that are available. The path covers both conventional and unconventional ground.

Chapter 1 sets out the requirements for a research design and anticipates the major elements to be discussed in detail in the following chapters. It also distinguishes between research designs and research proposals in terms of their purposes and the audiences to whom they are directed. In brief, a research design is a working document used by a researcher and close associates, while a research proposal is used mainly to obtain academic approval for a research project or to apply for research funds.

Chapter 2 begins with a review of conventional views on designing research in the social sciences, and the types of designs that are commonly discussed. An alternative view is then proposed in which the fundamental requirements and the eight core elements are elaborated. The implication of this view is that there is a wide variety of possible research designs rather than just a limited set. This variety is produced by the range of possible combinations of choices that can be made on each of the core elements. This is followed by a discussion of how to get started on a research design by stating the research problem to be investigated and formulating the topic. Some consideration is given to the possible influences on this process. The chapter concludes with a discussion of the differences between basic and applied research, and the various stances a researcher can take towards research and the researched.

The major design elements are dealt with in chapters 3 to 7. Chapter 3 commences with a discussion of the nature, role and development of research questions. This is followed by an elaboration of research purposes, and the links between research questions, and research purposes, hypotheses and the literature review. The rest of the book stands on the foundations laid in this chapter.

Chapter 4 outlines the four research strategies that are available to advance social scientific knowledge. Research strategies provide alternative procedures for answering research questions. Each strategy sets out a logic of enquiry, a series of steps for establishing knowledge about some part of the social world. The strategies embody particular combinations of ontological and epistemological assumptions, which provide a view of social reality and ideas on how knowledge can be generated. Researchers need to choose one or more research strategies to help them provide answers to their research questions. The choice of research strategy, or strategies, in conjunction with the research questions, will have a major influence on the decisions to be taken on the remaining design elements, and will largely determine the way the research proceeds. This chapter also includes a brief review of a range of ontological and epistemological positions and the research paradigms with which these and the research strategies are associated.

In chapter 5, four of the more complex and perplexing aspects of designing and undertaking research are explored: the role of concepts, theories, hypotheses and models. Different views of the role of concepts are discussed, followed by an examination of what constitutes 'theory' and a review of some classical and contemporary views on the relationship between theory and research. This leads to an examination of the major views on the use of models in social research. To conclude, the role of concepts, theories and models in the four research strategies is reviewed.

The next two chapters cover the more technical aspects of social research. Chapter 6 deals with the sources of and methods for selecting data: it examines the types and forms in which data are produced in the social sciences; it discusses the variety of contexts from which data can be obtained; it compares the techniques used to select data, particularly sampling methods; and it concludes with a critical review of the role of case studies.

Methods for collecting, reducing and analysing data are explored in chapter 7. This begins with a discussion of the important role that the timing of data collection has in determining the nature of a research design. Many discussions of research design focus almost exclusively on this element and its relationship to experimental procedures. In this book, timing is related particularly to data collection; decisions about it will follow from the form of particular research questions. The bulk of the chapter centres on the qualitative/quantitative distinction and the use of mixed methods. The chapter does not include a discussion of the actual techniques or methods used in social science research. Instead, attention is given to the links between research strategies and methods. The main argument is that while research strategies entail ontological assumptions, methods do not. In other words, at least some methods can be used in the service of different research strategies, and, hence, different ontological assumptions.

The final chapter presents four sample research designs on a set of related research topics, using the full range of research strategies. These designs are based on my own research programme, but modified to suit the present purposes. The intention of the designs is to illustrate how the individual choices about each of the core design elements can be brought together into a cohesive package.

The Nature of Science in the Social Sciences

It is a common practice in introductory books on sociology and social research methods to include a brief discussion of 'the scientific method' (see e.g. Chadwick *et al.* 1984; Kidder and Judd 1986; Sedlack and Stanley 1992; Ellis 1994; Kumar 2005; Neuman 2006). This usually includes an outline of a set of criteria that must be satisfied if social research is to be regarded as scientific. Unfortunately, many of these discussions perpetuate outdated notions of both science and social research. What is required is a discussion of the different research strategies, or logics of enquiry, that are available in the natural and social sciences.

It is not possible here to engage in a discussion of the nature of science. There is now an extensive literature on this topic, as well as on whether and, if so, how social science can be a science. (See e.g. Chalmers 1982; O'Hear 1989; and Riggs 1992 on the natural sciences, and Giddens 1976; Williams and May 1996; Hughes and Sharrock 1997; Smith 1998; and Blaikie 2007 on science in the social sciences.) However, the elaboration of the research strategies in chapter 4 will deal with some aspects of these issues.

This latter discussion is intended, among other things, to show that there are four possible views of science in the social sciences. Three of the logics that have been used in the natural and physical sciences have been advocated, by different scientific communities, as also being appropriate for the social sciences. In addition, there is another logic, with many versions, that has been presented as being exclusive to, and, according to some writers, the only one appropriate for, the social sciences.

For over one hundred years, advocates of these four views of social science have engaged in heated debates about their relative merits. The debates continue to rage. For those readers unfamiliar with these views and debates, all that is necessary for the moment is to recognize that there is no such thing as *the* scientific method, that there is a variety of logics of enquiry available in the social sciences, and that, in order to conduct social research, it is necessary to choose from among them. These logics, and the considerations relevant to choosing between them, form an integral part of what follows.

Key Concepts

This discussion of research design uses five key concepts: research questions, purposes, strategies, paradigms and methods. The first concept, *research questions*, should be uncontroversial. It refers to the questions researchers pose and which they try to answer by undertaking social research. While this is a straightforward idea, it is surprising how much research is conducted without them. Aims, objective and hypotheses are more commonly used. A core argument running through this book is that well formulated research questions are the peg on which all research activities hang.

The second concept, *research purposes*, identifies the types of knowledge a researcher wishes to produce, such as, descriptions and explanations. Research purposes are closely related to research questions as each of the three types of questions, 'what', 'why' and 'how', produces a particular type of knowledge. While 'aims' and 'objectives' are in common usage in texts on research design and methods, for the most part I have avoided using them. If attention is given to research questions and purposes, I consider 'aims' and 'objectives' to be superfluous in the process of designing social research. However, it may be necessary to discuss them in a research proposal (see chapter 1) to satisfy local requirements.

I used 'research objectives' in the first edition for what is now called *research purposes*. The reason for the change is to, hopefully, avoid confusion with the various uses of 'objectives' in the literature, and to focus on the type of knowledge that is desired rather than the activities to be undertaken or the goals to be achieved. Research questions identify what the research wishes to achieve, and a research design should make it very clear what activities are to be undertaken.

The fifth concept, *research methods*, is also not controversial. It is used here to include the procedures and activities for selecting, collecting, organizing and analysing data. Numerous texts cover this part of social research and many research methods texts cover very little else. Another core argument here is that the choice of methods occurs late in the process of designing social research. A number of fundamental decisions have to be made before methods of investigation can be considered. To focus attention on methods is to ignore the serious thinking and planning that needs to occur beforehand.

The third and fourth of these concepts, *research strategies* and *research paradigms*, require some clarification. I have coined 'research strategy' to identify a feature of social research that is usually overlooked, i.e. the logic used to generate new knowledge. This issue has received a great deal of attention in the philosophy of science literature and has generated much controversy. In this book and elsewhere (Blaikie 2007) I have identified four main logics of enquiry that are available to social researchers. This use of 'research strategies' needs to be distinguished from other more general uses, such as types of research design or methods of data collection and analysis.

An important aspect of a research strategy is the assumptions made about the nature of social reality and the ways in which we can come to know that reality, i.e. ontological and epistemological assumptions, respectively. Following the discussion of the four research strategies in chapter 4, six types of both ontological and epistemological assumptions are reviewed, based on my discussion of them elsewhere (Blaikie 2007). When you encounter this discussion, it is important to recognize that the range of types and the labels I have used for them, while following the literature in this field, include some types and concepts that I have devised to help elaborate the research strategies.

My use of the concept *research paradigm* may cause some controversy and confusion. Following the introduction of the concept of 'paradigm' into the literature of the history and philosophy of science by Thomas Kuhn (1970), and its application to sociology by Robert Friedrichs (1970), this concept has attracted a variety of usages and has since entered the popular vocabulary. I use *research paradigm* here in a manner that is consistent with some of Kuhn's uses. It refers to major traditions in the natural and social sciences that incorporate particular ontological and epistemological assumptions and one or more of the research strategies. Some also incorporate general theoretical ideas. The four classical and seven contemporary research paradigms that I have identified (see also Blaikie 2007) provide theoretical and methodological contexts within which research is frequently conducted. Some researchers adhere dogmatically to one of the paradigms for all their research, while others are comfortable with selecting a research paradigm to suit the research questions being investigated. This set of research paradigms reflects progressions and fashions in ways of thinking about ontology and epistemology, they reflect debates by protagonists from diverse points of view, some have been subjected to such severe criticism that they are unlikely to be considered to be useful, while others have been adhered to dogmatically.

In the first edition of *Approaches to Social Enquiry* (1993a) I used 'approaches' rather than *research paradigms*. I changed this in the second edition (2007) as I found the former concept to be rather too broad and it did not identify the features that the concept *paradigm* incorporates. Again, it is important to note that this latter concept has a specific meaning here and should not be confused with other usages.

A Manifesto for Social Research

The approach to social research taken in this book deviates in a number of ways from conventional wisdom and the views of social research expounded in many standard texts on the subject. Rather than leave the reader to discover these differences in the body of the text, I am setting them out here as assertions.

1 Social research is about answering research questions.
2 Three types of research questions can be asked: 'what', 'why' and 'how'.
3 All research questions can be reduced to these three types.
4 Social research can also address one or more of the following purposes: exploration, description, understanding, explanation, prediction, intervention (change), evaluation and impact assessment.
5 'Why' questions are concerned with understanding or explanation. 'How' questions are concerned with intervention. All other purposes involve the use of 'what' questions.
6 Hypotheses are possible answers to 'why' and some 'how' questions. They are normally expressed as statements of relationships between two concepts. Hypotheses direct the researcher to collect particular data.
7 'What' questions do not require hypotheses. Nothing is gained from hazarding an answer to a question that simply requires a description.
8 Research questions are answered by the use of four research strategies: Inductive, Deductive, Retroductive and Abductive (see Blaikie 2007).
9 The major characteristics of the research strategies are as follows: the Inductive strategy produces generalizations from data; the Deductive strategy tests theories by testing hypotheses derived from them; the Retroductive strategy proposes causal mechanisms or structures and tries to establish their existence; and the Abductive strategy generates social scientific accounts from everyday accounts.
10 When a research project includes a variety of research questions, more than one research strategy may be required to answer them.
11 Because research strategies entail different ontological and epistemological assumptions, they may only be combined in sequence.
12 Hypotheses are used mainly in the Deductive research strategy as part of the process of theory testing. While the testing of hypotheses commonly involves the use of quantitative methods, it need not do so. The Deductive strategy can also use qualitative methods, in which case hypothesis testing is more in terms of a discursive argument from evidence.
13 The Abductive research strategy may use hypotheses in the course of generating theory, but in a different way to the Deductive strategy. These hypotheses are possible answers to questions that emerge as the research proceeds, and are used to direct subsequent stages of the research.
14 The hypothetical models of possible causal structures or mechanisms that are developed in the Retroductive research strategy are not hypotheses. The researcher's task is to establish whether a postulated structure or mechanism exists and operates in the manner suggested.
15 Social science data normally start out in qualitative form, in words rather

than numbers. They may continue in this form throughout a research project or be transformed into numbers, at the outset, or during the course of the analysis. Ultimately, research reports have to be presented in words. When numbers are used, they need to be interpreted in words.

16 The use of tests of significance is only appropriate when data have been generated from a probability sample. These tests establish whether the characteristics or relationships in a sample could be expected in the population from which it was drawn. Tests of significance are inappropriate when non-probability samples are used, and are irrelevant when data come from a population.

17 As methods of data collection and analysis can be used in the service of different ontological assumptions, there is no necessary connection between research strategies and methods.

18 Methods of data collection can be combined, in parallel or in sequence. However, it is only legitimate to combine methods in parallel when they are used with the same or similar ontological assumptions. That is, data generated in the service of different ontological assumptions cannot be combined, only compared. It *is* legitimate to combine methods in sequence, regardless of their ontological assumptions. In this case, it is necessary to be aware of the implications of switching between assumptions.

19 Case studies are neither research designs nor methods of data collection. They constitute a method of data selection, and, as such, require particular procedures for generalizing from the results produced.

20 The results of all social research are limited in time and space. Hence, making generalizations beyond a particular time and place is a matter of judgement. While quantitative data from a probability sample can be statistically generalized to the population from which the sample was drawn, this type of research is in the same position as any other when it comes to moving beyond that population.

I trust that you will find the following arguments in support of these assertions to be both stimulating and convincing.

1

Preparing Research Designs

Chapter Summary

- A *research design* is a private working document that is prepared by a researcher or a research team before a research project is undertaken. It incorporates all the decisions that need to be made and provides justifications for these decisions. This should ensure that the decisions are consistent and it exposes them to critical evaluation. These decisions include:
  - the selection of the research problem and the researcher's motives and goals for investigating it;
  - the research question(s) that will address the problem and the purposes associated with it/them;
  - the choice of research strategy (logic of enquiry) to investigate each research question and justifications for these choices;
  - elaboration of the ontological and epistemological assumptions on which the research will be founded;
  - an outline of the research paradigm or paradigms within which the research will be conducted;
  - an elaboration of relevant concepts and theory and how they relate to the research process;
  - if relevant, a statement of the hypothesis or hypotheses to be tested, or an elaboration of the mechanisms to be investigated;
  - a discussion of data sources, types and forms;
  - a discussion of methods for selecting data from these sources;
  - an outline of the methods of data collection, reduction and analysis to be used;
  - and a discussion of the problems that might be encountered and the limitations of the design in its ability to answer the research questions.
- In contrast, a *research proposal* is a public document that is used to obtain necessary approvals for the research to proceed, including from an appropriate ethics committee, or for research funding applications. It addresses different audiences from a research design. While it includes many of the components in the associated research design, some of these may be presented in a different form. In addition, it will include the following:

o a statement of the aims and significance of the research (rather then researcher's motives and goals);
o some background that will justify the need to address the research problem;
o a budget and justifications for each item in it;
o a timetable for each stage of the research process;
o a statement of expected outcomes and benefits;
o identification of ethical issues and how they will be handled;
o and an indication of how the findings will be communicated to relevant audiences.

Introduction

The ultimate purpose in exploring the issues and processes covered in the following chapters is to facilitate the preparation of a detailed research design. In order to understand these processes, I shall begin by setting out some guidelines for the structure and content of a research design and compare this with the requirements for research proposals. While *research designs* and *research proposals* overlap considerably in their requirements, they are intended for different audiences. There is also likely to be a sequence to their development; the former informing the latter.

A *research design* is a technical document that is developed by one or more researchers and is used by them as a guide or plan for carrying out a research project. Decisions that need to be made at the beginning, or soon after some exploratory work has been completed, are stated, justified, related and evaluated. The aim is to:

• make these decisions explicit;
• spell out why they have been made;
• ensure that they are consistent with each other; and
• allow for critical evaluation.

In postgraduate[1] research, a research design is a working document that may be the outcome of courses in research methodology and methods, and the dialogue between student and supervisor/adviser. It should be the constant point of reference and guide throughout the research. If it is necessary to make changes as the research proceeds, or if it is necessary to allow some elements of the research design to evolve in the course of the research, this will happen in the context of the initial set of research design decisions. Amendments will need to achieve the same consistency between the research design elements.

Research proposals have different purposes and audiences. They can be used for:

• making public presentations and receiving feedback;
• obtaining official approval from appropriate university authorities for the project to proceed, including endorsement by a human ethics committee; or
• applying for research grants.

While research designs involve making and reporting a range of choices about *what* is to be studied and *how* it will be studied, research proposals require much more emphasis on *why* the research is to be conducted, including what it will contribute to knowledge and/or practical outcomes, and *why* it has been designed in a particular way. Where research funding is applied for, a proposal needs to state *what* funding is required for each aspect of the research and *why* it needs that level of funding.

Because research proposals have a number of purposes, they can be prepared in a number of versions. In addition, some information may be in a different form to that of research designs, and additional details may be required. A research proposal may be less technical than a research design, in that it may not include all the details of the decisions and justifications related to each design element. When a research proposal is intended for public presentation, it may include more details on it. Hence, it is likely to be a longer and a more discursive document than a research design. On the other hand, an application to a committee for approval of the project may be much briefer, and may emphasize the justification for the research and the more technical aspects of data sources, collection and analysis. An application for research funds may be similar to an approval version, but will usually require a detailed budget and justification for the various categories of expenditure.

Before proceeding to outline the requirements for research designs and, to a lesser extent, research proposals, I must point out that I am trying not to be prescriptive (although I certainly have been with my own students!). Rather, I offer two frameworks that will no doubt need to be adapted to local requirements and practices. In some situations, maybe only one document is required; in other situations, the distinctions between them may be drawn differently. My purpose is to identify the many elements that should be considered, and about which decisions may need to be made, in planning social research.

Two other important points need to be made at this stage. The first concerns the common view that social research consists of a set of linear stages. These stages commonly include the formulation of the problem, the statement of hypotheses, the development of measuring instruments (e.g. an attitude scale or a questionnaire), the selection of a sample, the collection of the data, the analysis of the data, and the preparation of the report (see e.g. Bailey 1994; Babbie 2004; Kumar 2005). I believe that such conceptions are not only simplistic but are also inappropriate for certain kinds of research.

In much the same way, the process of designing social research may also be represented as a linear sequence of decisions. While some of the diagrams used in this book could be interpreted in this way, I want to stress that, in practice, the preparation of a research design is likely to involve many iterations, and, like many types of research, is a cyclical rather than a linear process. Because the elements of a design must be intimately related, the process of making any decision will have an impact on other decisions. For example, early decisions may need to be reviewed and changed in the light of problems encountered in making later decisions, and decisions may need to be changed when the design is reviewed for consistency. In short, a complex process is required to make the various decisions consistent and compatible.

The second point is concerned with the view that all research design decisions need to be made before the research begins in earnest. In my view, every effort should be made to do this. The discipline of having to confront and make the decisions will be beneficial in the long run. To avoid doing this could mean losing control of the research, and, ultimately, failure to complete it satisfactorily. However, this ideal needs to be tempered with some practicalities. It is necessary to recognize that research designs differ in the extent to which it is possible to finalize all the design decisions before the major stages of a project commence. In some research projects, what is learnt at one stage of the research will help to determine what will be done at a later stage. Exploratory research projects, and those concerned with theory generation rather than testing, may have this character. Some research projects may require exploratory and developmental work in order to be able to make important research design decisions. In fact, to fail to do this may jeopardize the project. This exploratory work will usually occur at the beginning, but may have to be undertaken later, particularly if unanticipated problems are encountered. Therefore, while it is important to strive for the ideal of a fully worked out research design before serious research begins, the realities of a particular project must be taken into consideration.

It is inevitable that research projects will differ in the time needed to prepare the research design; some research topics are just more complex than others, or may be venturing into relatively uncharted territory. Hence, the time and effort required to produce a research design is usually much greater when a researcher starts a project from scratch, rather than by joining a research team or by picking up a project to which others have already made significant contributions. It seems to be a common feature of postgraduate research in the social sciences that students are expected to, or wish to, define and develop their own project. Consequently, the design stage of postgraduate social science research is more demanding and time-consuming than it appears to be in the natural and physical sciences. In the latter disciplines, students frequently become part of a research team, or make a contribution to their supervisor's research programme.

Research Designs

A research design is an integrated statement of and justification for the technical decisions involved in planning a research project. As already indicated, ideally, designing social research is the process of making all decisions related to the research project before they are carried out. This involves anticipating all aspects of the research, then planning for them to occur in an integrated manner. Designing a research project is the way in which control is achieved.

> To design is to plan; that is, design is the process of making decisions before the situation arises in which the decision has to be carried out. It is a process of deliberate anticipation directed toward bringing an expected situation under control. . . . If, before we conduct an inquiry, we anticipate each research problem and decide what to do before-hand, then we increase our chances for controlling the research procedure. (Ackoff 1953: 5)

This process is analogous to the activities of an architect in designing a building: it involves recording, relating and then evaluating the decisions that need to be made. Careful attention to detail, and a concern with the overall workability of the design, is required. Designing social research involves the same processes. In particular, it is necessary to make sure that individual design decisions are consistent and fit together. These decisions then need to be evaluated critically, and, to do this, the design decisions need to be made explicit. This book is about how to achieve this.

The components of a research design can be organized in many ways. The following framework is presented as an example of what the structure of a research design might look like. (Examples of four different research designs are presented in chapter 8.)

Title

The title or topic of a research project needs to be both concise and informative. It should capture the essence of what the project will be about and where and with whom it will be conducted. It is sometimes useful to divide the statement of the topic into two parts: the first part can refer to the issue under investigation; and the second part can locate the study. (See chapter 8 and the Appendix for examples of the wording of research topics.)

While it is useful to have a clear statement of the topic at the beginning of the research design process, this is not always possible. Not only is the nature of the research likely to be clarified during the course of preparing the research design, but also the best title may not emerge until after the research is completed. Therefore, it is unwise to waste time at the beginning trying to get the wording perfect. As we shall see, it is better to concentrate on stating the research problem clearly, and preparing the research questions and other elements of the design, and then return to the title later.

Research problem

A research problem is an intellectual puzzle that the researcher wants to investigate. The statement of the problem will normally consist of a few concise paragraphs. It may include reference to some literature, such as reports of previous research in the field and related areas, both academic and non-academic, theoretical discussions, official statistics, and, perhaps, newspaper articles. It might be informed by the findings of prior exploratory research.

A research design may set out with more than one problem or a related set of puzzles. As the work on the design proceeds, a choice of the one to be investigated will need to be made. To recapitulate, a research proposal is the product of a developmental process that is likely to involve a number of iterations. While it is important to try to get ideas on the topic clear as soon as possible, as with the title, it is possible that a precise statement of the problem cannot be formulated at the beginning of the design process. It is more likely to evolve as the design develops and may only become clear towards the end of the process. In addition, it is often necessary to make changes to the statement of the problem as the research proceeds (see chapter 2, 'Getting Started').

Motives and goals

The research design is the place where a researcher's personal motives and goals for undertaking the research can be stated. Academic researchers, including postgraduate students, will have personal reasons for choosing a particular topic. Personal reasons might include satisfying curiosity, solving a personal problem, achieving a credential or pursuing career goals. In addition, a researcher may have other more public or altruistic reasons, such as making a contribution to knowledge in a discipline, solving some social problem, or contributing to the welfare of some organization or a sector of society. Making these motives and goals explicit is a useful exercise and is often quite revealing.

Research questions and purposes

Research questions constitute the most important element of any research design. It is to answering them that the research activities are directed. Decisions about all other aspects of the research design are contingent on their contribution to this. In many ways, *the formulation of research questions is the real starting-point in the preparation of a research design.*

Research questions are essential and need to be stated clearly and concisely. They can be reduced to three main types: 'what', 'why' and 'how' questions. It is important to distinguish between these types of questions as they are related to different research purposes. In general, 'what' questions seek descriptions, 'why' questions seek explanations or understanding, and 'how' questions are concerned with interventions to bring about change.

In my view, it is not necessary to state aims or objectives in a research design. Research questions provide a better way of expressing what a research project is trying to achieve. However, aims and objectives have been included in the guidelines for research *proposals* as stating them is a useful way of communicating to various audiences what the research is about. In a research *design*, consideration might be given to listing research *purposes* instead. These are defined in a more technical way and specify what the research is intended to achieve: it may be to 'explore', 'describe', 'explain', 'understand', 'predict', 'change', 'evaluate' or 'assess the social impact of' some aspect(s) of the phenomenon under investigation. Such purposes help to define the scope of a study, and, together with the research questions, provide a clear direction.

Review of the literature

A research design should include a brief literature review. Its major function is to link the proposed research to the current state of relevant knowledge. Many areas of literature may need to be examined, for example, to provide the background and justification for the research, and to select theory, research strategies and methods. However, this section of the research design should *indicate clearly what is known from previous research about each of the research questions, or what could be anticipated in the light of existing social theory.* In the case of research for a thesis, a longer version will need to be produced and will probably become a chapter on this. Work on this will usually continue through-out the duration of the research. However, only a summary is normally included here.

The research questions can provide the framework for both this brief literature review and the chapter in the thesis; they determine the boundaries of what is relevant. Literature that is unrelated to a research question need not be included. Using this device can save endless hours of directionless activity in libraries.

Of course, consulting previous research and relevant theory may have inspired the project in the first place, or it may need to be consulted to define the research problem and develop the research questions. In addition, the language used to define and discuss the problem, and the key concepts that are used, are likely to be drawn from some theoretical perspective, the work of a particular theorist or a research programme.

Another purpose of the literature review is to find possible answers to research questions, particularly 'why' questions. In other words, we may need to search for possible hypotheses. If hypotheses are considered to be necessary, ideally they should be derived from a theory, either an existing one that will be included in the literature review (and might later form the basis of a separate theory chapter), or one that the researcher has constructed for the research at hand. The latter will normally modify an existing theory, or integrate ideas from a number of theories. There is always the remote possibility that the review of the literature will reveal that answers to all or some of the research questions are already available and that the research project is, therefore, unnecessary. Another topic will then have to be selected. For practical guides on preparing literature reviews see Hart (1998) and Fink (2005), as well as books on writing theses/dissertations, for example, Murray (2002), Kamler and Thomson (2006) and Hartley (2008) (see chapter 3, this volume, 'Research questions and the literature review', p.68).

Research strategies

Research strategies provide a logic, or a set of procedures, for answering research questions, particularly 'what' and 'why' questions. As the social sciences have developed, a number of ways of doing this have emerged.

In my view, the choice of research strategy, or a combination of them, con-stitutes *the second most important research design decision*. The reason for this is that I believe knowledge can only be advanced in the social sciences by using one or a combination of four research strategies, the Inductive, Deductive, Retroductive and Abductive (see Blaikie 2007).

In brief, the four research strategies provide distinctly different ways of answer-ing research questions. They present alternative starting- and concluding-points, and different sets of steps between these points. The Inductive research strategy starts with the collection of data and then proceeds to derive generalizations using some kind of inductive logic. The aim is to describe social characteristics and the nature of regularities, or networks of regularities, in social life. This strategy is essential for answering 'what' questions but rather limited in its capacity to answer 'why' questions.

The Deductive research strategy cannot be used to answer 'what' questions but is used exclusively for answering 'why' questions. Hence, it adopts a very different starting-point to the Inductive strategy and is concerned with explaining some social regularity that has been discovered and which is not understood. The researcher has to find or formulate a possible explanation, a theoretical argument for the existence of the behaviour or the social phenomenon under consideration. The task is to test that theory, by deducing one or more hypotheses from it, and then to collect appropriate data. Should the data match the theory, some support will be provided for its continuing use, particularly if further tests produce similar results. However, if the data do not match the theory, the theory must be either modified or rejected. Further testing of other candidate theories can then be undertaken. Therefore, according to this research strategy, knowledge of the social world is advanced by means of a trial and error process.

The Retroductive research strategy also starts with an observed regularity but seeks a different type of explanation. In this strategy, explanation is achieved by locating the real underlying structure or mechanism(s) that is/are responsible for producing the observed regularity, and identifying the context in which this happens. As structures and mechanisms may not be directly observable, it may be necessary to search for evidence of the consequences of their existence; should they exist, certain events can be expected to occur. Retroduction uses creative imagination and analogy to work back from data to an explanation.

The Abductive research strategy has a very different logic to the other three. The starting-point is the social world of the social actors being investigated: their construction of reality, their way of conceptualizing and giving meaning to their social world, their tacit knowledge. This can only be discovered from the accounts social actors provide. Their reality, the way they have constructed and interpreted their activities together, is embedded in their language. Hence, the researcher has to enter their world in order to discover the motives and meanings that accompany social activities. The task is then to redescribe these motives and meanings, and the situations in which they occur, in the technical language of social scientific discourse. Individual motives and actions have to be abstracted into typical motives for typical actions in typical situations. These social scientific typifications provide an understanding of the activities, and may then become ingredients in more systematic explanatory accounts.

A research design should include a brief description of the research strategy or strategies that have been selected, and justification for the selection in terms of its/their appropriateness for the task of answering the research questions. It is desirable to make explicit the ontological and epistemological assumptions entailed in the choice of research strategy or strategies, as these have a bearing on how the use of the methods of data collection and analysis will be interpreted (see chapters 4 and 7).

Research paradigms

Explicitly or implicitly, social researchers usually work within the context of a particular set of theoretical ideas and ontological and epistemological assumptions. Over the past one hundred years or more a number of traditions of ideas and assumptions have emerged and developed. In the first edition of this book, and *Approaches to Social Enquiry* (1993a), I referred to these traditions as Approaches. They are now referred to as Research Paradigms.

It is possible to conduct social research without making explicit reference to any of the research paradigms I have identified. Whereas choices made between research strategies and methods do not necessarily entail a commitment to a particular research paradigm, the reverse may be the case. In chapter 4, eleven research paradigms are identified, but it is necessary to go to Blaikie (2007) for detailed reviews and critiques.

Concepts, theories, hypotheses and models

Somewhere in a research design a discussion of concepts and theory is likely to be required. This may occur in a separate section (e.g. 'Conceptual Framework' or 'Theoretical Model'), or may be integrated in other sections (e.g. 'Literature Review'). Just what will be required, and how it will be handled, will depend on a number of things, including, particularly, the research strategy or strategies that are to be used.

All social research uses technical concepts; they form the special language of every discipline. Technical concepts are required at the outset of the research design process to state the topic, the research problem and research questions. However, after this, the way they enter into the research process differs, depending on the research strategy that is adopted. A research design may set out with some key concepts, perhaps even with a conceptual framework, and these concepts will become variables through the specification of procedures for their measurement. In other research, only sensitizing concepts will be used at the outset. Technical concepts will either emerge out of an intense examination of lay concepts, or will be created or borrowed to organize qualitative data.

The manner in which theory enters into research is a matter of great controversy and confusion, particularly for novice researchers. A common criticism of some research is that it is atheoretical, that it neither uses nor contributes to the development of social theory. On the other hand, some researchers may wish to argue that descriptive research does not need theory; that measuring variables and correlating them is a purely technical matter. However, I believe that it is impossible to avoid using theory in research. Even descriptive studies, which may be concerned with just a few concepts, cannot escape as all concepts carry theoretical baggage with them.

Social theory enters into social research in many ways. It may be a source of a theoretical language or specific concepts, and of general theoretical ideas or specific hypotheses. The four research strategies entail different views of what constitutes theory and its role in research. Focusing on these four views will help to reduce some of the complexity. The research strategies that are concerned with answering 'why' research questions also differ in terms of whether they set out with a theory to be tested, or whether their aim is to produce a new theory, i.e. whether they are concerned with theory testing or theory generation. Research that is concerned with theory generation may require sensitizing concepts but no hypotheses. On the other hand, research that is concerned with theory testing will require the researcher to borrow or construct a theory before the research begins. In this case, it is desirable to at least do some work on this theory at the research design stage; it can then be stated, its origins and relevance explained, and, if appropriate, hypotheses derived from it.

Hypotheses are tentative answers to certain kinds of research questions that use certain research strategies, particularly the Deductive strategy, to answer them. They are frequently stated in the form of a particular kind of relationship between two concepts. Testing them may involve seeing if the associated variables have the same relationship as that predicted in the hypothesis. However, not all research questions, or all research projects, require hypotheses. They are particularly relevant to the answering of 'why' questions, and perhaps to some 'how' questions, but they have no place in answering 'what' questions. In addition, the stating of hypotheses at the outset is only relevant when research is about theory testing, and they can play quite a different role when the concern is with theory development. The latter may use many tentative hypotheses in the trial and error process of developing theoretical ideas to account for the data at hand, but these cannot be formulated at the research design stage.

Unless a researcher is testing an existing hypothesis, the formulation of good hypotheses requires a great deal of theoretical work. The testing of personal hunches as hypotheses constitutes a much lower level of research activity and should, therefore, be avoided in good-quality research. Such hypotheses usually make very little contribution to the advancement of knowledge because they are not well connected to the current state of knowledge. But, let me repeat, hypotheses are more appropriate to some research strategies than others.

As with theory, the role of models in social research is a complex issue on which there is a diversity of ideas and practices. 'Model' can refer to a conceptual framework, a hypothesized set of relationships between concepts, a hypothetical explanatory mechanism, or a method for organizing research results. 'Theory' and 'model' are often used interchangeably, or even in combination, for example, in the phrase 'theoretical model'. Add the notion of 'modelling', and we have another range of activities and products to confuse the new researcher.

Some research strategies, particularly the Deductive and Retroductive, may require models to be developed at the outset. These may be conceptual models, theoretical models, or hypothetical models of causal mechanisms. Other research strategies, particularly the Inductive, can introduce models at the data analysis stage where they represent the patterns in the data in a simplified form.

This section of the research design is likely to be the most difficult to complete. A broad understanding of the role of concepts, theories, hypotheses and models is required, and, possibly, a detailed knowledge of a range of theories (see chapter 5).

Data, types, forms and sources

It is necessary to give consideration to the context or setting from which data will be collected, and to recognize the differences between them in terms of the nature of the data that they can produce. Data can be collected from four main types of sources, as well as from or about individuals, small groups and many kinds of larger groups. First, people can be studied in the context in which the activities of interest to the researcher occur, where people are going about their everyday lives, in their natural social environment. For example, family interaction may be studied in a home, or religious rituals in a church, mosque or temple. The size of the social unit studied in this way can range from individuals and small groups, through organizations and communities, to multi-national bodies. These are referred to as *natural* social settings.

Second, a great deal of research studies people in *semi-natural* settings, when they are not actually engaged in the activities of interest. For example, people may be interviewed individually *about* the activities in which they engage in their natural settings. Sometimes data are not particularly about a social setting at all, but may deal with the attitudes and values of individuals. The third context is *artificial* settings. The classical form is the experiment; focus groups, games and simulation research are similar.

Fourth, the wide range of data that do not come from people directly are usually referred to as *social artefacts*. They are the traces or products that individuals and groups leave behind them, directly or indirectly, as a result of activities in their natural settings. People in groups produce statistics and documents and keep records for a variety of purposes, and these may be of use to the researcher. They may come out of natural settings, or be about activities in these settings.

While a research project may draw on data from only one of these sources, the use of a combination of them is common. The choice of data source will normally be incidental to other research design decisions. It is included here to highlight the need to be aware of the consequences of this decision in terms of the number of steps that the researcher can be removed from where the relevant social activity occurs.

At a more concrete level, decisions about data sources are contingent on the researcher's ability to access them. It is vital at the design stage to obtain the approvals that are necessary from the relevant gatekeepers. This may involve getting written permission from some authority to enter a natural setting (e.g. school classrooms), to conduct interviews in a semi-natural setting (e.g. with members of a work organization) or to get access to some records (e.g. case files on welfare recipients). Of course, some forms of permission have to wait until the time of data collection (e.g. individual interviews with householders).

Before the decision is made about what methods to use to collect and analyse the data to be used to answer the research questions, it is useful to give consideration to the type of data needed and the form in which the data are required. This involves a number of related decisions, although these will not necessarily be made in the order in which they are discussed here.

Three main types of data can be used in social research: *primary*, *secondary* and *tertiary*. Primary data are collected by the researcher, secondary data have been collected by someone else and are used in their raw form, and tertiary data are secondary data that have also been analysed by someone else. Hence, researchers may generate their own data directly from the people being studied. Alternatively, it may be possible to use data from official government statistics, privately compiled statistics, or a previous research project. Sometimes these data may be available in raw form, for example as a data matrix or as interview transcripts, or they may have already been analysed and only be available in tabular or summary form.

Depending on the nature of the research topic and the research questions, a researcher may have little or no choice about the type of data that can be used. However, the critical issue is the distance of the researcher from the source of data. Each type of data implies a different degree of control by a researcher. The further the researcher is removed from the collection process, the more difficult it is to judge the quality of the data and to ensure that they are appropriate for the project. These matters need to be made explicit in the research design, and the problems associated with the particular decisions, and methods for dealing with them, discussed.

Consideration should also be given to the form or forms in which the data will be collected and analysed. The common distinction used for this is between *quantitative* and *qualitative* data, between data in numbers or in words (and sometimes in images). However, this is not a simple distinction. Data may remain in one of these forms throughout the research process, or they may be transformed from one to the other at later stages. Data may start out as words, be manipulated soon after into numbers, may be analysed numerically, be reported in numbers, and then be interpreted in words. Alternatively, data may start out as words, and then be recorded, analysed and reported as text. Research projects can use data in both forms and they can be combined in a variety of ways. In the case of quantitative data, the levels of measurement, nominal, ordinal, interval or ratio, should be specified for each of the variables to be used as these levels have a bearing on the kinds of analysis that are appropriate.

The reason why it is desirable to give consideration to this issue at the research design stage is to ensure that the methods for collecting and analysing data are selected appropriately, and that the technology, mainly computer hardware and software, is available (see chapter 6, 'Types of Data', 'Forms of Data' and 'Sources of Data').

Selection of data sources

A critical stage in any research is the process of selecting the people, events or items from which or about which data will be collected. This involves the definition of a population of such people, events or items. Some research projects will collect data from a whole population; others will select only certain members or items for study.

Textbooks on social research methods usually discuss data selection in the form of a review of methods of sampling. While data selection is a much broader topic than sampling, one or more sampling methods are frequently used in social research. This is true whether the study uses quantitative or qualitative methods of data collection.

If a decision is made to use a sample rather than a population, it is important to be aware of whether and how the selection process will impact on your ability to generalize the results. Will the selection process use random (probability) or non-random (non-probability) methods? Data from non-probability samples cannot be generalized statistically back to any population. A number of selection methods are available and these can also be used singly or in combination (see chapter 6, 'Populations and Samples').

Whether samples are intended to represent a population, and how this can be achieved, is a central design issue. However, a collection of people can be studied as the result of a selection process that is concerned with theory generation rather than representativeness.

Regardless of whether probability or non-probability sampling methods are to be used, the method should be elaborated in detail and the choice of method(s) justified. In addition, the source and size of the population or sample needs to be determined and justified. If some other method of selection is to be used, such as case studies, the procedures should also be stated and justified (see chapter 6, 'Selection of Data').

Data collection and timing

Collection and analysis of data are frequently regarded as the core activities in social research. Novice researchers have a tendency to want to launch into data collection as soon as a research topic has been selected, for example, to get on with constructing a questionnaire or to start interviewing. If this book does nothing else, I hope it will temper this practice and show that decisions about data collection and analysis must await many other considerations.

A wide array of quantitative and qualitative methods is available in the social sciences, and there are countless books available on how to develop and use them. These methods include:

- *observation*, ranging from highly structured to unstructured, and from a very detached position to a very involved position;
- *interviewing*, ranging from highly structured to unstructured or in-depth methods, and including both individual and group interviews;
- *questionnaire*, including pen and paper, and electronic forms; and
- *content analysis* of secondary sources of many kinds.

As there are countless texts available that deal with data collection methods, they are not dealt with in this book.

The research design needs to specify clearly the method or methods to be used to collect the data. It is extremely important in quantitative research to decide, before the research begins, how the data are to be collected and to do all that is necessary to prepare for this. This may seem obvious, but it is not always taken seriously. Just muddling through will not do. The same is true for many qualitative studies, although there will be exceptions where some of these decisions may have to be made as the research proceeds. However, as I have argued earlier, this should not be used as an excuse for avoiding careful planning.

If quantitative data are to be collected using an existing measuring instrument, its source should be stated and a copy should be attached. If a measuring instrument needs to be developed, such as an attitude scale or a questionnaire, the process by which this will occur, including any pre-testing and piloting of the instrument, needs to be outlined and justified. In the case of qualitative data, it is important to indicate what method or methods will be used to generate and record them, and to state why these are considered to be the most appropriate.

The time(s) at which data are collected is a critical element in a research design.

Data can be collected at one point in time or at a series of points over time. One of these points can be the present time, while others may have occurred in the past or be planned for some time in the future. Decisions about timing will determine whether the study is cross-sectional or longitudinal, retrospective or prospective, or historical. Experimental research also involves the collection of data at different times. Hence, the role that the timing of data collection will play in the project needs to be stated.

Data reduction and analysis

The final core element of a research design is the specification and justification of the methods to be used to reduce and analyse the data. Methods of data reduction transform raw data into a form in which they can be analysed. This may involve transforming qualitative data into quantitative data by some from of numerical coding, or re-coding existing numerical data into different categories. An example of the latter would be reducing the number of categories to be used, and/or reordering the categories. Coding may also be used to organize and simplify data that have been collected in the quantitative form, for example, by the creation of indexes, scales, factors or clusters. Alternatively, when qualitative data are collected, the processes of reduction and analysis may be integrated with data collection into a continuous and evolving process of theory construction. This will involve establishing categories and doing various kinds of coding.

There is another important stage between data reduction and analysis. Data have to be organized in such a way that they can be transferred into an appropriate database for manipulation by computer. The relevant design decisions here are who will do this and how the cost will be covered. Significant time and expense can be involved in this process. With quantitative data, it is usually a case of keying in responses to a questionnaire or structured interview. With some kinds of qualitative data, it may be necessary to transcribe cassette recordings of in-depth interviews and then format these for entry into a database. It has been estimated that an experienced transcriber, with clear recordings, will take at least three hours to do one hour of recorded interview.

Finally, we come to the choice of methods for analysing the data. If all the other design decisions have been made carefully and consistently, the decisions about the method of analysis should be straightforward. A variety of methods may need to be used, depending on the type of research questions, whether or not hypotheses being tested, and the type of data.

The quantitative/qualitative distinction is most evident when techniques of data analysis are discussed. Quantitative methods can be used for producing descriptions, for establishing associations, and, possibly, causal relationships between variables. They can also be used for making inferences from the results produced from a probability sample to the population from which the sample was drawn. For each of these aspects of quantitative analysis, an array of statistical techniques is available. Just which one is appropriate will depend on the level of measurement used to collect the data, and perhaps the size of the sample. Qualitative methods of analysis can also be used for description at various levels of abstraction (in words rather than numbers), and, more particularly, for theory generation. A number of techniques are now available for the latter analysis. When data are in the form of text, the methods generally deal with creating categories, indexing or coding documents, sorting data to locate patterns, describing the patterns, generating theories from the data, and validating these theories. For both qualitative and quantitative analysis, appropriate software packages, as well as suitable hardware, need to be identified and their availability confirmed.

I have observed a tendency in many research designs to discuss methods of data collection but to ignore both data reduction and data analysis techniques. At best, a computer program might be mentioned, but just how the data are to be prepared for entry into a database, and what manipulations will be undertaken to relate the data to the research questions, are often not mentioned.

Each method of data reduction and analysis selected should be identified, briefly described and its use justified. The important point is that the decision on methods of analysis needs to be made in conjunction with many other research design decisions, and before the research commences. It can be fatal to wait until after the data have been collected. Not only do the methods of analysis need to be appropriate for the research questions, and also hypotheses if they are being used, but they also need to match the type of data. Hence, a critical issue in research design is to achieve consistency between the type and form of the data, the source of the data, its selection, and the methods of collection, reduction and analysis. The possible combination of choices here can be overwhelming and should be given very careful attention. Finally, the choice of all these methods must make it possible to answer the research questions (see chapter 7).

Problems and limitations

An important step in the preparation of a research design is to stand back and evaluate it. First, it is useful to state what problems are likely to be encountered and how they will be handled. These will include both practical and theoretical problems, such as getting the co-operation of respondents, or knowing what further case studies will be required after the first one. The problems listed here should only be those that cannot be resolved at the design stage. However, getting permission to use a list of names and addresses, or getting access to the research site, are matters that cannot be left to chance after the research commences.

Secondly, it is a good idea for the researcher to make an explicit assessment of the particular strengths and weaknesses of the research design. Research projects usually have their secure and predictable aspects as well as their less secure and uncertain parts. In addition, those parts of the design that require further development as the research proceeds can be identified. If this assessment is done conscientiously, the researcher should be in a position to anticipate possible problems before they arise, rather than inadvertently ending up down a blind alley or falling in a great hole.

Some researchers seem to be reluctant to expose the weakness of their research design for fear that their work will be judged as being inadequate. The reverse is in fact the case. Lack of awareness of both the strengths and weaknesses of a research design can be interpreted as indicating a shallow understanding of research.

Research Proposals

While *research designs* are usually seen by only a few people close to the researcher, *research proposals* are public documents and may be presented in various contexts. Their purpose is to ensure that the research meets the requirements of the discipline and/or the institution in which it will be undertaken. It should communicate clearly and concisely what is to be studied, why it is being studied, and how the research will be conducted. This will normally require less detail than goes into a research design. However, these details are likely to receive close scrutiny. In the case of university research, it is also an opportunity for students to receive some feedback and advice from a wider audience than their supervisor(s)/adviser(s), for example, by a seminar presentation. While this feedback is not always sympathetic, and may produce confusing and conflicting recommendations, it is nevertheless very useful for a project to be subjected to such an examination before it proceeds.

Research funding proposals have different purposes. They are designed to persuade a funding body that the project is worthy of financial support. Committees that are set up for such purposes will look closely at the aims and justification of the research, at whether the design is sensible and feasible, at the budget details and the justification for each item, and at whether the project can be completed with the available resources and in the time allocated. In short, this is a rather different audience to the one involved in obtaining academic or research ethics approval. Hence more than one version of a research proposal may be required.

As the requirements for these and other versions of a research proposal vary considerably in terms of their purpose and local requirements, no attempt will be made here to provide models for each type. Rather, I shall simply identify the areas that normally need to be covered in most types of research proposals. Some sections are common to both research designs and research proposals, but may be given a different emphasis, while others are specific to only one version.

Where sections are shared by both designs and proposals, only the headings are shown. All or most of the following sections are typical of research proposals.

Title

Research problem

Aims and significance

Research proposals usually include a statement on what contribution the research is intended to make, and this will include one or more of the following:

- the development of a particular area of theory or methodology;
- the collection or accumulation of a new body of information or data;
- the development of research methods or techniques;
- knowledge about or understanding of an issue or problem; and/or
- policy and practice in a particular area.[2]

These should be stated in a manner that will make it possible to assess whether, or to what extent, they have been achieved at the end of the research.

The statement of aims is normally accompanied by some justification for pursuing them, i.e. why the topic is worth studying. All social research requires the use of resources, even if it is just the researcher's own time. In the context of postgraduate research, students may need to pay fees, and the university will devote considerable resources to supporting such students. As research resources are scarce, their allocation needs to be husbanded. Funding bodies will certainly want to know what contributions a study is likely to make. This is not to suggest that all research must be able to make immediate contributions to areas of priority established by public and/or private interests. However, good reasons for doing it should be articulated, even if it is just to satisfy the researcher's curiosity.

Background

Some versions of research proposals will normally require a discussion of how the research problem has arisen, who views it as a problem, evidence for its existence, the context in which it occurs and who are the stakeholders. In more theoretical research, it may be necessary to specify where the gap in knowledge exists and why it needs to be filled. In short, a concise review of some of the literature will connect the proposed project with the existing state of knowledge. In my experience, there is a tendency among postgraduate students to devote most of their proposal to a review of the literature. This may include erudite discussions of the ideas of a favourite or fashionable theorist. However, the connection between such discussions and the research project are often not very clear. Therefore, this version of the literature review, unlike that in the thesis itself, should be very concise, although its length will no doubt depend on the type of research being planned and local requirements.

Research plan and methods

The main aim of this section is to communicate to experts in the field, as well as lay audiences, what is to be studied and how the research will be conducted. This needs to include:

- a statement of the research questions;
- reference to theory and hypotheses (if appropriate); and
- an elaboration of the source of data;
- how they will be selected;
- how they will be collected; and
- how they will be analysed.

Whether or not reference is made to the choice of research strategies and paradigms will depend on who the audiences are and a judgement as to whether they will, or will need to, understand the nature and significance of logics of enquiry in social research.

The research design is invaluable for the preparation of this section of the proposal. If research design decisions have been made carefully, then summarizing them for the research proposal should be straightforward.

In some types of research it may be necessary to discuss how research instruments will be developed. For example, if an attitude scale is required, and if no suitable scale is available, an explanation should be given as to how existing scales might be adapted and supplemented, or a new one constructed, and how it will be pre-tested and/or post-tested for unidimensionality or multi-dimensionality. Similarly, proposed pilot studies should be outlined and their purposes clearly stated.

Budget

Regardless of whether the project is receiving support from a funding agency, a budget is normally required to indicate what funds are needed and how they will be spent. Even in postgraduate research it is useful to anticipate what the costs are expected to be and how they will be covered. In the case where an application for a research grant is to be made, a detailed budget is normally required. The following headings are standard:

- *personnel* (e.g. research assistance, interviewers, coders, data analysts, interview transcribers);
- *equipment* (e.g. major items such as computing, audio recording and transcribing equipment);
- *maintenance* (day-to-day running expenses such as stationery, telephone, photocopying, data storage discs, audio cassettes, interlibrary loans and purchase of reports);
- *travel and subsistence* (to research sites, for interviewing, or to libraries); and
- *publication and presentation expenses* (preparation of the report, printing, graphics, conference attendance, etc.).

Justification of the budget

Applications for research grants normally require justification for the need for and the amount of each item in the budget. Some research funders require the budget items to be prioritized, thus forcing the researcher to be very clear about their relative importance for the successful completion of the project. Where equipment (e.g. computers, software and cassette recorders) and other resources (e.g. personnel for data entry) are already available, and can be used on the project, these should be noted. Bodies that fund academic research usually expect that some costs (e.g. office space and furniture, and some basic equipment) will be covered by the university or research centre in which the researcher is located.

Budget items need to match the details of the research design. For example, if 200 interviews are to be conducted in dispersed locations, then realistic costing of these is necessary, in terms of equipment and consumables, interviewers' time for the interviews and travel to the sites, as well as the cost of travelling. It is here that the flaws in the research design and planning can become evident and will usually be spotted.

Timetable

In order to ensure that a research project is manageable and doable, it is useful to plan the duration of each of the components and stages within the time-frame allocated to it. The major components commonly include the following:

- preparation of the research design;
- review of the literature;
- selection of data sources (including sampling);
- development of the research instruments;
- collection of the data;
- analysis of the data; and
- writing the thesis/report.

Depending on the nature of the research, these components may need to be modified. In the case of research grants, the literature review and research design stages are assumed to have been completed before the application is prepared. However, they may apply in those universities that require a detailed research proposal to be prepared before a candidate is accepted into the programme. Where the development of the research design follows acceptance for candidature, it is desirable to include all stages, even if retrospectively, as the clock will have been running since the time of acceptance.

These components can overlap in time (e.g. the research design and literature review, or data collection and analysis), and some may occur at more than one time (e.g. the literature review) or extend over much of the life of the project (e.g. writing drafts). While it is difficult to be precise about how long each component will take, a realistic estimate should be made. This will help to reveal whether the project as planned can be completed within the time limits, and whether the workload is manageable in each time period. It is useful to do this diagrammatically in terms of a time line for each component.

One component that is usually underestimated is the writing. A good thesis needs many drafts (at least three in my opinion). If insufficient time is allowed for redrafting at the end, a poor product is likely to be the result. Writing can easily take between a third and a half of the total time, and will certainly take at least a quarter.

Some research funding bodies require the specification of definite 'milestones' so that progress can be checked. In these cases, the anticipated completion date for the major research stages (e.g. data collection) would need to be stated. If a project runs over an extended period, for example, two or three years, progress reports may be required at regular intervals. The work actually completed by a particular date can then be compared with the anticipated date in the proposal. Discrepancies may need to be satisfactorily accounted for if funding is to continue. I believe the same practice is desirable in postgraduate research programmes.

Expected outcomes or benefits

It has become a common practice, particularly in publicly funded research, for the anticipated benefits to be stated.[3] Traditionally, academic research has been about the pursuit of knowledge, which means that in some types of research the real benefits have to be left to posterity to determine. However, in this age of economic rationalism, even academic research may be expected to make some reasonably direct and useful contribution to some field of high priority in the public or private sectors. In the case of applied and policy research, someone other than the researcher may determine the expected outcome. If research funding bodies have their agenda and priorities, an application would need to address these.

Ethical issues

Most social research involves intervention in some aspects of individual and social life. There is always a risk that even asking someone quite innocent questions could be disturbing to that person. It has therefore become normal practice for the ethical implications of a social research project to be made explicit, together with the procedures to be used to deal with them. For research conducted within universities and independent research organizations, it may be mandatory to seek the approval of a relevant human ethics committee. Professional associations in the social sciences, both national and international, now usually have a code of ethics. Members of such associations are expected to abide by the association's code. In some countries, national research bodies also have codes of ethics. For example, the Economic and Social Research Council in the UK provides clear ethical guidelines to applicants for research funds (www. esrc.ac.uk/ESRCInfoCentre/Images/ESRC_Re_Ethics_Frame_tcm6-11291.pdf). Most textbooks on social research methods now have a chapter on research ethics.

The following points are usually included in codes of ethics.

- *Voluntary participation*. Research participants cannot be required to be involved, and, if they agree to, they must know that they have the right to withdraw at any time.
- *Obtaining informed consent of research participants*. This involves informing participants of the nature and purpose of the research, the methods that will be used, what will be required of them, and how the results will be used.
- *Protecting the interests of the research participants*. The research participants' privacy must be protected by ensuring that their anonymity is preserved and the confidentially of the data guaranteed.
- *Researching with integrity*. The researcher must ensure that the research is conducted according to acceptable standards of practice and without fraud, deception or dishonesty.

The Social Research Association in the UK has taken a broad view of codes of ethics by specifying four sets of obligations for social researchers: to society, to funders and employers, to colleagues, and to subjects (www.the-sra.org.uk/documents/pdfs/ethics03.pdf). Their statement also emphasizes the need to avoid undue intrusion in the lives of research participants and to enable the participation in research of individuals and groups who might be excluded for reasons of communication, disability, comprehension or expense.

It is important to note that ethical issues are not the same as the practical problems that the researcher expects to encounter.[4] The latter are dealt with in the next section. However, finding appropriate ways of dealing with the ethical aspects of a project can create practical problems. For example, the need to inform potential interviewees about the nature of a project may increase the refusal rate, and, hence, threaten the researcher's ability to produce useful results.

Scope and limitations

While the scope of a research project should be clear from the research plan and methods, a common requirement for research proposals is to state clearly both what is and what is not included, particularly as far as data sources and selection is concerned. Decisions on these latter matters have a large bearing on how widely the findings can be applied. Compromises inevitably have to be made in order to work within a budget and other resource constraints, and these place limits on the possible use of the findings. While it may not be appropriate to spell out all the problems and limitations that go into the research design, some reference to them may be necessary.

Communicating the findings

It has been argued that one criterion scientific research should satisfy is that it should be made public. It can be argued that researchers have a responsibility to communicate their findings to people who can benefit from them. How this is to be done should be considered as part of the research proposal. Research funding administrators may be keen to know how the researcher plans to do this, and they may be willing to cover or contribute to the costs.

The onus is also on thesis writers to consider ways of making the results of their research known to a wider audience than just those who read theses in university libraries. Following the completion of a thesis, some universities have a requirement that students make a public presentation to the university community and, perhaps, selected outside guests. Of course, traditional methods include conference presentations, journal articles and books. Some research lends itself to reporting in the media, such as newspapers and magazines. Now there are other possibilities in this electronic age.

Some kinds of research, such as applied, commissioned or sponsored research, may have more limited, in some cases even restricted, audiences. However, applied researchers might want to insist on retaining the right to publish at least some of the findings themselves before accepting such commissions.

Conclusion

Having proposed possible structures and content for *research designs* and *research proposals*, the next task is to find out how to prepare them. For the remainder of the book, I shall concentrate exclusively on the preparation of research designs. To set the scene, figure 1.1 presents the core elements and their component

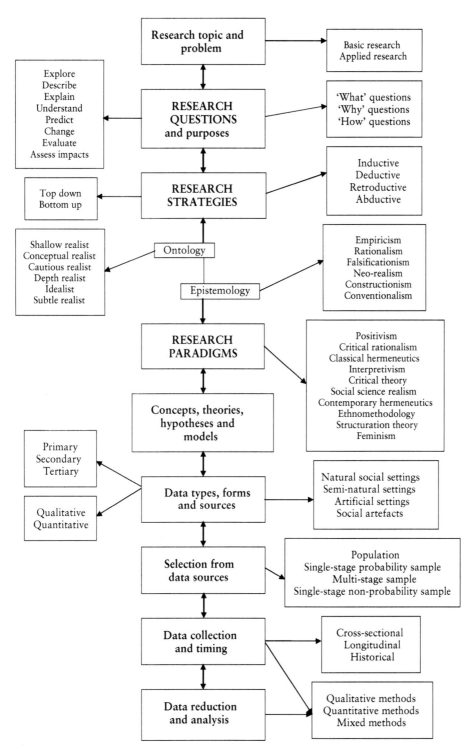

Figure 1.1   Elements of a social research design

choices. While many features of the elements and the choices have already been introduced, the components of the figure will now be elaborated step by step in the following chapters.

It is important to note that the connections between the elements of a research design (the centre column in figure 1.1) are shown with double-headed arrows to indicate that the design process is not linear and is bound to involve movement in both directions. In fact, the figure could have included many more such arrows linking all the core components with each other. While this would have more faithfully represented the iterative nature of the processes of research design, it would have turned the figure into an unintelligible spaghetti of connecting lines.

Further Reading

Punch, K. F. 2006. *Developing Effective Research Proposals.*
  Provides a more detailed coverage of the preparation of research *proposals* than is intended in this chapter. While there is considerable overlap, the author takes a different approach in some areas.
Kelly, M. 2004. 'Research design and proposals.'
  An overview of the structure and content requirements of research proposals.

2

Designing Social Research

Chapter Summary

- The research methods literature abounds with ideas on what constitutes a research design.
- However, many of these ideas are unhelpful as they:
  - deal with limited aspects of a research design;
  - are not mutually exclusive; and/or
  - are not comparable.
- Designing research involves giving consideration to a range of core elements, each with a number of choices, combinations of which lead to a wide variety of possible research designs.
- The basic aim in designing social research is to achieve maximum control over the research process.
- While a researcher's ability to achieve control will vary according to the nature of critical elements in the design, careful planning before the research commences makes it possible to evaluate the suitability and compatibility of the combination of decisions that need to be made; this will help to ensure a successful outcome.
- The preparation of a research design can start with different elements and proceed in a variety of sequences.
- While statements of the topic and research problem need to be produced, they will no doubt be reviewed and possibly modified as the research design evolves and the research itself proceeds.
- An important issue for all researchers is how to regard their relationship with the research participants.
- Various stances are possible, each with its particular ontological and epistemological baggage.
- It is essential to maintain consistency between the stance adopted and the assumptions entailed in the choices made about the research design elements, in particular, the research strategy and the methods of data collection.

Introduction

Social research is the use of controlled enquiry to locate, describe, understand, explain, evaluate and change patterns or regularities in social life. This control is achieved through a series of decisions that are made before the research commences and other decisions that may need to be made in the course of the research. This is not to suggest that complete control of all aspects of the research process is always possible. All eventualities cannot be anticipated, and, in some areas of research, control may be very difficult to achieve. For example, some methods of data collection, such as participant observation, are very unpredictable in terms of how they will develop and where they will take the researcher. However, there are many aspects of research that can and should be planned in advance. The aim is to achieve maximum control over all aspects, where possible.

The main reasons for designing research before it commences are to:

- make the research design decisions explicit;
- ensure that the decisions are consistent with each other and with the ontological assumptions adopted; and
- allow for critical evaluation of the individual design elements, and the overall research design, before significant research work commences.

Without such an overall plan, social enquiry cannot be controlled and the possibility of a successful outcome is severely jeopardized.

This chapter:

- sets the scene for what will follow in the later chapters;
- critically evaluates the common views and classifications of research design in the social sciences;
- presents an alternative view;
- discusses the fundamental requirements of a research design;
- provides an overview of the range of core elements of a research design;
- outlines the choices available for each element;
- reviews possible influences on these choices; and
- discusses the first steps in preparing a research design.

The subsequent chapters deal with the major research design decisions in detail.

Common Views of Research Design

The concept of 'research design' has a range of meanings, from narrow to broad. At the narrow extreme is the experiment, the type of design against which most other designs are regarded as compromises. Concern focuses on how to ensure that an experiment is capable of answering a particular 'why' research question, such that the effect of an independent variable, which is manipulated, can be assumed to be responsible for the observed changes in a dependent variable, the outcome. The design should rule out the possibility that some other features of the experimental situation can confound the independent variable. These design decisions are about the selection of experimental and control groups, the administration of the observations or measurements, and the type of statistical analysis to be used.

This approach to research design is very common in mainstream psychology. Texts on research methods frequently include a number of chapters on experimental methods (see e.g. Labovitz and Hagedorn 1976; Christensen 1988; Davis and Bremner 2006; Elmes *et al.* 2006; Shaughnessy *et al.* 2006; Goodwin 2008). Four criteria are commonly used to evaluate this type of research design: spatial control, temporal control, analysis of changes and representativeness. Spatial and temporal control is achieved by the use of one or more control groups in at least one of which the individuals do not receive the experimental treatment. The experimental and control groups can be made roughly equal in composition either by matching individuals in terms of relevant characteristics, or by assigning individuals to the experimental and control group by a random procedure. Analysis of change is achieved by comparing the individual responses in the pre-test and post-test groups, rather than the overall or average change for the group. Representativeness refers to the need to allocate individuals randomly to the experimental group if it is intended that the results are to be generalized to a wider population (Labovitz and Hagedorn 1976: 56–60).

An example of a broader but very conventional view of research design can be found in Kerlinger and Pedhazur (1973).

> Research design is the plan, structure, and strategy of investigation conceived so as to obtain answers to research questions and to control variance. The *plan* is the overall scheme or program of the research. It includes an outline of what the investigator will do from writing the hypotheses and their operational implications to the final analysis of the data. The *structure* of the research is more specific. It is the outline, the scheme, the paradigm of the operation of the variables. When we draw diagrams that outline the variables and their relation and juxtaposition, we build structural schemes for accomplishing operational research purposes. *Strategy*, as used here, is also more specific than plan. It includes the methods to be used to gather and analyse the data. In other words, strategy implies *how* the research objectives will be reached and *how* the problems encountered in the research will be tackled. (1973: 300)[1]

As Lincoln and Guba (1985) have pointed out, this view of research design requires the following to be spelt out before the research begins:

- the overall plan of the study;
- variables to be included;
- expected relationships between these variables (hypotheses);
- methods for data collection; and
- modes of data analysis.

They go on to suggest that this conventional view is narrower than it needs to be and that a more elaborate set of requirements are commonly used.

- State the problem, including justification for researching it and the objectives to be achieved.
- Outline the theoretical perspective.
- Indicate the procedures to be employed: sampling; instrumentation (operational definitions of the variables); data-analytic procedures (statistical tests to be used to test the hypotheses or answer the research questions).
- Establish a time schedule and 'milestones' to monitor progress.
- Designate agents who will undertake the various steps and tasks in the research.
- Provide a budget; give estimates of resources needed (time, people, funds).
- Indicate the expected end product(s): what the report will look like, including 'dummy tables'; and when the report will be available.

Research design requirements such as these have served countless research projects very well as a disciplined starting-point. However, some styles of research cannot be planned as precisely as this at the outset. Much of the information that is needed to make these decisions will not be known until the research has been in progress for some time. In addition, some of these requirements may not be relevant to certain styles of social research (e.g. specifying variables and their measurement, and using statistical tests). In the context of what they have called *naturalistic inquiry*, and what is more frequently referred to as qualitative research, Lincoln and Guba (1985: 224–5) have outlined why it may not be possible to meet these requirements in qualitative research.

- The focus of the study may change.
- Theory emerges in the course of the research rather than being stated at the beginning.
- Sampling serves different purposes; some samples need not be representative for the purposes of generalizing, but are concerned with the scope and range of information.
- Instrumentation is not about operational definitions but is a 'sensitive homing device that sorts out salient elements and targets in on them' (Lincoln and Guba 1985: 224).
- As the focus of the study changes, so do the procedures.
- Data analysis is open-ended and inductive rather than focused and deductive.[2]
- Statistical manipulations may have no relevance; the task is to 'make sense' of the data and to search for understanding.
- Timing cannot be predicted in advance because of the emergent nature of this kind of research.
- It is difficult to specify budgets precisely for the same reason.
- End products are difficult to specify, as the course of the research is unpredictable. All that can be said is that 'understanding will be increased'.

In short, 'the design of a naturalistic inquiry (whether research, evaluation, or policy analysis) *cannot* be given in advance; it must emerge, develop, unfold' (Lincoln and Guba 1985: 225).

Here, then, are three views of research design: the controlled experiment;

the planned linear stages based on a very quantitative view of research; and the developmental process characteristic of much qualitative research. In short, *experiments*, *social surveys*, and ethnographic or *field research* are all legitimate approaches to research design. However:

- few social scientists use experiments, mainly because they are either inappropriate or impossible to set up;
- many social scientists use the conventional linear approach to research design even when it is not appropriate; and
- some extreme types of naturalistic research may be as unpredictable as Lincoln and Guba have suggested.

The critical issue here is that the approach to research has to match the requirements of the research questions posed. Many design elements have to be considered in an attempt to answer these questions. As a wide variety of combinations of decisions on these elements are possible, there are many kinds of research designs. While the flexibility of a developmental approach to research design may be attractive, most research, particularly that conducted by postgraduate students, has to meet deadlines and needs some assurance of a useful outcome. Therefore, it is necessary to plan as carefully as possible at the outset, and to review the plan from time to time, as changes may be needed.

The importance of research design in answering research questions has been stressed by de Vaus in his concern with obtaining evidence that is as unambiguous as possible. '[W]hen designing social research we need to ask: given this research question (or theory), what type of evidence is needed to answer the question (or test the theory) *in a convincing way*? (de Vaus 2001: 9). Here, then, is the primary function of research design.

This position has been expressed in a more general way by Yin (2003a). *Research design* refers to the process that links research questions, empirical data, and research conclusions.

> Colloquially, a research design is *a logical plan for getting from here to there*, where *here* may be defined as the initial set of questions to be answered, and *there* is some set of conclusions (answers) about these questions. Between 'here' and 'there' may be found a number of major steps, including the collection and analysis of relevant data. (Yin 2003a: 20)

Common Classifications of Research Designs

Textbooks on social research methods and research design have reduced research designs to a few common types and usually devote a chapter or significant section to each one. Here is a list of common types.

- Experiments
- Social surveys
- Field work/ethnography

- Longitudinal study
- Cross-sectional study
- Case study
- Comparative/historical
- Secondary analysis
- Action research
- Evaluation research
- Impact assessment

(See, for example, Denzin 1970; Labovitz and Hagedorn 1976; Smith 1981; Chadwick *et al.* 1984; Sedlack and Stanley 1992; Bailey 1994; Hakim 2000; de Vaus 2001, 2006; Blaxter *et al.* 2002; Yin 2003a; Bell 2005; Sarantakos 2005; Neuman 2006; Bryman 2008.)

Many textbooks and book chapters confine their attention to only one of these designs. For example: **experiments** (e.g. Campbell and Stanley 1963a, 1963b; Aronson and Carlsmith 1968; Davis and Bremner 2006); **social surveys** (e.g. Rosenberg 1968; Moser and Kalton 1971; Marsh 1982; de Vaus 2002; Babbie 2004; de Leeuw *et al.* 2008; Fowler 2009); **field research or ethnography** (e.g. Burgess 1982a, 1984; Atkinson 1990; Atkinson *et al.* 2001; Hammersley and Atkinson 2007); **case study** (e.g. Gomm *et al.* 2000a; Yin 2003a, 2003b; Stake 2005; David 2006); **action research** (e.g. Winter 1987, 1989; Whyte 1991; Costello 2003; Cooke and Cox 2005; Kemmis and McTaggart 2005; McNiff and Whithead 2006; Whitehead and McNiff 2006; Somekh 2006; Stringer 2007; Reason and Bradbury 2008; McIntyre 2008; Schmuck 2009); **evaluation research** (Campbell and Stanley 1963a; Cronbach 1963, 1982; Weiss 1972, 1976; Cook and Campbell 1979; Weiss and Bucuvalas 1980; Rossi and Freeman 1985; Guba and Lincoln 1989; Pawson and Tilley 1994, 1997; Stern 2005; Pawson 2006); **impact assessment** (e.g. Wathern 1988; Vanclay and Bronstein 1995; Becker 1997).

Some classifications make a division between experimental, quasi-experimental and non-experimental designs. The latter include social surveys, sometimes referred to as *correlational* designs because they, unlike experiments, cannot establish causation.[3] De Vaus (2001, 2006) has expanded the four commonest types (experiment, longitudinal, cross-sectional and case study) into six types: experimental, panel, retrospective, cross-sectional, comparative/cross-national, and case study.

It has also become a common practice to group these different designs into two broad categories, quantitative and qualitative, with divisions within each category (see e.g. Punch 2005; Neuman 2006), and mixed methods have now been added to these (Creswell 2003, 2009). However, I shall question the usefulness of the quantitative/qualitative dichotomy in this context in chapter 7.

An Alternative View

At best, the concept of research design used in these classifications is very limited and confusing. Of course, social researchers can do surveys and conduct experiments, but surveys are about particular methods of data collection and analysis, and an experiment is about selecting groups and timing data collection. Similarly, secondary analysis is mainly about sources of data, and ethnography, comparative research, case studies, evaluation research and action research are particular approaches to research that can combine a number of methods of data collection and analysis. Hence, the first problem with these classifications is that each type of research design deals with some elements but none of them deals with them all.

A rare attempt to recognize these difficulties can be found in Chadwick *et al.* (1984). They have classified research designs according to six criteria:

- method of data collection;
- primary objectives (e.g. description, hypothesis testing, evaluation, social impact assessment);
- time orientation (cross-sectional, longitudinal, retrospective);
- whether the data are to be collected to answer a specific research question (primary and secondary); and
- the degree to which the methods impinge on the respondents (obtrusive and unobtrusive).

This view takes us part way to the approach adopted in this book.

The second problem is that the categories are not mutually exclusive. For example, surveys can be used in comparative studies, case studies and evaluation research; and experiments, comparative studies, case studies and evaluation research can use a number of methods of data collection and analysis. The third problem is that the categories are not exhaustive of the aspects of research that they do cover. For example, there are other ways of achieving control over variables, and there are many other sources of data and methods for producing and analysing data than those identified. These conventional categories mask the many choices that need to be considered in preparing a research design.

A research design contains many elements (see figure 1.1) and each element involves a choice from among alternatives. While some combinations of choices may be more common, and others may not be legitimate, potentially, there is a wide variety of possibilities. The resulting combinations of decisions produce a wide variety of actual designs that cannot easily be described by simple labels. For this reason, I do not follow the conventional classifications.

Adopting this approach avoids a ritualistic adherence to recipe book solutions. As a first step in this direction, I will examine in broad outline what any research design should achieve.

Fundamental Requirements

In general, a research design needs to answer three basic questions.

WHAT will be studied?
WHY will it be studied?
HOW will it be studied?

The last question can be broken down into five further questions.

WHAT research strategy will be used?
WHAT ontological and epistemological assumptions will be adopted?
WHERE will the data come from?
HOW will the data be collected and analysed?
WHEN will each stage of the research be carried out?

If these questions are answered satisfactorily, a researcher should be clear about how the research is to proceed. If they are written down in the form of a research proposal, others will be in a position to provide feedback on whether the project is sensible and feasible. In the case of postgraduate research, these others can include supervisors/advisers and academic research committees; for other social research they can include academic research committees, ethics committees, funders, sponsors and potential consumers.

In practice, however, to answer these eight questions, a number of aspects of research have to be addressed and many decisions need to be made. Because of the variety of types of research undertaken in the social sciences, it is not possible to be dogmatic about all the details to be considered in a research design. Nevertheless, some components are relevant to most designs.

Core Elements

I wish to propose a set of core design elements about which choices need to be made (see figure 2.1). Because the elements are connected in complex ways, a choice on one will have consequences for choices on other elements. The research design decisions that novice researchers usually give the most attention are 'data sources' and methods of 'data collection and analysis'. However, before these specific decisions can be made, several others must be considered.

The obvious starting-point in a research design is the statement of the 'research problem' that is to be investigated. Following closely behind is the consideration of two closely related research design elements, the 'research purposes'[4] and the all-important 'research questions'. The latter provide the focus and direction for the study; they are what the study will attempt to answer. Then follows the selection of a 'research strategy' or strategies that will be used to answer these questions, and the ontological and epistemological assumptions that will be adopted, usually in association with a particular 'research paradigm'. The decisions that are made about the 'research questions', 'research strategies' and 'research paradigms' will have a big influence on the decisions about 'data sources', 'data selection' and methods of 'data collection' and 'data reduction and analysis'.

Associated with these last four design elements are three others, the most fundamental of which concerns the timing of data collection. The role of time in a research design is frequently seen as being its defining characteristic. Two elements are concerned with the 'type of data' and the 'form of data' to be used. Choices related to the former are concerned with the proximity of the researcher

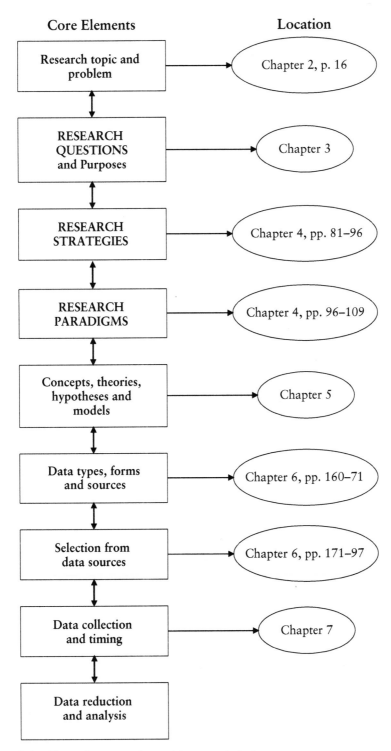

Figure 2.1 Core elements of a social research design

to the phenomenon being studied, and choices in the latter have to do with whether the data will be in words or numbers.

The order in which these core elements are discussed does not follow any particular logic. While the decisions made on the earlier ones may limit the decisions that can be made on the later ones, the process of designing research is spiral or cyclical in nature rather than being a set of linear steps. As the implications of the earlier decisions are explored, they may turn out to be impractical or unachievable. Therefore, the process is likely to require a number of iterations before a consistent and workable set of design decisions can be achieved.

The Ideal and the Practical

As I have argued earlier, all decisions that are concerned with the design of a research project should, if possible, be made before any substantial work has commenced. This *is* possible in studies conducted on topics that have already been well researched and for which there is adequate background information. Such studies may be the next step in a programme of research that has used well-tried methods and for which appropriate published reports are available. However, some studies may require preliminary or exploratory research to establish an adequate background against which choices can be made. This preliminary work may just involve the examination of statistical data, such as that produced in a census, but it may also require some field work, i.e. some contact with the site and the people who are to be involved in the research. In other studies, it may not be possible to make all the choices before the research commences, either because not enough is known about the field or the social context, or because the nature of the proposed methods requires a developmental process to be adopted. The latter involves the making of choices at the beginning of each stage of the research, based on what was learned in the previous stage. The fact that some kinds of research need to be done in this developmental mode is no excuse for failing to make choices that should and can be made at the outset, regardless of the category into which the project falls.

It is possible for researchers to avoid dealing with these choices if they operate within a research community that consistently adopts a particular research paradigm in a taken-for-granted manner. The need for choices will not be evident because those implicit in the paradigm will be adopted without discussion, or, perhaps, any awareness that choices have been made; the assumptions and methods to be used will be regarded as self-evident. Other researchers may avoid the need to examine critically the range of choices by simply adopting methods with which they are most familiar and comfortable, and designing the research project to use such methods.

Making the choices necessary to design a research project requires careful consideration of many factors, from fundamental philosophical and value positions to technical and practical matters. These choices are interdependent. The choice of research question(s), and the way it/they are worded, places limitations on the choices of research strategy. The choice of a particular research strategy may limit the choice of research methods. The choice of a particular method of data gathering limits the choices of methods of data analysis, and so on. However, choices made in the early stages of the research design process may have to be revised in the light of circumstances that require a change in the sample or methods of data collection. Problems with access to people, organizations or other data sources may require compromises from the ideal design, and these compromises require a revision of other choices. For example, a chain of choices may lead to a decision to use a mail questionnaire to gather data. However, if it is discovered that access to the required names and addresses cannot be obtained in order to draw a random sample and contact respondents, then it may be necessary to use snowball sampling, and in-depth interviews. Therefore, it will be necessary to choose a different method of data analysis, and, possibly, to reformulate the research questions and adopt a different research strategy. Hence, before settling on all the choices, it is usually necessary to go through the design decision sequence a few times in order to deal with the obstacles and limitations that are encountered.

Getting Started

Having now defined the fundamental requirements of a research design, and laid out the range of elements that need to be considered, we are now in a position to begin the task of preparing a research design. The selection of a research topic, and the statement of the problem to be investigated, usually constitutes the first or very early steps in setting out on a research project.

Research Topic and Problem

The starting point for social research is a problem, either *social* or *sociological*. A *social* problem is a state of affairs that is judged by someone, for example a social scientist or a policy-maker, to be unsatisfactory and in need of some form of intervention. A *sociological* problem is a puzzle that a social scientist considers needs to be solved, i.e. explained or understood.[5] Stating the research problem clearly is the first challenge, but it may need to be revised as work on the research design proceeds.

In conjunction with the selection and definition of the problem to be investigated, a statement of the research topic can be undertaken. The topic provides both a signpost and a set of boundary markers: it indicates that the research will follow a specific path; and it defines the territory to be explored. Hence, it is important to state the topic in a way that communicates the general nature of the research. However, while it is useful to try to state the topic clearly and concisely at the outset, it is not uncommon for the initial attempt to be rather vague and imprecise. Until the research design is completed, the researcher cannot be sure just what the project will be like. It may take much thought and reading, a number of trial runs, and even some exploratory research, before a clear and precise topic can be produced. The direction in which the signpost points, and the inscription on it, may change in the course of preparing the research design. In fact, the final version of the topic may not become clear until the time of writing the report or thesis. Therefore, novice researchers should not be concerned if difficulties are encountered in defining the topic in the early stages. Greater attention should be given to the problem statement.

Here are some examples of research topics.

Environmental Worldviews and Behaviour among Students and Residents.
Age and Environmentalism: a Test of Competing Hypotheses.
Gender Differences in Environmentalism: towards an Explanation.
Motivation for Environmentally Responsible Behaviour: the Case of Environmental Activists.

These topics will be used throughout the book, and, particularly, in chapter 8 where research designs for each one are outlined. They are part of a research programme on environmentalism that I have conducted. (See Appendix for examples of other research problems and topics.)

It is a common mistake to believe that, having stated the problem and defined the topic, the researcher is in a position to commence the project. Even well-formulated problem statements and topics provide very little direction for the design of a project. Something more is required. I argue in chapter 3 that this is achieved mainly by stating one or more research questions.

Influences on the Choice of Topic and Problem

An important aspect of any research project is the reasons why it is to be undertaken. Some social research requires a considerable investment of resources, and, even if this is mainly the researcher's time, justification for doing it is necessary. There are a number of dimensions on which this justification can be made, and these involve motives and goals of various kinds. Most projects will entail several of these. At the same time, there are various factors that can place limitations on the choice of topic.[6]

Motives

In an academic environment, lecturers/professors and students do social research for *personal*, *academic* and *social* reasons. *Personal* reasons include:

- satisfying curiosity;
- seeking credentials and/or pursuing career goals;
- trying to solve a personal problem; and
- pursuing personal interests and commitments.

Academic reasons for undertaking social research centre on making a *contribution to the discipline* or disciplines in which one works. These can include:

- contributing to knowledge in a particular field;
- seeking answers to current intellectual puzzles;

- participating in intellectual debates; and
- developing social theory.

Social researchers working in any context, be it in a university or in the public or private sectors, may wish to make a *contribution to the society*, or to some sector of the society, in which they are located. These motives may include:

- contributing to the solution of a social problem;
- helping some group, community or organization achieve its goals;
- assisting in the development of social policy; and
- contributing to public or private sector decision-making.

An examination of the motives behind the four sample research topics stated earlier will help to illustrate how *personal, academic* and *social* motives can be combined. The first of the research topics, 'Environmental Worldviews and Behaviour', was motivated by a personal curiosity about the kind and level of environmental attitudes and behaviour currently adopted by Australians. This arose from reading some of the American literature on environmental sociology. This curiosity was then translated into a desire to fill a gap in knowledge, and, at the same time, to compare the Australian situation with that in the United States and other parts of the world. The main motive for the second topic, 'Age and Environmentalism', was an academic concern to advance our knowledge of why some people have more favourable environmental attitudes and engage in higher levels of environmentally responsible behaviour than others. Of course, this knowledge could also have some practical benefits for the design of environmental education programmes and for groups and organizations that are committed to improving the quality of the natural and built environments. Topic three, 'Gender Differences in Environmentalism', was motivated by an academic desire to make more sense of the rather confused findings in previous research on gender and environmentalism. Are women more environmentally conscious than men, and, if so, what are the nature and origins of these differences? Again, the results of research on this topic could also benefit environmental education programmes, and, perhaps, make a contribution to the ultimate survival of the human race. The fourth topic, 'Motivation for Environmentally Responsible Behaviour', is essentially a theoretical puzzle: why do some people behave responsibly and others not? However, this puzzle is also related to specific social problems, for example, reducing litter and pollution, saving energy, and conserving non-renewable resources. It may be necessary to understand the motivation for environmentally responsible behaviour in those who practise it in order to know what would be necessary to change the behaviour of others. Hence research that is primarily directed towards solving a *sociological* problem can also assist in the solution of *social* problems.

Influences

Motives
    Personal interests and goals
    Discipline contribution
    Social contribution
The literature
Restrictions
    Audiences
    Political
    Funding bodies
    Practical considerations

It is important for researchers to articulate their motives for undertaking a research project, as different motives may require different research design decisions. This articulation will also help to reveal conflicts or inconsistencies in an individual's motives, within a research team, or between the researcher(s) and other stakeholders. It is sensible to resolve these differences before the research commences.

The literature

A major source of influence on the nature and choice of a research topic, particularly in basic or theory-oriented research, is the body of literature on theory and research related to the topic, in both the researcher's discipline and in related disciplines. A research project can be stimulated by the results of previous research and by problems posed by theorists. Even if the topic originates elsewhere, one or other of these bodies of literature is likely to help shape the way the topic and the problem are formulated. Of course, 'the literature' plays other roles in research, as we shall see in due course.

Restrictions

A number of factors can place restrictions on the choice of topic, including: a range of possible *audiences* the researcher has to, or wishes to, take into consideration; the *political* restrictions that may be imposed by authorities such as governments and universities; the types of research that *funding bodies* are willing to support; and practical factors, such as the ability to get access to desired research sites.

Audiences include:

- clients on whose behalf the research is being conducted (whether or not they are paying for it);
- sponsors who are funding the research;
- colleagues;
- scientific communities (particularly the editors of journals);
- employers; and
- potential future sources of funding (Smaling 1994).

Of course, each audience may have different expectations of and different degrees of influence on the design and execution of a research project, let alone what it might find. This is particularly important in the case of applied research as, in contrast to basic research, the researcher may have much less freedom in determining the topic and making other research design decisions. This can certainly occur if the sponsors, the main audience and the major benefactors coincide.

Basic and Applied Research

Motives for undertaking research are associated with the type of research, i.e. whether it is basic or theory-oriented research, or whether it is applied or policy oriented research.[7] The former is concerned with producing knowledge for understanding and the latter with producing knowledge for action. Both types of social research deal with problems: basic research with theoretical problems; and applied research with social or practical problems. *Basic* research is concerned with advancing fundamental knowledge about the social world, in particular, with the development and testing of theories. *Applied* research is concerned with practical outcomes, with trying to solve some practical problem, with helping practitioners accomplish tasks, and with the development and implementation of policy. Frequently, the results of applied research are required immediately, while basic research usually has a longer time-frame.

Basic and applied researchers have different orientations to their work. Basic researchers are more detached and academic in their approach, and tend to have their own motives. Applied researchers are more pragmatic and change-oriented, and generally have to pursue goals set by others. However, the issue of detachment is rather more complex than this simple comparison suggests. In some research traditions, detachment is considered to be necessary to achieve objectivity. In other traditions, it is claimed that detachment and, hence, objectivity is impossible. It is also important to note that the theoretical and/or political commitments of some researchers, for example critical theorists and feminist researchers with emancipatory commitments, can produce basic research from which detachment is absent. We shall come back to these issues later.

For an example of basic research, I draw on a research project conducted in New Zealand in the 1960s (Blaikie 1968, 1969, 1972). I was curious as to whether the relationship between religion and occupation that Weber (1958) had found in Germany about one hundred years earlier, and that Lenski (1961) and others had found in the United States in the early 1960s, was also present in New Zealand. If this relationship did exist, I wanted to know whether it was the result of the survival of the Protestant work ethic in this colonial outpost. This research clearly had no immediate practical value; it was designed to satisfy academic curiosity and to continue a tradition of research in the United States that was largely inspired by Weber's thesis.

An example of applied research comes from a commissioned study I did with some colleagues in the late 1970s. A developer wished to build houses on a site close to the Melbourne airport. He engaged a firm of architects and planners to assist him. Planning restrictions determined how close houses could be built to the flight paths associated with the runways. This restriction was established in terms of maximum decibel readings, and was shown as a line on a map down each side of the flight path. The developer was concerned about his ability to sell houses if they were built close to the flight path. Would purchasers be willing to live right up to the legal planning limit? If not, how close would they be willing to live? The firm of architects and planners engaged us to answer these questions. The study was done by interviewing residents who were living at different intervals from the flight path in an adjoining location, including some whose houses were built under the flight path before the airport was established there, and before the planning restrictions came into force. The developer would have liked us to draw a line on the map for him, but since people's responses to living close to aircraft noise were very varied this was not possible. We found that people differed considerably in the extent to which they could tolerate aircraft noise and the possible dangers of living close to an airport. Some people appeared to be willing to put up with aircraft noise if the price of the house was attractive. In the end, the developer adopted a conservative position and left some open space adjoining the planning limit.

In the social sciences, research is often a mixture of basic and applied: some stages of a project may have a basic flavour, while other stages may be more applied. For example, a researcher may be commissioned to assist the managers of an organization to change the organization's culture. After undertaking research to describe the existing culture of the organization, the researcher may then proceed to refine and test a particular theory of organizational change. Only when they are satisfied that this theory is relevant to this particular organization will the researcher proceed to engage in some form of action research that helps the members of the organization to bring about the changes desired by management.

Few if any social research projects are exclusively concerned with advancing knowledge for its own sake. While basic researchers may not be interested in the practical benefits, basic research can eventually produce such outcomes. Implicitly or explicitly, most social researchers appear to have some social issue or problem in mind when they undertake research. The fundamental question is whether the researcher chooses to define the problem and the research project, or whether the problem has been defined by someone else, for example, a sponsor who may also have a substantial say in how the project is to be conducted.

However, it is worth noting that in competitively funded basic research there are usually some constraints on research design. Funding bodies not only have expectations about what kinds of research projects are legitimate or important, but they are also likely to have prejudices about what are regarded as appropriate methods for data collection and/or analysis. In order to obtain research funds, prudent researchers need to take these expectations into account in designing a project, or be well prepared to defend less popular methods.

Researcher's Stance

An important choice that all social researchers have to make is what stance to take towards the research process and participants; what the relationship will be between the researcher and the researched. Elsewhere, I have suggested three basic positions a researcher can adopt: outside expert, inside learner and reflective partner or conscientizer (Blaikie 2007). Here, I want to elaborate these into six possible stances.

Researcher's Stance

Detached observer
Empathetic observer
Faithful reporter
Mediator of languages
Reflective partner
Dialogic facilitator

The traditional 'scientific' stance is that of *detached observer*. The researcher is regarded as an uninvolved spectator, particularly during the process of data collection. It is argued that the researcher's values and preferences can threaten the objectivity of the research, and, hence, the value of the results. Therefore, detachment is a requirement for producing reliable knowledge. This position is still widely advocated in spite of the many criticisms that have been raised against it.

The second position, the *empathetic observer*, still aims to achieve this kind of objectivity but insists that it is necessary for researchers to be able to place themselves in the social actors' position. Only by grasping the subjective meanings used by the social actors can their actions be understood. This is commonly referred to as *verstehen* (Weber 1964; Outhwaite 1975).

This second position has developed into a third, the *faithful reporter*, in which the researcher's stance is much less detached. The aim is to report a way of life by allowing the research participants to 'speak for themselves'. Thus, the researcher's task is to present the social actors' point of view. To do this, the researcher may have to become immersed in that way of life in order to grasp these meanings. This position is commonly referred to as 'naturalism' and was advocated by sociologists of everyday life (see e.g. Lofland 1967; Blumer 1969; Matza 1969; Denzin 1971; Douglas 1971; and Guba 1978). The researcher is required to study social phenomena in their 'natural' state, to be sensitive to the nature of the social setting, to describe what happens there and how the participants see their own actions and the actions of others. A related requirement is that the researcher 'retains the integrity of the phenomenon'. This means remaining faithful to the phenomenon under investigation by only producing reports in which the social actors can recognize themselves and others. Schütz presented this idea in his *postulate of adequacy*, in which he argued that social scientific concepts must be derived from and remain consistent with lay concepts.

> Each term in a scientific model of human action must be constructed in such a way that a human act performed within the life-world by an individual actor in the way indicated by the typical construct would be understandable for the actor himself [*sic*] as well as for his fellow-men [*sic*] in terms of commonsense interpretation of everyday life. (Schütz 1963b: 343)

In other words, if social actors cannot recognize themselves and their colleagues in the social scientist's accounts, then the latter must have produced a distortion of the social actors' world. This process of checking social scientific accounts with the social actors' accounts is sometimes referred to as 'member validation' or 'member checks' and is a major form of validity checking in qualitative research. However, this process is not without its difficulties.

A fourth position, which rejects the idea of detachment, is an extension of the third. In this case, the researcher becomes the *mediator of languages*, between everyday, lay language and social scientific or technical language (Giddens 1976; Gadamer 1989). Studying social life is akin to studying a text, and this involves interpretation on the part of the reader. The researcher actively constructs an account based on the accounts provided by the participants. This process of construction is not neutral; researchers have to invest something of themselves into their account. Social, geographical and historical locations, as well as the researcher's interests and assumptions, have a bearing on the nature of the account produced. Hence, detached objectivity is seen to be impossible as the author's voice will always be present in the researcher's account (Geertz 1988).

A fifth position is associated with critical theory. The researcher is viewed as a *reflective partner* who is committed to the emancipation of the participants from whatever kind of oppression they are experiencing (Habermas 1970, 1972). Following Husserl, Habermas rejected the 'objectivist illusion' of Positivism, according to which the world is conceived as a universe of facts independent of the 'observer' whose task is to describe them. He accepted the same premise as Interpretivism, that social and cultural reality is already pre-interpreted by the participants as a cultural symbolic meaning system, and that these meanings can be changed over time. Therefore, the process of understanding this socially constructed reality is 'dialogic'; it allows individuals to communicate their experiences within a shared framework of cultural meanings. In contrast, the process in the natural sciences is 'monologic'; it is the technical manipulation by the researcher of some aspect of nature. In the latter, the researcher is a 'disengaged observer' who stands in a subject-to-object relationship to the subject-matter while, in the former, the researcher is a 'reflective partner' whose relationship is that of subject to co-participant (Blaikie 2007: 135–6).

Another version of this fifth position is associated with feminist research and involves *conscious partiality*. Again, the concern is with emancipation, in this case of women. Much more than empathy is involved here. The researcher not only participates in women's struggles but is also expected to be changed by them. This view of research involves the conscientization of both the researcher and the researched (Mies 1983: 126). By conscientization is meant learning to perceive social, political and economic contradictions and to take action against oppressive elements of reality (Freire 1970).

The fourth and fifth positions have now culminated in a sixth postmodern view of the role of the researcher. In this case, the researcher is regarded as another actor in the social context being investigated. Rather than being the 'expert', as in the *detached* position, an *empathetic observer*, or a *faithful reporter*, the postmodern researcher takes elements from the positions of *mediator of languages*, *reflective partner*, and *conscientizer*, and seeks to reduce the researcher's authorial influence on the products of the research by allowing a variety of 'voices' to be expressed. These researchers

> still rely on their understanding of the situation, but they attempt to minimize their authorial bias by letting the natives speak for themselves as much as possible. The aim is to produce a 'polyphony' of voices rather than a single voice, in order to reduce bias and distortion. (Fontana 1994: 214)

The emphasis is on the dialogue between the researcher and the researched. Hence, this position might be described as *dialogic facilitator*.

Clearly, there are incompatibilities between most of these positions, and there is an extensive literature that debates their relative merits. As we shall see in chapter 4, these positions are associated with the four dominant research strategies used in social research. However, before we leave this discussion here, there is a related concept that needs to be discussed, that of reflexivity.

The notion of *reflexivity* is integral to the ethnomethodologist's views on how social actors make their actions and their social world meaningful to themselves and others. Giddens has incorporated this idea into his structuration theory as the 'reflexive monitoring' that social actors need to engage in to maintain continuity in their social practices. For Giddens, *reflexivity* is more than self-consciousness; it involves the active monitoring of the ongoing flow of social life.

> The reflexive monitoring of activity is a chronic feature of everyday action and involves the conduct not just of the individual but also of others. That is to say, actors not only monitor continuously the flow of their activities and expect others to do the same for their own; they also routinely monitor aspects, social and physical, of the contexts in which they move. (Giddens 1984: 5)

There is a growing acceptance of the idea that if reflexivity is an integral part of everyday social practices, then it must also be involved in the 'everyday' activities of social researchers. If the construction and maintenance of social worlds by social actors involves, among other things, reflexive monitoring, then the social researcher's creation of new social scientific knowledge will entail the same processes. In other words, wherever new knowledge is generated through a process of interaction between the researcher and the researched, the social researcher will draw on the same skills that social actors use to make their activities intelligible (Giddens 1976: 157–61).

Recognition of the need for social researchers to be reflexive can be found in the writings of qualitative researchers in general, and ethnographers in particular, as well as among feminist researchers (see Stanley and Wise 1993; Maynard and Purvis 1994). For example, Hammersley and Atkinson have argued that reflexivity implies that

> the orientations of researchers will be shaped by their socio-historical locations, including the values and interests that these locations confer upon them. What this represents is a rejection of the idea that social research is, or can be, carried out in some autonomous realm that is insulated from the wider society and from the particular biography of the researcher, in such a way that its findings can be unaffected by social processes and personal characteristics. (Hammersley and Atkinson 2007: 15)

Similarly, Mason (2002) has regarded *active reflexivity* as one of the essential features of qualitative research; researchers need to be active and reflexive in the process of generating data rather than being neutral data collectors.

> Qualitative research should involve critical self-scrutiny by the researcher, or *active reflexivity*. This means that the researcher should constantly take stock of their actions and their role in the research process, and subject these to the same critical scrutiny as the rest of their 'data'. This is based on the belief that a researcher cannot be neutral, or objective, or detached, from the knowledge and evidence they are generating. Instead, they should seek to understand their role in that process. Indeed, the very act of asking oneself difficult questions in the research process is part of the activity of reflexivity. (Mason 2002: 7)

Earlier, Mason also argued that 'we should be reflexive about every decision we take, and that we should not take any decisions without actively recognizing that we are taking them' (1996: 165). Therefore, *reflexivity* applies to the process of designing social research as much as to the research process itself.

The difference between adopting a reflexive stance in research and other possible positions is illustrated in the distinction that Mason has made between the three choices that qualitative researchers have in the way they 'read' their data: literal, interpretive or reflexive.

> If you are intending to 'read' your data *literally*, you will be interested in their literal form, content, structure, style, layout, and so on . . . . An interpretive reading will involve you in constructing or documenting a version of what you think the data mean or represent, or what you think you can infer from them . . . . A reflexive reading will locate you as part of the data you have generated, and will seek to explore your role and perspective in the process of generation and interpretation of data. (Mason 2002: 149)

Recognition of the impossibility of detachment, as well as the reflexive nature of social research, poses some difficult philosophical problems with regard to the status of social scientific knowledge. Part of this dilemma centres on different ideas as to whether objectivity and 'true' knowledge are possible. There seems to be a fear that giving up on the possibility of being an objective researcher means that all social research degenerates into the production of competing 'subjective' accounts, the relative merits of which can only be established by political processes. However, Hammersley and Atkinson have argued that a commitment to reflexivity does not imply 'that research is necessarily political, or that it should be political, in the sense of serving particular political causes or practical ends. For us, the primary goal of research is, and must remain, the production of knowledge' (2007: 15). On the other hand, critical theorists and feminist researchers see commitment to the cause of emancipation as an essential part of all social scientific activity. (See Blaikie 2007 for a brief review of these issues, and Hammersley 1992, Guba and Lincoln 2005, and Hammersley and Atkinson 2007 for discussions relevant to social research.)

I have not included the researcher's stance as a research design element as I suspect that adopting a particular stance is something that occurs independently of the research design. Of course, it is possible that an ideological commitment to a particular stance may have an influence on the research topics that are likely to be entertained, and on other design decisions. Having said this, in my view, reflexivity is not really a matter of choice. All social researchers should be reflexive, regardless of the stance they adopt. However, this will be easier for researchers who reject the detached stance.

We now turn to the first of two critical core design elements, the formulation of research questions.

Further Reading

de Vaus, D. A. 2001. *Research Design in Social Research*.
Adopts a very different approach to research design to the one presented here.

—— (ed.). 2006. *Research Design*.
  A comprehensive set of articles on many aspects of research design from a wide variety of positions.
Flick, U. 2007. *Designing Qualitative Research*.
  A brief introduction.
Marshall, C. and G. B. Rossman 2006. *Designing Qualitative Research*.
  Provides pragmatic, step-by-step guidance for developing and defending proposals in qualitative research.
Punch, K. F. 2006. *Developing Effective Research Proposals*.
  A concise and practical outline.
Silverman, D. 2005. *Doing Qualitative Research*.
  A broad coverage of the design, conduct, analysis, writing up, supervision, examination and publishing of postgraduate qualitative research.

3

Research Questions and Purposes

Chapter Summary

- All research projects are built on the foundation of research questions.
- Research questions define the nature and scope of a research project.
- Research questions can be grouped into three main types, 'what', 'why' and 'how' questions.
- The three types of questions form a sequence for the research process; 'what' questions followed by 'why' questions followed by 'how' questions.
- The importance of answering 'what' questions should not underestimated.
- The developmental nature of a research design should not be used as an excuse to avoid the effort required to formulate appropriate research questions.
- While the process of developing a set of research questions can be the most challenging part of any research project, techniques are available to assist the process.
- Research questions are what the research is designed to answer, not the questions asked of respondents or participants.
- The aim of the literature review is to indicate what the state of knowledge is with respect to each research question, or group of questions.
- Hypotheses are our best guesses at answering 'why' and, possibly, 'how' questions.
- If required, hypotheses should be derived from the literature review, particularly from theory or research results. Sometimes a theory may have to be generated.
- In some research, hypotheses may emerge, and be tested, in the course of the data collection and analysis.
- As an aid to the conception, clarification and classification of research questions, it is also useful to think about a research project in terms of its purposes.
- Social research can pursue eight major purposes: *explore*, *describe*, *understand*, *explain*, *predict*, *change*, *evaluate* and *assess impacts*.
- Many research purposes require 'what' questions. *Understand* and *explain*, and, to a lesser extent, *evaluate* and *assess impacts*, require 'why' questions. Only *change* requires 'how' questions.

- Research purposes are not a list of the activities the researcher is going to carry out: they are concerned with the type of knowledge researchers wish to produce.

Introduction

The use of research questions is a neglected aspect in the design and conduct of social research. This is surprising given that the fundamental purpose of social research is to provide new knowledge about the social world, to answer puzzles about what the social world is like and how it works, and to find ways to solve problems and bring about change. In my view, formulating research questions is the most critical component of any research design. It is only through the use of such questions that choices about the focus and direction of research can be made, that its boundaries can be clearly delimited, that manageability can be achieved and that a successful outcome can be anticipated. Establishing research questions also makes it possible to select research strategies and methods of data collection and analysis with confidence. In other words, *a research project is built on the foundation of its research questions*. However, getting these questions clear and precise requires considerable thought and sometimes some preliminary investigation.

This chapter discusses:

- three main types of research questions;
- the functions of research questions;
- how to develop and refine research questions;
- the relationship between research questions and hypotheses, and the functions of the latter; and
- how research questions can provide a guide and framework for the review of the literature.

As a way of elaborating research questions, consideration is also given to the research purposes behind the questions. Hence, there is a discussion of:

- the nature and range of research purposes that can be pursued; and
- the relationship between research purposes and research questions (see figure 3.1).

The aim of the chapter is not only to argue that research questions are necessary, but also that good research needs high-quality questions. A rare attempt to deal with the issue of the quality of research questions has been undertaken by Campbell *et al.* (1982). They reviewed articles in five journals in psychology, organizational behaviour and management, taking a two-year period for each journal. A list of the research questions was compiled and then researchers were surveyed in the fields covered to see what questions they thought should be asked. Their aim was to find gaps in research and to establish priorities for future research.

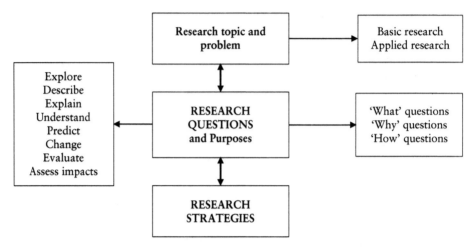

Figure 3.1   Research questions and purposes

Research Questions

Research questions are needed to define the nature and scope of the research. By selecting questions, and paying attention to their wording, it is possible to determine what is to be studied, and, to some extent, how it will be studied. The way a particular research question is worded can have a significant influence on how much and what kind of research activity will be required.

Conventional wisdom suggests that research should be guided by one or more hypotheses. According to this view, in order to get started on a research project the researcher should, first, select a research problem, second, state one or more hypotheses to be tested, and, third, measure and correlate the variables related to the concepts in the hypotheses. However, this procedure is only relevant to quantitative research conducted within the Deductive research strategy. While there is a role for hypotheses in particular kinds of research, they neither provide the foundation for a research design nor are they very useful for defining the focus and direction of a research project. In fact, the ritual of formulating and testing hypotheses can lead to unnecessary and unhelpful rigidities in the way in which research is conducted. In some kinds of research, it is impossible or unnecessary to set out with hypotheses. A much more useful procedure is to establish one or more research questions.

A Neglected Component of Social Research

Few textbooks on research methods give much attention to the formulation of research questions, and some ignore this vital part of the research process entirely. Exceptions can be found in some recent texts on research methods, for example, Hedrick *et al.* (1993); Miles and Huberman (1994); Blaxter *et al.* (2002); Mason (2002); Yin (2003a); Punch (2005); Maxwell (2005); Neuman (2006); Flick

(2006); Marshall and Rossman (2006); Creswell (2007); and Green (2008). It is interesting to note that these books are either concerned with qualitative research methods or include a significant discussion of them.

For example, Flick has argued for the importance of research questions in qualitative research.

> Experience from my own research and even more from supervising and consulting other people in their research has shown how decisive it is for the success of a project to have a clear and explicitly formulated research question. (Flick 2007: 22)

> [A] first and central step, and one which essentially determines success in qualitative research, but tends to be ignored in most presentations of methods, is how to formulate the research question(s). (Flick 2006: 105)

Creswell (2007) has argued that in a qualitative study, research questions are central, not objectives (goals for research) or hypotheses (predictions involving variables and statistical tests). I concur wholeheartedly with Flick's statement and would argue that what he and Creswell say about qualitative research applies to all social research.

Mason set her discussion of research questions in the context of intellectual puzzles that seek some kind of explanation. These puzzles take a variety of forms, depending on the ontological and epistemological positions adopted by the theoretical and intellectual traditions from within which they emerge. Intellectual puzzles then lead to research questions that she regarded as forming the backbone of a research design and as having much greater significance than hypotheses or propositions, particularly in qualitative research. For her, research questions

> should be clearly formulated (whether or not you intend to modify them or add to them later), intellectually worthwhile, and researchable (both in terms of your epistemological position, and in practical terms), because it is through them that you will be connecting what it is that you wish to research with how you are going to go about researching it. They are the vehicles which you will rely upon to move you from your broad research interest to your specific research focus and project, and therefore their importance cannot be overstated. Research questions, then, are those questions to which you as researcher really want to know the answers, and in that sense they are the formal expression of your intellectual puzzle. (Mason 2002: 19–20)

I hope these examples are sufficient to reinforce my argument about the pivotal role played by research questions in social research.

Types of Research Questions

Research questions can be grouped into three main types, 'what' questions, 'why' questions and 'how' questions. I have restricted research questions to 'what', 'why' and 'how' to maintain simplicity and to achieve a correspondence with the three main categories of research purposes: *description*, *explanation/understanding* and *change* (see figure 3.1).

What questions require a descriptive answer; they are directed towards discovering and describing the characteristics of and patterns in some social phenomenon, for example, categories of individuals, social groups of all sizes, and social processes. They include the following types of questions.

- What types of people are involved?
- What characteristic knowledge, beliefs, values and/or attitudes do they hold?
- What is their characteristic behaviour?
- What are the patterns in the relationships between these characteristics?
- What are the consequences of these activities?

Why questions ask for either the causes of, or the reasons for, the existence of characteristics or regularities in a particular phenomenon. They are directed towards understanding or explaining the relationships between events, or within social activities and social processes. For example:

- Why do people think and act this way?
- Why did these patterns come to be this way?
- Why do the characteristics or social process change, or remain stable?
- Why does this activity have these particular consequences?

How questions are concerned with bringing about change, with practical outcomes and intervention. For example:

- How can these characteristics, social processes or patterns be changed?
- How can they be made to stop changing, or to slow down or speed up their rate of change?

These three types of research questions form a sequence: 'what' questions normally precede 'why' questions, and 'why' questions normally precede 'how' questions. We need to know what is going on before we can explain it, and we need to know why something behaves the way it does before we can be confident about intervening to change it. However, most research projects will include only one or two types of research questions, most commonly 'what' and 'why' questions.

Some research may not proceed beyond one or more 'what' questions. While there may be a strong desire to include 'why' and possibly 'how' questions in a research project, the significance of producing good answers to 'what' questions should not be underestimated. In some fields, and on some topics, little research may have been undertaken anywhere, or recently, or in the context of interest. Before 'why' questions can be tackled, a good description of what is going on is needed. This may be an opportunity to make an important contribution to knowledge. In addition, some social scientists have argued that good description is all that is needed for an adequate understanding of many topics. Certainly, in comparative studies, description is the fundamental task. In short, good description is a vital part of social research.

Some writers have proposed more than three types of research questions. Yin (2003a), for example, has discussed seven types: 'who', 'what', 'where', 'how many', 'how much', 'how' and 'why'. However, he does acknowledge that 'who', 'where', 'how many' and 'how much' questions are different forms of a 'what' question. Blaxter *et al.* (2002) have suggested five types of questions: 'how', 'who', 'what', 'when' and 'why'. Similarly, the first four of their questions can all be transposed into 'what' questions: 'what individuals' in 'what places', at 'what time', in 'what numbers or quantities' and in 'what ways'.

Other writers have taken a different approach to research questions. Hedrick *et al.* (1993: 23–32) have identified four types of research questions that are relevant to applied research: descriptive, normative, correlative and impact. Marshall and Rossman (2006) have classified research questions as theoretical, as focusing on particular populations and as being site-specific. These categories relate to the context in which they are examined. While these categories may be useful, throughout the book, I shall discuss only the three types of research questions, 'what', 'why' and 'how'.

The process of developing research questions will inevitably produce a range of question wording similar to that discussed by Yin (2003a: 5–7). However, I believe the discipline of reducing all questions to these three types helps to make the links between research questions and research purposes clear.

Examples of Research Questions

Let us return to the four research topics discussed in chapter 2 and examine some possible research questions for each one.

Environmental Worldviews and Behaviour among Students and Residents

1 To what extent do students and residents hold different environmental worldviews?
2 To what extent is environmentally responsible behaviour practised?
3 What is the level and type of involvement in environmental movements?
4 To what extent, and in what ways, is environmental behaviour related to environmental worldviews?
5 In what ways and to what extent will environmental worldviews and behaviour change over the next five years?

As these are all 'what' questions, the study will have only *descriptive* purposes. It seeks to describe the distributions of environmental worldviews and behaviour in these populations, and the pattern of the relationship between these variables, now and in the future.

Age and environmentalism: a test of competing hypotheses

1 To what extent is age related to environmental worldviews and environmental behaviour?
2 If there are relationships, what are their forms?
3 Why do these relationships exist?

These are straightforward research questions, two 'what' questions followed by a 'why' question. The study wishes to establish the nature of these relationships and to explain them.

Gender differences in environmentalism: towards an explanation

1 To what extent do women hold more favourable environmental attitudes than men?
2 To what extent are women more willing than men to engage in environmentally responsible behaviour?
3 Why do these gender differences in environmentalism exist?

Again, this is a combination of 'what' and 'why' questions seeking descriptions of relationships and explanations for them.

Motivation for environmentally responsible behaviour: the case of environmental activists

1 In what range and types of behaviour do environmentally responsible individuals engage?
2 Why do these people act responsibly towards the environment?
3 Why do some of these people manage to sustain this behaviour?
4 How can the incidence of this type of behaviour be increased?

Now we come to a combination of all three types of research questions. The study seeks to describe environmentally responsible behaviour, and then to explain why people engage in and manage to sustain that behaviour. Then comes the sting in the tail – how to get more people to engage in this behaviour. It will be unlikely that a study of this kind could do anything more than point in the direction of possible answers to this last question, using the answers to questions 2 and 3. But it could also suggest ideas for further research to pursue it. (See the Appendix for examples of different and more complex sets of research questions.)

Developing and Refining Research Questions

The process of translating a research problem into a set of research questions can be the most challenging part of any research project. This is particularly the case when the researcher initiates the project, as is the case in much academic and postgraduate research in the social sciences. However, the problem still exists in research that is commissioned by someone else for problem-solving or policy-related purposes. Organizations or groups that commission research are very often vague about what they want done, and usually need some assistance to clarify the research questions.

It is very rare to commence a project with clearly formulated research questions already provided. This might occur where a researcher has joined a research programme in which the research questions have already been established, or if a researcher is taking up questions posed in previous research. However, it is much more common in the social sciences to approach a topic or field in which previous research is limited or has used an approach different from the one the researcher wants to use, or considers to be appropriate.

All researchers have to devise their own way of developing research questions. What I offer here is a process that I have used myself and found to work success-fully with many postgraduate students. Note that every step may not be required in every project. Creswell (2007, 2009); Maxwell (2005); Neuman (2006); and Punch (2006) offer other techniques.

1   Write down every question you can think of that relates to the research problem   The list will include all kinds of questions; some will be seeking descrip-tions, some explanations, some will be concerned with action, and so on. There is no need to try to achieve any order or consistency in the list; simply record the questions as they arise. One question will usually stimulate other questions; they should all be recorded. This activity may produce a long list. The purpose is to try to expose all the ideas that you have on the research problem, particularly those that may be taken for granted and which later you wish you had been fully aware of at the design stage. No question should be censored, even if it may seem to be marginal, outrageous or impractical.

2   Review the list of questions   Once you are satisfied that you have pretty well exhausted all the ideas you have on the research problem, you should review your list. There are a number of strategies for doing this.

- Group the questions under similar themes or topics, if such exist in your list. This is likely to reveal overlaps between questions which will make it possible to eliminate some and to consolidate others. Part of this consolidation can be achieved by developing a single, general or abstract question that summarizes a group of more specific questions.
- Set aside questions that seem to be marginal to the research problem, that *are* too outrageous, or that seem to take you in directions that may be too difficult or too demanding. You can always review these questions later if you decide to change the direction of the research.

3   Separate 'what', 'why' and 'how' questions   Within each group of questions, begin to identify those that appear to be 'what', 'why' and 'how' questions. Of course, some studies may be concerned ultimately with only one type of question, for example one or more 'what' questions, or just a 'why' question.

The wording of 'what', 'why' and 'how' questions requires very careful con-sideration, as the way a question is stated initially can be deceptive: 'what' and 'why' questions can begin with 'How', and 'how' questions can begin with 'What'. For example: 'How are environmental behaviour and environmen-tal worldview related?' This needs be transposed into a descriptive question, as: 'What is the relationship between environmental behaviour and environ-mental worldview?' or 'To what extent, and in what ways, is environmental behaviour related to environmental worldview?' The question, 'How do some people manage to behave in an environmentally responsible way?' needs to be transposed into an explanatory question: 'Why do these people act responsibly towards the environment?' The question, 'What can be done to increase the incidence of environmentally responsible behaviour?' needs to be transposed into an intervention question: 'How can the incidence of environmentally responsible behaviour be increased?'

Make sure each question is worded as clearly and as simply as possible and that each one can be identified unambiguously as a 'what', 'why' or 'how' question. Complex questions may need to be broken down into a series of questions. For example, the question, 'What is the incidence of student plagiarism?' would be better broken down into at least two questions: 'What has been the extent of detected student plagiarism over the past five years?' and 'In what types of plagiarism have students engaged?' (See the Appendix).

4 Expose assumptions   Check each question to see what it assumes. Many questions, particularly 'why' questions, presuppose other questions. It is important to expose the 'what' question that must be answered before a 'why' question can be asked, or, perhaps, even formulated.

'How' questions may presuppose both 'what' and, particularly, 'why' questions. A research project may need to examine all three types of questions. Rather than reducing the number of questions on the list, this part of the process may add further questions.

5 Examine the scope of the questions   Now is the time to get practical and ask yourself how many groups of questions, and questions within groups, can be tackled in the project. A judgement has to be made about what is going to be manageable within the time and with the other resources available. There is an inevitable tendency to try to do too much; the questions for the topic on student plagiarism are a good example (see the Appendix). Therefore, it is advisable at this stage to reduce the project to what may appear to be an extremely limited or even trivial set of questions. Such innocent-looking questions usually have other questions lurking in their shadows.

6 Separate major and subsidiary questions   Once the list of questions has been reduced to what appears to be a manageable set, further work can be done on them. It may be useful to separate the questions into two broad categories, *major* questions and *subsidiary* questions.[1] Major research questions are those that will form the core of the research project, the key questions that are to be answered. They may also be stated more abstractly than some of the other questions. Research projects may have only one major research question. However, most are likely to have a combination of major questions: 'what' questions and a 'why' question, or a set of 'what', 'why' and 'how' questions. About five or six major research questions is probably more than enough for any project. Subsidiary questions will include those that deal with background information or issues that are presupposed by one or more major questions that, while being necessary, are not absolutely central to the project. Here is an example of a set of major and subsidiary questions.

Major research question

• To what extent is environmentally responsible behaviour practised?

Subsidiary research questions

• To what extent are household waste products recycled?
• To what extent is buying environmentally damaging products avoided?
• To what extent is public transport and cycling used in preference to private motor vehicles?

In this example, the subsidiary questions can be used to specify categories of environmental behaviour and thus focus the study.

7 Is each question necessary? As your set of questions begins to take shape, you need to subject them to critical scrutiny by asking of each question: 'Why am I asking this question?' 'Is it related to the research problem?' 'Why do I want to know this?' 'What will I do with the results from it?' 'How does it relate to other questions?' 'Is it researchable?' 'Can I manage all these questions?' This process needs to be taken very seriously and not glossed over quickly. It is very easy to include questions because 'that would be interesting to explore', or 'I would really like to know about that'. This critical examination needs to be ruthless.

A common mistake in drafting research questions is to confuse them with questions used to elicit information from respondents or participants, for example, interview questions, or questions that would go into a questionnaire. Research questions are what you want the research project to answer. Questions you ask respondents can provide the basis for answering research questions, but their style and scope are very different. A wide variety of data may contribute to the answering of any research question.

Many postgraduate students seem to have a desire to do the definitive piece of research on their topic. This is not only an unrealistic expectation for a fully research-based PhD; it is impossible in research for any other kind of postgraduate degree. The problem is most acute for students undertaking a coursework (taught) master's degree in which there is a minor thesis/dissertation/project component. Because of its limited duration, such a research project is very difficult to design.

In short, the number and nature of the questions selected has got to reflect the available time and resources. This is the stage at which the scope of the project is determined, and bad decisions can produce serious problems later.

It is important to recognize that while it is highly desirable to produce a well formulated set of research questions as part of an integrated research proposal or design, this may not always be possible without some preliminary research being undertaken. In addition, what is discovered in the process of undertaking the research is likely to require a review of the research questions from time to time. No research design can completely anticipate how a research project will evolve. It may turn out that some research questions cannot be answered because it is not possible to obtain the necessary data. What the researcher assumed or was led to believe about the availability of or access to the necessary data may turn out to be wrong. Consequently, the design may require some revision, and part of this may involve a change to one or more research questions. Hence, while it is necessary to be as clear as possible about the scope and direction of the research at the beginning, what the researcher learns in the course of undertaking the research may necessitate some changes. This is simply the nature of research in any discipline.

Research projects differ in the extent to which it is possible to be able to produce precise research questions. This is certainly true of exploratory research, the aim of which can be to provide information to assist in the development of research questions. It might also be argued that some studies that use qualitative or ethnographic research methods involve the researcher in a learning process, of discovering research questions as well as answering them. In these cases, the research questions may evolve in the course of the research. However, even this kind of research requires careful consideration of scope and direction at the beginning in order to ensure that it will be manageable and will have a high probability of successful completion. The developmental nature of a research design should not be used as an excuse for avoiding the effort required to formulate appropriate research questions.

Staying on Track

A common feature of the research process is for the researcher to be deflected or distracted from their original intentions. Many influences may be at work:

- encountering new ideas, for example, in published research, in conference papers or presentations, in previously unfamiliar theory, or in the media;
- discussion with colleagues;
- changing academic fashions;
- changing political agendas; and, more particularly,
- learning that takes place during the course of the research, for example, from observations, from interviews and discussions, and from working with data.

It is very easy to lose one's way and to forget or neglect the original research questions. Changes to research questions should be made only after careful consideration and not by just drifting away from them. One way to counter this drift is to print the questions in large type and display them in prominent places, such as in your regular work space, or in the front page of your field book or journal. They should be read regularly to keep the focus of the research clear.

Research Questions and Hypotheses

As we have seen, it is a common view that social research should be directed by one or more hypotheses. However, in some types of research this is impossible or inappropriate. When hypotheses are considered to be essential, it is not always clear what their role is or where they are to come from. In some traditions of research, it is expected that hypotheses will be stated very precisely, in the null and directional forms, to facilitate statistical testing. In other traditions, hypotheses are stated much more loosely, and their acceptance or rejection is based on evidence and argument rather than tests of significance. In practice, hypotheses are drawn from a variety of sources, such as hunches or intuition, previous research, discursive argument and carefully formulated theories. While the latter is advocated in some traditions (see the discussion of the Deductive research strategy in chapter 4), their source is frequently vague and their purpose unclear.

Lundberg's early textbook on social research (1942) provides a classical view of the role of hypotheses. He argued that there are four steps in 'the scientific method': the formulation of a working hypothesis, the observation and recording of data, the classification and organization of the data collected, and the production of generalizations that apply under given conditions. In this context, Lundberg defined a hypothesis as 'a tentative generalization, the validity of which remains to be tested. In its most elementary stages, the hypothesis may be any hunch, guess, imaginative idea or intuition whatsoever which becomes the basis for action or investigation' (1942: 9). This view of a hypothesis simply requires the researcher to have a guess at what they think the data might reveal, and then proceed to see if it is the case. So conventional has this view become that the novice researcher feels compelled to make such guesses, even if it makes no sense to do so; one feels naked without a hypothesis for a fig leaf. The fear of not being able to 'prove' their hypothesis hangs like the sword of Damocles over the novice's head; guessing the wrong hypothesis, or the wrong version of it, can be regarded as a disaster. The stress in this tradition of research is on having a hypothesis, not always on where it comes from, what it might be connected to, and what purpose it serves. It is not uncommon to invent such hypotheses after the research has been completed.

Some writers conflate hypotheses and research questions. For example, Mitchell and Jolley stated that research is done to answer questions, but then went on to say that such questions are usually stated as hypotheses (1992: 38). They have quite rightly argued (2007: 52) that research does not begin with variables, equipment and participants, and encourage students to learn how to generate questions and develop them into workable hypotheses. However, in the discussion that follows this injunction, there is no mention of questions, only hypotheses, variables and relationships between variables.

It is my view that *hypotheses are tentative answers to 'why' and, sometimes, 'how' research questions*. They are our best guesses at the answers. But *they are not appropriate for 'what' questions*. There is little point in hazarding guesses at a possible state of affairs. Research will produce an answer to a 'what' question in due course, and no amount of guessing about what will be found is of any assistance; it might even prejudice the answer. Therefore, hypotheses should be reserved for the role of tentative answers to 'why' and 'how' questions, and particularly 'why' questions. While it may not always be possible to produce a hypothesis for such research questions, to do so is to give research a much clearer sense of direction; decisions about what data to gather, and how to analyse them, are easier to make. However, it is important to note that some traditions of research that are concerned with 'why' questions may not set out with hypotheses. In grounded theory, for example, hypotheses are proposed in response to the patterns in the accumulating data, and they will be tested in a continuing trial and error process, being refined and, perhaps, discarded along the way.

A central issue that researchers confront at the stage of formulating research questions and hypotheses (if required) is what concepts to use and how to define them. How this is handled will depend largely on the particular research strategy or strategies, and theories or theoretical perspectives, adopted. This issue will be introduced in the next section and will be discussed in more detail in the early part of chapter 5.

Research questions and the literature review

A literature review is a customary component of any research report or thesis. Its main purpose is to provide a background to and context for the research, and to establish a bridge between the project and the current state of knowledge on the topic. This review may include:

- background information that establishes the existence of the problem to be investigated;
- previous research on the topic, or related topics;
- theory of relevance to the 'why' question(s);
- research paradigm(s) as a source of ontological and epistemological assumptions;
- methodological considerations of relevance to the selection of a research strategy or strategies; and
- a review and/or elaboration of the methods to be used.

These components of the literature review may end up in various places in the thesis or research report. The first may be part of the introductory chapter; the last two may appear in a methodology and methods chapter; and the fourth may be part of a discussion on the choice of research strategy or strategies. It is the second and third, on previous research and theory, that are particularly relevant to the research questions.

A major dilemma in any research project is to establish what literature to review – what literature is relevant. This can be a daunting and confusing task, particularly for novice researchers. I have observed many students spending an excessive amount of time reading rather aimlessly. Some will not really be satisfied until they have read 'everything', but the problem is to know what to include in 'everything'.

One solution to this problem is to use the research questions to guide and structure the review of previous research and relevant theory. Each question can be used to put a boundary around a body of literature, be it theory, published research or reports. *The aim of the literature review is to indicate what the state of knowledge is with respect to each research question, or group of questions.* In support of this position, Marshall and Rossman (2006: 39) have argued that research questions 'should forecast the literature to be reviewed.'

If hypotheses are used, they should have some connection with this literature. In some cases it may be possible to derive such a tentative answer to a 'why' question from existing theory, or it may be necessary to construct a new theory for the purpose. As we shall see, within the Deductive research strategy, the development of a theory from which a hypothesis or hypotheses can be deduced is an essential part of answering 'why' questions. In the Retroductive research strategy, the literature review may provide some assistance in the construction of hypothetical explanatory models. When the Abductive research strategy is used for theory generation, hypotheses are an integral part of the continuing process of data collection and analysis, of observation, reflection, hypothesizing and testing. However, advocates of this strategy usually argue that research should *not* begin with hypotheses.

Research Purposes

In contrast to the researcher's personal motives and goals for undertaking a particular research project, research purposes are concerned with the types of knowledge a researcher wants to produce. Social research can have a number of purposes, ranging from relatively simple to very complex, and encompassing both basic and applied research. Research can set out to *explore, describe, explain, understand, predict, change, evaluate* and *assess impacts* (see figure 3.1).

A research project can pursue just one of these purposes or, perhaps, a number of them in sequence. For example, a study may set out to *describe*, or it might begin with a descriptive stage and then proceed to *explain* and then to *change*. Basic research focuses on the first five purposes, to *explore, describe, explain, understand* and *predict*, but particularly *describe, explain and understand*. While applied research may include some of these 'basic' purposes, it is particularly concerned with *change, evaluation* and *impact assessment*.

Types of Purposes

Basic research

To *explore* is to attempt to develop an initial, rough description or, possibly, an understanding of some social phenomenon.

To *describe* is to provide a detailed account, or the precise measurement and reporting, of the characteristics of some population, group or phenomenon, including establishing regularities.

To *explain* is to establish the elements, factors or mechanisms that are responsible for producing the state of or regularities in a social phenomenon.

To *understand* is to establish reasons for particular social action, the occurrence of an event or the course of a social episode, these reasons being derived from the ones given by social actors.

To *predict* is to use some established understanding or explanation of a phenomenon to postulate certain outcomes under particular conditions.

Applied research

To *change* is to intervene in a social situation by manipulating some aspects of
it, or to assist the participants to do so, preferably on the basis of established
understanding or explanation.

To *evaluate* is to monitor social intervention programmes to assess whether they
have achieved their desired outcomes, and to assist with problem-solving and
policy-making.

To *assess social impacts* is to identify the likely social and cultural consequences
of planned projects, technological change or policy actions on social structures,
social processes and/or people.

Similar classifications of research purposes have been presented by Marshall
and Rossman (2006) – exploratory, explanatory, descriptive and emancipatory
– and by Neuman (2007) – exploratory, descriptive, explanatory, evaluation,
action and social impact assessment.

In case you might be wondering why *comparison* is not included as a research
purpose, I regard it either as a form of description or as a technique for arriving at
explanation or understanding, i.e. for theory generation or testing. In fact, comparison is one of the best methods for generating theory, as is evident in grounded
theory (Corbin and Strauss 2008). As such, it is not a research purpose but can
be a means for achieving such purposes. Therefore, a list of purposes should not
include statements like 'To compare the environmental attitudes of university
students and logging contractors'. A research project might set out to *describe* the
attitudes of each group, and to try to *explain* why they hold particular attitudes.
A comparison of their attitudes can be part of either of these purposes.

Explore   Exploratory research is necessary when very little is known about
the topic being investigated, or about the context in which the research is to be
conducted. Perhaps the topic has never been investigated before, or never in that
particular context. Basic demographic characteristics of a group of people, or
some aspects of their behaviour or social relationships, may need to be known
in order to design the study. The relevance of particular research questions, or
the feasibility of using certain methods of data gathering, may also need to be
explored. Essentially, exploratory research is used to get a better idea of what is
going on and how it might be researched. The methods used to conduct exploratory research need to be flexible but are not usually as rigorous as those used to
pursue other purposes.

While exploratory research is usually conducted at the beginning of a research
project, it may also be necessary at other stages to provide information for critical design decisions, to overcome an unexpected problem, to better understand
an unanticipated finding, or to establish which avenues of explanation would be
worthwhile pursuing.

In the context of his advocacy of symbolic interactionism, Blumer (1969) gave
exploratory research a substantial role. He believed this was necessary to counter
the common tendency to move straight into research without an adequate understanding of the sector of social life being investigated. He saw the exploratory

phase as being necessary to sharpen the focus of the research; not as an optional extra, but as an essential part of any project. 'The purpose of exploratory investigation is to move towards a clearer understanding of how one's problem is to be posed, to learn what are the appropriate data, to develop ideas of what are significant lines of relation, and to evolve one's conceptual tools in the light of what one is learning about the area of life' (Blumer 1969: 40). Blumer has left us in no doubt about how essential exploratory research is to the development of a good research design.

Describe Descriptive research seeks to present an accurate account of some phenomenon, the characteristics in some demographic category, group or population, the patterns of relationships in some social context, at a particular time, or the changes in those characteristics over time (Bulmer 1986: 66). These descriptive accounts can be expressed in words or numbers and may involve the development of sets of categories or types.

In practice, the boundary between exploratory and descriptive research is blurred. Descriptive research is more rigorous and is usually narrower in its focus; it should be directed by clearly stated research questions. However, both types of research require the use of concepts and they will be structured by at least some theoretical assumptions.

Explain and understand Explanatory research seeks to account for patterns in observed social phenomena, attitudes, behaviour, social relationships, social processes or social structures (Bulmer 1986: 66–7). Explanation is making intelligible the events or regularities that have been observed and which cannot be accounted for by existing theories. Explanations eliminate puzzles and provide intellectual satisfaction. To explain some phenomenon is to give an account of why it behaves in a particular way or why particular regularities occur. Detailed description can provide the beginnings of an explanation.

Explanations make the obscure plain to see. This is true of both semantic and scientific explanation. Semantic explanation is concerned with the meanings of words and phrases, while scientific explanation seeks the causes for the occurrence of a particular event or regularity. However, making something intelligible is not just a subjective matter.

> There is a difference between *having* an explanation and *seeing* it. In the case of semantic explanation, we do not have one unless and until we see it, but in the case of scientific explanation either the having or the seeing may occur without the other. That an explanation is often resisted when it is first offered is a commonplace of the history of science – men [*sic*] have it, but do not see it. The reverse is characteristic of the sort of explanations occurring in myths, paranoia, the occult 'sciences', and the like. . . . They provide a certain intellectual satisfaction, but it is one unwarranted by the actual state of affairs. Those who accept them only see an explanation, but do not have one. (Kaplan 1964: 330)

I follow the distinction between *explanation* and *understanding* that has been discussed by writers such as Taylor (1964) and von Wright (1971) and, subsequently, Giddens (1979: 258). The difference between them is a matter of how intelligibility is achieved; by *causal* explanation or by *reason* explanation. Explanations identify causes of events or regularities, the factors or mechanisms that produced them, whereas understanding is provided by the reasons or accounts social actors give for their actions. The latter is also associated with the meaning of an event or activity in a particular social context, either that given by social actors or the meaning that researchers derive from social actors' accounts. Explanations are produced by researchers who look at a phenomenon from the 'outside', whereas understanding is based on an 'inside' view in which researchers grasp the subjective consciousness, the interpretations, of social actors involved in the conduct (Giddens 1976: 55).

The distinction between explanation (*erklären*) and understanding (*verstehen*) has a long history in German scholarship. While some writers (e.g. Winch 1958) have argued that causal explanation is appropriate in the natural sciences and reason explanation is appropriate in the human or social sciences, other writers have argued either that both can be used in the social sciences (e.g. Habermas 1972), or that characterizing the two fields of science as being exclusively concerned with only one of these is inappropriate (e.g. Giddens 1976). The position adopted here is that both explanation and understanding are appropriate purposes in the social sciences, but that they produce rather different kinds of intelligibility.

In both the natural and social sciences, various strategies have been advocated to achieve explanation or understanding, based on different assumptions and the use of different logics of enquiry. These strategies look in different places, and in terms of different factors or mechanisms, for answers to their research questions. In chapter 4, three of these explanatory strategies (the Inductive, Deductive and Retroductive), and one that is used to achieve understanding (the Abductive), are outlined and compared in terms of their relevance to the design and conduct of social research.

Predict   Prediction in research makes claims about what *should* happen if certain laws or mechanisms operate under certain conditions. This needs to be distinguished from prophecy, which makes claims about what will happen in the future (Popper 1961: 128). The possibility of prediction is dependent on the state of knowledge at a particular time.

Prediction can be achieved in two ways: in terms of well-established patterns of association between concepts (as in the Inductive research strategy); or by shifting the emphasis in a theoretical argument (as in the Deductive research strategy). In the case of established patterns, whenever one part of a relationship is present, it can be expected that the other part will also be present. For example, if it has been consistently established that juvenile delinquents come from broken homes, then locating particular juvenile delinquents can lead to the prediction that they will be found to have come from broken homes, or, alternatively, that children from broken homes are likely to become delinquents.

Some writers have argued that the logic involved in explanation and prediction is essentially the same; it is just a matter of where the emphasis is put and what can be taken as given (Popper 1959, 1961; Hempel 1966). This claim is based on the assumption that a set of propositions that has been used as an explanation of an observed pattern can also be used to predict another pattern. For example, if an explanation has been constructed to explain why the suicide rate is low in a country in which a particular religion is predominant, and if religion has been shown in a deductive argument to be related to suicide rates (as Durkheim claimed to have established), then it is possible to predict that other countries of a similar religious composition will have similar suicide rates (see the discussion of Homans's (1964) reconstruction of Durkheim's (1951) theory of suicide in chapter 4).

Writers who have advocated the Retroductive research strategy (e.g. Bhaskar, 1979) have argued that prediction is only possible in closed systems, perhaps only under experimental conditions. As social scientists have to work in open systems, it follows that prediction is not possible in the social sciences. While explanation in terms of causal mechanisms is possible, there is no scope for prediction because the conditions under which a mechanism operates can never be fully established. As the natural sciences also operate in open systems, apart from artificially controlled experiments, the advocates of this position also claim that prediction is not possible in the natural sciences.

Change　Research that is concerned with change endeavours to intervene in the social world to bring about partial or major changes, either in conjunction with the research itself, or as a consequence of research outcomes. Change can only be achieved with confidence if the actions taken are based on those that a well established explanation or understanding would suggest. However, the process of intervention itself can be used as a learning process. Knowledge of a phenomenon can be developed in a trial and error process, as intervention is conducted in stages. What is learnt from one stage can be used to decide what action to take in the next stage. The outcome can be explanation as well as change. In fact, some philosophers of science (e.g. Popper) have argued that this trial and error process, rather than gigantic leaps into unknown territory, is the only way scientific knowledge can be advanced. Nevertheless, it is possible to distinguish between intervention that is used primarily for the purpose of advancing knowledge, and intervention that tries to change the social world; between purely scientific concerns or essentially social or political concerns; between basic research and applied research.

The 'action research' tradition has the joint purposes of increasing knowledge and changing some aspect of the world at the same time. It differs from more conventional research in that the researcher may take the role of facilitator or resource person who helps a group of people change their own situation from the inside, rather than the researcher adopting the role of outside expert who tries to bring about change by 'external' intervention.

In some research paradigms (e.g. Critical Theory and Feminism) it is argued that change is the fundamental purpose of social science; all other purposes must serve that of the emancipation of oppressed groups. Therefore, while the purpose of *change* may be regarded as an add-on stage in research, it has been regarded by some as being either the only way to generate scientific knowledge, or the only legitimate form of social science.

Hence, intervention research may adopt 'outside' or 'inside' methods; it may be done to a group or community at the researcher's initiative, or on behalf of someone else, or it may be done in conjunction with, or as a result of, the initiative of a group or community. In the latter case, it is directed towards the goals *they* have defined or have been helped to define. This type of research is usually referred to as 'participatory action research' (see Whyte 1991).

Intervention research can also be done 'top down', thus serving the needs of the powerful, or 'bottom up' by serving the needs of the powerless. Hence, it may be viewed loosely as either 'radical' or 'conservative'. Radical interventionist research is emancipatory research that is designed to improve the conditions of less powerful sections of society and to replace oppressive regimes, and is frequently associated with some version of critical theory (Habermas 1971, 1987; Fay 1975, 1987; Bhaskar 1979, 1986). More conservative versions of intervention research can be found in fields such as organizational change. While some organizational research may be concerned with producing a more humane working environment, and with the welfare of employees, generally the ultimate concern is to bring about changes that will achieve greater productivity and efficiency.

Evaluate   Evaluation research, as well as *impact assessment* of various kinds, is concerned with policy and programme development and implementation in particular, and with problem-solving and decision-making in general. It seeks answers to questions posed by decision-makers, not academics. Evaluation research seeks to examine the consequences of the adoption of particular courses of action. It sets out to determine whether a particular policy or programme has been effective in achieving certain policy or programme goals. Evaluation research compares 'what is' with 'what should be' (Weiss 1972: 6): 'The purpose of evaluation research is to measure the effects of a program against the goals it set out to accomplish as a means of contributing to subsequent decision-making about the program and improving future programming' (Weiss 1972: 4).

Two types of evaluation research are commonly discussed: *formative evaluation*, in which built-in monitoring or continuous feedback is used during the implementation of a policy as a basis for helping to improve it; and *summative evaluation*, which is conducted after a policy has been implemented to establish its overall effectiveness in achieving the original goals.

Pawson and Tilley (1997) have identified four main perspectives on evaluation research: the *experimental* (Campbell and Stanley 1963a; Cook and Campbell 1979); the *pragmatic* (Weiss 1972, 1976; Weiss and Bucuvalas 1980); the *naturalistic* (Guba and Lincoln 1989); and the *pluralist* (Cronbach 1963, 1982; Rossi and Freeman 1985). The first on the scene in the 1960s, the *experimental* perspective, used classical or quasi-experimental procedures to try to establish whether change is the result of the planned intervention. In the wake of disappointing results from this first phase, the *pragmatic* perspective became less ambitious and advocated the careful use of any kind of sound research. The *naturalistic* perspective took a different turn and saw evaluation as a matter of negotiation between stakeholders with different interpretations (constructions) of a programme. The *pluralists* called for greater depth and breadth in programme evaluation by examining the way programmes are conceptualized, dealing with both institutional and individual diagnoses of the problem and focusing on outcome effectiveness. Pawson and Tilley (1997) have added a fifth perspective, *realistic evaluation*, based on scientific realism (see 'social realism' in chapter 4), for which they claim superiority over the other perspectives. They have provided eight rules for the conduct of evaluation research. More recently, Pawson (2006) has taken this approach further in his argument for evidence-based policy.[2]

Commonly used tools in both *evaluation* research and *impact assessment* are *needs analysis* and *cost-benefit analysis*. However, it is because of the deficiencies in cost-benefit analysis, due to its narrow economic focus, that the development of both *social impact assessment* and *environmental impact assessment* has occurred.

Assess impacts   Impact assessment (IA) has been defined as '*the process of identifying the future consequences of a current or proposed action*' (Becker 1997: 2). In the case of social impact assessment (SIA), these consequences are related to '*individuals, organizations, institutions and society as a whole*' (Becker 1997: 123). Following the definition of SIA in the United States by the Inter-organizational Committee on Guidelines and Principles (1994), Burdge and Vanclay have included cultural as well as social impacts: Social impacts are the consequences of

> any public and private actions that alter the way in which people live, work, play, relate to one another, organize to meet their needs, and generally cope as members of society. Cultural impacts involve changes to norms, values, and beliefs of individuals that guide and rationalize their cognition of themselves and their society. (Burdge and Vanclay 1995: 32)

SIA can be concerned with assessing or predicting the demographic, socio-economic, institutional, community and psychological impacts of resource development and large-scale construction projects, as well as social or economic policies and programmes (Becker 1997; Bulmer 1986). The tasks of SIAs are to:

- assess and predict potential impacts;
- mitigate and monitor these impacts; and
- audit and analyse the impacts of past actions.

For example, a major road construction scheme may lead to population movements, the fragmentation of social communities, psychological stress and changes in property values. Similarly, a new social welfare policy may lead to disadvantages among groups that it was supposed to benefit. SIA will endeavour to identify the range and extent of such impacts; it can be used to trade off the benefits of the project (e.g. reduced traffic congestion and accidents) against social costs. An important aspect of *social impact assessment* is the relative gains and losses that particular groups in a community or society are likely to experience as the result of a construction project. Some form of compensation for such losses might then be built into the costing of the project (see also Finsterbusch 1983, 1985).

In many ways, SIA has grown out of the related and increasingly significant field of *environmental impact assessment* (EIA). While the latter's primary concern is with the natural and biophysical impacts of major physical projects, it is now generally accepted that EIA and SIA are complementary and that the latter must accompany the former.

Relationships among Research Purposes

The four research purposes, *explore, describe, explain* and *predict,* can occur as a sequence in terms of both the stages and the increasing complexity of research. Exploration usually precedes description, and description is necessary before explanation or prediction can be attempted. Exploration may be necessary to provide clues about the patterns that need to be described in a particular phenomenon. The sequence, beginning with the description of patterns, and followed by an explanation of why they occur, is central in any form of social research. Description of what is happening leads to questions or puzzles about why it is happening, and this calls for an explanation or some kind of understanding.

The importance of description is often underrated in research, with explanation being seen as the ultimate goal. However, without adequate description there may be nothing to explain; it is necessary to be sure what the patterns or regularities are before any attempt is made to explain them. It has been argued that explanation works 'not by involving something beyond what might be described, but by putting one fact or law in relation to others' (Kaplan 1964: 329). This is known as the 'pattern' model of explanation and is characteristic of the Inductive research strategy (to be discussed in chapter 4). Hence, some forms of explanation, such as pattern explanations, are nothing more than complex descriptions.

There are a variety of views on the relationship between explanation and prediction. It is possible to make predictions without having an explanation of a phenomenon. This kind of prediction relies on well-established generalizations about patterns of relationships between concepts. While some philosophers have argued that these patterns provide a basis for explanation, others have argued that it is necessary to find the mechanism that produces such patterns before explanation can be achieved (see chapter 4). However, the description of patterns or relationships between concepts can be used for prediction.

The purposes of *evaluate* and *assess impacts* share much in common. They, together with *change,* constitute the main fields of applied research. As we have seen, a major distinguishing feature of applied research is that it has a sponsor and/or client. Its goals are either set by the sponsor, or are the outcome of negotiation between the sponsor and researcher, and its outcomes have to address the concerns of the client. While it may be possible to attempt evaluation and impact assessment from an atheoretical point of view, by building on only a descriptive research base and side-stepping explanation or understanding, sophisticated evaluation and impact assessment need to use existing theories. If relevant theories are not available, they will need to be developed. Because applied research is normally done within strict time and resource constraints, there is pressure to take short cuts to avoid these essential components. Good applied research has to draw on well-established theories, because, after all, there is nothing as practical as a good theory.

It is unlikely that the whole gambit of research purposes can be or need to be tackled in most research projects, and certainly not within the limitations of postgraduate research. Previous research can and should be used as a background to a research project. For example, if good descriptive research has already been done in the field, it may be possible to begin with an explanatory purpose, or if well-established and relevant theories are available, it may be possible to engage directly in the purposes of *change, evaluation* or *assess impacts*. But, to repeat an earlier point, without an adequate descriptive base, it is not possible to begin to pursue the other research purposes.

Research Purposes and Questions

Each of the eight research purposes is related to a particular type of research question. If we take some imaginary social process as an example, the three types of research questions would be associated with the eight research purposes as follows.

Explore	**What** might be happening?
	What people are involved? In **what** way?
Describe	**What** is happening?
	What people are involved? In **what** way?
Understand	**Why** is it happening?
Explain	**Why** is it happening?
Predict	**What** is likely to happen?
Change	**How** can it be made to be different?
Evaluate	**What** has happened? **Why** did it happen?
Assess impacts	**What** have been, or are likely to be, its individual, social and environmental consequences? **Why** have these consequences occurred?

The purposes of *understand* and *explain*,[3] and, to a lesser extent, *evaluate* and assess *impacts*, are the only ones that require 'why'-type questions. *Change* is the only purpose that requires 'how'-type questions. All the other purposes have questions beginning with 'what', or their questions can be transposed into this form. They are, therefore, either descriptive in nature, or involve comparisons between situations in the present, between a present and a past situation, or between a present situation and a desired future. To avoid the confusion that can result from other question wording, for example, pursuing description or explanation with questions that commence with 'how', this three-category classification of questions should be followed.

Further Reading

Andrews, R. 2003. *Research Questions*.
   A brief and readable discussion of research questions from the point of view of educational research.

Flick, U. 2006. *An Introduction to Qualitative Research.*
  Argues for the importance of research questions and offers some useful advice.
Green, N. 2008. 'Formulating and refining a research question.'
  An excellent discussion that draws on ideas presented in this chapter.
Mason, J. 2002. *Qualitative Researching.* Chapter 1.
  A brief but highly pertinent discussion of research questions and their relationship to intellectual puzzles.
Punch, K. F. 2005. *Introduction to Social Research.* Chapters 3 and 4.
  A detailed discussion of the nature and role of research questions.

4

Strategies for Answering Research Questions

Chapter Summary

- When social researchers set out to answer research questions, they are faced with the task of choosing the best research strategy or strategies to answer them.
- Four fundamentally different research strategies are available, each with its unique logic of enquiry and its particular combination of ontological and epistemological assumptions.
- The research strategies differ in the types of research questions and purposes they can answer.
  - The Inductive and Abductive strategies are the only ones that can answer 'what' questions and are useful for *exploration* and *description*, although they each achieve these purposes in different ways and with different outcomes.
  - The Deductive and Retroductive research strategies specialize in answering 'why' questions and are the most suitable for pursuing the purpose of *explanation*; they achieve this using different procedures based on different assumptions.
  - The Abductive research strategy can answer both 'what' and 'why' questions, and, together with the *constructionist* version of the Retroductive strategy, can deal with the purpose of *understanding* with their particular ontological and epistemological assumptions and logics of enquiry.
- Research strategies are normally used in the context of a research paradigm; some are closely associated with a particular research paradigm while others can be used with a number of them.
- Choice of research strategy can be influenced by:
  - a researcher's familiarity or lack of familiarity with the strategies;
  - a researcher's preference for certain ontological and epistemological assumptions;
  - a researcher's perceived link between preferred research methods and research strategies;
  - preferences of audiences and consumers of the research, and associated politics; and

○ a range of pragmatic factors such as time, cost and availability of equipment.

Before proceeding to a consideration of the research methods that may be suitable for selecting, collecting and analysing data to answer research questions, within a particular research strategy, we need to backtrack to consider a set of fundamental issues. These are the roles of concepts, theories, hypotheses and models in social research.

Introduction

Having established a set of research questions, the next task is to devise ways to answer them. How this is done depends on the type of question. Answering a 'what' question is usually easier than answering a 'why' or 'how' question. 'What' questions can be dealt with by making appropriate observations or measurements, i.e. collecting appropriate data, and then producing quantitative and/or qualitative descriptions based on them. However, this process is not as simple as it sounds; descriptions of what we believe we have observed may not be, perhaps cannot be, pure descriptions. The observer, as an active participant in the process, has to make many decisions before a description can be produced, and cannot avoid using someone's concepts and categories.

Answers to 'how' questions require a different kind of description; a possible state of affairs has to be described and ideas about how to get there have to be provided. As we saw in chapter 3, 'how' questions usually require answers to related 'what' and 'why' questions, either in the research being undertaken, or in previous research. Unless a good understanding of the nature of the phenomenon being investigated has already been achieved, and why it behaves the way it does, it is difficult, undesirable and possibly dangerous to begin to propose any form of intervention. However, the monitoring of limited interventions in 'safe' situations (i.e. ones that will not have ethically undesirable or socially unacceptable consequences) is one way of discovering answers to 'why' and 'how' questions. Action research is such a learning process. I will come back to the ways of answering 'what' and 'how' questions later in the chapter. In the meantime, I want to concentrate on how to answer 'why' questions.

The main problem in answering 'why' questions is where to look for the answers. How we deal with this will determine where the research process begins and how it will proceed. Answering them involves dealing with theory in one form or another; *explanation* and *understanding* require either a theory or a very complex description. Hence, 'why' questions present us with complex issues and choices.

This chapter:

• outlines the four research strategies that can be used to answer research questions;
• reviews six types of both ontological and epistemological assumptions;
• indicates which of these two kinds of assumptions are associated with the four research strategies;

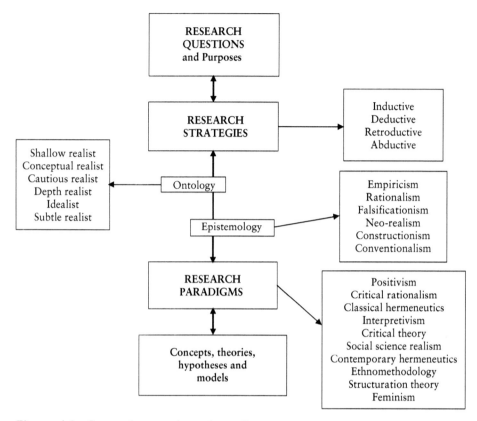

Figure 4.1   Research strategies and paradigms

- reviews four classical and seven contemporary research paradigms that provide a background to the research strategies;
- indicates which types of research questions and research purposes each research strategy can answer;
- indicates which of the researcher's stances are associated with the research strategies; and
- discusses issues involved in choosing a research strategy.

Four Research Strategies

A daunting array of possibilities is available for answering research questions. Are the answers to be found by collecting data and generalizing from them, by finding a suitable theory that will provide some hypotheses to test, by searching for underlying causal mechanisms, or by seeking social actors' meanings and interpretations? The choice made from alternatives such as these will depend on the research strategy that is adopted. A research strategy, or logic of enquiry, provides a starting-point and set of steps by means of which 'what' or 'why' questions can be answered. Research strategies differ in their:

- ontological assumptions;
- starting-points;
- steps or logic;
- use of concepts and theory;
- styles of explanation and understanding; and
- the status of their products.

Each strategy has connections with particular philosophical and theoretical traditions, i.e. research paradigms (see Blaikie 2007).

The concept of 'research strategy' has been used for various purposes in the literature. It is important to note that my usage here, and in my *Approaches to Social Enquiry* (Blaikie 2007), focuses on the major logics of social enquiry, not on such things as types of research designs or the range of methods of investigation.

I shall discuss four research strategies; the Inductive, Deductive, Retroductive and Abductive (see figure 4.1).[1] The discussion is illustrated by reference to two of the research questions from topic 4 in the Appendix:[2]

1 What kinds of young people engage in juvenile crime?
2 Why do young people engage in these activities?

The first requires a description of juvenile delinquents, and the second requires an explanation or an understanding for their behaviour.

To answer the first question it is necessary to identify individual characteristics and then summarize the most common ones, perhaps ordered in terms of the frequency with which they occur. Hence, we move from characteristics of individuals to summaries of, or generalizations about, the characteristics of a collection of individuals. For the second question it is necessary to go beyond generalizations to search for causes or reasons for this behaviour. As we shall see, summary descriptions begin to take us some way along this path.

It is important to note that description requires considerable input from the researcher. For a start, we need a definition of juvenile crime, and then descriptions of the characteristics of juvenile delinquents require a selection by the researcher from a wide array of possibilities. Of course, the social sciences have developed traditions on what is considered to be appropriate individual and social characteristics that should be examined in such a situation. These are likely to include *demographic* characteristics (e.g. age, gender, religion, area of residence), *socio-economic* characteristics (e.g. education, social class, employment status), *social* characteristics (family circumstances, peer group affiliation) and some *individual* characteristics (e.g. personality, academic ability). There was a time when *physical* characteristics were the focus of attention, in particular head shape, on the assumption that criminals' heads were shaped differently from non-criminals'. While we no longer regard such characteristics to be relevant, it should be clear that what is considered to be relevant is a matter of agreement and can change.

The issue of researchers making choices about what to include in descriptions is not a trivial one. Not that long ago philosophers argued that objective descriptions were jeopardized by observers choosing what to observe (see Blaikie 2007, chapter 4). However, today we know that pure description is impossible and that researchers have no alternative but to make choices about what characteristics to study. The consequence is that different choices lead to different answers to 'what' research questions.

Let us see how each of the four research strategies could provide suitable logics for answering these questions.

Inductive Research Strategy

Social researchers need descriptions of social phenomena in order to answer 'what' research questions. The aim of the Inductive research strategy is to establish limited generalizations about the distribution of, and patterns of association amongst, observed or measured characteristics of individuals and social phenomena (see Table 4.1) .

While it is possible to produce elementary descriptions that refer to single individuals or events, researchers also need more general descriptions to answer their questions, descriptions about the characteristics of groups or collectivities of people. To answer the research question – 'What kinds of young people engage in juvenile crime?' – this research strategy requires the researcher to choose a set of characteristics, collect data related to them and then draw generalizations from them. From the point of view of this research strategy, the social world can only be observed or measured through the use of researcher-defined concepts.

How do we know what characteristics to look for? We have to decide this in advance – although we may stumble across some other characteristics in the course of our research – and we have to limit our data collection to a specific location, however narrow or extensive. The answer to our 'what' question will be influenced by our background knowledge, from both theory and previous research, as well as from traditions within our discipline, and it will be limited in time and space.

If the data are to be quantitative, further decisions will need to be made about how to define and measure each characteristic. For example, characteristics as basic as 'age' and 'education' can be defined and measured in different ways.

In addition to the use of individual characteristics, descriptions can also be made of the patterns of association between these characteristics. For example, if family circumstances have been determined, it would be possible to compare the family backgrounds of young criminals and other young people to see if there is any support for the conventional view that 'juvenile delinquents come from broken homes'. While such generalizations are never universal in the social sciences, patterns in distributions, or substantial associations between such concepts, can be established at a certain time and in certain places.

In one philosophical position, known as Positivism (see section on research paradigms in this chapter), claims were made that causal explanations are not possible. Rather, all that can be established are sequences between events, or patterns of association between phenomena. This led to what is known as the *pattern model of explanation*. For example, if research has consistently established that 'juvenile delinquents come from broken homes', then it is possible to offer an

Table 4.1 The logic of four research strategies

	Inductive	Deductive	Retroductive	Abductive
Aim:	To establish descriptions of characteristics and patterns	To test theories, to eliminate false ones and corroborate the survivor	To discover underlying mechanisms to explain observed regularities	To describe and understand social life in terms of social actors' meanings and motives
Ontology:	Cautious, depth or subtle realist	Cautious or subtle realist	Depth or subtle realist	Idealist or subtle realist
Epistemology:	Conventionalism	Falsificationism Conventionalism	Neo-realism	Constructionism
Start:	Collect data on characteristics and/or patterns	Identify a regularity that needs to be explained	Document and model a regularity and motives	Discover everyday lay concepts, meanings
	Produce descriptions	Construct a theory and deduce hypotheses	Describe the context and possible mechanisms	Produce a technical account from lay accounts
Finish:	Relate these to the research questions	Test hypotheses by matching them with data explanation in that context	Establish which mechanism(s) provide(s) the best	Develop a theory and elaborate it iteratively

explanation for juvenile delinquency in terms of family circumstances. In this tradition, it is unnecessary to try to discover what it is about 'broken homes' that produces delinquent children. Establishing the association is all that is seen to be necessary.

While searching for patterns in our data is important, there is something unsatisfactory about only establishing patterns. Such pattern explanations are really only the first step. It is for this reason that I have argued that other research strategies are more appropriate for answering 'why' questions. However, the Inductive research strategy is an essential tool, although not the only one, for answering 'what' questions.

It is important to stress that descriptions produced by the Inductive research strategy are limited in time and space and are not universal laws as claimed by its original proponents. Also, while they are commonly quantitative, they are not restricted to data of this type. However, the selection of characteristics to be studied, and their definition and measurement, are conducted from the researcher's point of view. (See Blaikie 2007: 59–70)

Deductive Research Strategy

Social researchers have to be able to answer 'why' research questions in order to explain patterns that they or others have observed. Using an existing theory, or inventing a new theory, is one way of achieving this. The aim of the Deductive research strategy is to find an explanation for an association between two concepts by proposing a theory, the relevance of which can be tested. The association itself can be established by using the Inductive research strategy, although descriptions produced by the use of the Abductive research strategy can also provide the starting point (see Table 4.1).

In its original formulation, the Deductive research strategy was seen to have a number of essential steps.

1 Begin by putting forward a tentative idea, a conjecture, a hypothesis or a set of hypotheses that form a theory.
2 With the help, perhaps, of other previously accepted hypotheses, or by specifying the conditions under which the hypotheses are expected to hold, deduce a conclusion, or a number of conclusions.
3 Examine the conclusions and the logic of the argument that produced them. Compare this argument with existing theories to see if it constitutes an advance in our understanding. If you are satisfied with this examination, then:
4 Test the conclusion by gathering appropriate data; make the necessary observations or conduct the necessary experiments.
5 If the test fails, i.e. if the data are not consistent with the conclusion, the theory must be false. If the original conjecture does not match the data, it must be rejected.
6 If, however, the conclusion passes the test, i.e. the data are consistent with it, the theory is temporarily supported; it is *corroborated*, but not proven to be true (Popper 1959: 32–3).

The important point is that a theory has to be invented or borrowed and expressed as a deductive argument, the conclusion of which is the proposition that is to be explained. The theoretical ideas that lead to the conclusion provide the explanation. These ideas have to be tested to see if they can be accepted as an adequate explanation.

If inductively oriented research had produced a conclusion that there is an association between juvenile delinquency and type of family, then the Deductive research strategy could be used to explain this association. The first step is to borrow or construct a theory to explain the association.

A theory could be proposed using the idea that it is inadequate socialization into acceptable social norms in 'broken homes' that makes a young person susceptible to the influences of deviant peer groups. The concept of 'broken home' could include families where the father is absent and the mother is unable to be an adequate substitute as far as socializing children is concerned. In addition, it could be argued that it is the absence of an authority figure, the lack of good adult role models or the presence of bad role models that are responsible for this inadequate socialization. These theoretical ideas can be expressed as a deductive argument as follows.

1 Lack of adequate *socializing agents* (authority figures and role models) in the family is associated with inadequate *socialization* into acceptable social norms.
2 Inadequate *socialization* in the family is associated with susceptibility to deviant *peer group influence*.
3 Deviant *peer group influence* is associated with *juvenile delinquency*.
4 Therefore, *juvenile delinquency* is associated with the lack of adequate *socializing agents* in 'broken homes'.

It should be clear that this theoretical argument contains many assumptions about families and peer groups and their influences on young people. It is the spelling out of these assumptions into a theoretical argument that allows for their testing. Whether or not this is a good theoretical argument will depend on this testing.

Note that there is no causal language in the propositions in the theory; each proposition only expresses an association between two concepts. However, as a whole, these propositions provide a possible explanation for the association that has, presumably, been established between juvenile delinquency and type of family.

This argument moves logically from one proposition to the next, and ends up with the conclusion that needs to be explained. The originator of this logic of explanation has argued that all that needs to be tested is one or more hypotheses that can be deduced from such theoretical arguments, in this case, the last proposition (see Blaikie 2007: 72–4). However, it would be possible to do research on all or most of the propositions, thus subjecting the theory to very rigorous testing. Such testing may require separate research projects for each proposition.

Therefore, the second step is to collect data on the concepts in the theory and do appropriate analyses on the relationships between the concepts in the propositions. It is at this point that a host of research design decisions have to be made.

Concepts have to be defined, measurements for them determined, populations or samples selected, and so on. In this particular case, these decisions are not straightforward.

The third step is to relate the findings from the research to the propositions in the theory. It is necessary to establish some kind of measure of association between pairs of concepts and then compare this with the form of the statement of association in the theory. In other words, some or all of the propositions in the argument are compared with the patterns and strengths of association in the data. As conclusive refutations of a theory are not possible, a judgement has then to be made as to the extent to which the theoretical argument answers the 'why' research question.

In its original form, the Deductive research strategy was seen to produce explanations that were regarded as being tentative, and, therefore, subject to modification or replacement. Nevertheless, the ultimate aim was to find the 'true' explanation. However, my version of the strategy is less ambitious and more pragmatic. Rather than searching for *the* truth, any deductive explanation should be regarded as one amongst other possible explanations. If it meets the research objectives in a particular context, satisfies the stakeholders, and produces useful outcomes, it can be accepted until something better comes along (see Blaikie 2007: 70–9).

Retroductive Research Strategy

The aim of the Retroductive research strategy is to discover underlying mechanisms that, in particular contexts, explain observed regularities. The logic of retroduction refers to the process of building hypothetical models of structures and mechanisms that are assumed to produce empirical phenomena (Bhaskar 1979: 15). It involves working back from data to a possible explanation.

The first stage is to provide an adequate description of the regularity to be explained. As with the Deductive research strategy, this stage requires the use of either the Inductive or Abductive research strategies. What follows after this is likely to include an examination of the characteristics of the context under investigation, and a consideration of possible contending mechanisms. The relevance of these mechanisms needs to be investigated and the features of the context, in terms of the ways in which it facilitates or inhibits the operation of the mechanism(s), needs to be established (see table 4.1).

The central problem for the Retroductive research strategy is how to discover the structures and mechanisms that are proposed to explain observed regularities. Is there an appropriate mode of reasoning that will assist the researcher to find these ideas? Is there a logic of discovery? This issue has been a matter of some dispute. However, there is general agreement that it requires disciplined scientific thinking aided by creative imagination, intuition, and guesswork.

The Retroductive research strategy comes in two versions, a *structuralist* one following the work of Bhaskar (1979), and a *constructionist* one following the later work of Harré (1974, 1977) and Harré and Secord (1972). The former version locates explanatory mechanism in social structures, while the latter

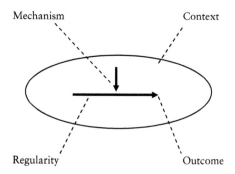

Figure 4.2   Explanatory model (*Source:* Pawson and Tilley 1997:72)

is concerned with cognitive mechanisms. The strategy has been elaborated into a combination of mechanisms and social contexts, and translated into research practice by Pawson (2000; Pawson and Tilley 1997) (see Blaikie 2007: 82–8).

To return to the research questions, let us assume that the first question has been answered and that we wish to answer the second question with regard to the association between juvenile delinquency and family circumstances. In using the Retroductive research strategy, we have to imagine what mechanism(s) might be responsible for this association and the context in which it/they operate. We have to construct a model of how it/they might work, and then we have to look for evidence that it/they behave as imagined.

So the challenge is to apply the knowledge we have of social processes to this particular problem. In contrast to the use of this strategy in the natural sciences, where the problem may require the creation of previously unknown mechanisms, in dealing with a research problem such as this in the social sciences we are more likely to be choosing from amongst known mechanisms.

Returning to the ideas used in the Deductive research strategy, we can create a model of the **regularity** between *type of family* and *juvenile delinquency* (the **outcome** to be explained), with inadequate *socialization* as the **context** and deviant *peer group influence* as the **mechanism** (see Figure 4.2).

Hence, this model offers an explanation for juvenile delinquency (the outcome), and its regular association with type of family (the regularity), by hypothesizing that, in the context of inadequate socialization in the family, a particular kind of peer group influence (mechanism) is the trigger for the behaviour. It suggests that inadequate socialization is a characteristic of a particular type of family, but this on its own does not lead to juvenile delinquency. A mechanism has to be added, and this will only produce the outcome in the context of inadequate family socialization. It is the combination of context and mechanism that is central to the explanation.

The model presents a clear view of how these concepts are connected theoretically. Rather than seeing them as a logical set of associations, as happens in the Deductive research strategy, they are seen in terms of a combination of socially relevant influences. The researcher's task is now to test the model by establishing whether it is the combination of this mechanism operating in this context that produces delinquent children.

The Retroductive research strategy can be summarized as follows.

1 In order to explain observable phenomena, and the regularities that obtain between them, social scientists must attempt to discover appropriate mechanisms and the contexts in which they operate.
2 A model is constructed of the location of the observed regularity and its outcome in a social context in which one or more mechanisms operate.
3 The model is such that, were it to represent correctly the mechanism and the context, the regularity would than be causally explained.
4 We then proceed to test the model as a hypothetical description of actually existing social phenomena and their relations.
5 If these tests are successful, this gives good reason to believe in the relevance of the context and mechanism.
6 The whole process of model-building can then be repeated in order to explain how such mechanisms work (adapted from Harré (1961); Keat and Urry (1975: 35); and Pawson and Tilley (1997) for relevance to the social sciences).[3]

Abductive Research Strategy

Whereas the Inductive research strategy can be used to answer 'what' questions, and the Deductive and Retroductive strategies can be used to answer 'why' questions, the Abductive research strategy can answer both types of questions. However, it answers 'why' question by producing understanding rather than an explanation, by providing reasons rather than causes.

This research strategy involves constructing theories that are derived from social actors' language, meanings and accounts in the context of everyday activities. Such research begins by describing these activities and meanings and then deriving from them categories and concepts that can form the basis of an understanding of the problem at hand.

The Abductive research strategy incorporates what the Inductive and Deductive research strategies ignore – the meanings and interpretations, the motives and intentions, that people use in their everyday lives, and which direct their behaviour – and elevates them to the central place in social theory and research. As a consequence, the social world *is* the world perceived and experienced by its members, from the 'inside'. The social scientist's task is to discover and describe this 'insider' view, not to impose an 'outsider' view on it. Therefore, the aim is to discover why people do what they do by uncovering the largely tacit, mutual knowledge, the symbolic meanings, intentions and rules, which provide the orientations for their actions. Mutual knowledge is background knowledge that is largely unarticulated but which is constantly used and modified by social actors as they interact with each other.

According to Giddens, the mutual knowledge social actors use to negotiate their encounters with others, and to make sense of social activity, is the fundamental subject matter of the social sciences. The social scientist cannot begin to describe any social activity without knowing what social actors know, either what they can report or what they tacitly assume, while engaging in social activity. The techniques available to a researcher to learn a way of life are the same as those available to any person who wishes to become a member of a group or community. Understanding the meaning of what other people say and do is a skilled accomplishment of competent social actors, not the preserve of the professional social investigator. Hence, social scientists must draw on the same 'mutual knowledge' that social actors use to make sense of their activity. Social research has to deal with a social world that is already constituted as meaningful by its participants. In order to grasp this world it is necessary to get to know what social actors already know, and need to know in order to go about their daily activities (Giddens 1976, 1979). Therefore, it is to the process of moving from lay descriptions of social life, to technical descriptions of that social life, that the notion of abduction is applied.

The Abductive research strategy has many layers to it. The basic access to any social world is the accounts that people can give of their own actions and the actions of others. These accounts contain the concepts that participants use to structure their world, and the 'theories' they use to account for what goes on. However, much of the activity of social life is routine, and is conducted in a taken-for-granted, unreflective attitude. It is when enquiries are made about their behaviour by others (such as social scientists), or when social life is disrupted, and/or ceases to be predictable, that social actors are forced to search for or construct meanings and interpretations. Therefore, the social scientist may have to resort to procedures that encourage this reflection in order to discover the meanings and theories.

Therefore, the first stage of the Abductive research strategy is to discover how social actors view and understand that part of their world of interest to the researcher. To begin with, the researcher needs to both discover the everyday concepts that social actors use to typify features of their world and discover the meanings they have given to them. It may also be necessary to discern the social actors' motives and their ways of interpreting and understanding their own actions, others' actions and social situations (see table 4.1).

For some social scientists, reporting social actors' accounts is all that is possible and necessary in order to understand social life. The task is to report these concepts, meanings, motives and interpretations in language that stays as close as possible to that of the social actors. However, if research stops at this point, abductive logic has not really come into play.

Those researchers who wish to go further than this have a choice between one or two more stages. The first of these, and the second stage in the sequence, is for the researcher to abstract or generate technical concepts from these lay concepts. While this technical language removes the researcher somewhat from the social actors' world, it is necessary to constrain the process of generating social scientific concepts in order to maintain a close connection with it. Social actors need to be able to recognize themselves and others in the researcher's account. There are a number of reasons for this: first, the researcher needs to know whether the social actors' world has been adequately grasped; and second, that the social scientific account has not been overly 'contaminated' by the researcher's constructions. The researcher's account needs to have 'integrity'. A method for establishing this has been described by ethnomethodologists as 'member checking', a process in which social actors are invited to respond to the researcher's account of some aspects of their world. While this feedback process is not without its problems and critics, researchers have no real alternative if they wish to ensure that their account remains faithful to social actors' accounts.

At the third stage, the understanding obtained in the second stage can be taken in at least two directions. One is the refinement and further elaboration of this understanding by the continuing use of the Abductive research strategy, perhaps with other social actors in the same context, or by moving into similar or contrasting social contexts.

The other possibility is to take the understanding obtained in the second stage and translate it into a form that can be used either in the Deductive research strategy or a version of the Retroductive strategy. This would involve supplementing understanding derived from the social actors' point of view with further input from the researcher's point of view. Taken together, such a combination of research strategies could provide rich answers to research questions. Whether it is necessary to move to another research strategy, will depend on the way the research questions have been formulated and whether the use of something other than the Abductive strategy is considered to be necessary.

It is important to note that the Abductive research strategy answers research questions differently to the other three (although the constructionist version of the Retroductive strategy is the exception). The Abductive strategy adopts a 'bottom up' rather than a 'top down' approach. It tries to present descriptions and understanding that reflect the social actors' points of view rather than adopting entirely the researcher's point of view.

It is possible that a researcher might accept the answer to the first research question provided by the use of the Inductive strategy, and then proceed to answer the second question using the Abductive strategy. However, if the Abductive strategy was also used to answer the first research question, the logic used would be quite different to that of the Inductive strategy. For example, the researcher might spend time with a reasonable number of juvenile delinquents in order to develop a picture of the kind of people they are. The number will be determined by the point at which the researcher considers that nothing new is being learnt about the characteristics of these young people. The descriptions produced will be mainly in words rather than in numerical distributions.

To deal with the second research question, this process is simply extended. Detailed descriptions of the social contexts and social relationships in which these young people are involved will be produced. An attempt will be made to establish categories or types of young people, their social contexts and their social relationships. These will evolve through an iterative process of immersion in these social worlds and reflection on what is discovered. In time, these descriptions will begin to provide an answer to the 'why' research question, not in terms of causal explanations but, rather, in terms of an understanding that is based on how these young people see themselves and their social worlds, and their meanings and motives for their actions.

Hence, the Abductive research strategy is based on the following principles.

1 The basic access to any social world is the accounts that people can give of their own actions and the actions of others.
2 These accounts are provided to the social scientist in the language of the

participants and contain the concepts that the participants use to structure their world, the meanings of these concepts, and the 'theories' that they use to account for what goes on.

3 However, much of the activity of social life is routine and is conducted in a taken-for-granted, unreflective manner.

4 It is only when enquiries are made about their behaviour by others (such as social scientists) or when social life is disrupted, and/or ceases to be predictable, that social actors are forced to consciously search for or construct meanings and interpretations.

5 Therefore, the social scientist may have to resort to procedures that encourage this reflection in order to discover the meanings and theories.

6 Ultimately, it is necessary to piece together the fragments of meaning that are available from their externalized products.

In other words, the Abductive strategy involves developing descriptions and constructing theory that is grounded in everyday activities, and/or in the language and meanings of social actors. It has two stages:

- describing these activities and meanings; and
- deriving categories and concepts that can form the basis of an understanding of the problem at hand. (See Blaikie 2007: 88–104)

Ontological and Epistemological Assumptions

In addition to the different logics used in the four research strategies, they also differ in the ontological and epistemological assumptions on which they are based. Ontological assumptions are concerned with the nature of social reality. These assumptions make claims about what kinds of social phenomena do or can exist, the conditions of their existence, and the ways in which they are related. Epistemological assumptions are concerned with what kinds of knowledge are possible – how we can know these things – and with criteria for deciding when knowledge is both adequate and legitimate. Each of the research strategies entails a particular combination of ontological and epistemological assumptions. As I have elaborated six types of each set of assumptions elsewhere (Blaikie 2007: 12–24) they are reviewed here only briefly.

I need to point out that the range of these types of assumptions is more elaborate than can be found in most of the literature. Nevertheless, each one, and its content, has been derived from a wide range of literature with the aim of identifying further characteristics of the research strategies. The content of some types overlaps with well-known categories, while others bring alongside these other or more recent ideas. While some of the labels used for the types may look familiar, others are either my own creation or are adaptations of those used in the literature. It is therefore important to treat the types and their definitions on their own merits and not read into them related concepts or content with which you may be familiar. Space does not permit a discussion of other classifications and their relationships with these ones.

Ontological Assumptions

The six types of ontological assumptions are: shallow realist, conceptual realist, cautious realist, depth realist, idealist and subtle realist.

Shallow realist

- Phenomena we study exist independently of us.
- They can be observed (experienced by the senses), and only that which can be observed is relevant to science.
- There are patterns or sequences in observable phenomena, and the challenge for science is to discover and describe them.

Conceptual realist

- Reality has an existence independent of human minds.
- It is not the property of any individual or the construction of a social community.
- It is a collective consciousness, or structure of ideas, and is not directly observable.

Cautious realist

- Reality has an independent existence
- However, because of imperfections in human senses, and the fact that the act of observing is an interpretive process, it cannot be observed directly or accurately.
- Hence, a cautious and critical attitude must be adopted.

Depth realist

- Reality consists of three domains ranging from what can be observed (*empirical* domain), through what exists independently of the observer (*actual* domain), to an underlying domain of structures and mechanisms that may not be readily observed (*real* domain).
- Therefore, reality is stratified and has ontological depth.
- Unlike natural structures, social structures are less enduring and do not exist independently of the activities they influence or social actors' conceptions of what they are doing in these activities.

Idealist

- Reality consists of representations that are the creation of the human mind.
- Social reality is made up of shared interpretations that social actors produce and reproduce as they go about their everyday lives.
- Idealist ontologies take a variety of forms: one considers there is a reality that exists independently of socially constructed realities; another sees such an external reality placing constraints on or providing opportunities for reality

constructing activities; and in a third, constructions of reality are regarded as different (multiple) perspectives on an external world.

Subtle realist

- An independent, knowable reality exists independently of social scientists.
- Cultural assumptions prevent direct access to this world.
- As all knowledge is based on assumptions and purposes, and is therefore a human construction, it is not certain.

Epistemological Assumptions

The six types of epistemological assumptions are: empiricism, rationalism, falsificationism, neo-realism, constructionism and conventionalism.

Empiricism

- Knowledge is produced and verified by the use of the human senses.
- A neutral, trained observer, who has undistorted contact with reality, can arrive at reliable knowledge.
- Knowledge is certain when it accurately represents the external world.

Rationalism

- Knowledge comes from the direct examination of the structure of human thought.
- Evidence for an unobservable collective consciousness can be found in the consequences it has on people's lives, or in thought processes and structures of the mind itself.
- Logic and mathematics provide the standards for judging knowledge claims.

Falsificationism

- Knowledge is produced by a process of trial and error in which theories are proposed and tested against empirical evidence.
- Because of our inability to observe reality directly, tests of theories must be directed towards trying to falsify rather than confirm them.
- As it is not possible to establish whether knowledge is true, it must be regarded as tentative and, therefore, open to revision.

Neo-realism

- Knowledge of the causes of observed regularities is derived from the structures and/or mechanisms that produce them.
- The discovery of these structures and/or mechanisms may necessitate the postulation or selection of entities and process that go beyond surface appearances.

- This view of causation allows for the possibility that competing or cancelling mechanisms may be operating when no event or change is observed.

Constructionism

- Everyday knowledge is the outcome of people having to make sense of their encounters with the physical world and other people, and social scientific knowledge is the outcome of social scientists reinterpreting this everyday knowledge into technical language.
- Because it is impossible for fallible human beings to observe an external world unencumbered by concepts, theories, background knowledge and past experiences, it is impossible to make true discoveries about the world; all social enquiry reflects the standpoint of the researcher and all observation is theory-laden.
- Hence, there are no permanent, unvarying criteria for establishing whether knowledge can be regarded as true.

Conventionalism

- Scientific theories are created by scientists as convenient tools for dealing with the world.
- Theories do not describe reality; they determine what is considered by the scientist to be real.
- Decisions about what are good theories, or which is the better of two competing theories, is a matter of judgement, not proof.

Ontological and Epistemological Assumptions in the Research Strategies

We now turn to the place of ontological and epistemological assumptions in the four research strategies. In five instances, these two sets of assumptions form pairs. In fact, it is not really possible or sensible to think of them as being independent. The purpose of the separation was simply to highlight the fact that there *are* two types of assumptions and that other combinations are possible and might be sensible. Here are the common combinations.

Ontology	*Epistemology*
Shallow realist	Empiricism
Conceptual realist	Rationalism
Cautious realist	Falsificationism
Depth realist	Neo-realism
Idealist	Constructionism

The *subtle realist* ontology and the epistemology of *conventionalism* do not combine in the same way. They are alternatives to some of the others, and are used to produce variations in the above combinations. As a result of extensive criticism over many decades, the combination of *shallow realist/empiricism* is no longer tenable, and the combination of *conceptual realist/rationalism* is not relevant to social research. This leaves us with the last three combinations to work with, plus the *subtle realist* ontology and the epistemology of *conventionalism*.

In Table 4.1, we can see the ontological and epistemological assumptions that can be used with each of the four research strategies. The Inductive strategy is viable with three types of ontological assumptions, *cautious*, *depth* and *subtle*. It might be argued that *idealist* assumptions could also be used, but I have reserved these for the Abductive strategy. The Inductive strategy, as I have revised it, works best with the epistemology of *conventionalism*.

The Deductive research strategy is most likely to be used with the *cautious realist* ontology and the *epistemology* of falsificationism. However, the *subtle realist* ontology and *conventionalism* work just as well, either together or cross-linked with the other two types of assumptions. In fact, the founder of this research strategy, Karl Popper, supported many aspects of the epistemology of *conventionalism*.

The Retroductive research strategy is most likely to be used with the *depth realist* ontology and the epistemology of *neo-realism*, the latter perhaps with some minor modifications to its original formulation, as shown here. This change involves the choice from amongst known mechanisms in the social sciences rather than a search for unknown ones. This is not to suggest that we cannot look for new mechanisms for our explanations, or that the natural sciences cannot also offer explanations using known mechanisms. It is just that the original formulation of the research strategy placed exclusive emphasis on the need to discover previously unknown entities, such as atoms and viruses.

As the *subtle realist* ontology is compatible with some versions of the Retroductive research strategy, it may also be used. In addition, the *constructionist* version of this strategy blends in with much of what is included in the Abductive strategy. This illustrates that, in practice, the research strategies are not watertight compartments, and can be modified by practitioners to suit their purposes. However, maintaining consistency in the combination of ontological and epistemological assumptions is vitally important.

The Abductive research strategy is most likely to be used with a combination of *idealist* ontological assumptions and the epistemology of *constructionism*. However, I can see no reason why the *subtle realist* ontology could not also be used.

Research Paradigms

Social research is usually conducted against a background of some tradition of theoretical and methodological ideas. These traditions, which have developed and mutated over more than a hundred years, are referred to here as *research paradigms*. They are the source not only of theoretical ideas but also of ontological and epistemological assumptions. While researchers may have strong commitments to particular research paradigms, I prefer to view them as possible sources of ideas and assumptions for use where appropriate. It is possible to choose a research paradigm for a particular research project just as it is possible to make choices between research strategies to answer research questions.

The choice of a research strategy does not necessarily entail a commitment to a particular research paradigm, but the reverse may be the case. However, some research paradigms, such as Critical Theory and Feminism, require or allow the use of more than one research strategy. We will return to this issue shortly.

Elsewhere (Blaikie 2007) I have provided a detailed elaboration and critique of four classical and six contemporary research paradigms. I have also reviewed them with regard to the ontological and epistemological assumptions associated with them. Hence, all that is necessary here is to identify the research paradigms and review their main characteristics.[4]

I am very aware that there is a danger in using the concept of 'paradigm' for this purpose. I previously used 'approaches' (Blaikie 1993) but found that it, like 'strategies', had developed a wide range of uses in the context of social theory and research. From its specific use by Kuhn (1970), the concept of 'paradigm' has entered both the social science and everyday vocabulary with the result that its meaning has been widened and trivialized. My usage here has a close affinity with Kuhn's broadest use. My focus is on the role that theoretical and methodological traditions play in providing social researchers with an intellectual context in which to conduct their research, and, therefore, as a source of assumptions and ideas.

It is important to point out that the relationships between the four research strategies and the ten research paradigms that I am about to elaborate, are not neat and tidy. Some research paradigms do fit closely with one of the research strategies, while others may draw on more than one strategy. Similarly, each research paradigm does not necessarily incorporate just one combination of ontological and epistemological assumptions, although some do. Hence, the role of the research paradigms in social research is much broader, and less clearly defined, than is the case for the research strategies. In my view, the latter are an essential component of social research, while the former are not.

Classical Research Paradigms

Four classical research paradigms have been identified. They represent the earliest attempts at either applying the methods of the natural sciences in the social sciences, or rejecting such an application. Most of the contributors were writing during the nineteenth century and the early part of the twentieth century, although many of the ideas predate this period. The classical research paradigms are: Positivism, Critical Rationalism, Classical Hermeneutics and Interpretivism.

Positivism

Positivism regards reality as consisting of discrete events that can be observed by the human senses. The only knowledge of this reality that is acceptable is that which is derived from experience. The language used to describe this knowledge consists of concepts that correspond to real objects, and the truth of statements in this language can be determined by observations that are uncontaminated by any theoretical notions.

It is assumed that there is order in this reality and that it can be summarized in terms of constant conjunctions between observed events or objects. These regularities, which are considered to apply across time and space, constitute general laws but not causes. Explanations are achieved by demonstrating that any regularity is a specific case of some more general law. Positivism, but particularly the version known as logical positivism, rejects all theoretical or metaphysical notions that are not derived from experience. In the same way, value judgements are excluded from scientific knowledge as their validity cannot be tested by experience. Anything that cannot be verified by experience is meaningless (see Blaikie 2007: 110–17; 183–5).

Critical rationalism

Critical Rationalism rejects sensory experience as a secure foundation for scientific theories thus making 'pure' observation impossible. Observations are always made within a frame of reference, with certain expectations in mind. Hence, it is argued, generalizing from a limited set of 'impure' observations is not a satisfactory basis for developing scientific theories. Observation is used in the service of deductive reasoning and theories are invented to account for observations, not derived from them. All theories are regarded as being tentative rather than absolutely true.

The process of explanation must begin with a tentative theory, an idea that could account for what has been observed. Such a conjecture must then be subjected to critical examination and rigorous testing against 'reality'. Rather than scientists waiting for nature to reveal its regularities, they must impose regularities (deductive theories) on the world, and, by a process of trial and error, use observations to try to reject false theories. This is done by collecting data relevant to the theory. If these data are not consistent with the theory, the theory must be rejected, or at least modified and retested (see Blaikie 2007: 113–17; 185–7).

Classical hermeneutics

Classical Hermeneutics arose as a way of discovering the meaning of ancient texts and then, through a number of phases, developed into alternative positions. Initially, the emphasis shifted away from texts to an understanding of how members of one culture or historical period grasp the experiences of a member of another culture or historical period. This involved the re-experiencing of the mental processes of the author of a text or speaker in a dialogue. The emphasis then shifted from mental states to socially produced systems of meaning, from introspective psychology to sociological reflection, from the reconstruction of mental processes to the interpretation of externalized cultural products. It was argued that as an interpreter's prejudices inevitably distort his/her understanding, it is necessary to extricate oneself from entanglement in a socio-historical context.

A fundamental issue, which came to divide Classical Hermeneutics, concerned the possibility of producing 'objective' knowledge freed from the limitations of the social and historical location of the observer. One branch became concerned with experts establishing the path to pure consciousness, and hence to pure truth. This aspiration gave way to a fully blown recognition that this is not only impossible, but that it is also undesirable. Understanding came to be seen as being fundamental to human existence, and, therefore, the task of ordinary people. It was argued that there is no understanding outside of history; human beings cannot step outside of their social world or the historical context in which they live. Therefore, the social world should be understood on its own terms in the same manner as its participants do, from the inside as it were, not from some outside position occupied by an expert (see Blaikie 2007: 117–24; 195).

Interpretivism

In Interpretivism, social reality is regarded as the product of its inhabitants; it is a world that is interpreted by the meanings participants produce and reproduce as a necessary part of their everyday activities together. This ontology requires the use of a different logic of enquiry to that used in the natural sciences.

The founders of Interpretivism followed the branch of Classical Hermeneutics that sought to establish an objective science of the subjective, with the aim of producing verifiable knowledge of the meanings that constitute the social world. Attention focused on the nature of meaningful social action, its role in understanding patterns in social life, and how this meaning can be assessed. Rather than trying to establish the actual meaning that social actors give to a particular social action, these Interpretivists considered that it is necessary to work at a higher level of generality. Social regularities can be understood, perhaps explained, by constructing models of typical meanings used by typical social actors engaged in typical courses of action in typical situations. Such models constitute tentative hypotheses to be tested. Only social action that is rational in character, i.e. which is consciously selected as a means to some goal, is considered to be understandable.

The question of whose meanings are used to construct this understanding has been a matter of some dispute. Can the observer's point of view be used to attribute likely meanings to social actors, or must meanings be taken from the social actor's point of view? Later contributors to Interpretivism argued that meanings used in social theories must be derived from social actors' concepts and meanings (see Blaikie 2007: 124–31; 187–9).

Contemporary Research Paradigms

The six contemporary research paradigms are critical of or entirely reject both Positivism and Critical Rationalism, and, to varying degrees, use or build on Classical Hermeneutics and/or Interpretivism. The contemporary research paradigms are Critical Theory, Ethnomethodology, Social Realism, Contemporary Hermeneutics, Structuration Theory and Feminism.

I have chosen not to discuss Postmodernism as a research paradigm as it is has not led to a research programme and lacks its own social scientific research area. Amongst many other things, it has offered a radical critique of traditional views of science, and some of these critiques have been adopted in a number of the contemporary research paradigms (see Blaikie 2007, chapter 2, for a review). However, I am adding a seventh contemporary research paradigm here, Complexity Theory.

Critical theory

The Critical Theory of Habermas (1970, 1972) supports the view that, as the subject matters of the natural and social sciences are fundamentally different, the use of a common logic of enquiry must be rejected. In common with Interpretivism and Structuration Theory, Habermas accepted the preinterpreted nature of social reality and its methodological implications. He argued that the natural sciences can only use observation but the social sciences can use communication. However, he rejected the possibility of 'objective' observation in the natural sciences, arguing that the assumptions embedded in both theoretical constructs and common-sense thinking determine what will be regarded as reality rather than producing knowledge of it directly (conventionalism); 'cognitive interests' can influence what is produced as knowledge, even in the natural sciences.

For Habermas, scientific enquiry falls into three categories based on different interests: the *empirical–analytic* sciences, which are interested in technical control over nature and social relations; the *historical–hermeneutic* sciences, which are based on practical interests of communicative understanding; and *critical theory*, which has an emancipatory interest in human autonomy. While the first is characteristic of the natural sciences, it can also be applied to social life. According to Habermas, all three need to be used in the social sciences.

Critical Theory rejects the interests of the *empirical–analytic* sciences, but not necessarily all its methods, and it uses *historical–hermeneutic* methods and rational criticism in the interest of human emancipation. A later development of Critical Theory (Fay 1975, 1987) stressed the need for the social sciences to expose the nature and origins of false consciousness, to describe the nature and development of social crises, to identify what needs to be done to resolve such crises, and to provide a plan of action on how people can effect the transformation of society. (See Blaikie 2007: 135–40; 189–90)

Ethnomethodology

Ethnomethodology took as its rationale the study of the way ordinary members of society achieve and maintain a sense of order in their everyday practical activities. The idea that social order is achieved by the passive acceptance of socialized norms and values was rejected in favour of a continuous process by which members create or adapt norms and use them in their activities together. Maintaining order becomes a practical problem that members have to solve together in particular circumstances.

In addition to rejecting Parson's solution to the problem of order, Garfinkel

(1952, 1967) also rejected Durkheim's notion of 'social facts' as constituting external constraints that determine social behaviour. Instead, social facts are regarded as the creations of members in and through their practical, everyday activities. Instead of using these social facts to explain social activity and individual actions, Ethnomethodologists endeavour to explicate how they come into being and how they are used by members to maintain social order.

Because so much of what goes on in the dynamics of maintaining social order in everyday activities is taken for granted, Ethnomethodologists have had to resort to the use of various techniques to help members become aware of their assumptions and the norms to which they are implicitly relating. Breaching experiments have been used to demonstrate the presence and relevance of what is being taken for granted (see Blaikie 2007: 140–5; 190–2).

Social realism

The versions of Social Realism (also known as Critical Realism) that have come to dominate contemporary philosophy of science are designed to replace both Positivism and Critical Rationalism with a view of science that, it is claimed, reflects what scientists do. The view of reality advocated by Positivism, based on what can be perceived by the senses, becomes for Bhaskar (1978) but one domain of reality. Reality consists not only of events that are experienced but also of events that occur whether experienced or not, and of the structures and mechanisms that produce these events. The aim of science is to discover these structures and mechanisms, some of which may be reasonably accessible by the use of instruments that extend the senses. However, inaccessible mechanisms require the building of hypothetical models of them and a search for evidence of their existence. Structures and mechanisms, as the causal powers or the essential nature of things, are independent of the events they produce; they exist at a 'deeper' level of reality and may counteract each other to produce no observable event. Therefore, the constant conjunctions of Positivism are merely the observed regularities that need to be explained by establishing what links them.

However, the advocates of Social Realism disagree on the ontological status of social structures and mechanisms, and this has resulted in two versions of the research paradigm, the *structuralist* and the *constructionist* (see Blaikie 2007: 145–51; 192–5).

Contemporary Hermeneutics

Contemporary Hermeneutics has further developed the two traditions of Classical Hermeneutics, but with the majority of attention being given to the last version discussed in 'Classical Hermeneutics'. Instead of looking for what the author of a text intended, or the 'real' meaning, Gadamer (1989) argued that the text must be engaged in dialogue. Understanding involves the 'fusion of horizons' of the text and the interpreter, a process in which the interpreter's horizon is altered and the text is transformed; it is about mediation and translation of languages. Different interpreters at different times are likely to produce different understandings.

Unlike his predecessors in the hermeneutic tradition, Gadamer was not concerned with methodological questions. Rather, he saw the task of his philo-sophical hermeneutics as being ontological, as addressing the fundamental condi-tions that underlie all modes of understanding, be they scientific or everyday. He was not concerned with methods of gaining knowledge, but with the openness required of interpreters of literary or historical texts. Gadamer's hermeneutics takes as 'reality' the ever-changing world in which people are participants. He was not concerned with their individual, subjective meanings but with the mean-ings they share. Neither was he interested in traditional views of 'objectivity' and 'truth'. For him, shared meanings are 'objective' and their 'truth' can be communicated.

Ricoeur (1981) distinguished between language and discourse, between the objective study of a text by structural linguistics and its interpretive study. He extended Gadamer's position by arguing that texts create a distance from spoken discourse. As texts have no social context, an unknown audience, and no dialogue is possible between the reader and the author, they can be read in many ways. Interpretation is achieved by the reader recovering what the text points to and, in the process, achieving self-interpretation. Social action can also be decontextual-ized and can also have a variety of interpretations, inferior interpretations being eliminated by argumentation. (See Blaikie 2007: 151–7; 195)

Structuration theory

Structuration Theory was developed by Giddens (1976, 1979, 1984) as an attempt to establish a bridge between traditions of social theory concerned with the experiences of social actors (agency), and traditions concerned with the exist-ence of forms of social totalities (structure). This requires a theory of the human agent, an account of the conditions and consequences of social action, and an interpretation of 'structure' as dealing with both conditions and consequences (Giddens 1979: 49). It dispenses with the notion of 'function', as developed by Parsons, and is based on the view that dualities such as 'subject' and 'object', or 'action' and 'structure', need to be reconceptualized under the concept of *duality of structure*.

This key concept recognizes that social actors are engaged in both producing and reproducing their social world. Therefore, in addition to arguing that social actors are knowledgeable and capable of acting differently, that they have the capacity reflexively to monitor their continuing actions and to rationalize their actions, and that they can have unconscious motives, Giddens recognized, unlike Interpretivists, that these actions occur within a framework of unacknowledged conditions and unintended consequences.

Giddens' idea of the *double hermeneutic* was sympathetic with Gadamer's notion of the 'fusion of horizons', and he argued that the language of social science is parasitic on lay language. However, Giddens wished to differentiate between 'mutual knowledge', used as a basis for everyday activity, and 'common sense' (social actors' justifications for what they 'know'). Social scientists must respect the authenticity of the former but are free to critique the latter.

Giddens argued that 'explanation' and 'understanding' are relevant to both the natural and social sciences. Nevertheless, he rejected the possibility of universal laws in the social sciences in favour of generalizations limited by time and space. The latter is a consequence of the preinterpreted nature of social reality and the fact that a basic element in all social contexts is the knowledge social actors have about their actions. As this knowledge can change, so too can generalizations produced by social scientists about social actors' actions. Giddens insisted that all social research requires immersion in a form of life and a process in which the social scientist explicates and mediates divergent forms of life within the meta-language of social science (see Blaikie 2007: 157–63; 195–7).

Feminism

The foundation of feminist methodology is a critique of the natural and social sciences as being androcentric. It is argued that research questions, theories, concepts, methodologies and knowledge-claims, which are supposed to be gender-free, provide a distorted understanding of both nature and social life and omit or distort women's experiences. In the social sciences, this has meant that important areas of social enquiry have been overlooked.

Feminist methodologists have received support from the debates that have raged in the philosophy of science during the second half of the twentieth century. This has resulted in the development of three major traditions: feminist empiricism, standpoint feminism and feminist postmodernism.

Feminist empiricism represents an attempt to reform traditional science rather than replace it. However, this position has been difficult to maintain in the face of the devastating criticisms of empiricism as it is practiced within the Positivist research paradigm. A partial solution has been presented in 'philosophical feminist empiricism' in which the notion of universal norms of science is replaced by the recognition that scientific communities are the creators of knowledge and the arbiters of rules regarding such things as what counts as objectivity and evidence (conventionalism).

Feminist standpoint methodology rejects the legitimacy of traditional scientific norms and practices and recognizes that a researcher's background and location has a critical bearing on research outcomes. Initially, it was argued that members of oppressed groups have a clearer understanding of the problems that need to be investigated, and have had experiences that provide a more appropriate foundation for knowledge than those of dominant groups. Hence, basing knowledge on women's experiences was regarded as providing more reliable knowledge on which to base political action.

A major difficulty with this approach was to find a criterion that would make such knowledge defensible in the face of opposition. This was further exacerbated when it was recognized that women have diverse experiences related to race, class and geographic location, and, hence, have a plurality of standpoints. This recognition forced feminist methodologists to re-examine the notion of objectivity. 'Dynamic objectivity' (Keller 1985) and 'strong objectivity' (Harding 1993) have been proposed as solutions.

These attempts at reforming traditional science, and revising the notions of objectivity and truth, have been rejected as unsatisfactory by feminists of a postmodern persuasion. They recognize that knowledge is local and situated,

contextual and historical rather than universal, and that as there are no criteria for establishing truth and falsity. They have raised serious questions about
attempts to establish a feminist science and are sceptical about the possibility of
establishing any kind of science that can avoid replicating undesirable forms of
human existence.

For example, Haraway, as far back as 1988, argued that all knowledge is 'situated', located and embodied, based on partial perspectives due to the inevitability
of limited vision. Knowledge is seen to emerge from situated conversations. This
position contrasts with a totalized, single vision (as in Positivism) and views from
nowhere that are regarded as equal (as in relativism) (see Blaikie 2007: 163–76;
197–8).

Complexity theory

Complexity Theory refocuses our attention on system analysis, something that
much of social science has either rejected or ignored since the demise of Parsonian
structural functionalism in the 1970s. It does this by overcoming the deficiencies
in structural functionalism, and, at the same time, taking account of developments
in the philosophies of science and social science over the last fifty or so years.

While Complexity Theory is primarily concerned with presenting a new scientific ontology, it also rejects the epistemology of traditional science based
around notions of universal knowledge, experimental control, determinism and
a linear logic of causal explanation. Instead, it offers explanatory accounts based
on limited and contextual knowledge, open and unpredictable systems, and
complex, non-linear interaction between elements that leads to emergent properties and self-organizing structures and processes. This non-linear analysis places
emphasis on interaction and feedback loops. The influence between components
in a system can go in both directions at different times, and feedback iterations
can change the whole system over time.

Complexity Theory is seen as steering a course between modernism and
postmodernism. It rejects the traditional view of science, while at the same time
rejecting the anti-scientific doctrines of postmodernism. It confronts the subjective relativism of the latter by asserting that explanation is possible, and it
draws heavily on the ontological assumptions of the research paradigm of Social
Realism (see Blaikie 2007, Postscript).

Research Strategies, Questions and Purposes

As we have seen, the four research strategies provide different ways of answering
research questions; each one sets out a logic of enquiry; a starting point, a series
of stages and a finishing point. The Inductive and Abductive research strategies
are the only ones that can answer 'what' research questions, but they do so in
quite different ways. If a 'realist' rather than 'idealist' ontology is desired, then the
alternative is the Inductive strategy.

The Inductive strategy is weak on answering 'why' questions and only some
versions of the Abductive strategy can be used for this purpose. The Inductive

Table 4.2   Research strategies, questions and purposes

Purpose	Research Strategy				Type of Research Question
	Inductive	Deductive	Retroductive	Abductive	
Exploration	***			***	What
Description	***			***	What
Explanation	*	***	***		Why
Prediction	**	***			What
Understanding				***	Why
Change		*	**	**	How
Evaluation	**	**	**	**	What and Why
Assess impacts	**	**	**	**	What and Why

Key: *** = major activity; ** = moderate activity; * = minor activity. These 'weightings' of the connections between objectives and research strategies are indicative only.

strategy explains by means of well-confirmed generalizations, the Deductive strategy explains by means of well-tested theories that represent the current state of knowledge, the Retroductive strategy explains by means of mechanisms operating in contexts, the Abductive strategy produces understanding based on 'thick' descriptions and social scientific concepts that have been derived from everyday concepts and accounts.

Answering a 'how' question requires a different kind of description that is built on previous answers to both 'what' and 'why' questions, a description of a desired state of affairs, and the specification of stages and procedures for getting from an existing situation to the desired situation. Clearly, this type of description is complex and requires a great deal of knowledge of the social phenomenon and the context. All four strategies would claim to be able to answer 'how' questions, although there are disagreements about which ones are the most effective. In some cases, a combination of strategies might be useful.

Differences exist between the research strategies in the purposes they are able to pursue (see table 4.2). *Exploration* and *description* are confined to the Inductive and Abductive strategies. While the Deductive and Retroductive strategies need description as their starting-point, they must rely on the other two strategies for this. The major task of the Deductive and Retroductive strategies is *explanation*, although Inductivists also claim to be able to do it, and some Abductivists would like to be able to do it. *Prediction* is confined to the Inductive and Deductive strategies, again being achieved in different ways. Some Abductivists may be interested in *prediction*, based on 'thick' descriptions, but this is of minor concern. *Understanding* is the exclusive preserve of the Abductive strategy and the *constructionist* version of the Retroductive strategy. Some users of the Retroductive and Abductive strategies are interested in *change*, particularly researchers concerned with emancipation. *Evaluation* research is practised by followers of all four research strategies, with a common division between positivist and constructivist approaches (Guba and Lincoln 1989) and quantitative and qualitative methods. Social *impact assessment* can use the Inductive strategy, perhaps in combination with the Deductive strategy, the Retroductive strategy or the Abductive strategy (see table 4.1).

The selection of a research strategy does not determine the kind of research design that is adopted. While some research strategies tend to be associated with particular types of research, such as the Inductive strategy with social surveys, the Deductive strategy with the experimental method, and the Abductive strategy with case studies, there is no necessary connection. The logic of any of the four research strategies can be implemented using a variety of research designs.

As we shall see in chapter 7, while there may be conventions about quantitative methods being used with some strategies, for example, the Inductive and Deductive, and qualitative methods being used in others, for example, the Abductive, there is no necessary association. Methods can be used in the service of a number of research strategies. However, they will need to be used, and can be used, with different ontological assumptions. For example, observation can be used in the service of all four research strategies, although just how it is used might vary; the same is true of interviewing. The critical issue is the need to be aware of the ontological and epistemological assumptions within which a method is used.

Research Strategies and the Researcher's Stance

To conclude this discussion of the four research strategies, we need to return to an issue raised in chapter 2 regarding the stance a researcher takes towards the research process and the participants. Because of its particular ontological and epistemological assumptions, each research strategy entails a particular stance.

In the classical version of the Inductive research strategy, the ideal was for the researcher to take a *detached observer* position and avoid allowing personal values or political commitments to contaminate the research. If objectivity cannot be achieved, then the generalizations produced cannot be trusted as representing the regularities in social life; it would not be possible to achieve the aim of arriving at true statements about the world. However, as we have seen, the necessary revisions to the classical version of this strategy recognize that this ideal is not fully achievable.

While the aim of the Deductive research strategy is also a search for the truth, it is recognized that the culture, language, knowledge and previous experiences of a researcher make presuppositionless data collection impossible. However, even though 'observation' may be theory-laden, it is still necessary to endeavour to exclude personal values and political commitments from the research process. Again, detachment is the ideal, even though it is recognized that its complete achievement is impossible.

The two branches of the Retroductive research strategy, the *structuralist* and the *constructionist*, deal with this issue differently. The *structuralist* version essentially follows the stance adopted in the Deductive strategy. The aim is to establish the existence of real structures and mechanisms even in the face of the 'theory-dependence of observation' (see Pawson 1989). In the *constructionist* version, the stance of the researcher is likely to be one of those adopted in the Abductive strategy.

It is in the Abductive research strategy that very different views of the stance of the researcher are adopted. These include the *faithful reporter*, the *mediator of languages*, the *reflective partner*, the *conscientizer*, and the postmodern 'narrative dialogue'. The reflexive nature of this type of social research requires a very different stance to that advocated in both the Inductive and Deductive research strategies.

In spite of their sympathy for one or more of these latter stances, some writers have expressed reservations about their implications for the social scientific enterprise (e.g. Geertz 1988; Hammersley and Atkinson 2007). The acceptance of these stances can lead the researcher in a number of directions, including the abandonment of any concern with the production of new social scientific knowledge. The fear is that research will just become a form of journalism or part of a political programme, or will lead to 'methodological paralysis'. While I sympathize with the view that social science should include emancipatory concerns, I am also committed to seeking better understanding of social life, preferably by incorporating the social actors' point of view. In any case, without sound understanding, emancipation becomes problematic. Of course, it is necessary to accept the idea that such knowledge will be limited in its relevance in terms of both time and space. However, accepting this degree of relativity in the nature of the knowledge we produce does not invalidate the social research enterprise. An example of the adoption of a middle position can be found in Hammersley and Atkinson (2007: 1–19).

Choosing a Research Strategy

To arrive at a decision on what will be the best research strategy or strategies, the capabilities and the relative strengths and weakness of each strategy must be understood. This requires a reasonably sophisticated understanding of the philosophies of social science and the research paradigms with which each research strategy is associated (see Blaikie 2007).

The principal aim in choosing a research strategy, or strategies, is to achieve the best procedure(s) for addressing a research problem, and, particularly, for answering the research questions formulated to deal with it. However, it is important to reiterate that it may be necessary to use different strategies for different research questions. For example, the Inductive strategy could be used to answer 'what' questions, and then the Deductive, Retroductive or Abductive strategies used to answer 'why' questions. The Abductive strategy has the advantage that it can be used to answer both 'what' and 'why' questions.

Research questions can usually be answered by using more than one research strategy. For example, in the research topic on 'Absenteeism' (see the Appendix), the research question – 'Why does absenteeism occur?' – could be answered by selecting an appropriate theory and putting it to the test in this context (the Deductive strategy), or, alternatively, by trying to understand work and life from the nurses' points of view (the Abductive strategy).

The two strategies are likely to produce different accounts of absenteeism, and it may be difficult, if not impossible, to decide which is the best one. One criterion might be to see which account leads to interventions that produce the greatest reduction in absenteeism. However, situations like this are always complex and changing, interventions are never simple, and outcomes may not be easy to establish conclusively. It has been argued that there are no completely neutral criteria for making such choices (see e.g. Kuhn 1970). Hence, ultimately, the choice of research strategy has to be a matter of judgement, and judgements involve both acceptable criteria and personal preferences.

A number of other factors can influence the choice of research strategy. When a researcher is contributing to a particular research programme, a decision might be made to select the strategy or strategies already in use. This may be a conscious choice or may simply be taken for granted, particularly if a researcher is trained in the research traditions used in that research programme, and in the particular paradigm within which it is located. Not to follow these traditions may lead to conflict with colleagues, and, ultimately, to reduced career prospects.

It is also possible that a preference for, or familiarity with, certain research methods will influence the choice of strategy. For example, if a researcher believes that particular quantitative methods are best, and has received training in only these methods, s/he may opt for a strategy in which it is believed these methods are used. For example, the Deductive strategy might be selected because it is believed that quantitative methods, such as questionnaires, are used in this strategy. Similarly, students who have received training in the use of a new computer package for analysing textual data may assume that it must be used within the Abductive strategy.

Another set of possible influences has to do with the audiences that a researcher considers to be important and the assumptions that are made about their methodological preferences. These audiences can include funding agencies, book publishers and journal editors, discipline colleagues and consumers of the research, such as book buyers, journal readers, clients and respondents. In the case of research students, supervisors/advisers and examiners are important. Perceptions of the preferences of these audiences may need to be taken into account, although conflict between audience expectations can obviously be a problem.

In the last analysis, practical considerations, such as time, cost and availability of equipment, may have an influence. While these factors are more directly associated with research methods, views about links between research strategies and methods, whether correct or not, may lead to the rejection of a particular strategy. For example, in-depth interviewing may be seen to be associated with the Abductive research strategy, and as this method can be time-consuming, both the method and the strategy may be rejected.

The possible influence of all these factors, and the difficulty involved in establishing the relative merits of the four research strategies, would seem to undermine my case of the need for a detailed knowledge of the strategies and careful consideration in their selection. My concern is about making informed choices based on adequate knowledge of what is being selected and rejected, and on an understanding of the ontological and epistemological assumptions that go with such choices. The fact that personal, social and practical factors may also have an influence makes it necessary not only to be aware of these, but also of the consequences of allowing them to influence the choices.

Further Reading

Blaikie, N. 2007. *Approaches to Social Enquiry*.
   In addition, the following references deal with various aspects of the topics covered in the chapter.
Bhaskar, R. 1979. *The Possibility of Naturalism*.
Giddens, A. 1976. *New Rules of Sociological Method*.
Harré, R. and P. F. Secord 1972, *The Explanation of Social Behaviour*.
Keat, R. and J. Urry 1982. *Social Theory as Science*.
Outhwaite, W. 1987. *New Philosophies of Social Science*.
Pawson, R. 2000. 'Middle-range realism.'
Popper, K. R. 1961. *The Poverty of Historicism*.
Ramazanoğlu, C. and J. Holland 2002. *Feminist Methodology*.
Sayer, A. 2000. *Realism and Social Science*.
Thompson, J. B. 1981. *Critical Hermeneutics*.

5

Concepts, Theories, Hypotheses and Models

Chapter Summary

- The nature of the research questions, and the choice of research strategy or strategies, will determine how concepts are used, whether hypotheses are used, and the role of theory and models.
- Four traditions represent the ways concepts are used in social research.
  - *Ontological* tradition – concepts identify the basic features of some social phenomenon and the relationships between them.
  - *Operational* tradition – concepts are translated into variables by devising ways to measure them.
  - *Sensitizing* tradition – concepts provide initial ideas of what to look for, and these ideas will be refined as the research proceeds.
  - *Hermeneutic* tradition – concepts that a researcher uses to describe and understand any social phenomenon are derived from everyday concepts and meanings.
- The adaptive alternative seeks concepts that integrate agency and structure, as well as micro and macro-analysis, and social and sociological conceptions, with general theory.
- The four research strategies tend to use concepts in different ways.
- Theory can be regarded as being of two main types – theoreticians' and researchers' – and as existing at different levels of abstraction, ranging from classificatory schemes, through conceptual frameworks to theoretical systems.
- The place of theory in social research has been described in a variety of ways.
  - As occupying the space between empirical generalizations and grand theory, theories of the middle-range (Merton).
  - As producing an understanding of personal troubles and public issues by focusing on the intersection of biography and history (Mills).
  - As occupying various levels of abstraction between data and general theoretical ideas (Turner).
  - As being both inputs and outputs in ongoing cycles of induction and deduction (Wallace).

- ○ As being generated from data (Glaser and Strauss).
- ○ As being the outcome of a dialogue between research data and unfolding conceptualizations and theoretical reflections (Layder).
- Hypotheses play a limited role in social research, only being relevant to the answering of 'why' research questions with the Deductive research strategy.
- Various types of models are used in social research. They are:
  - ○ abstract descriptions;
  - ○ synonym for theory;
  - ○ conceptual models;
  - ○ theoretical models;
  - ○ analogue for mechanisms;
  - ○ diagrammatic representations; and
  - ○ mathematical representations.

Introduction

The social science literature is replete with ideas about the role of concepts, theories, hypotheses and models in social research. Some of these ideas have come to be accepted uncritically. For example, many textbooks on social research methods regard the core of social research as being the definition and measurement of concepts, with theories stating relationships between concepts and models consisting of networks of such relationships. Hypotheses are regarded as potential relationships between concepts that can be tested by measuring the key concepts in them and analysing the data so produced. This view is attractive because of its simplicity. However, while it is very common, it is only relevant to two of the research strategies, the Inductive and Deductive, and then it is used differently in each one. Other views also need to be considered.

This chapter examines:

- views on how concepts are used in social research;
- ideas on the nature and use of theory;
- classical and contemporary views on the relationship between theory and research;
- the role of hypotheses and their connection with theory;
- types of models and their uses; and
- the role of concepts, theories, hypotheses and models in the four research strategies (see figure 5.1).

The Role of Concepts

A concept is an idea that is expressed in words or as a symbol. Technical concepts in any discipline form the language by means of which it deals with its subject-matter. They range in generality from the very specific to the highly abstract, and from the simple to the complex. Concepts are regarded as the building blocks of social theories. Theories, in turn, specify the relationships between concepts

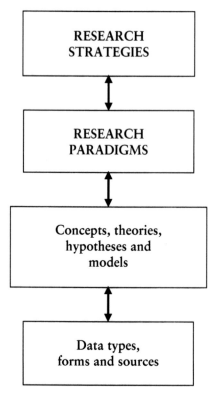

Figure 5.1   Concepts, theories, hypotheses and models

and why these relationships exist. Good theories are supposed to represent what happens in the social world.

A commonly held view of the role of concepts in social research, and their place in social theory, is embodied in the Positivist research paradigm. Blumer (1969) describes this view as follows.

> Theory is of value in empirical science only to the extent to which it connects fruit-fully with the empirical world. Concepts are the means, and the only means of estab-lishing such connection, for it is the concept that points to the empirical instances about which a theoretical proposal is made. If the concept is clear as to what it refers, then sure identification of the empirical instances may be made. With their identifica-tion, they can be studied carefully, used to test theoretical proposals and exploited for suggestions as to new proposals. Thus, with clear concepts theoretical statements can be brought into close and self-correcting relations with the empirical world. (Blumer 1969: 143)

In addition to this role of establishing some kind of link with the social world, Blumer saw concepts as being important in the theoretical framework that sets a context for the research, as being involved in the statement of the research problem, as determining the data that will be collected and how they will be categorized, and as being essential in describing the findings (1969: 26). However, he proceeded to scrutinize this view, in particular, to question whether concepts used in this paradigm actually match the empirical world to which they are supposed to refer (1969: 28). His solution was to use sensitizing rather than definitive concepts, a distinction to be discussed shortly.

It is differences in views about the sources of concepts and their definitions that distinguish the research strategies. For example, in the Inductive and Deductive research strategies, it is the researcher's responsibility to select the relevant concepts and to define them before the research commences. However, in the Abductive research strategy, the concepts and their definitions may be derived initially from those used by social actors in the context of the topic under investigation. Technical concepts are derived from these lay concepts by a process of abstraction during the course of the research. Because of these different usages, *we cannot set out with just a single view of the role of concepts in social research*.

In the Inductive and Deductive research strategies, concepts and their definitions have various origins. For example, they may come from:

- a theoretical perspective or research paradigm that is dominant within a discipline or social scientific community (e.g. conflict theory or Interpretivism);
- a specific research programme (e.g. social mobility);
- commonly used theoretical concepts that are given a new definition (e.g. social class); or
- everyday concepts that are given precise meanings.

All of these sources involve the researcher in deciding what concepts and definitions are the most appropriate.

To explore these differences, five traditions in the use of concepts in the social sciences are discussed: the *ontological*, the *operationalizing*, the *sensitizing*, the *hermeneutic* and the *adaptive*. The *ontological* tradition is concerned with establishing the main features of social reality, the *operationalizing* tradition with specifying and measuring concepts to produce variables for a particular research project, the *sensitizing* tradition with refining an initial flexible concept in the course of the research, the *hermeneutic* tradition with deriving technical concepts from lay language, and the *adaptive* alternative with using both technical and lay concepts to link structure and agency.

The Ontological Tradition

The *ontological* tradition is concerned with establishing a set of concepts that identifies the basic features of the social world, and that are essential for understanding societies, major social institutions or, perhaps, small-scale social situations. Elements of the ontological tradition can be found in the work of classical and modern social theorists. Classical theorists, such as Marx, Weber and Durkheim, each developed a battery of key concepts that provided a view of reality and were used in their theorizing. However, it was a modern theorist, Talcott Parsons, who turned the ontological analysis of concepts into a major

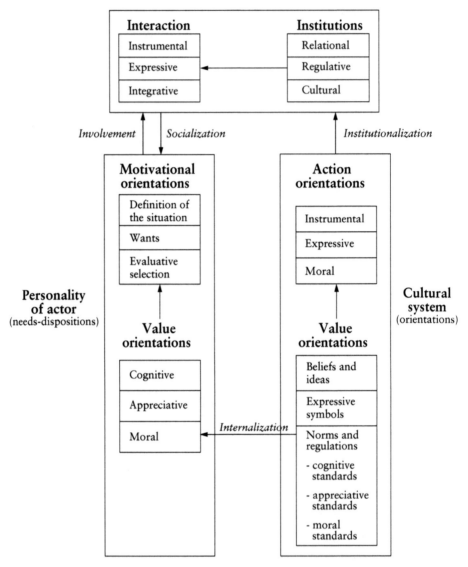

Figure 5.2   Parsons's theory of the system of action (*Source*: Waters 1994: 145)

preoccupation. A modification of part of Parsons's conceptual scheme will serve as an illustration of this tradition (see figure 5.2).

More recent attempts at theoretical synthesis, such as those by Habermas and Giddens, also include a strong ontological emphasis. Giddens, for example, has reorganized and redefined some of the basic concepts used by Parsons and others (e.g. society, social system, institution, structure), and has arranged them around the concept of 'structuration'. The foundation concepts in his scheme are 'agency' and 'structure', and the interplay of these leads to the process of structuration. While it is not possible to elaborate Structuration Theory here (see Giddens 1979, 1984 as well as: Cohen 1989; Bryant and Jary 1991; Craib 1992; Layder 1994;

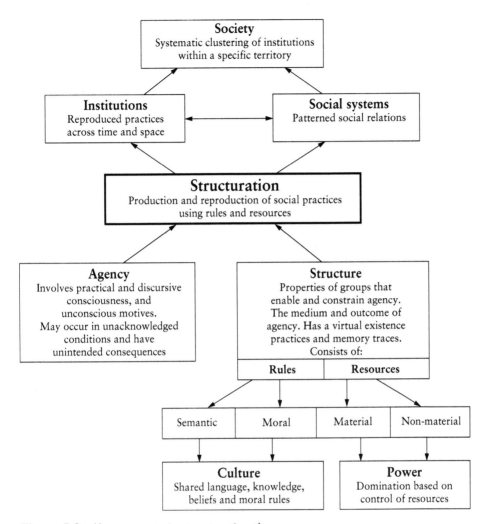

Figure 5.3   Key concepts in structuration theory

Scott 1995; Blaikie 2007), figure 5.3 is my attempt at setting out the relationships between Giddens's basic concepts.

The Operationalizing Tradition

The operationalizing tradition is concerned with turning concepts into variables, with identifying the key concepts to be used in a particular study, and then defining them and developing ways of measuring them.

From Durkheim on, it has been argued that as concepts are the basic building blocks of theory, they must be defined precisely and consistently. The imprecision of ordinary language must be superseded by a technical use of concepts. This has led to the view that science has two languages (see e.g. Blalock 1968; Sedlack and Stanley 1992; Babbie 2004; Neuman 2006): one is the language of *conceptualization* and the other is the language of *operationalization* used in quantitative measurement and testing of theories.

The language of *conceptualization* is the language that social scientists use to communicate their theoretical ideas and research findings to each other; it is the language of both abstract theoretical notions and a means of identifying observable phenomena. In the context of a research project, this language is used to identify key concepts and to state relationships between these concepts; to state research questions and hypotheses. Thus, some authors refer to this language as 'theory'. For example: 'Theories are built from concepts [and] . . . concepts are constructed from definitions' (Turner 1991: 5).

Researchers are required to define these concepts precisely in terms of how they will be used in a particular research project. The aim is to maintain a consistent theoretical language, although this is unlikely to be achieved. Turner has certainly adopted an optimistic view on this.

> Hence the verbal symbols used to develop a concept must be defined as precisely as possible in order that they point to the same phenomenon for all investigators. Although perfect consensus may never be obtained with conventional language, a body of theory rests on the premise that scholars will do their best to define concepts ambiguously. (Turner 1991: 5)

These meanings are usually referred to as *formal definitions.*

The second language, *operationalization*, is used to transform theoretical language into empirical concepts. This is done by specifying the procedures by which the 'theoretical' concept will be measured, by indicating what will count as an example of, or what will have to change to produce different values for, the theoretical concept, i.e. the indicators that will be used to measure the concept to produce data related to it. These are commonly called *operational definitions.*

The concept of 'social class' is an example of such an abstract concept. Social class might be defined as 'a category of individuals who occupy a similar position in a structure resulting from the distribution of economic resources'. While there are other meanings, this is what social class could mean in a particular research project. Thus defined, the concept might then be measured in terms of the income a person receives from wages or salary. This operationalization relates to only one part of the total economic resources to which an individual may have access, such as interest on savings, dividends from shares, rental income from property, capital gains from property or other assets, a pension or superannuation. To faithfully measure the concept as defined, these and maybe other data would be required. However, the researcher might decide that some sources of income (e.g. capital gains) are too difficult to measure reliably, or that individuals in the study may have little or no idea how much of such income they receive. Hence, operationalization may be kept to something that is readily measured (although experienced researchers will know that obtaining accurate information about a person's annual wages or salary can be far from straightforward).

When a concept can have a number of values, the measurement of it produces a *variable.* A variable is 'a *concept* which can have *various values*, and which is defined in such a way that *one can tell by means of observations which value it has in a particular occurrence*' (Stinchcombe 1968: 28–9). In research that stresses the importance of operationalism, variables are the focus of research activity.

A great deal of attention has been given to the problems of operationalizing some of the major concepts in social science. Debates about defining and operationalizing concepts have sometimes been regarded as a theoretical activity. For example, some time ago, discussions on the appropriate meaning of the concept of 'role' kept many writers busy. The purpose seems to have been to arrive at the 'right' definition and to somehow persuade others to use it (see Biddle 1979).

A major difficulty encountered in defining and operationalizing concepts is that they differ in their level of abstractness. Some concepts relate to concrete phenomena in specific times and places (e.g. the suicide rate). Other concepts deal with phenomena that span time and place, that are very general (e.g. deviant behaviour). These latter concepts may be difficult to operationalize unless they are translated into more specific concepts.

This tradition of two languages also identifies a particular relationship between theory and research. Theoretical activity is essentially about identifying the most useful concepts and finding the right formal meanings for them, while research is about selecting the best method of operationalizing a concept and then proceeding to collect appropriate data and analyse them. As C. Wright Mills pointed out many years ago, this is a very restricted view of both theory and research.

> 'Theory' becomes the variables useful in interpreting statistical findings; 'empirical data' . . . are restricted to such statistically determined facts and relations as are numerous, repeatable, measurable. . . . There are no philosophical grounds, and certainly no grounds in the work of social science . . . so to restrict these terms. (Mills 1959: 66)

The relationship between theory and research will be taken up later in this chapter.

Blumer was a major critic of the operational tradition. He depicted the tradition thus.

> 'Operational procedure' rests on the idea that a theoretical assertion or a concept can be given both empirical reference and validation by developing a specific, regularized procedure for approaching the empirical world. The given procedure or operation may be the use of a test, a scale, a measuring instrument, or standardized mode of inquiry. The procedure 'operationalizes' the theoretical proposition or concept. If the given operation meets tests of reliability the operation is taken as a sound instrument for disengaging specific empirical data. In turn, these data are thought to be valid empirical referents of the concept or proposition that is operationalized. (Blumer 1969: 30–1)

He objected to the idea of measuring concepts by selecting only a limited aspect of the relevant phenomenon and assuming that it reflected all aspects. Take the measurement of intelligence for example. In everyday life, intelligence manifests itself in many ways and is present in such varied things as the skilful military planning of an army general, the ingenious exploitation of a market situation by a business entrepreneur, effective methods of survival by a disadvantaged slum dweller, the clever meeting of the problems of his world by a peasant or a primitive [*sic*] tribesman, the cunning of low-grade delinquent-girl morons in a detention home, and the construction of telling verse by a poet. It should be immediately clear how ridiculous and unwarranted it is to believe that the operationalizing of intelligence through a given intelligence test yields a satisfactory picture of intelligence. To form an empirically satisfactory picture of intelligence, a picture that may be taken as having empirical validation, it is necessary to catch and study intelligence as it is in play in actual empirical life instead of relying on a specialized and usually arbitrary selection of one area of its presumed manifestation. (Blumer 1969: 31)

As a symbolic interactionist, Blumer argued that an adequate understanding of social life requires recognition of the fact that individuals and groups find their way about by defining and interpreting objects, events and situations that they encounter. The operational tradition either ignores this or takes it for granted as not needing to be considered (Blumer 1969: 133). However, Blumer was not completely against the operational tradition as long as it was only used 'for those areas of social life and formation that are not mediated by an interpretive process' (Blumer 1969: 139). He was also prepared to accept that in areas where interpretation is involved, variable analysis might unearth patterns that cannot be detected by the direct study of people as is required in the interpretive approach to social enquiry. These patterns can then be investigated for the interpretations that lie behind them.

The Sensitizing Tradition

Blumer's major solution to the deficiencies of the operational tradition was to suggest the use of sensitizing concepts.[1] He argued that in getting close to the social world we discover what social phenomena have in common. However, these similarities are usually expressed in a distinctive manner, with individual and group variations. Therefore, concepts need to be sensitizing rather than definitive in order for a researcher to be able to explore the nature of what is common.

Sensitizing concepts provide clues and suggestions about what to look for. The task is to reshape the concept to identify the nature of common aspects within the diversity of other features. Until this is done, it is premature to impose predefined (definitive) concepts on the phenomenon. A researcher sets out with one or a few rather general and vaguely defined concepts that are needed to provide an orientation to the research problem. Initially, their meaning will be established by exposition rather than by definition. However, as the research proceeds, the meaning of the concepts will be refined to make them more relevant for their purpose.

In their exposition of grounded theory, Glaser and Strauss (1967) referred to theoretical sensitivity as the continual development of theory from data. Grounded theory combines 'concepts and hypotheses that have emerged from the data with some existing ones that are clearly useful. . . . Potential theoretical sensitivity is lost when the sociologist commits himself [*sic*] exclusively to one specific preconceived theory' (1967: 48). The notion of *sensitivity* here refers to openness on the part of a researcher to different ideas, to a process of interrelating theoretical insights and data.

Drawing on the ideas of Glaser and Strauss (1967) about grounded theory, Denzin has taken the middle ground with regard to sensitizing concepts. He has argued that within his version of symbolic interactionism, the use of sensitizing concepts precedes operationalization. In fact, he defined sensitizing concepts negatively: 'By *sensitizing concepts* I refer to concepts that are not transformed immediately into *operational definitions* through an attitude scale or check list. . . . The sensitizing approach merely delays the point at which operationalization occurs' (Denzin 1970: 14).

Two points need to be noted here. First, Denzin included the meanings that social actors give to the concept being investigated in order to arrive at his meaning for it. Second, the subsequent *operationalizing* of the concept may be looser and much more diverse that would normally be the case in the operationalizing tradition.

The defining characteristic of the *sensitizing* tradition is that a researcher sets out with a loosely defined concept and then refines its meaning during the course of the research. While some help might be obtained from the people involved in the study, the concept remains the researcher's. Even if another concept is substituted, the concept and its ultimate meaning are based on the researcher's decisions. The *hermeneutic* tradition presents a radical alternative to this view.

The Hermeneutic Tradition

The *hermeneutic* tradition differs from the *sensitizing* tradition in that concepts the researcher uses to describe and understand *any* social phenomenon (i.e. technical concepts) have their origin in the everyday language of the social actors under investigation, not in the language of the discipline.

Advocates of this tradition argue that, initially, accounts of social life need to be derived from the accounts that social actors give of their activities; the language used by the social scientist must be derived from everyday language. This requires a hermeneutic process in which the researcher tries to grasp the meaning of everyday language by becoming immersed in the relevant sector of the social world (Giddens 1976). As the process advances, the researcher has to mediate between the particular everyday language and some version of the technical language of social science in order to produce concepts that are relevant to the research topic. The process of mediation is akin to the hermeneutic reading of a text; it is a matter of interpretation rather than translation (Gadamer 1989).

While a researcher may need sensitizing concepts at the outset, these must give way to the everyday concepts that social actors use to discuss and relate to this phenomenon. For example, if the topic for investigation is the 'care of the aged', then a researcher has to discover what language old people, their families and professionals use to discuss the problem of what should be done about old people who have lost the capacity to care for themselves. A range of concepts might be used by different actors in different contexts, and none of these may correspond to the ones a researcher has derived from the literature. The researcher's task is to make sense of this diversity of language by producing a typology, a set of categories (types) that capture the different concepts and their meanings. The labels for such types may be invented or borrowed from the literature, but their meaning will be generalized from those used by the social actors (see Stacy 1983; Blaikie and Stacy 1982, 1984; Blaikie 2007: 97–9).

Hence, the *hermeneutic* tradition also differs from the *operational* tradition in terms of the source of concepts. The *operational* tradition works 'top down' in the sense that it imposes a researcher's concepts on everyday life, the assumption being that the researcher is in a position to judge what concepts will be relevant because of the theoretical model or perspective that has been adopted. In the *hermeneutic* tradition, researchers work 'bottom up' by adopting the position of learner rather than expert. Social actors have to teach the researcher how they understand their world, i.e. what everyday concepts and interpretations (lay theories) they use to make sense of it. By a complex process, researchers can use these lay concepts and methods of understanding as the ingredients for their accounts. From lay concepts technical concepts can be generated. This may require the invention of new concepts, the adaptation of existing technical concepts, or the borrowing of the latter. In the process, a more general and abstract account than the individual accounts of social actors is produced.

To use concepts as advocated by this tradition is to be reflexive: to allow concepts to evolve through a process of re-examination and reflection. The meaning of a concept does not remain static; it changes as the concept evolves from the data and is applied to them. Whether concepts developed in this way can be applied in other contexts is a matter for investigation. Of course, a researcher has to stop somewhere and freeze the meaning of a concept for a while. The aim of all this is to generate concepts that fit the problem at hand and work to provide useful description and understanding.

The Adaptive Alternative

Later in the chapter we will encounter an approach to the relationship between theory and research proposed by Layder (1998). As part of this proposal, he discussed the types of concepts that he considers enter into social research.

His primary concern was to establish a link between theoretical concepts and ideas, and empirical materials (data and information), a link that did not give preference or priority to one or the other. The *ontological* tradition is clearly on the theoretical side while the *operational* tradition leans towards the empirical side. In their own ways, the *sensitizing* and *hermeneutic* traditions try to establish bridges between the theoretical and the empirical. However, Layder wanted to go much further by establishing concepts that bridge aspects of individual social agency and reproduce social relations and practices. In other words, he wanted concepts that integrate agency and structure as well as the micro and macro levels of social analysis. At the same time, he wanted to blend social actors' conceptions with sociological conceptions.

He saw these concepts as merging 'the subjectively experienced world of research subjects with the analytic and conceptual predilections and directives of the researcher.' These concepts 'are not simply grounded in data of lived experiences or local narratives, but are also anchored to a chain of reasoning and an analytic advantage point which gives their conceptual representation of the behaviour in focus a rather different basis' (Layder 1998: 82).

To achieve this, Layder identified four types of concepts: *behavioural, systemic* or structural, *bridging* or mediating, and *general* or theoretician's. *Behavioural* concepts are concerned with individual social agency and with describing the everyday world from an 'insider' point of view. They include types of social actors in particular types of social activities or social settings, types of interpersonal relationships in such settings, and the meanings and interpretations people give to such activities, settings and relationships. 'The point about behavioural concepts is that they directly describe some aspect of a participant's behaviour, predisposition or attitude and include some reference to his or her identity or the quality and meaning of the relationships in which he or she is involved' (Layder 1998: 85).

Layder is willing to allow behavioural concepts to be either member-defined or observer-defined. However, if the latter, they need to be 'subjectively adequate' (Schütz 1963b; Bruyn 1966), 'retain the integrity of the phenomenon' (Douglas 1971) or be relevant to the people involved (Glaser and Strauss 1967). This means that behavioural concepts 'must be recognizable, make sense and be understandable to those who are the subjects of the study (even if not routinely employed by them)' (Layder 1998: 86).

Systemic or structural concepts refer to the reproduced social relations that confront social actors as an external reality. They represent

> the historically emergent standing conditions of an ongoing society. To say that they are standing conditions does not mean that they are static and unchanging or that they are somehow beyond the reach and influence of human agents. Such things as institutions, language, culture and various forms of knowledge are all susceptible to the transformative powers of individuals and social groups, but they nonetheless confront particular individuals and groups as the products of previous generations. (Layder 1998: 88)

At this point, Layder draws on Giddens's notion of 'duality of structure', that social structures are both constituted by human agents and provide the conditions for social life. They provide the rules and resources that people draw on in their routine social activities, and such activities contribute to the reproduction of these structures through time and space. They are the settings and conditions that constitute the social environment in which social life takes place. Therefore, while the systemic or structural aspects of society are intimately linked with the behavioural aspects, they constitute a second area of attention for the theorist and social researcher.

Layder goes on to argue that a third category of concepts is required as *bridging* or mediating concepts between the behavioural and systemic. He referred to these concepts as typifications. This notion is derived from Schütz (1963a), although Schütz regarded typifications as being both social (social actors' everyday concepts) and sociological (theorists' and researchers' technical concepts). Layder has confined his use to sociological concepts.[2] He wanted these concepts to be an amalgam, and to have an equal measure of agency and structure, or behavioural and systemic aspects. Because bridging concepts are not defined entirely in terms of everyday social activities, they may not be recognizable to social actors without their sociological meaning being explained.

Layder has proposed that bridging concepts indicate and focus on three broad kinds of phenomena. The first is the linkage between subjective and objective phenomena. Some concepts refer both to subjective behaviour and the objective social conditions in which it takes place. He used the concepts of 'career' and 'emotional labour' as examples. The second kind of concept indicates that certain social actors occupy strategic positions of control and can therefore mediate the effects of systemic aspects on the behaviour of others. Examples are managers and professionals. Third, some concepts characterize the nature of social relations that are influenced by systemic features and also express people's involvements and motivations. Concepts such as 'calculative' or 'alienative' involvement in organizations are examples (Etzioni 1961).

The fourth type of concept is those produced by *general* theorists. Shortly we shall encounter a distinction between *theoretician's* and *researcher's* theories. This fourth type fits in the theoretician's category. We only have to turn to the many books on social and sociological theory to find examples of concepts that have been invented by both classical and contemporary social theorists and that are embedded in their theories of society and social life. The illustrations of the *ontological* conceptual tradition discussed in this chapter provide examples.

Layder lamented the fact that researchers tend to neglect these general concepts, perhaps because they are seen to be unconnected with the 'real' empirical world. He rejected this notion. 'In my view, all general theory is connected with the empirical world in some way. However, . . . general theories differ in terms of their degree of abstraction . . . as well as in relation to the question of how they may be tested or adjudicated' (Layder 1998: 95). He acknowledged that the notion of 'subjective adequacy' has little relevance to general concepts, as they are not meant to be social actors' concepts. Instead, their value has to be judged on the basis of, 'first, the broader context of reasoning in which they are embedded and secondly, their relation to other competing or complementary concepts or theories' (Layder 1998: 95). He argued that researchers need to move beyond the immediate substantive concerns in research and pay attention to the ontological features of social life. This is where theoreticians' concepts and theories come into play.

The research paradigms that were identified in chapter 4, along with the vast body of work of social theorists, provide ontological assumptions and general concepts that social researchers can use to locate their research in existing ways of understanding social life. Just which research paradigms or social theories a researcher chooses to draw on, and how they are used, are the critical issues.

Concepts and Research Strategies

There are some connections worth noting between the research strategies outlined in chapter 4 and these five conceptual traditions. The ontological tradition provides a background to all research, although it is less relevant to, and
may be rejected by, researchers who use the Abductive research strategy. While
Deductivists may find conceptual schemes very useful as a source of variables,
Abductivists may resist the imposition of such 'top down' schemes and prefer to
generate their own concepts in a hermeneutic, 'bottom up' manner.

It is in the Inductive and Deductive research strategies that the operationalizing
tradition has been most evident.[3] In the Inductive strategy, concepts need to be
selected, defined and operationalized. In the Deductive strategy, hypotheses are
deduced from a theory, and concepts in a hypothesis are measured in order to
test whether or not a hypothesized relationship exists. While it is possible to test
hypotheses using other methods, this research strategy has been dominated by
the operationalizing tradition. It is worth noting that the sensitizing tradition can
also be used in these two research strategies, for example, in an exploratory phase
when relevant concepts and their definitions are being sought.

The connection between the Retroductive research strategy and the conceptual
traditions is rather complex. Strictly speaking, concepts are not operationalized in
this research strategy. Rather, structures and mechanisms are hypothesized and discovered by direct and indirect observations and experiments. Of course, to hypoth-
esize the existence of a structure or mechanism requires the use of language; you have
to have some idea of what you are looking for. This may involve adopting or adapt-
ing an existing concept, or inventing a new one, to identify it. In this regard, it would
be interesting to know how concepts such as 'atom' and 'virus' came to be used.

These comments on the Retroductive strategy apply particularly to the *structuralist* version. The situation is rather different in the *constructionist* version,
and is similar to that in the Abductive research strategy. It is in this latter strategy
that both the sensitizing and hermeneutic traditions are used, but in different
branches. Nevertheless, it is the hermeneutic tradition that is most appropriate for
genuine Abductive research. This is because the generation of technical concepts
from lay concepts is a hermeneutic process.

Aspects of the 'adaptive alternative' provide the possibility for a more sophisticated use of concepts in all traditions of research but, particularly, when the
Deductive and Abductive research strategies are used. Linking the hermeneutic
tradition and the use of the Abductive research strategy with *structural* and
general concepts can lead to more productive theory generation. In addition, the
incorporation of both *behavioural* and *structural* concepts, and the bridging of
social actors' and sociological concepts in the context of general theory, can only
lead to more productive theories to test using the Deductive strategy.

Clearly, these five views of the role of concepts in social research are very different. As a result, researchers have to make choices about which tradition or
traditions to use, and, in the process, to make sure that their use is consistent with
other research design decisions. While the choice of research strategy will have a
big influence on the way concepts are used, a researcher may use concepts in more
than one way in a particular research project.

The Role of Theory

One of the most vexed problems for novice researchers is how to use theory in research. Atheoretical research is usually condemned; good research is supposed to involve the use of theory in some way. However, there are many views, and much confusion, about where and how theory should enter into the research process. No doubt, part of the reason for this uncertainty is the fact that the concept 'theory' itself refers to a variety of activities and products.

> Like so many words that are bandied about, the word theory threatens to become meaningless. Because its referents are so diverse – including everything from minor working hypotheses, through comprehensive but vague and unordered speculations, to axiomatic systems of thought – use of the word often obscures rather than creates understanding. (Merton 1967: 39)

The problem is what kind of theory to use, and for what purpose. The situation is further complicated by the existence of a diversity of perspectives in social theory, and differences in the ways in which theory is used in the four research strategies.

Some Definitions of Theory

In order to examine the role of theory in research, we must first be clear about what constitutes social or sociological theory. While the answer to this question may appear to be self-evident, an examination of the literature indicates that there are numerous uses of the concept.

At a general level, theory has been described as 'a heuristic device for organizing what we know, or think we know, at a particular time about some more or less explicitly posed question or issue' (Inkeles 1964: 28), or as 'a "story" about how and why events in the universe occur' (Turner 1991: 1). More specifically, theories 'attempt to answer why and how questions' by 'relating the subject of interest (e.g. riots) to some other phenomena (e.g. heat and crowding)' (Bailey 1994: 41).

Some definitions of theory are even more specific. 'A theory is a set of concepts plus the interrelationships that are assumed to exist among these concepts' (Seltiz *et al.* 1976: 16). 'Sociological theory refers to logically interconnected sets of propositions from which empirical uniformities can be derived' (Merton 1967: 39). 'A theory highlights and explains something that one would otherwise not see, or would find puzzling' (Gilbert 2008: 25).

Therefore, theories provide:

- explanations
- of some aspects of human experience
- that form non-random patterns.

In other words, *social theories are explanations of recurrent patterns or regularities in social life.* They are answers to questions or puzzles about why people behave in the way they do in particular social contexts, and why social life is organized in the way it is. In the context of research design, *a theory is an answer to a 'why' question*; it is an explanation of a pattern or regularity that has been observed, the cause or reason for which needs to be understood.

Types of Theory

Out of this array of definitions of theory it is possible to identify two types in terms of the activities engaged in by practitioners: *theoreticians'* theory and *researchers'* theory (Menzies 1982). This distinction helps us to understand the common complaint that there is a gap between theory and research in the social sciences. This gap refers to the lack of connection between what theoreticians and researchers do, between the ideas discussed in books on social theory and the theoretical ideas that are used in research. Some researchers try to bridge this gap by setting their research within a theoretical perspective. However, the connection is often very tenuous; a perspective may be reviewed in a theory chapter of a thesis and then largely ignored as the research proceeds. Alternatively, an attempt may be made at the end of the research to interpret the results within a theoretical perspective in the hope of staving off accusations of the research being atheoretical. While theory is commonly used in this way, some writers have argued that *post hoc* theorizing is an unsatisfactory use of theory (see, for example, Merton 1967: 147–9).

Theoreticians' theory

Theoreticians' theory is that produced by writers whose aim is to develop an understanding of social life in terms of basic concepts and ideas. Such concepts and ideas are neither derived from social research, nor are they systematically tested by means of research. Their status may be so abstract that they constitute a broad perspective on social life rather than explanatory accounts of it. The *ontological* conceptual tradition discussed earlier in this chapter is an example of *theoreticians'* theory, as is most of the work usually discussed as classical and modern social/sociological theory.

Theoreticians' theory can be both at the macro and micro; it can deal with both large-scale and small-scale social phenomena. Theoreticians feed off each other in the sense that much of their work attempts to synthesize and/or build on earlier theorizing.

Theoreticians' theory can be examined from a number of points of view.

- *The history of social thought*: developments in the understanding of social life and society (e.g. Barnes and Becker 1938; Bogardus 1940; Barnes 1948; Martindale 1960; Becker and Barnes 1961).
- *The work of great theorists*: original works, plus reviews and commentaries (e.g. Aron 1965, 1968; Raison 1969; Coser 1971; Giddens 1971; Beilharz 1991; Ritzer 2003; Craib 1997; Appelrouth and Edles 2008).
- *Theoretical schools or perspectives*: clustering of classical and contemporary

theorists into schools based on common ontological assumptions (e.g. Cuff and Payne 1979; Ritzer 1980, 2005; Jones 1985; Giddens and Turner 1987; Turner 1991; Craib 1992; Scott 1995; Wallace and Wolf 2006; Cuff *et al.* 2006; Ritzer and Goodman 2007a, 2007b)

- *Theorizing strategies*: the establishment of broad categories of theorizing in terms of both ontological and epistemological assumptions (e.g. Johnson *et al.* 1984; Waters 1994; Blaikie 2007).

As the most relevant aspect of *theoreticians'* theory in the present context is *theoretical perspectives*, only these will be discussed here.

Theoretical perspectives provide a way of looking at the social world; they highlight certain aspects while at the same time making other aspects less visible. A shift in theoretical perspective changes the shape of the social world. They provide a particular language, a conceptual framework, or a collection of 'theoretical' concepts and related propositions, within which society and social life can be described and explained. Some perspectives attempt to establish a set of principles that provide the ultimate foundation for social life and a basis for its explanation. In general, theoretical perspectives provide images of society or social life (ontologies), but they do not provide rigorously developed and logically organized theoretical statements (Turner 1991: 29–30).

Classical and contemporary theorists who share similar ontological assumptions and ways of understanding social life are grouped together, and the common elements of their theories abstracted. The concept of *theoretical perspective* is equivalent to the notions of 'general theoretical orientation' (Merton 1967), 'general model' (Willer 1967), 'meta-theory' (Turner 1991), 'foundationalist theory' or 'formal theory' (Waters 1994), and even 'paradigm' (Kuhn 1970; Freidrichs 1970; Krausz and Miller 1974).

Theoretical perspectives are sometimes regarded as paradigms because they include ontological and epistemological assumptions and associated practices for the pursuit of social knowledge (Kuhn 1970; Friedrichs 1970). The advocates of these perspectives differ in the kinds of 'stories' that they tell about social life. They tend to disagree on:

- what topics should be studied (subject matter);
- what the social world looks like and how it works (ontological assumptions);
- what kind of knowledge about human interaction and social organization is possible (ultimate purpose);
- what kinds of questions can be asked;
- what logic of enquiry should be used and how knowledge can be developed (epistemological assumptions); and
- what this knowledge should be used for (objectives) (Wallace and Wolf 2006: 3–13).

Ontological assumptions, which are invariably implicit, include:

- the basic components of social life, including individuals, social processes or social structures;

- how these components relate to each other;
- what human nature is like, i.e. whether human behaviour is essentially determined and therefore predictable, or whether human beings are relatively autonomous and create their own social life, thus making prediction difficult; and
- whether human beings are motivated essentially by interests or by values.

A simple set of major theoretical perspectives has been arrived at by using two overlapping dichotomies, structural vs. interpretive and consensus vs. conflict. This is mainly a British way of viewing social theories and has been used in introductory texts on sociology and social theory (e.g. Cuff and Payne 1979; Jones 1985; van Krieken *et al.* 2005; Haralambos and Holborn 2004; Cuff *et al.* 2006). Three perspectives are commonly identified in these texts:

- structural-consensus (Functionalism);
- structural-conflict (Marxism);
- interpretive (Interpretivism).[4]

Theoretical perspectives have been categorized in other ways. A common set of categories can be found in texts from the United States on social/sociological theory (e.g. Turner 1991; Wallace and Wolf 2006; Ritzer and Goodman 2007a, 2007b), in more recent British texts (e.g. Craib 1992; Scott 1995), and in the North Atlantic collaboration by Giddens and Turner (1987). These classifications include categories such as:

- *functionalism* (Durkheim, Malinowski, Radcliffe-Brown, Parsons, Merton);
- *neo-functionalism* (Luhmann, Alexander);
- *conflict theory* (Marx, Weber, Dahrendorf, Coser, Collins, Rex);
- *rational choice and exchange theory* (Frazer, Malinowski, Mauss, Weber, Homans, Blau, Elster);
- *phenomenology* (Husserl, Schütz, Tiryakian, Bruyn, Berger, Luckmann, Douglas, Psathas);
- *ethnomethodology* (Garfinkel, Cicourel, Sacks, Schegloff, Zimmerman);
- *symbolic interactionism* (Mead, Dewey, Cooley, Thomas, Blumer, Strauss, Becker, Denzin);
- *dramaturgy* (Goffman);
- *structuralism and post-structuralism* (Saussure, Lévi-Strauss, Foucault, Lacan, Althusser, Derrida);
- *critical theory* (Adorno, Horkheimer, Marcuse, Habermas, Fay);
- *structuration theory* (Giddens);
- *feminist theory* (Barnard, Smith, Harding); and
- *complexity theory* (Reed and Harvey, Cillers, Bryne, Capra, Urry).

I am sure you will have noticed an overlap between some of these categories and the research paradigms discussed in chapter 4. The emphasis here is on their theoretical idea whereas the research paradigms concentrate on their methodological contributions, particularly reference to logics of enquiry and ontological and epistemological assumptions. While this distinction between theory and methodology is not always clear-cut, I selected the set of research paradigms from those in which the methodological considerations are particularly strong.

The Role of Theoreticians' Theory in Research

In spite of the division of labour between *theoreticians'* theory and *researchers'* theory, the former, and, particularly theoretical perspectives, have much to offer the researcher. They can provide:

- a way of viewing the social world, including ontological and epistemological assumptions;
- a language with which to describe and explain aspects of the social world;
- general theoretical ideas to set the context and direction for research; and
- possible explanations or tentative hypotheses.

The first contribution overlaps with a key element of research paradigms. Social reality may be viewed as either 'material' or 'ideal' (Johnson *et al.* 1984), or as either 'subjective' or 'objective' (Waters 1994; Ritzer and Goodman 2007b). People's actions may be regarded as the result of either choice or constraint (humanistic vs. deterministic assumptions), and their relationships based either on agreement about norms and values or on different interests (consensus vs. conflict assumptions). Perspectives also include different epistemological assumptions about how the social world can be known. Social reality can be approached from a nominalist or realist epistemology (Johnson *et al.* 1984), or explained in individualistic or holistic terms (Waters 1994). However, such ontological commitments are not always fully recognized or made explicit.

The second role of *theoreticians'* theory in research, to provide a language, facilitates the statement of research questions and answers to them. Like everyday language, theoretical language provides a vocabulary and meanings for concepts. While the meanings may be more precise than in everyday language, they are still subject to multiple definitions and disputes within and between paradigms. There are fashions in theoretical perspectives, and, therefore, in theoretical language. Such language both facilitates dialogue between adherents to a perspective and excludes the outsider. While the relationship between a theoretical language and everyday language is regarded as the most fundamental methodological issue in the social sciences (Bhaskar 1979; Blaikie 2007), it is also a highly contested one.

The third role of theory is an extension of the second. It provides a context of ideas, or a theoretical framework, which is the source of the focus and direction for the research. The review of a theorist's ideas on an issue, such as Marx's discussion of 'alienation', can set the scene for the collection of particular types of data from particular sources, for example, from factory workers who were formerly rural peasants in a developing country. While the theoretical ideas may not suggest specific hypotheses, they provide the inspiration to pursue research in a particular way.

The final role of theory concerns the source of hypotheses. Theory can be used either to provide general explanatory ideas to guide research, or, more specifically, to provide possible answers to 'why' questions, i.e. as a source of hypotheses to be tested. The Deductive research strategy has taken the latter to the limit by requiring that hypotheses be logically deduced from a set of theoretical propositions. In this case, a hypothesis is the conclusion to a theoretical argument that provides a tentative answer to a 'why' question. Of course, hypotheses can come from other sources, including previous research.

It is clear that researchers rely on *theoreticians'* theory in a number of ways. However, the extent to which theoreticians use the results of research is much less clear. Certainly, there would appear to be few explicit connections in the literature. The exceptions are the rare cases where a researcher is also a theoretician (e.g. Bourdieu).

Researchers' Theory

Researchers' theory is either theory that produces specific hypotheses to be tested, or theory that is generated in the course of the research. It is possible to construct a composite definition of *researchers'* theory as consisting of:

- a related set of statements
- about relationships between concepts
- with a certain level of generality
- which are empirically testable; and which,
- when tested, have a certain level of validity.

These theories provide explanations of regularities in social life at a level that is directly relevant to research.

Each of the research strategies gives a particular interpretation of this definition. In the Inductive strategy, general statements are related in networks, while in the Deductive strategy, these statements are related logically and have different levels of generality. Although the Retroductive research strategy only requires a description of the generative structure or mechanism, it may require discursive support for their operation. This may take the form of a theoretical argument, but less formalized than in the Deductive strategy. In the Abductive research strategy, theory may take many forms, from tight logical arguments to loose discussions. However, in the end, theories in all four research strategies need to be reduced to statements of relationships between concepts. We will return to these differences between the research strategies towards the end of the chapter.

An important issue for a researcher is where to get a suitable theory. In the absence of a good existing theory, Stinchcombe has argued that you should make them up yourself, a task that he regarded as being manageable even for students: 'A student who has difficulty thinking of at least three sensible explanations for any correlation that he [*sic*] is really interested in should probably choose another profession' (Stinchcombe 1968: 13).

Levels of Theory

Another way of approaching the diversity in theoretical activity is to view theory as occupying different levels. Denzin (1970), for example, has slightly elaborated the scheme developed by Parsons and Shils (1951) by proposing five levels:

- *ad hoc* classificatory systems;
- categorical systems or taxonomies;
- conceptual frameworks;
- theoretical systems; and
- empirical-theoretical systems.

These five levels are intended to move from 'mere' description, through patterns of relationships, to explanatory schemes, and then to empirical testing of the theoretical ideas.

Ad hoc classificatory systems are used to summarize data. The classes or categories are more or less arbitrary and no attempt is made to establish relationships between them. They are just labels for particular observations or data, and are normally not derived from any theory. For example, students might be classified as 'very bright', 'serious', 'average', 'lazy' and 'dumb', as well as 'older' and 'younger', and 'female' and 'male'. Such classifications are not theoretical but may later be incorporated into a theoretical scheme.

A categorical system or taxonomy moves beyond *ad hoc* classification, although it is still tied closely to a particular context or limited range of phenomena. Now the relationships between the classes or categories are stated. For example, the classification of students into their level of ability and attitude to their work (a mixed classification that would need to be refined into at least two separate dimensions) could be related to their age or gender. Research might then match the relationships with some data, but the activity remains at the level of description.

Conceptual schemes take us to a higher level by presenting a systematic image of the world (as in the *ontological* tradition). These schemes lend themselves to the development of propositions about relationships between concepts, and are intended to apply to a wide range of situations. Some conceptual schemes claim to represent society and its constituent parts (see figures 5.2 and 5.3). A more limited example might deal with concepts involved in predicting 'academic performance': 'level of ability', 'attitudes to study', 'age', 'gender', 'social class background', 'type of schooling' and 'career aspirations'. These concepts could be developed into a scheme of relationships, including some assumptions about causal connections.

Theoretical schemes bring together combinations of taxonomies and conceptual schemes into a theoretical argument. Now explanation is the aim. However, these schemes are likely to be rather abstract and not in a form that can be used directly in research. This requires another step, the establishment of empirical–theoretical schemes that are formulated precisely and in such a way that they can be tested. Hence, only these last two levels in the list can be regarded as being truly theoretical, and only the last connects theory with research.

Another basis for differentiating between levels of theory is to consider their scope. Again, Denzin (1970) has proposed four main levels: *grand* theories, *middle-range* theories, *substantive* theories and *formal* theories. *Grand* theories, or system theories, present a master conceptual scheme that is intended to represent the important features of a total society. These are often referred to as macro-theories because they apply to large-scale social phenomena. Merton referred to these as 'general sociological orientations' that

> involve broad postulates which indicate *types* of variables which are somehow to be taken into account rather than specifying determinate relationships between particular variables. . . . The chief function of these orientations is to provide a general context for inquiry; they facilitate the process of arriving at determinate hypotheses. (Merton 1967: 142)

Middle-range theories, a notion coined by Merton, lie between grand theories and empirical generalizations.

> [M]iddle range theories have not been logically *derived* from a single all-embracing theory of social systems, though once developed they may be consistent with one. Furthermore, each theory is more than a mere empirical generalization – an isolated proposition summarizing observed uniformities of relationships between two or more variables. A theory comprises a set of assumptions from which empirical generalizations have themselves been derived. (Merton 1967: 41)

Nevertheless, these theories (e.g. a theory of reference groups – Merton's example) are intended to apply to a variety of contexts and research problems. I shall elaborate Merton's ideas on middle-range theories in the next section of this chapter.

The third level referred to by Denzin, *substantive* theories, does apply to specific problem areas such as race relations and juvenile delinquency. Both middle-range theories and substantive theories are stated at a level that a researcher can use. They can also be combined, for example, by using reference group theory as part of a theory of race relations.

Finally, the development of *formal* theory is based on the now contested idea that universal explanations of social life can be developed. While the content may be different in different contexts, the form of these theories will be the same. Simmel, Goffman and Homans were all committed to the idea that the development of formal theory is possible. Homans, for example, claimed that social behaviour could be explained in terms of a few psychological principles. One of his principles was: 'For all actions taken by persons, the more often a particular action is rewarded, the more likely the person is to perform that action' (Homans 1974: 16).

Relationship between Theory and Research

The relationship between theory and research was a topic of considerable interest in the United States during the 1950s and the 1960s, largely as a result of the seminal work of Merton (1967), whose views on this first appeared in 1949, and the provocative writings of C. Wright Mills (1959). Merton and Mills lamented the state of the sociological enterprise at that time and proposed their own broad solutions, 'middle-range theory' and the 'sociological imagination', respectively. Towards the end of this period, Willer (1967) elaborated a methodological framework in which the concepts of 'theory' and 'model' were given precise meanings. His work was followed immediately by a spate of rather technical writing on theory construction by, for example: Stinchcombe (1968); Dubin (1969); Blalock (1969); Reynolds (1971); and Hage (1972). Later editions of some of these works (e.g. Dubin 1978), and other contributions (e.g. Chafetz 1978), followed a decade later to consolidate a particular view of the relationship between theory and research.

More recent attempts to link theory and research have done so either in a series of *linear* steps or levels, or in a *cyclical* process used to construct and test theories. Both approaches are used to move from abstract theory to the empirical products of research, or from data to theory. Turner (1991) and Alexander (1982) have discussed the linear view of the relationship, and Wallace (1971, 1983), Lin (1976) and de Vaus (2002) the cyclical view.

I will limit the discussion here to a consideration of Merton's advocacy of middle-range theory, Mills's use of the sociological imagination, Turner's scheme of levels and linear stages, Wallace's proposal to integrate induction and deduction into a cyclical process, Glaser and Strauss's theory generation from data, and Layder's attempts to modify and synthesize the views of Merton and the grounded theorists.

Merton: middle-range theory

Merton's arguments were directed towards the two unsatisfactory extremes that he had observed in the practices of sociologists about sixty years ago. This is captured in his oft-quoted passage from the beginning of the chapter in which he discusses the various uses of theory.

> The recent history of sociological theory can in large measure be written in terms of an alternation between two contrasting emphases. On the one hand, we observe those sociologists who seek above all to generalize, to find their way as rapidly as possible to the formulation of sociological laws. Tending to assess the significance of sociological work in terms of scope rather than the demonstrability of generalizations, they eschew the 'triviality' of detailed, small-scale observation and seek the grandeur of global summaries. At the other extreme stands a hardy band who do not hunt too closely the implications of their research but who remain confident and assured that what they report is so. To be sure, their reports of facts are verifiable and often verified, but they are somewhat at a loss to relate these facts to one another or even to explain why these, rather than other, observations have been made. For the first group the identifying motto would at times seem to be: 'We do not know whether what we say is true, but it is at least significant.' And for the radical empiricist the motto may read: 'This is demonstrably so, but we cannot indicate its significance.' (Merton 1967: 139)

Throughout his work on the nature of sociological theory, Merton's main target was theorists such as Marx, Parsons and Sorokin and their concern for all embracing theory. What he wanted was theories that were of use to the researcher who was trying to deal with more practical problems, theories that could be part of the research process.

> [A] large part of what is now described as sociological theory consists of *general orientations toward data, suggesting types of variables which theories must somehow take into account, rather than clearly formulated, verifiable statements of relationships between specified variables.* We have many concepts but fewer confirmed theories; many points of view, but few theorems; many 'approaches' but few arrivals. (Merton 1967: 52)

Merton's solution to the excesses of these two contrasting positions was to advocate what he called *theories of the middle range*,

> theories that lie between the minor but necessary working hypotheses that evolve in abundance during day-to-day research and the all inclusive systematic efforts to develop a unified theory that will explain all the observed uniformities of social behaviour, social organization and social change. (Merton 1967: 39)

He summarized his arguments as follows:

1 Middle-range theories consist of limited sets of assumptions from which specific hypotheses are logically derived and confirmed by empirical investigation.
2 These theories do not remain separate but are consolidated into wider networks of theory. . .
3 These theories are sufficiently abstract to deal with differing spheres of social behaviour and social structure, so that they transcend sheer description or empirical generalization . . .
4 This type of theory cuts across distinctions between micro . . . and macro-sociological problems . . .
5 Total sociological systems of theory – such as Marx's historical materialism, Parsons' theory of social systems and Sorokin's integral sociology – represent general theoretical orientations rather than the rigorous and tightknit systems envisaged in the search for a 'unified theory' in physics.
6 As a result, many theories of the middle range are consistent with a variety of systems of sociological thought.
7 Theories of the middle range are typically in direct line of continuity with the work of classical theoretical formulations . . .[5]
8 The middle range orientation involves the specification of ignorance. Rather than pretend to knowledge where it is in fact absent, it expressly recognizes what must still be learned in order to lay the foundation for still more knowledge . . . (Merton 1967: 68)

When Merton presented his ideas on middle-range theory, he was, understandably, criticized by the grand theorists. In time, the notion of *middle-range theory* has entered the consciousness of many sociologists and lip-service has been paid to it by succeeding generations. It has become the flag under which many self respecting researchers wish to be seen marching. However, research practice has frequently fallen short of Merton's ideal and has tended to become ritualized in the testing of isolated or trivial hypotheses. The linking of research to theory has tended to be achieved through theories being reduced to simple and isolated statements of relationships.

A major critic of Merton's idea of middle-range theory has argued that grand theory and small-scale empirical research are not really at the ends of a continuum, and, even if they were, middle-range theory is not intermediate between them (Willer 1967: p. xiv). Willer has suggested that Merton equated a middle range of generality with the scientific adequacy and testability of a theory. For concepts to be testable, they do not need to be at a middling level of generality, or modest in scope. According to Willer, what they need to be is precise and measurable, and it must be possible to connect them in a meaningful way. He supported Merton's call for testable theory but was critical of him for not providing a methodology for constructing and testing theory (Willer 1967: xvi).

This latter criticism seems to be rather unfair, as Merton had very clearly advocated the use of the Deductive research strategy; he constantly reiterated the need to derive hypotheses from theory. While his ideas on theory testing are consistent with those of Popper, as a practical researcher, unlike Popper, he paid attention to the process of theory generation. His ideas on this may have been too 'woolly' for Willer as they reflect the rather messy process that seems to be inevitable in most research.

What Merton clearly recognized was the complex interplay between theory and data, and he saw research findings as being a major source of stimulus for theory development. His views were made clear in his paper entitled 'The Bearing of Empirical Research on Sociological Theory', a paper that has been given less attention than his statements on middle-range theory. Merton has suggested that: 'Under certain conditions, a research finding gives rise to social theory' (1967: 157). He called this the *serendipity* pattern, 'the fairly common experience of observing an *unanticipated, anomalous and strategic* datum which becomes the occasion for developing a new theory or for extending an existing theory' (1967: 158). The observation of something that is inconsistent with existing theory provokes curiosity, stimulates the researcher to try to make sense of it in terms of a broader theoretical framework, and leads to new observations. 'The more he [*sic*] is steeped in the data, the greater the likelihood that he will hit upon a fruitful direction of inquiry' (1967: 159). However, Merton suggested that it is not the data themselves that provide the stimulation but the application by the researcher of some general theoretical ideas: Therefore, serendipity is not the discovery of a new idea accidentally, but the presence of an unexpected anomaly that excites curiosity and puts pressure on the researcher to think creatively in new directions by matching different theoretical ideas to the situation. This process is at the core of theory generation in the later stages of the Abductive research strategy.

Another stimulus to theory construction that Merton discussed concerns data overlooked by the conceptual framework being used. The repeated recording of these data can stimulate the researcher to extend the conceptual framework to include other concepts. Merton gave the example of how Malinowski observed the differences in the way the Trobriand Islanders went about fishing in the inner lagoon, compared to the open sea. This led Malinowski to incorporate new elements into existing theories of magic. The theory was extended by an observant, curious and creative researcher who, recognizing that the existing theory had something missing, used his observations to stimulate the filling of the gap.

A third way in which empirical data affect theory occurs when new research procedures shift the foci of theoretical interest by providing previously unavailable data. However, there is a danger that these new research techniques will divert attention to problems that are theoretically and socially less important.

Finally, Merton has suggested that the process of doing research can lead to the clarification of concepts. He regarded a large part of theoretical work as involving such clarification. He argued that research stimulates this clarification as the result of the need to establish indices of the variables being used, i.e. the need, in the kind of quantitative research with which he was familiar, to find the best, the most precise way to operationalize a concept. According to Merton, it is this pressure to measure concepts that is instrumental in clarifying them in a way that cannot occur in purely theoretical activity.

In summarizing these four ways in which the process of research stimulates theoretical development, Merton suggested that

> an explicitly formulated theory does not invariably precede empirical inquiry, that as a matter of plain fact the theorist is not inevitably the lamp lighting the way to new observations. The sequence is often reversed. Nor is it enough to say that research and theory must be married if sociology is to bear legitimate fruit. They must not only exchange solemn vows – they must know how to carry on from there. Their reciprocal roles must be clearly defined. (Merton 1967: 171)

Given that Merton was writing some time ago (his work was first published in 1949 with a major revision in 1957), the reader may be curious as to why so much space has been devoted to his three short articles. The reason is that not only have they been common reference points over recent decades, but they have also provided some practical methodological wisdom that is still very relevant today. The problems with which Merton was wrestling, of how to relate theory and research, and what kind of theory is relevant to research, are matters that still perplex researchers and cause disputes among the proponents of the various theoretical, methodological and research traditions. While Merton's commitment was clearly to the Deductive research strategy and quantitative methods, his view of theory construction shares much in common with that used in the Abductive research strategy. His view of research is not that of a rigid, linear set of stages, but involves the researcher as an active and creative agent in the complex interplay between ideas and data. He was reflecting on his own research experience in attempting to understand important and practical problems, and that is why he objected so strongly to the work of the 'armchair' theorists.

Mills: sociological imagination

A slightly later attempt to discuss similarly conceptualized extremes in sociology can be found in the writing of C. Wright Mills (1959). Mills lamented the state of sociology in the 1950s because of the two extreme tendencies that had developed. On the one hand, there was the interest in what he called 'grand theory', and, on the other hand, there was the concern with research methods and empirical studies, what he called 'abstracted empiricism'. He acknowledged that considerations of theory and method are essential to the task of the sociologist, but he argued that these two dominant versions of them were a hindrance to understanding and resolving 'the personal troubles of milieu' and 'the public issues of the social structure' (Mills 1959: x).

Mills divided grand theory into two types, both of which have been discussed earlier in this chapter. The first, in the work of Comte, Marx, Spencer and Weber, tried to develop 'a theory of man's [sic] history'. He described this kind of sociology as

> an encyclopedic endeavor, concerned with the whole of man's [sic] social life. It is at once historical and systematic – historical, because it deals with and uses the materials of the past; systematic, because it does so in order to discern 'the stages' of the course of history and the regularities of social life. (Mills 1959: 22)

The second type of grand theory is concerned with producing a systematic theory of the nature of man and society, as in the work of Simmel and von Weise.

> Sociology comes to deal in conceptions intended to be of use in classifying all social relations and providing insight into their supposedly invariant features. It is, in short, concerned with a rather static and abstract view of the components of social structure on a quite high level of generality. (Mills 1959: 23)

Mills was critical of both of these traditions: the first because it can become distorted into 'a trans-historical strait-jacket' into which human history is forced and which is used to predict the future; and the second because it can become 'an elaborate and arid formalism in which the splitting of Concepts and their endless rearrangement becomes the central endeavour' (1959: 23).

Mills regarded Parsons as the leading exponent of the second tradition. To illustrate how this kind of grand theory makes unnecessarily complex what are essentially simple ideas, he reduced Parsons's classic text, *The Social System*, to four paragraphs that take up no more than a page. In fact, he claimed it could be summarized in two sentences – 'How is social order possible? Commonly accepted values.' Mills was simply trying to illustrate what he thought was the limited value that such a theoretical endeavour has in aiding our understanding of the human condition, of the intersection of 'biography and history, and the connections of the two in a variety of social structures' (1959: 32). Another aspect of his criticism was that grand theorists have attempted to produce one universal scheme by which to understand the nature of society and social life. This, he argued, is impossible.

It would be easy to conclude from his damning criticisms that Mills was developing an argument for the use of systematic research rather than grand theory as the central activity of sociology. However, this was not his intention, as he was equally critical of the dominant kind of social research that was conducted in his day. Both, he argued, are ways of avoiding the task of the social sciences, dealing with personal troubles and public issues. The former he described as producing a 'fetishism of the Concept' and the latter as leading to 'methodological inhibition'.

For Mills, abstracted empiricism is equivalent to crude survey research, atheoretical data gathered by interview or questionnaire from a sample of individuals. He argued that it is an activity that can be done by administrators and research technicians, although the practitioners like to regard themselves as scientists. The problems selected for consideration, and the way they are formulated, are severely limited by what the practitioners regard as 'the scientific method', which means some version of Positivism. Theory is equated with variables that help to interpret statistical findings, and data are restricted to statistically determined facts and relations. This is the *operationalizing* conceptual tradition discussed earlier in this chapter.

According to Mills, the major characteristic of the abstracted empiricists is that they are methodologically inhibited, and this is what accounts for the thinness of their results. Their concern is with statistical rituals and pseudo precision. Mills did not deny the value of statistical procedures, when they are appropriate, but he argued that there are also other ways of doing research.

In spite of the fact that it is now fifty years since Mills expressed these concerns, what he had to say can still be applied to a great deal of social research. The techniques may have become more sophisticated, and there may be more effort to avoid the appellation of being atheoretical, but methodological inhibition is still rampant. With the advent of postmodernism, 'methodological paralysis' has taken over.

Mills's solution to these extremes was rather different from Merton's. It was not a case of finding some middle ground between the lofty heights of theory and the mundane activities of data collection, but, rather, the use of the *sociological imagination*.

The sociological imagination enables its possessor to understand the larger historical scene in terms of its meaning for the inner life and the external career of a variety of individuals. . . .

The first fruit of this imagination – and the first lesson of the social science that embodies it – is the idea that the individual can understand his own experience and gauge his own fate only by locating himself [*sic*] within his period, that he can know his own chances in life only by becoming aware of those of all individuals in his circumstances. . . . We have come to know that every individual lives . . . out a biography, and that he lives it out within some historical sequence. By the fact of his living he contributes, however minutely, to the shaping of his society and to the course of its history, even as he is made by society and by its historical push and shove.

The sociological imagination enables us to grasp history and biography and the relations between the two within society. That is the task and its promise. (Mills 1959: 5–6)

Turner: linear elements

Turner (1991) viewed the relationship between theory and research as being facilitated by a series of levels or steps, from data produced by research, through theory at different levels of abstraction, to general ideas and assumptions. For him, theory is constructed from several basic elements: *concepts*, *statements* and *theoretical formats*. *Concepts* identify phenomena in the social world, both in everyday language and social scientific or technical language. Concepts need to be defined, preferably in a consistent way by all researchers to ensure that they refer to the same phenomenon (Turner 1991: 5). These concepts can then be formed into *statements* of relationships, and sets of statements constitute *theoretical formats*. Hence, research is seen to proceed in a linear manner, beginning with concepts and moving to theoretical formats. However, the latter have been viewed in a variety of ways. As

- *meta-theoretical* schemes,
- *analytical* schemes,
- *propositional* schemes, and
- *modelling* schemes (Turner 1991: 7–12).

Meta-theory is concerned with discerning underlying ontological and epistemological assumptions that a body of theory or a theoretical perspective uses. By *analytical* schemes, Turner referred to conceptualizations of the key properties of and relationship in the social world; they give the social world a sense of order. This is equivalent to the *ontological* conceptual tradition discussed earlier in the chapter.

Turner has divided *analytical* schemes into two types: *naturalistic* schemes and *sensitizing* schemes. *Naturalistic* schemes 'try to develop a tightly woven system of categories that is presumed to capture the way in which the invariant properties of the universe are ordered' (e.g. the work of Parsons). *Sensitizing* schemes are 'more loosely assembled congeries of concepts intended to sensitize and orient researchers and theorists to certain critical processes' (Turner 1991: 10). Apart, perhaps, from some very general concepts, the authors who advocate sensitizing schemes do not assume that they apply across time and space. They accept that as social arrangements are subject to change, concepts and their arrangements may also have to change; they are always provisional. Some writers have argued that *analytical* schemes are a prerequisite for the development of theory to be used in research; that they provide a framework and an orientation to a research problem. Turner, on the other hand, has argued that the *naturalistic* variety may be too rigid and elaborate to stimulate theorizing, and that *sensitizing* schemes may be more useful.

Turner's third type of format, *propositional* schemes, is more directly related to the business of research. A proposition is a statement of a relationship between two or more concepts; it claims that a variation in one concept is associated with a variation in another concept. For example, as Durkheim might have argued, an increase in the level of individualism among members of a group or society is associated with a rise in the suicide rate. Propositional schemes vary along two dimensions, in their level of abstraction and in the way the propositions are organized. Some are highly abstract and do not relate to any empirical instance, while others may simply summarize relations between observed phenomena.

Turner's fourth type of scheme involves the use of diagrammatic or pictorial representations of social events or processes. These have been labelled *modelling* schemes and will be discussed later in this chapter.

According to Turner, it is also possible to view theory construction as a movement from one theoretical format to another. He clearly saw the movement between them as occurring in both directions, although his preference was for working from the middle to the ends: 'Start with sensitizing schemes, propositions and models, and only then move on to the formal collection of data or to meta-theorizing and scheme-building' (Turner 1987: 167).

Turner pointed out that the proponents of these formats have engaged in a great deal of debate about which one is the best. He expressed some strong views on the value to the researcher of the various approaches to theorizing just reviewed. At one extreme, he regarded *meta-theory* as interesting but counterproductive. At the other extreme, he rejected the idea of mechanically abstracting theory from empirical findings. While he regarded familiarity with empirical regularities as being crucial to the development of theoretical statements, he argued that a 'much more creative leap of insight is necessary, and so I do not suggest that theory building begin with a total immersion in the empirical facts. I suspect that, once buried in the facts, one rarely rises above them' (Turner 1991: 23–4).

Wallace: ongoing cycles

Wallace first developed the idea of research as a cyclical process in his *Logic of Science in Sociology* (1971) and modified it in a later publication (1983). The idea has been taken up by a number of writers (e.g. Lin 1976; de Vaus 2002). Wallace argued that the logics of *induction* and *deduction* should be combined in an ongoing cycle. Or, to put this in my language, the Inductive and Deductive research strategies should be combined to provide an explicit link between theory and research. While these two research strategies can be viewed as presenting opposing logics of enquiry, these authors have suggested that, in practice, theory and research can be combined in a never-ending alternation between induction, deduction, induction, and so on. Hence, the process of theory construction and theory testing are seen to occur in this cyclical process (see figure 5.4).

The starting-point for theory construction could be data collection, at the bottom of the figure, to be followed by data analysis, from which empirical generalizations are derived. According to inductive logic, a new theory is constructed from these generalizations. Further testing could follow.

The starting-point for theory testing is at the top of the figure with the 'theory' box. Hypotheses are deduced, their concepts operationalized, statements of relationships between concepts formed, the data collected and analysed, and the results compared with the original hypothesis (represented by the 'test of a theory' box). In other cycles around this process, the step from 'empirical generalizations' to 'theory' can be used to refine an existing theory. Hence, the process can be used in at least three ways: to generate a new theory, to test a theory, or to refine a theory.

The extent to which researchers follow these processes is an open question; much research is done in less systematic ways than the figure would require. Perhaps researchers who use the Deductive research strategy might benefit from

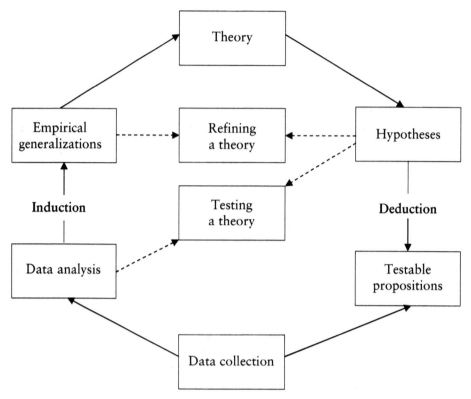

Figure 5.4   The cycle of theory construction and testing (*Source*: Adapted from Wallace 1971, 1983; de Vaus 2002)

recognizing the cyclical rather than linear nature of their kind of research, and for those who use the Inductive strategy it is important to recognize that induction cannot stand on its own as a method of theory development.

The strength of this scheme is the recognition of the developmental nature of theory construction. However, I would argue that the inductive phase of the cycle is much too simplistic a representation of the creative side of research. What should occur is a complex trial and error process, more akin to that used in the Abductive research strategy and by grounded theorists. The other major deficiency of the scheme is that it provides no place for the social actors' concepts and meanings to enter into the process; it uses the ontology of both Positivism and Critical Rationalism, and a combination of their epistemologies.

Glaser and Strauss: grounded theory

A different view of the relationship between theory and research has been presented by Glaser and Strauss (1967). They shifted the emphasis from the testing of theories to their generation. While recognizing that theories need to be verified, their proposal for this is very different from that advocated by Merton and Wallace, and goes against Turner's views. For Glaser and Strauss, theory generation and verification are both part of the same process and occur in a much more flexible way.

Grounded theory originated in the United States at the time middle-range deductive theorizing was being advocated by Merton. It emerged out of the research Glaser and Strauss had conducted on 'dying patients' (1965).

Glaser and Strauss have offered a radical critique of the Deductive research strategy by arguing that, at the time they were writing, there was 'an over-emphasis in current sociology on the verification of theory, [with] a resultant de-emphasis on the prior step of discovering what concepts and hypotheses are relevant for the area that one wishes to research' (1967: 1–2). They believed that 'good' theory is systematically discovered from and verified with the data of social research.

Glaser and Strauss advocated the use of an inductive process, which, they argued, produces a theory that will fit and work, i.e. its concepts and categories will be appropriate, and it will be meaningfully relevant to, and will be able to both explain and predict, the phenomena under study.

> In contrasting grounded theory with logico-deductive theory and discussing and assessing their relative merits to fit and work (predict, explain, and be relevant), we have taken the position that the adequacy of a theory for sociology today cannot be divorced from the process by which it is generated. Thus one cannon for judging the usefulness of a theory is how it was generated – and we suggest that it is likely to be a better theory to the degree that it has been inductively developed from social research. (Glaser and Strauss 1967: 5)

Hence, theory generation is seen to be intimately involved in the process of research, rather than being something that precedes or occurs apart from it. 'Generating a theory from data means that most hypotheses and concepts not only come from the data, but are systematically worked out in relation to the data during the course of the research' (Glaser and Strauss 1967: 6). Theoretical ideas that come from other sources are not simply tested during the course of the research, as is the case with the Deductive research strategy, but have to be worked out in relation to the data in a much less formal trial and error process. Theory generation is therefore an ever-developing process.

The method advocated by Glaser and Strauss is *comparative analysis*. As conceptual categories (or concepts) and their properties are generated from data gathering in one social context, their relevance can be explored in other contexts. This requires the use of 'a multitude of carefully selected cases, but the pressure is *not* on the sociologist to "know the whole field" or to have all the facts "from a careful random sample." His [sic] job is not to provide a perfect description of an area, but to develop a theory that accounts for much of the relevant behavior' (Glaser and Strauss 1967: 30).

Comparative analysis is used to generate two types of theory, *substantive* and *formal*. Substantive theory is generated in specific contexts and will be related to a specific social process. Formal theory, on the other hand, is generated at a higher level of generality and involves concepts that can be applied to a number of substantive areas.

> By substantive theory, we mean that developed for a substantive, or empirical, area
> of sociological inquiry, such as patient care, race relations, professional education,
> delinquency, or research organizations. By formal theory, we mean that developed
> for a formal, or conceptual area of sociological inquiry, such as stigma, deviant
> behavior, formal organization, socialization, status congruity, authority and power,
> reward systems, or social mobility. (Glaser and Strauss 1967: 32)

While substantive and formal theories differ in their level of generality, this is
only a matter of degree. Glaser and Strauss use the example of the concept of
'nonscheduled status passage', which was generated from the substantive area of
dying. Comparative analysis at this level can be made across different hospitals,
or with other examples of status passage such as marriage, which may help to
illuminate the dying process.

These theories have two elements: conceptual categories and their properties;
and hypotheses or generalized relations among the categories and their properties.
Categories and properties are concepts indicated by the data and can vary in their
level of abstraction. A category stands by itself as a conceptual component of the
theory while a property is a conceptual aspect of a category. For example, the category of social loss, which is related to the care of dying patients, was generated by
observing differences in the way in which patients of different socio-economic and
ethnic backgrounds were cared for. The greater the loss of the person to society,
the better the care, and *vice versa*. Nurses were found to develop 'loss rationales'
to explain the death of a patient whom they saw as a high social loss, and to help
them to maintain 'professional composure' (another category) when facing the
person's death. A 'loss rationale' is a property of the category of 'social loss'.

While it is possible to borrow categories from existing theory, provided it can
be demonstrated that they fit the data, Glaser and Strauss preferred that new categories be developed. They were aware that borrowed categories can be used to
select data that fits the category rather than using data to produce the category.
They argued that there are many areas of everyday life for which there are no
appropriate categories, and even if borrowed categories are used, their meanings
are likely to undergo radical transformation.

As the research proceeds, and categories and properties begin to emerge, possible links between them are likely to suggest themselves. This involves a process
of observation and reflection, of trial and error, of on-going comparative analysis.
As the process continues, emerging hypotheses may be integrated into a more
formal theory, with hypotheses at different levels of generality. The form of the
theory is not important; it may be either a set of propositions or a discursive
argument.

Glaser and Strauss illustrated these various features of a theory with reference
to the concept of 'social loss' (1967: 42).

Elements of Theory	*Types of Theory*	
	Substantive	*Formal*
Category	Social loss of dying patients	Social value of people

| Properties of Category | *Calculating* social loss on basis of *learned* and *apparent* characteristics of patient | Calculating social value of person on basis of *learned* characteristics of patient |
| Hypotheses | The higher the social loss of a dying patient, (1) the better the care, (2) the more nurses develop loss rationales to explain away the death | The higher the social value of a person the less delay s/he experiences in receiving services from experts |

The authors used the concept of 'verification' of a theory ambiguously and uncritically; it is not clear whether they are referring to the inductive process of adding support, or the deductive process of testing. In practice, however, they considered the process of generation to also be a process of testing, and that no 'ultimate' critical testing is required. Grounded theories, they argued, are not easily refuted because they are intimately linked to data, but they are likely to be modified and reformulated as the research process continues. The publication of a report on the research is only a pause in the never ending process of theory generation.

The question of how a researcher selects appropriate comparative groups is determined by *theoretical sampling*, a process of data collection that is controlled by emerging theory. It is their relevance to theory generation, not verification, that is important. Initially, the process of data collection and analysis is guided by the research topic or problem (and, more importantly, research questions). However, as the research proceeds, the emerging categories and theory will direct the data collection. The simplest comparisons are made between different groups of the same substantive type (e.g. public libraries in a particular city). The theory generated will apply to these situations. Somewhat more general substantive theory is achieved by comparing different types of groups (e.g. public and university libraries). The scope of the theory can be further increased by comparing different types of groups within various larger groups (e.g. public libraries in a number of major cities within a country). Generality is further increased by making comparisons between countries (e.g. public libraries in major cities in different countries). The question of how many groups should be studied at each stage is not something that can be determined before the study begins as it is heavily influenced by the kinds of categories and hypotheses that emerge. 'The criterion for judging when to stop sampling the different groups pertinent to a category is the category's *theoretical saturation*. *Saturation* means that no additional data are being found whereby the sociologist can develop properties of the category' (Glaser and Strauss 1967: 61).

In summary then, research conducted from a grounded theory point of view is not a pre-planned linear process of testing hypotheses, but rather an evolving process in which what has been 'discovered' at any point will determine what happens next. An understanding of any phenomenon is seen as a developing process involving the collection of a variety of data, by a variety of methods, from a variety of situations. As concepts and insights emerge they will be explored and 'tested' by adding comparative groups to the study until such time as an adequate account or explanation of the problem at hand has been achieved.

Grounded theory, as presented by its founders, has had its critics. I begin with some of my own. First, it has strong empiricist tendencies. 'Facts' and 'data' are treated as being unproblematic; they are simply there to be observed and collected. There is a failure to recognize that observation is always theoretically saturated. Second, the role of the observer is also regarded as being unproblematic, although it is accepted that 'he [*sic*] must have a perspective that will help him see relevant data and abstract significant categories from his scrutiny of the data' (1967:3n). Third, no consideration is given to the problem of meaning or to social actors' constructions of reality. In striving to discover useful concepts, the authors have suggested beginning with 'local' concepts, but these simply designate 'a few principal or gross features of the structure and processes in the situation' (1967: 45). For example, in studying a hospital, concepts like 'doctors', 'nurses', 'wards' and 'admission procedures' might be useful starting points. There is no suggestion that the concepts used by the social actors in the situation, or the meanings they give to them, might serve this purpose, although it is accepted that the meaning of key words constantly used by people might be 'tracked down' in the course of the research (1967: 166). Fourth, the logic of generating theories is claimed to be inductive, but it is much more than generalizing from data. The process appears to have a closer affinity to abductive logic, but without the strong reliance on the social actors' point of view. Fifth, it is accepted that grounded theory will 'combine mostly concepts and hypotheses that have emerged from the data with some existing ones that are clearly useful' (1967: 46). However, Layder has argued that the rejection of general social theory, and the need to generate new theory in every research context, is both a waste of good theoretical ideas and also leads to very fragmented overall theory development (1998: 19, 37, 47).

The original version of grounded theory has since been elaborated by both authors independently (e.g. Strauss 1987; Glaser 1978, 1992, 2001) and in a series of editions by Strauss and Corbin (1990, 1998; Corbin and Strauss 2008). However, the deficiencies just reviewed remain in these later versions. A growing number of sympathetic critics have argued for a social constructionist foundation and the adoption of a more pragmatic approach (see, for example, Seale 1999; Charmaz and Mitchell 2001; Clarke 2005; Charmaz 2005, 2006).

Layder: the adaptive alternative

A more recent and practical proposal for linking theory and research has been proposed by Layder (1998). It steers a course between middle range and grounded theory, between pre-existing theory and theory generated from data analysis. At the outset, Layder rejected all anti-theoretical and atheoretical approaches in social science. The anti-theoretical arguments have come from strands of postmodernism, feminism and relativism as well as from the anti-formalism of grounded theory and some research with a social problem or policy-oriented focus.

Layder, like me, is committed to the accumulation of sociological knowledge. While rejecting the ideas that there are pure facts from which objective truths can be derived, and that it is possible to produce one universal, objective truth about any social phenomena, he regarded the purpose of social enquiry to be the production of ever more accurate knowledge and ever more powerful explanations of social phenomena.

> [A]daptive theory proposes that greater adequacy and validity should be understood as the best approximation to truth given the present state of knowledge and understanding. It is not a once-and-for-all notion, and in this respect, adaptive theory, fully formed, simply represents the 'latest stage' in the elaboration of theory. It is always, potentially at least, revisable in terms of future research and theoretical developments. (Layder 1998: 9)

Layder has argued that, as it is not possible to engage in research in a theory-neutral manner, it is necessary to acknowledge the use of, to make explicit and to control the inputs from, pre-existing concepts and theory in the research process. In this way, these prior concepts and theory shape the data that are collected, and the theory that emerges from the data can be used to modify the prior theory.

Layder was critical of both sides of many of the key methodological polarities. First, he rejected both naive positivism, with its emphasis on objective knowledge, and naive interpretivism, in its exclusive concern with subjective knowledge. He argued for an understanding of social life based on both objective and subjective components.

Second, this latter polarity is also expressed in a number of other ways, such as between system and life-world, between structure and agency or between social context and social activity. Whereas some traditions in social science concentrate exclusively on only one of these alternatives, Layder, along with others, has argued that as both are intertwined in social life they must be recognized as being independent elements and be given equal weight in social analysis.

Third, the activities of theory-testing and theory-generation, which are commonly viewed as being opposed research activities, should be combined in an on-going manner. Layder's proposal for this is perhaps less formal than Wallace's and is much broader than theory-generation in grounded theory. He has modified both middle-range and grounded theory, to overcome their limitations and to capitalize on their strengths, and has then used them in an integrated manner.

Fourth, Layder rejected the traditional view that theorizing occurs at discrete stages in the research process, say at the beginning as in middle-rage theory, or as an outcome as in grounded theory. He has argued that theorizing is a continuous aspect of social research and can occur at any stage in the process.

Fifth, he rejected the opposition between general theory and substantive theory, between theoretician's theory and researcher's theory. Whereas Merton and Mills rejected grand theory, and, more recently, postmodernists have rejected grand or meta-narratives as being irrelevant distortions of social reality, Layder wants to reserve a place for any form of theorizing as possible sources of input into the research process. He has included in this not only the work of classical theorists, such as Marx, Durkheim, Weber and Simmel, who concerned themselves with empirical enquiry as well as conceptual and theoretical frameworks, but also more abstract theorists, such as Parsons, Habermas, Foucault and Giddens. However, he argued that general theories should be open to revision and reformulation in the light of the results of empirical research. This has certainly not been the case for the latter category of theories, perhaps because they tend to present ontologies of the social world rather then explanatory accounts. It is probably easier to modify explanations, such as Durkheim's (1951) theory of egoistic suicide, than it is to alter an elaborate ontological scheme.

Adaptive theory requires a very flexible approach to the research process both in terms of the order in which activities are carried out and also in their role in the process of theorizing. '[T]he notion of theorizing itself has to be understood as an integral part of the overall research process as well as organically connected to the wider literature and findings of previous research and scholarship' (Layder 1998: 49). While research conducted in this way has to be systematic and disciplined, it also has to use a wide range of resources and be tolerant of a diversity of standpoints.

Layder has set out some practical ideas on how to move from existing concepts and theory to data and how to analyse data with theory in mind. He sees adaptive theory as using both *general* and *substantive* theory as well as *existing* and *emergent* research data. We have already encountered *general* and *substantive* theory. *Existing* data include previous research findings as well as documents, both visual and linguistic. Literature from disciplinary and popular sources, films and theatre, photographs, advertisements and sporting events, all qualify. In short, 'any aspect of social life that is capable of representation in a form which allows it to be offered or referred to as evidence of social trends, customs, habits, types of work or recreation, and so forth' (Layder 1998: 165). *Emergent* research data refers to the immediate findings from a current research project. It can suggest new concepts and theoretical ideas. This is not to suggest that data are somehow pure sources. 'All data is already theoretically saturated either through "contamination" by prior theorizing or through the preconceptions and commonsense presuppositions imported by the researcher (or generations of researchers)' (Layder 1998: 166).

While this view of the constructed nature of data flies in the face of traditional approaches to social research, it is now recognized in more recent traditions. In defending this position, Layder also gets to the heart of his view of the connection between theory and research, which rejects traditional views that consider concepts and theoretical propositions as directly representing reality.

> Thus, to speak of the manner in which adaptive theory attempts to capture or fashion an 'organic' connection between theorizing and data collection and analysis is not to imply an essentialist link. Although adaptive theory allows for and indeed encourages a dialectical relation between the formulation of theoretical concepts, clusters and models and their reformulation or revisability in the light of emergent data collection and analysis, there is no implication that this presupposes some kind of pre-theoretical (or epistemologically neutral) basis which is reflected in the term 'organic'. In this sense 'organicism' simply refers to the uncovering of research data and the simultaneous unfolding of conceptualization and theoretical reflection.
> (Layder 1998: 166)

Reminiscent of Giddens (1976), Layder proposes a new set of rules of method. These include an elaboration of his ontological and epistemological assumptions.

In summary, then,

> adaptive theory focuses on the construction of novel theory in the context of ongoing research by utilizing elements of prior theory (both general and substantive) in conjunction with theory that emerges from data collection and analysis. . . . The adaptive theory that results from such an interchange and dialogue always represents an attempt to depict the linkages between lifeworld and system elements of society. . . . Adaptive theory is accretive, it is an organic entity that constantly reformulates itself both in relation to the dictates of theoretical reasoning and the 'factual' character of the empirical world. Prior theoretical concepts and models suggest patterns and 'order' in emerging data while being continuously responsive to the 'order' suggested or unearthed by the data themselves. (Layder 1998: 27)

The Role of Hypotheses

It should be clear by now that hypotheses play a specific but limited role in social research. They are only relevant when 'why' questions are being investigated, and, then, mainly when the Deductive research strategy is being used to answer them. Hypotheses are not appropriate in the Inductive strategy and have a very particular role in the Abductive strategy. In the Retroductive strategy, it is models of structures and/or mechanisms that are hypothesized rather than statements of relationships between concepts. If quantitative methods are being used, a hypothesis will be tested by operationalizing the concepts in the hypothesis, collecting the appropriate data, and then exploring the nature of the relationship between the measures of the concept by some form of statistical analysis, such as correlation or regression.

It is extremely important to distinguish between the theoretical and statistical uses of hypotheses. Theoretical hypotheses are tentative answers to 'why' research questions, regardless of where they come from. Statistical hypotheses are used to establish whether a relationship between two variables that have been measured in a probability sample could be expected to exist in the population from which the sample was drawn. This latter use is narrowly technical and is irrelevant when non-probability samples or populations are used. Decisions about whether data confirm or refute a theoretical hypothesis cannot be settled by the use of tests of statistical significance. Hence, consideration of null and alternative hypotheses is only relevant to statistical hypotheses, not theoretical hypotheses (see Blaikie 2003 for a more comprehensive discussion of these issues).[6]

If qualitative methods are being used in the Deductive research strategy – and there is no reason why they should not be – the testing process will be less formal and is likely to rely more on arguments from evidence and the manipulation of concepts and categories in textual data.

Hypotheses also have a role in the Abductive research strategy, and in grounded theory. However, their use here is less formal and is an integral part of the process of generating theory from data. Questions will arise from the analysis of some of the data, and hypotheses may be used to explore these questions, within the same body of data, or to stimulate further data collection. This will not involve either the measurement of concepts or the statistical testing of relationships.

To reiterate a point made in chapter 3, 'what' questions do not require hypotheses to guide the data collection, and they may also be unnecessary for 'how' questions. 'What' questions need concepts, and descriptions can be produced using these concepts, with either quantitative or qualitative data, without the need to guess at what the outcome might be. Such guessing of answers to 'what' questions adds nothing to the quality or sophistication of the research.

The Role of Models

Like *theory*, the concept of *model* has a variety of meanings and uses in the context of creating new knowledge and understanding social life. Calling something a model seems to be regarded as adding sophistication or legitimacy to one's research. A discussion of the role of *models* and *theory* in research is complicated by the fact that the concepts are sometimes used interchangeably. Some writers even combine them to produce 'theoretical models'.

In this section of the chapter, I will review the major types of models used in the social sciences. However, before doing this, it is necessary to set aside two everyday uses of *model* that are not relevant to our discussion: three-dimensional representations of objects, and ideals of some kind. Examples of representations include model aeroplanes, or an architect's model of a proposed building. The first is a model *of* an actual aeroplane, while the second is a model *for* a new building. Such models are not relevant to social research.

The other everyday use of model, again not relevant to research, is in the normative or ideal sense, for example, a model parent or a model organization. These models may never exist in reality but are presented as ideals for which to strive. However, they could be studied as a research topic.

Types of Models

Models are used in social research in a variety of ways. They provide a conceptual or theoretical framework, they can represent a hypothetical explanatory structure or mechanism, perhaps derived by the use of analogies, or they can be a method of organizing and communicating research results

Types of Models

Abstract descriptions
Synonym for theory
Conceptual models
Theoretical models
Analogues of mechanisms
Diagrammatic representations
Mathematical representations

Abstract descriptions

The most elementary but not trivial use of models in social research is as abstract descriptions. While not usually thought of as models, abstract descriptions can be regarded as models *of* some aspects of social reality. Casual or systematic observation and data may inform them.

Two examples of models as abstract descriptions can be found in the work of Schütz and Harré. Schütz elaborated the way models are used in the Abductive research strategy and Harré on how they are used in the *constructionist* version of the Retroductive strategy. Schütz's project (1963a, 1963b), like that of Weber and Dilthey before him, was to find a way 'to form objective concepts and objectively verifiable theory of subjective meaning structures' (Schütz 1963a: 246). He attempted to do this by establishing a bridge between the meanings social actors use in everyday activities and the meaning the social scientist must attribute to these activities in order to produce an adequate theory. He argued that social life is possible to the extent that social actors use typifications. Typifications are everyday categorizations of typical persons, social actions and social situations. They are socially constructed and transmitted, and they are refined and changed by processes of trial and error in everyday activities. Typifications that social actors use are related to their biographically and situationally determined system of interests and circumstances (Schütz 1963a: 243). According to Schütz, the intersubjective meanings that social actors use – motives, goals, choices and plans – can only be experienced in their typicality (1963a: 244). It is these typical meanings that the social scientist must discover, describe and use as ingredients in sociological ideal types.

Schütz distinguished between everyday typifications and sociological typifications, or ideal types. The critical difference between them is that they are constructed with different purposes in mind. Everyday typifications are part of the social stock of knowledge which, while often taken for granted, makes social life possible. Sociological typifications are constructed by social scientists to supersede everyday typifications and to understand some aspects of social life (Schütz 1963a: 246).

Schütz argued that all knowledge of the social world is indirect; people cannot be understood theoretically in their uniqueness but only as impersonal ideal types existing in impersonal and anonymous time. He regarded sociological typifications as *models* of typical social actors, typical social actions and typical social situations, not as descriptions of actual human beings, actions and situations. The elements of Schütz's models of the social world can be manipulated and the logical outcomes compared. They are the building blocks of theory and the source of testable hypotheses.

In their version of social psychology, Harré and Secord (1972) focused on 'episodes' involving one or more people. Episodes involve a beginning and an end as well as some internal structure or unity. 'Everything of interest that occurs in human life happens in the course of, or as the culmination of, or as the initiation of an episode' (Harré and Secord 1972: 153). In order to grasp such an episode it is necessary to construct a *model* of it, a critical or abstract description of its structure and its principle of unity, of the pattern of relationships and social processes. This type of model has been referred to as a *homeomorph* (Harré and Secord 1972; Harré 1977). However, the explanation of the episode requires the use of a different kind of model, a *paramorph*, which identifies the mechanism(s) that produced it. This second kind of model is based on the use of analogies and will be discussed shortly.

Synonym for theory

The concept of *model* has been used by some writers as a synonym for 'theory', or, more particularly, for a particular view of theory. For example, Lave and March (1975) regarded *model* as being not only interchangeable with 'theory' but also 'paradigm', 'hypothesis' and even 'ideas'. Another example can be found in Inkeles's (1964) discussion of evolutionary, structural-functional and conflict theories as models of society. The sociologist 'carries in his [*sic*] head [models that] greatly influence what he looks for, what he sees, and what he does with his observations by way of fitting them, along with other facts, into a larger scheme of explanation' (Inkeles 1964: 28).

We should note, however, that Inkeles went on to suggest that a *model* is a general theory with a strong ontological component, while a 'theory' is an answer to a specific research question.

> It is not always possible to distinguish precisely between a scientific model and a scientific theory, and the terms are sometimes used interchangeably. A model may generate a host of theories but one theory may be so powerful as to become, in effect, a general model. . . . [W]e use model to refer to a rather general image of the main outline of some major phenomenon, including certain leading ideas about the nature of the units involved and the pattern of their relations. A theory we take to be a heuristic device for organising what we know, or think we know, at a particular time about some more or less explicitly posed question or issue. A theory would, therefore, be more limited and precise than a model. A theory can ordinarily be proved wrong. In the case of a model, it can usually only be judged incomplete, misleading, or unproductive. (Inkeles 1964: 28)

I suggest that to use *model* and 'theory' synonymously is to add confusion to concepts that already have a variety of other uses. This practice is to be avoided.

Conceptual models

Model is also associated with the idea of a conceptual scheme. This usage is closely related to both 'theoretical perspectives' and the *ontological* conceptual tradition discussed earlier in this chapter. A *conceptual model* attempts to represent the social world in terms of an array of related concepts, or a conceptual scheme (see e.g. Krausz and Miller 1974: 5). Further examples of conceptual schemes will be discussed in the section 'Diagrammatic representations' later in this chapter.

A *conceptual model* may be an important component of a theoretical perspective. However, theoretical perspectives tend to use different sets of concepts. If the same concepts *are* used, they will usually be given different meanings. For example, structural-functionalism uses concepts such as norms, values, roles, socialization, social control, equilibrium, adaptation and system, while the conflict perspective uses concepts such as economic base, superstructure, alienation, contradiction, interests, class, power and structure. These two theoretical perspectives share some concepts, such as institution, and may use them in a similar way, but, overall, the concepts in each perspective entail very different assumptions about and ways of viewing the social world. The former is based on the idea that consensus on norms and values is the basis of social order, and the latter that conflict and power are characteristic of all social relationships, including those between social classes. 'Role' is a good example of a concept that is used very differently in two perspectives such as structural-functionalism and symbolic interactionism. In the former, roles are occupied by social actors whose behaviour is determined by the associated norms. In the latter, roles are negotiated and renegotiated as social interaction proceeds; they are not predetermined.

Theoretical models

Another common use of *model* is to combine the word with 'theory' to form 'theoretical model'. This is frequently done in a very imprecise manner. However, Willer (1967) has attempted to use the combined concept precisely in an elaboration of the relationship between theory and research. He saw this relationship as a hierarchy of levels with 'general model' at the top. My concept of Research Paradigm comes close to what he had in mind, a source of broad theoretical ideas and assumptions. The second level down consists of a 'theoretical model', which contains concepts and explanatory ideas related to a particular phenomenon. It is the source of specific hypotheses that can be tested in the course of research. 'General models' may be a source of 'theoretical models', but not the only one. They provide 'theoretical models' with the background that is essential in theory construction and testing. Below this is a 'formal system', which consists of set of statements that represent the key relationships within a phenomenon; it is a compact, systematized and internally consistent set of statements of relationships that identify the core ingredients of a 'theoretical model'. The logic of moving from 'general model' to 'theoretical model' to 'formal system' is deductive. Then, when the nominally defined concepts and the statements of the relationships of the 'formal system' are translated into measurable relationships between concepts it becomes the 'operational system'. (See the earlier discussion on the *operationalizing* tradition.) If the 'operational system' survives the testing, the 'formal system' can be called a 'theory'.[7]

Analogues of mechanisms

In both the natural and social sciences, many theories have been developed by drawing on ideas from another field of science. An example from the natural sciences occurred when physicists tried to understand the structure of the atom. They developed the idea of electrons and neutrons by drawing from astronomy the idea of the orbits of the planets around the sun. In sociology, Spencer's (1891) evolutionary theory of social change viewed society as being like an evolving organism. He argued that evolutionary growth is accompanied by changes in society's structure and functions, that an increase in size produces an increase in differentiation and structural complexity. His theory has employed what is commonly called the 'organismic analogy'; an idea that can be traced back to ancient and medieval writings. Hence, as the discipline of sociology developed to provide a 'scientific' understanding of human societies, it drew on familiar and well established ideas from the discipline of biology. A theory in biology was used as a model for a theory of society.

Many other examples can be found of the use of a theory from a better-developed field as a model for a theory in a field where knowledge is still limited. The process is one of taking the concepts, and the established relationships between them, from the better-developed field and translating them into concepts and statements of relationships in the new field. For the model to be most useful, a one-to-one correspondence has to be established between the concepts and statements of relationship in both fields. If this is achieved, then hypotheses can be developed and tested in the new field. For example, in order to understand how rumours spread, it is possible to use as a model a theory about the spread of diseases. If the resulting hypotheses are corroborated, theories in the two fields will have the same form.

Some writers (e.g. Black 1962; Brodbeck 1968) have argued that analogies are the only genuine kinds of models in science. They considered all other uses of 'model' are unnecessary because there are perfectly good alternative concepts available; other uses simply create ambiguity and confusion.

Diagrammatic representations

Models of this type are designed to indicate patterns of relations, time sequences, or causal connections between aspects of social life. Concepts are arranged in a visual space to reflect their ordering in the social world, and symbols, such as lines and arrows, are used to represent the form and direction of the relationships. These models include arrangements of abstract concepts about generic aspects of the social world, and more specific summaries of relations among a number of variables. The former have been described as *abstract-analytical* models and the latter as *empirical-causal* models (Turner 1987: 164–5; 1991: 17).

Mathematical representations

While this is not the place for a detailed discussion of the role of mathematics in the social sciences, a few comments are in order. The use of mathematics is essential in physics, and to a certain extent in biology, but social scientists are very divided about the extent and manner in which it should be used in the social sciences. Of course, the application of mathematics to the social sciences is not completely new: economics is very dependent on the use of mathematical modelling, and psychologists have applied mathematics to certain aspects of their work, particularly in psychometrics. It is in the areas of social psychology, sociology and political science that the use of mathematics is a more recent and controversial development.

At a very basic level, however, whenever we count some aspect of the social world, and then apply some form of statistical analysis to the data, we are assuming that regularities in the social world conform to the rules of arithmetic. However, this kind of mathematical modelling is largely taken for granted.

It is other activities to which the label of *mathematical modelling* is usually applied, such as:

- formalizing theories by providing a language that clarifies assumptions and consequences embedded in the use of ordinary language;
- organizing, sifting through and finding systematic patterns in data;
- providing substitutes for theories from which consequences can be drawn and tested; and
- playing 'what if' games with sociological ideas (Lazarsfeld and Henry 1966; Leik and Meeker 1975).

The first of these activities is concerned with developing a precise language for social theory. However, this has not been the major use of mathematics in sociology (Sorensen 1978). The second use is the more common. It includes descriptive, correlational and inferential statistics at one extreme, and, at the other extreme, attempts to achieve causal explanations. The latter includes the use of regression and other forms of structural equation modelling (e.g. path analysis). In this activity, the aim is either to find a line or curve that represents a relationship in data, or to establish the extent to which a network of relationships conforms to a perfect model of them. The third and fourth uses involve constructing a theory in the form of a set of mathematical (algebraic) equations, exploring its implications by substituting parameters (possible values for the variables), and seeing what the model would predict. (See Coser 1975 for a critique of mathematical sociology, and Featherman 1976 and Treiman 1976 for defences.)

It is hard to find an article in any issue of *The American Sociological Review* over recent years that does not use some form of structural equation modelling, particularly regression. Generally, the aim is to find a set of independent variables that can best predict variations in a dependent variable. In regression analysis, independent variables are progressively added or manipulated in various combinations, each combination being described as a model. The other dominant form of modelling involves the use of mathematical equations of various kinds, including log linear and logit variations, to express a complex theoretical statement (such as that involved in rational choice theory) or the relations among dependent and independent variables.

Whether or not consideration needs to be given to mathematical modelling in a research design will depend on a number of other choices. These choices are likely to be influenced by the various audiences that a researcher needs or wishes to take into account as well as the paradigms that are regarded as being appropriate in one's discipline or research community. In some kinds of research, the development of a mathematical model may only be relevant after the data have been collected. In other kinds of research, such as most qualitative studies, mathematical models will be completely irrelevant.

Theories, Models and Research Strategies

To summarize the discussion in this chapter, I shall review the role of theory and models in each of the research strategies. Two issues will be discussed. The first is the contrast between theory development and theory testing; whether research sets out with a well-developed theory or whether theory is the end product of

Table 5.1 Research strategies, theory and models

Research strategy		Nature of theory	Use of models
Inductive	Form:	Generalizations	Abstract descriptions
		Networks of propositions	Mathematical representations
	Process:	Generated by induction from data	Conceptual frameworks
Deductive	Form:	Deductive argument produces hypotheses	Theoretical models
	Process:	Hypotheses tested by matching against data	Diagrammatic representation Mathematical representation
Retroductive	Form:	Generative structures and/or mechanisms	Abstract descriptions
	Process:	Modelling of hypothetical mechanisms	May involve use of analogies
Abductive	Form:	Social scientific accounts	Abstract descriptions
	Process:	Generated from everyday accounts	(ideal types)

research. The second is concerned with the way explanation or understanding is achieved. The four research strategies present us with contrasting positions on these issues (see table 5.1).

Inductive and Deductive Strategies

The relationship between theory and research is viewed differently in the Inductive and Deductive research strategies. Insofar as explanation is considered to be possible at all in the Inductive research strategy, theory consists of generalizations derived by induction from data. Hence, research starts with the collection of data, and, hopefully, ends up with abstract descriptions of patterns in the data. If strong support is achieved for a generalization from many studies, its status is enhanced. A specific instance of a particular phenomenon can be explained by regarding it as an instance of such a regularity, i.e. it is seen to fit the pattern. Hence the idea of *pattern* explanations. In short, research within the Inductive strategy involves collecting data by operationalizing concepts, and then searching for patterns in the data. Patterns become generalizations, and networks of generalizations is considered to be a theory. Theory development consists of accumulating generalizations and producing further support for them.

The use of models in the Inductive research strategy is confined to abstract descriptions and mathematical representations. The former consists of relatively low-level generalizations and possible networks of such generalizations, while the latter involves the mathematical modelling of data. This modelling can range from basic statistical summaries, such as measures of central tendency, dispersion and association, to more complex mathematical simplifications of patterns of relationships.

As we have seen, the logic of the Deductive research strategy is the reverse of the Inductive strategy. Rather than theory being the outcome of research, it has to be produced, borrowed or invented at the outset. Theory takes the form of a deductive argument. Depending on the purpose at hand, the conclusion to the argument can be a hypothesis, a prediction, or the regularity that is to be explained. Hence, this strategy requires a great deal of theoretical work before data are collected.

A Deductive theory can come from many sources, or a combination of them. An existing *researchers'* theory could be used in its original or a modified from. Alternatively, theory might be constructed using elements from *theoreticians'* theory and/or the findings of previous research. The latter clearly requires a great deal of knowledge of the field, as well as creativity. However, according to Popper, it matters not from whence a theory comes; it is the logic of its construction and the rigour of its testing that are important.

The Deductive strategy lends itself to the use of various types of models. It is possible to regard a deductive argument as a 'theoretical model' and to set it in the context of a 'general model', a 'formal system' and an 'operational system' (Willer 1967). Alternatively, it is possible to represent the relationships between the concepts contained in the propositions of the argument in diagrammatic and/or mathematical forms. This is now common practice among quantitative researchers.

Retroductive and Abductive Strategies

The Retroductive and Abductive research strategies do not lend themselves to conceptual or logical ways of linking theory and research. In the Retroductive strategy, a theory or explanation is achieved by establishing the existence of the hypothesized structure or mechanism that is responsible for producing an observed regularity. Alternatively, and probably more commonly in the social sciences, the task is one of establishing which one of a number of possible known structures or mechanisms is responsible, and the conditions under which it operates. Whether it is a structure or a mechanism on which the researcher focuses will depend on whether the *structuralist* or the *constructionist* version is used. However, as we have seen, Pawson and Tilley (1997) and Layder (1998) have argued that it is possible, perhaps necessary, to incorporate both structures (context) and mechanisms in our explanations.

Models play a vital role in the Retroductive strategy. They are used to provide abstract descriptions of the regularities or episodes under consideration (*homeomorphs*), and they are then used to construct 'images' of mechanisms (*paramorphs*). It is in this latter use that analogies may be employed as a stimulus to the creative process involved in discovering unknown mechanisms. In the end, the connection between a hypothetical model, and the process of establishing its existence, is more a matter of arguing from evidence than of engaging in the statistical testing of hypotheses (as in the Deductive strategy).

To demonstrate the existence of a particular structure may involve documenting many possible consequences of its existence, and then arguing for the plausibility of the connection between the evidence and the theory. For example, to establish the existence of a particular type of class structure as an explanation for patterns of alienated behaviour at work will require an argument of the kind that connects evidence other than the work behaviour in question to both that behaviour and a possible class structure. Such arguments will obviously be a matter of persuasion based on evidence.

The relationship between theory and research in the Abductive research strategy is very different from that in the other three strategies. In this case, the two are intimately intertwined; data and theoretical ideas are played off against one another in a developmental and creative process. Regularities that are discovered at the beginning or in the course of the research will stimulate the researcher to ask questions and look for answers. The data will then be reinterpreted in the light of emerging theoretical ideas, and this may lead to further questioning, the entertainment of tentative hypotheses, and a search for answers. *Research becomes a dialogue between data and theory mediated by the researcher.* Data are interpreted and reinterpreted in the light of an emerging theory, and, as a result, change in the process. The emerging theory is tested and refined as the research proceeds. While this dialogue could continue forever, a satisfactory explanation will have been produced when theoretical saturation is achieved and satisfying answers to the research questions have been arrived at.

The process used to generate theory in the Abductive research strategy is sometimes described as inductive. However, this is misleading for a number of reasons. Abduction is a process by means of which the researcher assembles lay accounts of the phenomenon in question, with all their gaps and deficiencies, and, in an iterative manner, begins to construct her or his own account. The central characteristic of this process is that it is iterative; it involves the researcher in alternating periods of immersion in the relevant social world, and periods of withdrawal for reflection and analysis. This alternating process means that theory is generated as an intimate part of the research process; it is not invented at the beginning nor is it just produced at the end. The form of this theory can vary, depending on the particular branch of Interpretivism within which the researcher is working. Following Weber, Schütz and Becker, my preference is for the construction of ideal types as the abstract second-order descriptions, i.e. models. The rich detail in ideal types can then be used to produce theoretical propositions, which, in turn, may be tested by the further use of the Abductive strategy, or, possibly, within the Deductive strategy. The latter case does not necessarily entail the use of quantitative methods; it is possible to test deductively derived hypotheses using any type of data.

Ideal types as models can look very much like the models of mechanisms developed in the *constructionist* version of the Retroductive research strategy. I have argued (Blaikie 1994) that Weber's ideal type of the Protestant work ethic, particularly the typical meaning given to work by the early Calvinists, is equivalent to a model of a mechanism. In this case, the mechanism explains the relationship between religion and occupation that Weber claimed existed in Germany over a hundred years ago. However, it is not clear whether Weber arrived at this ideal type cum model by abduction or retroduction. Given the historical nature of his study, his ability to use the logic of abduction, as used in the Abductive research strategy, was rather restricted. Perhaps he used a combination of both, thus reinforcing the idea of the possible close association between these two research strategies.

Further Reading

Blaikie, N. 2007. *Approaches to Social Enquiry.*

Layder, D. 1998. *Sociological Practice: Linking Theory and Social Research*
  Discusses the issues related to the relationship between theory and research and offers
  some practical procedures for achieving this.

Turner, J. H. 1991. *The Structure of Sociological Theory.*
  Presents formal views of the relationship between theory and research.

The following references, written between 1959 and 1972, deal with some classical issues
  and present various points of view.

Blumer, H. 1969. *Symbolic Interactionism.*

Glaser, B. G. and A. L. Strauss 1967. *The Discovery of Grounded Theory.*

Harré, R. and P. F. Secord 1972. *The Explanation of Social Behaviour.*

Merton, R. K. 1967. *On Theoretical Sociology.*

Mills, C. W. 1959. *The Sociological Imagination.*

Wallace, W. L. 1971. *The Logic of Science in Sociology.*

Willer, D. 1967. *Scientific Method: Theory and Method.*

6

Sources and Selection of Data

Chapter Summary

- The discussion of types and forms of data is often glossed over in designing social research.
- Data are of three types: primary, secondary and tertiary.
- These types reflect the distance researchers are from the original source of the data.
- This distance has consequences for the ability of the data to represent the social phenomenon to which they relate.
- Data can be in two main forms: words and numbers.
- At various stages in a research project, data may be transposed between these two forms, commonly from words to numbers.
- Data can come from a variety of settings:
  - natural social settings;
  - semi-natural settings;
  - artificial settings; and
  - social artefacts.
- An essential part of every research design is the choice of method of selection of data from its source.
- Data can come from populations, samples from populations and individuals.
- Populations consist of single members or units, such as, people, social actions, social situations, events, places, times or things.
- Researchers are usually free to define a population in a way considered appropriate for answering the research question(s).
- A sample is a selection of elements (members or units) from a population, and may be used to make statements about that population.
- A sample can be selected by either probability or non-probability methods.
- Probability samples give every population element a known (usually equal) and non-zero chance of being selected.
- Non-probability samples do not meet this requirement.
- While the aim in probability samples is to achieve a perfect representation of the population, this method of selection does not do this automatically; an imperfect representation is quite possible.

- However, inferential statistical procedures make it possible to estimate, with varying degrees of accuracy, the characteristics of a population, with a determined level of confidence.
- There are two major methods of selecting probability samples: simple random and systematic.
- Population elements can be organized into strata before the selection occurs, thus making it possible to have particular categories in the population represented in the sample in the same proportions.
- Either individual population elements, or clusters of elements, can be selected.
- Sampling can also occur in single or multiple stages.
- Multi-stage sampling can use different methods of selection at each stage.
- The main methods of non-probability sampling are: accidental or convenience, quota, judgemental or purposive, and snowball.
- In probability samples, particularly those involving people, it is imperative that as high a response rate as possible is achieved if accurate estimates of population characteristics are required.
- In order to estimate population characteristics, the optimum size of a probability sample is determined by:
  - degree of accuracy required in estimating population characteristics;
  - distribution in the population of key characteristics;
  - level(s) of measurement being used; and
  - extent to which sub-groups in the sample are to be analysed.
- The size of non-probability samples is influenced by the purpose of the research and the type of analysis to be undertaken.
- Case studies:
  - are another method for selecting units for study, only one or a small number, usually studied in depth in natural settings;
  - should *not* be thought of as a particular kind of research design, or as requiring the use of particular methods of data collection;
  - can be used to make wider generalizations, but with methods that are different from that used with probability samples; and
  - can play a major role in theory development.
- Choices made from among the elements of a research design discussed in this chapter have serious consequences for research outcomes, and, therefore, need to be made with the research questions in mind.
- These choices, like many others, are also influenced by pragmatic factors, such as proximity, access and cost.
- While compromises may be necessary, care must be taken not to jeopardize the possibility of answering the research questions.

Introduction

Before decisions can be made about how to collect the data required to answer research questions, consideration needs to be given to the kind of data to be collected, where they will come from, and how they will be selected. Hence, this chapter discusses:

- types of data used by social researchers, i.e. primary, secondary and tertiary;
- forms in which data are produced in the social sciences, i.e. in either words or numbers;
- sources of data in terms of the settings from which they will be obtained, i.e. natural social settings, semi-natural settings, artificial settings, and social artefacts;
- selection of data, with particular reference to sampling; and
- the role of case studies in social research.

Types of Data

Data used in social research can be of three main types: *primary*, *secondary* and *tertiary*. *Primary* data are generated by a researcher or researchers who is/are responsible for the design of the study, and the collection, analysis and reporting of the data. These are 'new' data, used to answer specific research questions. The researcher can describe why and how they were collected. *Secondary* data are raw data that have already been collected by someone else, either for some general information purpose, such as a government census or other official statistics, or for a specific research project. In both of these sources, the original purpose in collecting such data could be different from that of the secondary user, particularly in the case of a previous research project. *Tertiary* data have been analysed either by the researcher(s) who generated them or by a user of secondary data. In this case the raw data may not be available, only the results of this analysis (see figure 6.1).

While *primary* data can come from many sources, they are characterized by the fact that they are the result of direct contact between a researcher and the source. Primary data are generated by the application of particular methods, and as

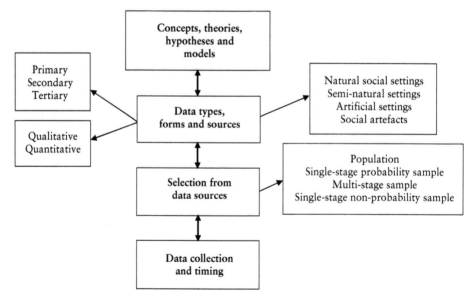

Figure 6.1 Data sources and selection

researchers have control over the production and analysis they are in a position to judge their quality. This judgement is much more difficult with secondary and tertiary types of data.

Secondary data can come from the same kind of sources as primary data; researchers are just one step removed. The use of secondary data is often referred to as secondary analysis. It is now common for data sets to be archived and made available for analysis by other researchers. Such data sets constitute the purest form of secondary data. Most substantial surveys have potential for further analysis because they can be interrogated with different research questions.

> **Types of Data**
>
> **Primary**
>   Generated by the researcher
> **Secondary**
>   Generated by another researcher
> **Tertiary**
>   Analysed by another researcher

While there are obvious advantages in using secondary data, such as savings in time and costs, there are also disadvantages. The most fundamental drawback stems from the fact that this previous research is likely to have been done with different aims and research questions. It may also have been based on assumptions, and even prejudices, which are not readily discernible, or which are inconsistent with those of the current research. Secondly, there is the possibility that not all the areas of interest to the current researcher may have been included. Thirdly, the data may be coded in an inconvenient form. Fourthly, it may be difficult to judge the quality of secondary data; a great deal has to be taken on faith. A fifth disadvantage for some research stems from the fact that the data may be old. There is always a time lag between collection and reporting of results, and even longer before researchers are prepared to archive their data set. However, this time lag may not be a problem in some research, such as historical, comparative or theoretical studies.

With *tertiary* data, the researcher is two steps removed from the original primary data. Published reports of research and officially collected 'statistics' invariably include tables of data that have summarized, categorized or otherwise manipulated raw data. Strictly speaking, most government censuses report data of these kinds, and access to the original data set may not be possible. When government agencies or other bodies do their own analysis on a census, they produce genuine tertiary data. Because control of the steps involved in moving from the original primary data to tertiary data is out of the hands of researchers, such data must be treated with caution. Some sources of tertiary data will be more reliable than others. Analysts can adopt an orientation towards the original data, and they can be selective in what is reported. In addition, there is always the possibility of academic fraud. The further a researcher is removed from the original primary data, the greater the risk of unintentional or deliberate distortion.

Forms of Data

Data are used in two main forms, as *numbers* or *words*. There seems to be a common belief among researchers, and the consumers of their products, that numerical data are needed in scientific research to ensure objective and accurate results. Somehow, data in words tend to be regarded as being not only less precise but also less reliable. These views still persist in many circles, although non-numerical data are now more widely accepted. As we shall see later in this chapter, the distinction between words and numbers, between qualitative and quantitative data, is not a simple one (see figure 6.1).

It can be argued that all primary data start out as words. Some data are recorded in words, they remain in words throughout the analysis, and the findings are reported in words. The original words will be transformed and manipulated into other words, and these processes may be repeated more than once. While the level of the language may change, say from lay language to technical language, throughout the research the medium is always words. In addition, some data may start out as images, such as photographs or video recordings. However, words must be used to describe and interpret such images before analysis can begin.

In other research, the initial communication, say on a questionnaire or between interviewer and research participant, will be transformed into numbers immediately, or prior to the analysis. The former involves the use of pre-coded response categories, and the latter the post-coding of answers provided in words, as in the case of open-ended questions. Numbers are attached to both sets of categories and the subsequent analysis will be numerical. The findings of the research will be presented in numerical summaries and tables. However, words will have to be introduced to interpret and elaborate the numerical findings. Hence, in quantitative studies, data normally begin in words, are transformed into numbers, are subjected to various kinds of statistical manipulation, and are reported in both numbers and words; from words to numbers and back to words. The interesting point here is whose words are used in the first place and what process is used to generate them? In the case where responses are made to a predetermined set of categories, the questions and the categories will be in the researcher's words; the respondent *only* has to interpret both. However, this is a big 'only'. As Foddy (1993) and Pawson (1995, 1996) have pointed out, this is a complex process that requires much more attention and understanding than it has normally been given.

Sophisticated numerical transformations can occur at the data reduction stage of analysis. For example, responses to a set of attitude statements, in categories ranging from 'strongly agree' to 'strongly disagree', can be numbered, say, from 1 to 5. Subject to some test of unidimensionality, scores from each statement can be combined to produce a total score for an attitude scale. Such scores are well removed from the respondent's original reading of the words in the statements and the recording of a response in a category with a label in words.

Forms of Data

Words
  At source
  During analysis
  For reporting
Numbers
  Soon after source
  For analysis
  For reporting

In studies that deal with large quantities of textual data, as in the case of transcribed in-depth interviews, manipulation can occur in two main ways: in the generation of categories in which segments of text are coded (as in grounded theory); or in the abstraction of technical language from lay language (as in the case of Schütz's and Giddens's versions of the Abductive research strategy). In both of these forms of analysis, it is possible to do simple counting, for example, to establish the number of times a category occurs in a body of text, or the number of respondents who can be located in each of a set of ideal types.

So far, this discussion of the use of words and numbers has been confined to the collection of primary data. However, these kinds of manipulations may have already occurred in secondary data, and will certainly have occurred in tertiary data.

The controversial issue in all of this is the effect that any form of manipulation has on the original data. To reiterate earlier arguments, we need to be clear at the outset that it is impossible to produce any data without researchers having an influence on it. If all observation is interpretation, and concepts are theoretically saturated, then manipulation is involved from the very beginning. Even if a conversation is recorded unobtrusively, any attempt to understand what went on requires interpretation and the use of concepts. How much manipulation occurs is a matter of choice. Researchers who prefer to remain qualitative through all stages of a research project may argue that it is bad enough abstracting lay language into technical language without translating either of them into the language of mathematics. A common fear about such translations is that they end up distorting the social world out of all recognition, with the result that research reports based on them become either meaningless or, possibly, dangerous if acted on. We shall encounter arguments in favour of quantification later in the chapter.

Sources of Data

Regardless of whether data are primary, secondary or tertiary, they can come from four different types of settings: *natural social settings, semi-natural settings, artificial settings* and from *social artefacts* (see figure 6.1). In research conducted in a *natural social setting*, researchers enter an area of social activity and study people going about their everyday lives. In a *semi-natural setting*, individuals are asked to report on their activities that occur in natural settings, while in an *artificial setting*, social activity is contrived for experimental or learning purposes. The fourth kind of social setting is in the past and involves the examination of records or traces left by individuals or groups. A fundamental distinction here is whether social activity is studied as it occurs *in situ*, or whether it will be artificially or historically reconstructed in some way. This fourth type of research setting introduces a time dimension, and this will be examined shortly.

Natural Social Settings

Natural social settings involve three main levels of analysis: micro-social, meso-social and macro-social.[1] These levels vary in scale from individuals and small social groups, through organizations and communities, to institutions and large-scale social situations, such as cities and regions, nations and multi-/transnational bodies. Obviously, it is very difficult to use 'naturalistic' methods in large-scale social units. In these cases, it may be possible to regard the unit of analysis as social, i.e. as involving continuing social activity, but accept that it may not be possible to study this activity directly.

Sources of Data

Natural social settings
Micro
   Individuals
   Small groups
   Social episodes
Meso
   Organizations
   Communities
   Crowds
   Social movements
Macro
   Social institutions
   Social structures
   Nations
   Multinational bodies
Quasi-experiments
Semi-natural settings
Individuals' characteristics
Individuals as informants
Representative individuals
Life histories
Individuals as case studies
Artificial settings
Experiments
   Categories of individuals
   Groups
Simulation and games
Social artefacts
Official statistics
Public documents
Private documents
Personal records

Micro-social phenomena

In its most basic form, the micro-social level is made up of individuals in their everyday social settings. However, unlike a great deal of research in psychology, this interest in the individual is as a participant in some small-scale social unit rather than as an individual *per se*. These social units include the dyad and small primary social groups.[2] Micro-social relations are normally characterized by face-to-face social interaction in which social actors give meaning to their own actions, and the actions of the others involved, and take these others into account when making decisions about their own actions. Another important feature of these small units is their continuity; they have a history and, usually, a relatively permanent membership, and they develop and reproduce patterns, structures and institutions.

The other major type of micro-social phenomenon is the social episode, those social interactions that are limited in time and space, such as social gatherings of various kinds. Most of the participants in these situations may not meet again or certainly not in the same circumstances or with the same membership. Intersubjective meanings develop and then dissipate, and the structuring of social relations is fleeting. The number of people involved in social episodes can vary considerably, from two to hundreds, thus making their inclusion under this category of social phenomenon somewhat arbitrary. However, the processes involved in understanding such phenomena are likely to be social–psychological in nature and similar to those used for small groups.

Meso-social phenomena

Meso-social phenomena include organizations, communities, crowds and social movements. As relatively permanent, large social groups with established goals, organizations can be public or private, for business or pleasure, legal or illegal. The social relationships in organizations are largely secondary in nature, with membership that may be compulsory (e.g. in a prison) or voluntary (e.g. in a sporting club), full-time or part-time, paid or unpaid, long-term or short-term. While organizations change, at times rapidly, the structure of relations and forms of authority and leadership are likely to be relatively enduring.

'Community' has been included to refer to a diverse range of social phenomena. Like 'society', this concept has many uses; for example, we refer to 'local' communities, 'the' community, 'ethnic' communities, 'regional' communities and 'the world' community, all of which are very different. The notion of community being used here refers to looser forms of social organization in which either space or common interests are the defining characteristics. These social collectivities are different from organizations, and remove us one step further from primary and even secondary relationships.

Forms of collective behaviour, such as crowds and social movements, can also be included here. A crowd consists of a reasonably large collection of people gathered together in a public place. As their reason for being together varies, different types of crowds have been identified: *casual*, *conventional*, *expressive* and *active* (Goode 1992). *Casual* crowds are loosely structured and are made up of people who just happen to be in the same place at the same time and who enter and leave at any time. A *conventional* crowd comes together for a specific purpose, for example for a lecture or a concert, and is governed by normative rules. Members of an *expressive* crowd gather for the specific purpose of belonging to the crowd itself, to cheer, clap, scream or stomp. Membership is an end in itself. An *acting* crowd engages in overt behaviour, such as a demonstration or a riot. While a crowd can be regarded as a type of group, it is frequently characterized by emergent behaviour that can spread rapidly from one person to another and from one situation to another. Even though crowds form and change suddenly and unexpectedly, their members may have a high degree of personal engagement (Marx and McAdam 1994).

'Social movements' lie somewhere between crowds and organizations or institutions. They are reasonably organized collectivities, fairly long-lasting and stable, with emerging rules and traditions, and an indefinite and shifting membership. Social movements 'attempt to further common interests through collective action outside the sphere of established institutions' (Giddens *et al.* 2003). Leadership positions are 'determined more by the informal response of the members than by formal procedures for legitimating authority' (Turner and Killian 1972: 246).

Macro-social phenomena

Macro-social phenomena are much larger social entities than those already discussed and are abstractions of some kind. Examples of such abstract phenomena are social institutions and social structures, both of which are the products of the theorizing by experts. While institutions and structures are usually discussed in the context of some society, or nation,[3] it is also possible to use them in the analysis of cross/inter/multi-national bodies, such as trans-national corporations, international non-government organizations, and the United Nations.

At the macro level, it is becoming increasingly necessary in social science to move beyond nations, or even comparisons between nations, to deal with social phenomena that span the globe. We are witnessing a developing paradox in which national and regional boundaries are becoming both less important and more important at the same time. In terms of world economics and migration, national boundaries have become less significant, but in terms of politics and social identity, national and regional boundaries are assuming greater significance.

The boundaries between micro, meso, and macro-social settings are not rigid;

the three categories are intended to indicate a range of possible research sites that vary in terms of the number of people involved, the nature of their social relationships and their relative geographical concentration or dispersion.

Quasi-experiments

The category of quasi-experiment is included under *natural social settings* to identify research in which experimental procedures are used outside the laboratory. Rather than contriving an experiment, researchers may use opportunities as they arise in natural settings. An example comes from a before-after study of a town in which a change of circumstances was introduced that was outside the researcher's control. Many years ago, I participated in a study of an isolated town on the west coast of the South Island of New Zealand. A thriving gold-mining centre in the late nineteenth century, the town was located on a narrow coastal strip between mountains and the sea. It was isolated at the end of a road. A decision was made to extend the road across a mountain pass to a popular tourist resort area, thus creating the potential for the town to be included in a tourist route. A project was designed to study the town before and some time after the road was constructed to assess the impact of tourism. While the design of this study did not satisfy experimental ideals, the natural setting and fortuitous timing made a quasi-experiment possible. Many social impact studies are of this kind.

Semi-Natural Settings

Probably the most common form of research in the social sciences involves asking individuals to report on their own and/or other people's activities, attitudes and motives, or on social processes and institutionalized practices.

Individuals' characteristics

Three main kinds of data are collected in these studies: demographic characteristics; orientations to the world; and reported behaviour. Demographic characteristics are an essential part of data collected in censuses and social surveys. These include age, gender, marital status, education, income, occupation, place of residence, ethnic background and religion. While these characteristics may have social origins and social consequences, the analysis undertaken on them searches for connections between such variables and other variables. The social processes or structures on which these connections might depend are left very much in the background, although assumptions about them may be made.

The second common focus in studies of individuals is their orientation to the world or, more narrowly, their perceptions, knowledge, attitudes, beliefs, values, etc. The aim is usually to use this information to explain reported behaviour. Not only are such data taken out of the context in which they might be relevant, but the connection between attitudes and behaviour is often extremely tenuous.

The third feature of this type of research is to ask individuals to report behaviour. This is either the individual's own behaviour (e.g. the number of times they make a call on the telephone, or the number of hours they watch television in a particular week), or the behaviour of others (e.g. the number of times particular categories of people telephoned them, or the number of hours their children watched television in a particular week).

A major difficulty in asking people about themselves is the gap between what they say they do and what they actually do. In addition, the reports individuals give about their views and behaviour are likely to be interpreted differently by the researcher if they had studied social actors in their natural settings. For example, a respondent may be asked about their occupation, which is then used by the researcher to establish a status hierarchy. In everyday life, occupation might enter into the structuring of social relationships quite differently. What goes on in the natural setting may be either ignored or distorted by the researcher.

Individuals as informants or representatives

Individuals can also be studied as special persons (e.g. in the case of political biographies), as representative of a particular type of social actor (e. g., 'indulgent parent' or 'rebellious teenager'), or as informants who report on their beliefs, values, norms, social activities and, possibly, their motives. They can also be studied as categories (e.g. youth, pensioners, members of the working class, tertiary-educated), as populations (e.g. residents eighteen years old and over living in the city of Montreal on 1 August, 2008, or all newly enrolled full-time students at the University of London in the 2008/9 academic year) or as samples from a population (either probability or non-probability).

Individuals as case studies

The study of single persons, perhaps as in-depth case studies, lies on the boundary of *social* science, particularly if the person's social context is given little or no attention. It is possible to assess an individual's perceptions of the social world and to get them to report their social experiences, i.e. their interaction with other people. However, when the emphasis is placed more on cognitive processes, as in psychoanalytic studies of political leaders, the research might be more correctly classified as psychological or behavioural rather than social.

Artificial Settings

A limited range of social research places people in experimental or simulated conditions in order to study some form of social behaviour in a controlled environment.

Experiments

For many social scientists, to be able to hold some variables constant while others are manipulated, and then to observe the outcome, is considered to be the only way to explain any social phenomenon conclusively.[4] All other research designs are regarded as deviations. However, in practice, very little social research involves the use of genuine experiments. Hence, they will be given only a brief treatment here. Rather, pseudo-experimental language is used in other types of research such that 'independent' and 'dependent' variables have become almost universally adopted in a great deal of social research.

> The purpose of the simple experiment is to test whether a treatment causes an effect. . . . To determine that a treatment causes an effect, you must create a situation where you show that (1) the treatment comes before the effect, (2) the effect occurs *after* the treatment is introduced, and (3) nothing but the treatment is responsible for the effect. . . . [T]he ideal setup for demonstrating causality would be to find two identical groups of subjects, treat them identically except that only one group gets the treatment, test them under identical conditions, and then compare the behavior of the two groups. (Mitchell and Jolley 1992: 169)

Simple experiments are particularly suitable where a single cause is assumed to produce an effect. However, it is possible to extend an experimental design to deal with different levels of treatment, and with more than one kind of treatment.

There are a number of possible threats to the validity of the relationship between treatment and effect in experiments. This is commonly referred to as *internal validity*.

1 *Selection bias*: without random assignment, there is a risk that groups will not be equivalent.
2 *History*: specific events that occur during the experiment may influence the experimental variable.
3 *Maturation*: biological, psychological or emotional changes, like growing older, or becoming hungry, tired or bored, can occur if experiments extend over long periods.
4 *Testing*: the effects of taking a test on the scores on a second test.
5 *Instrumentation*: changes in the calibration of a measuring instrument, or in the observers or scorers used.
6 *Statistical regression*: the tendency of subjects who receive extreme scores on the pre-test to receive less extreme scores on the post-test, and thus move the results towards the average.
7 *Selection*: comparing groups that are different.
8 *Mortality*: subjects dropping out of the study.
9 *Selection–maturation interaction*: groups naturally maturing at different rates. Because they scored similarly at the beginning of the study does not mean that they would have scored identically at the end of the study, had the treatment not been applied to one group.
10 *Diffusion of treatment*: subjects in different groups may communicate and learn about the other's treatment.
11 *Compensatory behaviour*: a specific example of the diffusion of treatment occurs if one group receives something of greater value than another group; if this becomes known, resentment may lead to a distortion in responses.
12 *Experimenter expectancy*: unintentional, perhaps non-verbal, communication

between the experimenter and the subjects can give clues about what the experimenter hopes to find. This can be reduced by the use of assistants, who have limited knowledge of the logic of the experiment, to do the measurements (Campbell and Stanley 1963a: 5; Neuman 2006: 260–4; Mitchell and Jolley 2007: 132, 527–9).

The effects of the experimental process on the subjects can also threaten the representativeness (*external validity*) of the results. However, the most serious threat to the possibility of generalizing results obtained in social experiments comes from the fact that people may behave differently in experimental situations than they do in natural situations.

Simulation and games

Social life has been simulated for a number of reasons, perhaps the most common being for educational purposes. Such *simulations* or *games* allow the participants to:

* experience features of social life under controlled conditions;
* experience and be involved in initiating co-operation and conflict;
* experience what it is like to be a particular type of person, for example, to be wealthy or poor, to have high status or low status; and
* learn about how power is acquired and used.

However, it is the use of simulation and games as a way of modelling some aspect of social life and as a research technique that is of interest here.

Such games require a set of rules. While some factors are held constant by the controller of the activity, the participants are able to manipulate others in the course of their activity together. The effects of changing what is controlled and what can be manipulated can be observed and analysed. Therefore, games are a form of experimentation in artificial settings. However, they differ from experiments in that they attempt to replicate some real social situation; they may be less concerned with establishing causation and more concerned with recognizing and understanding the complexities of social processes.

The use of simulation as a method for investigating social phenomena has been stimulated in recent years by the advent of small powerful computers and developments in computer science and information technology. Now people need not be involved; social processes that are not directly accessible, or are of too large a scale to be observed directly, can be modelled. The logical possibilities of a set of specifications or assumptions can be explored when the values of certain variables are changed. An early example of such a simulation was conducted by Markley (1964) in which he simulated Caplow's theory of organizational behaviour to test the claim that the system would reach a stable equilibrium. Through a series of iterations Markley discovered the reverse.

Another form of computer simulation involves a theoretically informed selection of aspects of some social phenomenon that are then manipulated by means of a selected computer language. Simulations are run and the output compared with data from such a social situation. The model of the phenomenon can be modified gradually by running a series of simulations to provide the best approximation to the data. Unlike statistical analysis, where the data are manipulated, computer simulation is a process by which a simplified and abstract representation of some part of the social world is developed to fit the data as closely as possible. A recent development in computer modelling of relevance to the social sciences is the simulation of cognitive processes and communication between people using techniques drawn from artificial intelligence. (See also Gullahorn and Gullahorn 1963; Inbar and Stoll 1972; Hanneman 1988; Ragin and Becker 1989; Brent and Anderson 1990; Garson 1990; Anderson 1992; Gilbert and Doran 1993; Lee 1995; Gilbert 1995.)

Social Artefacts

The fourth main source of data, *social artefacts*, involves neither natural nor artificial situations. Rather, it involves the traces of social activities left behind by participants. Records of past social activities can be found in various places. Some are kept officially – such as censuses, publicly available minutes of meetings, or biographies and autobiographies – while others have been kept for private purposes – such as internal reports and correspondence of a company or organization, and diaries, private letters or family photographs and genealogies. Unlike public records, these latter records are defined as 'private' because there is no legal obligation to provide open access to them. In addition, some individuals keep personal records, such as diaries or journals, which, during their lifetime, are intended for no one else's eyes but the author's. It is usually only after their death, or by special permission, that access to them can be gained. While social artefacts are the sources on which historians have to rely, they can also be invaluable, and, in some cases, the only data available to other social scientists.

A Dilemma

A major dilemma that researchers face in studying any social phenomenon is the assumptions that are made about its ontological status. As we have seen, there is essentially a choice here. One is for the researcher to define the phenomenon in terms of the technical concepts and ideas of some theoretical perspective within a discipline. The other is to adopt the social actors' construction of reality, at least as the starting-point in the investigation. For example, what constitutes a social episode or a social group is not simply a matter of observation; it is either a product of the way social actors consider their social world to be organized, or it is the result of a social scientist's way of organizing the social world; it is either a *social* construction or a *sociological* construction. In both cases, information may be sought from the social actors; the difference is how that information is regarded.

More abstract social entities, such as social institutions and social structures, are usually *sociological* constructions, the inventions of social scientists. Nevertheless, as with social groups and social processes, data can be obtained both from researchers' observations and experience, as well as from social participants' knowledge, perceptions and experiences. However, there is no guarantee that social actors will see their world in the same way as social scientists. In fact, their views are invariably different because they are coming from different directions and have different intentions. For example, social scientists have conceptualized structures of inequality in various ways, such as three social classes (upper, middle and lower) or as a hierarchy of occupations, but the social actors concerned may not share these conceptions. They may have a very different way of 'structuring' their world (e.g. in terms of 'insiders' and 'outsiders', or as a set of concentric circles around their own position in society). Differences between *social* constructions and *sociological* constructions pose a fundamental methodological problem for researchers. In short, the issue is whose construction of reality should provide the foundation for understanding social life. It is on this issue that the four research strategies adopt different positions.

Selection of Data

All social research involves decisions about how to select data from whatever the source or sources may be. This is true regardless of the purposes of the research, the research setting, the time dimension, the type of social phenomenon being studied, the type of data, the form of the data, and the methods of data collection, reduction and analysis. When data are obtained separately from a number of individuals, social units or social artefacts, the researcher has a choice of either taking a whole population, or selecting a sample from a population. However, whether a population or a sample is used, a selection must be made, and when sampling *is* used, other forms of selection will precede it, such as the research site and the population. When a decision has been made to include sampling in the selection process, a choice must be made from a variety of sampling methods.[5]

Sampling is a common but not universal feature of social research. When it is used, it is frequently the weakest and least understood part of research designs. The type of sample selected, and the method used to do so, can have a bearing on many other parts of a research design, and these decisions can determine the kind of conclusions that can be drawn from a study.

This section begins with a discussion of some of the key concepts in sampling, in particular, technical meanings of 'population' and 'sample'. This is followed by a review of the major sampling methods, commonly referred to as random and non-random, but identified here as probability and non-probability methods. The idea of 'random' methods has the disadvantage of being associated with 'accidental' sampling rather than with the idea of representativeness and the ability to statistically estimate population characteristics from a sample.

As part of this review, consideration is given to how different methods can be combined, and how the size of a sample can be established. In addition, some comments are made on the connection between the use of tests of significance and probability sampling methods. Details of the techniques used in the major methods of probability sampling, and the associated mathematics, will not be elaborated here. (See e.g. Kish 1965 and Scheaffer *et al.* 1996 for technical details.) Rather, an overview is provided of the major sampling methods, and consideration is given to the implications that the choice of sampling method can have for other research design decisions.

Populations and Samples

First, it is necessary to clarify the concepts of *population* and *sample*. In order to apply a sampling technique, it is necessary to define the population (also called the target population, universe or sampling frame) from which the sample is to be drawn. A *population is an aggregate of all cases that conform to some designated set of criteria*. Population elements are single members or units of a population; they can be such things as people, social actions, social situations, events, places, time or things. The researcher is free to define a population in whatever way is considered appropriate to address the research question(s). For example, a population might be defined as:

- the citizens of a country at a particular time;
- first-year university students at a particular university;
- telephone subscribers in a particular city;
- people of a particular age;
- all the issues of a newspaper published over a twelve-month period;
- only the Saturday issues of this newspaper during this period; or
- only articles in these newspapers that report domestic violence.

A *census is a count of all population elements* and is used to describe the characteristics of the population.

A *sample is a selection of elements (members or units) from a population and may be used to make statements about the whole population*. The ideal sample is one that provides a perfect representation of a population, with all the relevant features of the population included in the sample in the same proportions. However, this ideal is seldom achieved. In a probability sample, *every population element must have a known and non-zero chance of being selected*. Most types of probability samples will also give every element an equal chance of being selected. Non-probability samples do *not* give every population element a chance of selection. The relationship between the size of the sample and the size of the population is the *sampling ratio*.

While sampling can introduce many complexities into the analysis of data, it is used for a variety of reasons. Studying a whole population may be slow and tedious; it can be expensive and is sometimes impossible; and it may also be unnecessary. Given limited resources, sampling can not only reduce the costs of a study, but, given a fixed budget, can also increase the breadth of coverage.

Methods of Sampling

A range of methods for drawing a sample is available. Some methods aim to represent the population from which the sample is drawn, while other methods involve a compromise on this ideal. The nature of the research, the availability of information, and cost will determine the choice of a particular method. Sampling methods have been divided along two dimensions: probability versus non-probability, and single-stage versus multi-stage.

Single-stage probability sampling

Simple random sampling

If a decision is made to use probability sampling, then a choice of methods must be made.[6] Simple random sampling is the standard against which all other methods are judged. It involves a selection process that gives every possible sample of a particular size an equal chance of being selected.

Sampling Methods

Single-stage probability
   Simple random
   Systematic
   Stratified
   Cluster
Multi-stage
Single-stage non-probability
   Accidental/Convenience
   Quota
   Judgemental/Purposive
   Snowball

However, even simple random sampling does not guarantee an exact representation of a population; it is possible to draw very 'biased' samples. What simple random sampling does is to allow the use of probability theory to provide an estimate of the likelihood of such 'deviant' samples being drawn. The other probability sampling methods provide different kinds of compromises with simple random sampling, each with its own advantages, in terms of cost or convenience, and degree of sacrifice in terms of accuracy.

Simple random samples require that each element of a population be identified and, usually, numbered. Once the size of the sample has been determined, a list of computer-generated columns of random numbers can be used to make the selection from the population.[7] For samples between 10 and 99, two columns of numbers will be used; between 100 and 999, three columns; between 1,000 and 9,999, four columns, and so on. Not all combinations of digits in the selected columns will be relevant as they may lie outside the range of the desired sample size. However, by scanning the column, the numbers that are relevant can be noted until the desired sample size is reached. These numbers then determine the population elements to be selected.

Systematic sampling

Systematic sampling provides a method that avoids having to number the whole population. If the population elements can be put in a list, they can be counted and a sampling ratio decided to produce the desired sample size, for example, one in five, or one in sixteen. In effect, the list is divided into equal zones the size of the denominator of the sampling ratio (e.g. five or sixteen), and one selection is made in each zone. The only strictly random aspect to this method of selection is determining which element in the first zone will be selected. Then it is a matter of counting down the list in intervals the size of the denominator (e.g. five or sixteen).

The systematic sampling procedure is simple and foolproof. However, it does have some potential dangers. Should the size of the zone correspond to a regular pattern in the list, the method may produce a very biased sample. For example, if houses in a regular pattern of city blocks are being selected, with a sampling ratio of one in sixteen, and if there happened to be sixteen houses in each block, and if the first house was randomly selected in the first zone, then the sample would consist only of corner houses. The subject of the study, for example traffic noise pollution, may affect corner houses differently than others in the block. There are two ways to protect a sample from such bias. One is to make a random selection more than once, thus changing the selection within the zones from time to time. Another is to double or treble the size of the zones and then to make two or three random selections within each zone. It is desirable to use either or both of these methods as they introduce a greater degree of randomness into the selection.

Stratified sampling

Stratified sampling is used for two main purposes. Firstly, when a researcher wishes to ensure that particular categories in the population are represented in the sample in the same proportion as in the population, for example, gender, age or ethnic identification. In order to do this, it must be possible to identify the population elements in terms of the relevant characteristic. If this is possible, the population elements can be grouped into the desired categories, or strata, before selections are made. By using the same sampling ratio in each stratum, the population distribution on this characteristic will be represented proportionately in the sample. The second major use of stratified sampling is to ensure that there are sufficient numbers in the sample from all categories that are to be examined. For example, if people are to be compared in terms of their religious affiliation, and a particular minority religion is considered to be important for this purpose, simple random sampling, and stratified sampling with the same sampling ratio in each stratum, may produce insufficient numbers from this category for later analysis. Assuming that this is the only underrepresented stratum, one solution is to lower the sampling ratio for this stratum (say, 1:3 rather than, say, 1:15 for the other strata). Another solution is to draw equal numbers from each stratum, by varying the sampling ratios. Once the number that is required from each stratum is decided, the denominator of the sampling ratio is arrived at by dividing that number by the number in the stratum. For example, if there are four strata of 5,000, 1,500, 1,000 and 100, and 50 are required from each stratum, the sampling ratios would be 1:100, 1:30, 1:20 and 1:2.

It is important to note that if the same sampling ratios are not used in all strata, the resulting sub-samples cannot be combined for analysis, as every member of the population did not have an equal chance of being selected. The strata are, in effect, separate populations. This problem can be overcome by weighting each stratum in the sample to restore it to the original relative proportions of the population strata. In the example just used, as the ratios between the population strata are 50:15:10:1, the numbers on which the data in each stratum are based would need to be multiplied by its respective ratio figure, or some multiple of it. The main disadvantage with this procedure is that any lack of representativeness in the initial sample will be magnified in the 'reconstituted' sample, particularly in cases where large weights are used. This kind of weighting procedure can also be used in simple random sampling when the population proportions on some variable are known, and the sampling proportions differ considerably from these.

Cluster sampling

All other forms of probability sampling use one or a combination of simple random sampling, systematic sampling or stratified sampling. The fourth common sampling method is cluster sampling, one version of which is known as *area sampling*. A cluster is a unit that contains a collection of population elements. Cluster sampling selects more than one population element at a time, for example, a classroom of students, a city suburb of households, a street or block of residences, a year of issues of a newspaper, or a month of applications for citizenship. Cluster sampling is generally used when it is impossible or very difficult to list all population elements. It also has the advantage that it can reduce the cost of data collection by concentrating this activity in a number of areas, rather than being scattered over a wide area. However, as clusters are unlikely to be identical in their distribution of population characteristics, cluster sampling will normally be less accurate than simple random sampling. It is not difficult to select a very biased set of clusters, and this problem is exacerbated if only a few are selected.

Multi-stage sampling

Cluster sampling is often the first stage, or perhaps one of the stages, of multi-stage sampling designs. The selection of the clusters themselves, and later selections within clusters, can use any of the three probability sampling methods. It is preferable that clusters are of equal size, otherwise each population element will not have an equal chance of being selected. However, this is not always achievable as natural clusters may vary considerably in size. One rather complex method for overcoming this is to stratify the clusters roughly according to size, and use a sampling ratio in each cluster that will give each population element a more or less equal chance of selection. Weighting can also be used, although this adds to the complexity.

Multi-stage sampling is commonly used in surveys of householders. For example, if householders in a large metropolitan area have been defined as the population, the first stage could be a random selection of administrative areas (e.g. local city councils), perhaps stratified by size, and/or mean socio-economic status of the residents. The second stage could be based on subdivisions that are used in census collection (perhaps using simple random procedures, or stratified procedures if the areas vary considerably in size). This could be followed by a random sample of households (perhaps using the systematic method while walking along each street). Finally, a member of the household could be selected by a random procedure. This sampling design does not require the identification of households and householders until the very last stages, and even then they need not be listed. Efficiencies in data gathering can be achieved as interviewers can concentrate their efforts and save a great deal of time and money in travelling. However, at each stage in this sampling design sampling errors can creep in. In order to compensate for this, a larger than the minimum desirable sample could be used. Nevertheless, this design represents an example of how practical problems (e.g. not having access to lists of householders) can be overcome, and how a compromise can be struck between precision and cost.

It is possible to combine probability and non-probability methods in a multi-stage sample. For example, the selection of initial clusters, such as areas of a city based on the demographic characteristics of the residents, could be based on a judgement of how typical each area is of the range of these characteristics. Subsequent sampling in each cluster could then use probability methods. Judgemental sampling will be discussed shortly.

Single-stage non-probability sampling

So far I have concentrated on issues related to probability sampling. Such sampling may be necessary in order to answer certain kinds of research questions with large populations. However, in addition to the use of populations rather than samples, some studies either do not need to generalize to a population, or cannot adequately identify the members of a population in order to draw a sample. For example, research on people who are infected with HIV/AIDS faces the problem that lists of such people are unlikely to be available. To insist on the use of random sampling would make the research impossible. Therefore, in such cases, it will be necessary to compromise with the ideal and use a non-probability sampling method. This research design decision can be justified in the terms of it being better to have some knowledge that is restricted because of the type of sample than to have no knowledge of the topic at all.

Having said this, it must be stressed that social researchers usually hope that what they find in a sample or group has wider relevance or value. This issue will be taken up in the next main section on 'Case Studies'. However, even when non-probability samples are used, they can be selected in such a way that it is possible to make a judgement about the extent to which they represent some population or group. What the researcher hopes to achieve is a sound basis for making such a judgement.

Decisions about whether or not to use a probability sample, and how it should be done, are not confined to quantitative studies; they are also necessary in studies that intend to gather qualitative data.[8] Invariably, because qualitative methods are resource-intensive, smaller samples must be used. Here the compromise is between having data that can be applied to large populations, or having in-depth and detailed data on, perhaps, an unrepresentative sample or just a single case. Qualitative researchers may argue that they are not really involved in a compromise, and that their methods can produce a richer understanding of social life than is possible by more superficial methods used by quantitative researchers. The relative merits of qualitative and quantitative methods will be discussed in chapter 7. In the meantime, we need to confine our attention to the role of sampling in both types of data gathering and analysis.

There is no necessary connection between the type of research method used (quantitative or qualitative) and the type of sample that is appropriate. As in quantitative studies, qualitative studies can also work with populations, although they are likely to be much smaller. For example, it would be possible to study neighbouring behaviour through participant observation in a city street (block) in a middle-class suburb. Defining a population in this way may restrict the statistical generalizability of the results, but the richness of the data may allow generalizations, based on a judgement about how typical the chosen research site is, or whether other suburbs in other cities are similar in important respects. If the research also included a variety of sites in the same city (e.g. working-class, upper-class, ethnically homogeneous, etc.), then generalizability may be enhanced. Here the sampling issue becomes one of which city, and which streets/blocks, to select. The method of selection may be based on judgement rather than probability, although probability sampling should not be overlooked.

Accidental or convenience sampling

The idea of randomness in sample selection should not be confused with the selection of respondents by accident. The method of accidental or convenience sampling is the most extreme and unsatisfactory form of non-probability sampling as it is likely to produce very unrepresentative samples. The use of such methods may be an indication of laziness or naivety on the part of the researcher, or may be used in 'quick and dirty' commercial research. A typical convenience sample is obtained when an interviewer stands on a street and selects people accidentally as they pass. Such respondents are representative of no particular population, not even of people who passed that spot during a particular period of a particular day. The views obtained in such a study do not even represent the mythical 'person in the street'. Doing accidental interviews at a random selection of spots in a city is no help; the population can neither be defined adequately nor its members be given an equal or known chance of selection.

A similar kind of accidental sample is obtained when readers of a newspaper or magazine are asked to complete a short questionnaire that is then cut out and mailed in. While the population might be defined as the readers of that particular issue of the newspaper or magazine, the self-selection process gives no guarantee that the respondents are representative. A similar process can occur when a researcher advertises in the print media for people with particular characteristics to volunteer to participate in a study; there is no way of knowing how representative they might be of that population. However, in some circumstances a researcher may have to use such a sampling method as a last resort, but results from such a study would need to be heavily qualified.

Quota sampling

A commonly used non-probability method is quota sampling. It is certainly an improvement on accidental sampling and is commonly practised when it is impossible, difficult or costly to identify members of a population. This method has the advantage that it can produce a sample with a similar distribution of characteristics to those that are considered to be important in the population that it is supposed to represent. A set of selection criteria is identified because of their relevance to the research topic, although the establishment of these criteria may not be a simple matter. For example, in a study of undergraduate university students, three selection criteria might be used: gender (male and female), year at university (e.g. 1, 2, 3 and 4 or more), and type of degree being undertaken (e.g. arts, social science, science, engineering, medicine, law, economics and education). These three criteria would produce sixty-four selection categories.[9] The researcher would then have to decide how many respondents are to be selected in each category. There are two main possibilities: equal numbers in each category or numbers proportional to incidence in the population (if this is known). The first option can ensure sufficient numbers for analysis, while the second has some of the advantages of proportional stratified random sampling. However, in neither case can the population characteristics be estimated statistically, as the selection into each category will be accidental. In an interview survey, for example, interviewers are only required to fill up the categories with the quota of respondents who meet the selection criteria. The advantages of quota sampling are that it is economical, easy to administer and quick to do in the field. It can also produce adequate results, although the degree to which it does this may not be known. As has already been mentioned, it may be no worse than using a probability sample with a poor response rate.

Judgemental or purposive sampling

Judgemental or purposive sampling is another commonly used non-probability method. One use is to deal with situations where it is impossible or very costly to identify a particular population, i.e. where there is no available list of the population elements. For example, a study of intravenous drug users could find respondents by a number of means: by contacting users in the field, through police and prisons, and through public and private agencies such as drug rehabilitation centres. Depending on the particular research questions being investigated, it would be possible to contact a significant number of drug users from a variety of contexts, and to include at least the most common types of drug users. A second use of the judgemental sampling method is for selecting some cases of a particular type. For example, a study of organizational behaviour may use a few cases of organizations that have been particularly successful in achieving what a researcher is interested in. The selection will be a matter of judgement as to which organizations would be most appropriate. A variation on this would be to select cases that contrast in some way, for example successful and unsuccessful organizations. Another use would be to select a variety of types of cases for in-depth investigation. For example, a study of 'problem' families could seek the assistance of experts in a social welfare agency to provide a list that includes a variety of such families, or, perhaps, families that differ on a set of criteria. The expert, with directions from the researcher, will make a judgement about the appropriateness of families for the study. These judgements may be informed by theoretical considerations.

Snowball sampling

A fourth type of non-probability method is snowball sampling, also known as network, chain referral or reputational sampling. The analogy is of a snowball growing in size as it is rolled in the snow. This method has two related uses. In a difficult to identify population, such as intravenous drug users, it may be possible to contact one or two users who can then be asked for names and addresses of other users, and so on. Another example would be in a study of people who regard themselves as social equals; the respondents' definitions of social equality can be used to build up a sample. Snowballing can also be used to locate natural social networks, such as friendship networks. Once contact is made with one member of the network, that person can be asked to identify other members and their relationships. In this way a sociogram can be built up, and, perhaps, the members of the network interviewed.

Theoretical sampling

Finally, a common sampling method used in qualitative research is theoretical sampling. When a researcher collects, codes and analyses data in a continuous process, as in grounded theory, decisions about sample size are made progressively. The initial case or cases will be selected according to the theoretical purposes that they serve, and further cases will be added in order to facilitate the development of the emerging theory. As theory development relies on comparison, cases will be added to facilitate this. An important concept in this process is 'theoretical saturation'. Cases are added until no further insights are obtained; until the researcher considers that nothing new is being discovered. Another grounded theory concept related to sampling is 'slices of data', defined as 'different kinds of data [that] give the analyst different views or vantage points from which to understand a category and to develop its properties' (Glaser and Strauss 1967: 65). A variety of slices is desirable to stimulate theory development. Just what slices are selected, and how many, is a matter of judgement. An important point about this method of sampling is that any notion of representativeness is irrelevant.

Accuracy, Precision and Bias

Three important sampling concepts need to be discussed briefly.[10] They are concerned with the ability of a particular sample, and a particular method of sampling, to be able to estimate a population parameter from a sampling statistic. A population parameter is the actual value of a particular characteristic, such as the percentage of females, or the mean age. A sample statistic is the value of such characteristics obtained from the sample. The aim, of course, is to draw a sample in which the value of the characteristic is the same as that in the population.

The concept of *accuracy* refers to the degree to which a particular sample is able to estimate the true population parameter. A sample value is inaccurate to the extent that it deviates from the population value. This is referred to as the *sampling error*. While it is usually not possible to establish the level of accuracy of an estimate, it is possible to calculate from any one sample value the likely distribution of all possible sample values. This possible distribution indicates the fluctuations in sample values that result from random selection. In other words, the probable accuracy or *precision* can be calculated and used as a basis for estimating the population parameter.

Sampling *bias* refers to the systematic errors of a particular sampling method. These errors affect the capacity of the method to estimate population parameters. Here we are dealing with not just one sample estimate, but with all possible samples that the method can produce. The mean value of all sample statistics produced by a particular method is compared with the population parameter. If this mean corresponds to the population parameter, the sampling method can be regarded as being unbiased. Some of the methods we have discussed are better at this than others; the compromises made against the method of simple random sampling may be responsible.

There are, therefore, two important considerations in selecting a sampling method. The first is the likely *bias* of the method itself, and the second is the possible *accuracy* of its estimates of population parameters. The researcher can deal with the former by selecting a method that minimizes bias and with the latter by making sure that the sample size is appropriate. In general, the larger the sample, the narrower is the distribution of possible sample values, and hence the more precise the estimates. Sample size will be discussed shortly.

Response Rate

Ultimately, the usefulness of any sampling design will be determined by the extent to which all sampled units are included in the study. A poor response rate can destroy all the careful work that has gone into devising an appropriate sampling design. Many years ago a statistician colleague advised me that there is no point in trying to estimate population parameters from sample statistics if the response rate is below about 85 per cent. Lower response rates, he suggested, make nonsense of the application of probability theory because of the possible biases that can be introduced. When I have quoted this figure to my students, they usually reel in horror as they have little confidence in achieving anything like this response. A casual reading of research reports will show that this level of response is very rarely achieved.[11] What my colleague was claiming was that it is pointless to apply tests of significance to sample data that are based on poor response rates. Nevertheless, this statistical ritual *is* applied to samples with response rates of well below 50 per cent. To use probability sampling is one thing; to achieve a high response rate is another. Both are needed to estimate population parameters from samples. It is therefore essential that every effort be made to achieve as high a response rate as possible, whether the study is based on a sample or a population, but particularly for samples.

As human populations have become saturated with social surveys and opinion polling, low response rates have become increasingly common. What can a practising social researcher do? The problem with low response rates is the risk of unrepresentativeness. If data are available on population distributions on critical variables (e.g. from the census), sample distributions can be compared with them. If the distributions are similar, then tests of significance can be used with some confidence. When a very poor response rate is anticipated, it may be better to use a carefully designed non-probability quota sample. This will at least ensure that sample distributions will be similar to those in the population, even if representativeness cannot be guaranteed.

Sampling and Tests of Significance

Tests of significance are designed to apply probability theory to sample data in order to draw conclusions as to whether characteristics, differences or relationships found in a sample can be expected to have occurred, other than by chance, in the population from which the sample was drawn. Of course, these statistical tests are only relevant when probability sampling has been used, and then only when there is a very good response rate.

There appears to be a great deal of misunderstanding about the use of tests of significance with populations and samples. It is not uncommon for social researchers to call whatever units they are studying a sample, even when the units constitute a population. This can lead to the use of certain statistical tests (e.g. the chi-square test for nominal data and the *t* test for interval or ratio data) with population data (parameters) when they are only necessary if sample data (statistics) are being analysed. The fact that these tests are called 'statistical' tests is the clue that they should be applied only to sample 'statistics'.

It is because tests of significance are frequently misinterpreted as indicating whether there is any difference or relationship worth considering in the data, that they are applied inappropriately to data from populations or non-probability samples. Any differences or relationships found in a population are what the data tell you; applying a test of significance is meaningless. The researcher has to decide on the basis of the evidence if the difference or relationship in a population is worthy of consideration. It is the strength of association between variables, in both samples and populations, that is relevant to this decision, and then it is a matter of judgement about whether the relationship is important. If a non-probability sample is used, it is not possible to estimate population characteristics. Hence, the use of tests of significance is inappropriate.

A critical research design decision for the researcher is whether to use a population or sample. This decision will be influenced by the need to strike a compromise between what would be ideal in order to answer the research questions, and what is possible in terms of available resources and other practical considerations, such as accessibility of population elements. The decision will then have a big bearing on the kinds of analysis that will be necessary.

Sample Size

This brings us to the research design question that I have been asked more than any other: 'How big should my sample be?' Of course, the question might mean,

'How big should my population be?' There is no easy answer to this question, as many factors have to be considered. In addition, the answer will vary depending on whether probability or non-probability samples are being used.

Probability sample size

There are four important factors to be considered in deciding the size of probability samples:

- the degree of accuracy that is required, or, to put this differently, the consequences of being wrong in estimating the population parameters;
- how much variation there is in the population on the key characteristics being studied;
- the levels of measurement being used (nominal, ordinal, interval or ratio), and, hence, the types of analysis that can be applied; and
- the extent to which sub-groups in the sample will be analysed.

A common misunderstanding is that a sample must be some fixed proportion of a population, such as 10 per cent.[12] In fact, it is possible to study very large populations with relatively small samples. While large populations may need larger samples than smaller populations, the ratio of population size to an appropriate sample size is not constant. For example: for populations around 1,000, the ratio might be about 1:3 (a sample of about 300); around 10,000, the ratio may be about 1:10 (1,000); around 150,000, the ratio may be 1:100 (1,500); and, for very large populations (say over ten million), the ratio could be as low as 1:4,000 (2,500) (Neuman 1997: 221–2). It is not uncommon for opinion pollsters to use samples of 1,000–2,000 with populations of 5–10 million. For such populations, increases beyond 1,000 produce only small gains in the accuracy with which generalizations can be made from sample to population, and beyond 2,000 the gains are very small (see Blaikie 2003: 176–7). However, the analysis undertaken in opinion polls is usually very simple. The factors mentioned in the previous paragraph may require larger samples. It is in small populations that care must be taken in calculating the sample size, as small increases in size can produce big increases in accuracy, or alternatively, samples that are too small can produce inaccurate generalizations. *It is the absolute size of a sample, not some ratio to the population size, which is important in determining sample size.*

In any attempt to generalize from a sample to a population, it is necessary to decide on what is technically called a 'level of confidence'. What this means is the degree to which we want to be sure that the population parameter has been accurately estimated from the sampling statistic. All such estimates of population parameters have to be made within a range of values around the sample value. This is known as the 'confidence limits'. Just how big this interval is depends on the level of confidence set. If you want to have a 95 per cent chance of correctly estimating the population parameter, the interval will be smaller than if you want to have a 99 per cent chance. For example, if in a sample of 1,105 registered voters, 33 per cent said they would vote for a particular candidate at the next election, we can estimate the percentage in the population to be between 30.2 and

35.8 (a range of 5.6 per cent) at the 95 per cent level of confidence, and between 29.4 and 36.6 (a range of 7.2 per cent) at the 99 per cent level.[13] Therefore, *setting the level of confidence high will reduce the chance of being wrong but, at the same time, will reduce the accuracy of the estimate* as the confidence limits will have to be wider. The reverse is also true. If narrower confidence limits are desired, the level of confidence will have to be lowered. For example, if you only want to be 80 per cent sure of correctly estimating a population parameter, you can achieve this with very narrow confidence limits, i.e. very accurately. In the example above, the confidence intervals would be between 31.2 per cent and 34.8 percent (a range of 3.6 per cent). However, this more accurate estimate has limited value, as we cannot be very confident about it. Hence, there is a need to strike a balance between the risk of making a wrong estimate and the accuracy of the estimate. (See Blaikie 2003: 171–7)

Unfortunately, there is no other way of generalizing from a probability sample to a population than to set a level of confidence and estimate the corresponding confidence limits. The commonly used levels of confidence are 95 per cent (0.05 level) or 99 per cent (0.01 level), but these are conventions that are usually used without giving consideration to the consequences for the particular study. It is worth noting again that these problems of estimation are eliminated if a population is studied. As no estimates are required no levels of confidence need to be set; the data obtained *are* the population parameters.

Various formulae are available to calculate a suitable sample size. However, they are limited in their ability to take into account all the factors mentioned above. One approach in studies that work with sample statistics in percentages is to estimate the likely critical percentage as a basis for the calculation. For example, if we have an idea that the voting between two candidates at an election is going to be very close, then a poll prior to the election could select a sample to give the best estimate assuming each candidate will get about 50 per cent of the votes. Foddy (1988) has provided a formula for this.

$$\text{Sample size} = \frac{pqZ^2}{E^2}$$

where p is the expected percentage (say 50), q is p subtracted from 100 (in this case 50), Z is the t value for the chosen confidence level (say 95 per cent), and E is the maximum error desired in estimating the population parameter (say 5 per cent). In this example the sample would need to be 384, say 400. However, when a population is likely to be split about 50:50 in their answers to a question, such as the one above, the sample size will have to be larger than when the support for two candidates is uneven.

Hence, two important factors enter into the determination of sample size: the desired accuracy, i.e. the tolerable sampling error, in the estimation of the population characteristics; and, the distribution of answers to a question, such as voting preferences. The higher the desired accuracy, the bigger the sample. For example, when a population is likely to be split about 50:50 in their answer to a critical question, and the acceptable sampling error is 1 per cent, a sample of 10,000 would be required (at the 95 per cent level of confidence). However, if the desired level of accuracy is 5 per cent with the same level of confidence, a sample of 400 would be sufficient. If the percentage split is anticipated as 5:95, a sample of 1,900 would be required to achieve a 1 per cent level of accuracy and only 73 at a 5 per cent level, at the same level of confidence. Hence, the anticipated distribution of answers to a question is also relevant. (See de Vaus 2002: 82 for a table that covers the range from 1 to 10 per cent accuracy.)

There is another way that the distribution of population characteristics can influence sample size. The characteristics of a relatively homogeneous population can be estimated with a much smaller sample than a heterogeneous population. Take age for example. If the population is all the same age, it is possible to estimate that age from a sample of one. However, a wide age distribution would require a substantial sample. Hence, the wider the distribution of a key population characteristic, the larger will be the sample required.

A third factor that influences sample size is the effect of the level of measurement and the associated method of analysis (see Blaikie 2003: 22–33). In general, the more precise or higher the level of measurement, the smaller the sample required, and vice versa. Interval and ratio measures require smaller samples than nominal measures. The reason for this is that nominal measures have to use cumbersome forms of analysis, and, therefore, usually need larger samples to achieve satisfactory results. However, the distribution of population characteristics affects all levels of measurement, but they are more difficult to deal with when lower levels are used. There is no simple rule of thumb for making this decision. What is necessary is to know before the study commences what levels of measurement are going to be used and what methods of analysis can be applied to them (assuming they are both quantitative). Most good statistics textbooks will indicate what the minimum number is for using a particular statistical procedure, particularly for interval and ratio data. When results are presented in tabular form (usually cross-tabulations), a rule of thumb is that the sample size needs to be ten times the number of cells in the table. This rule is based on the requirement for chi-square analysis and the measures of association derived from chi-square. The number of cells will be determined both by the number of categories on each variable, and the need to meet chi-square requirements in terms of minimum expected frequencies. Other methods of analysis will have different implications for sample size. However, the complicating factor in all of this is the possibility that in any study a variety of levels of measurement will be used. The sample size will have to meet the requirements of the lowest level of measurement.

A fourth factor emerges if it is intended that analysis will be undertaken on a sub-sample. The total sample must be big enough to make this possible. For example, if a study is conducted with a population of ethnic communities whose members migrated to a particular country before the age of eighteen, and if analysis is to be done on each group separately, then there must be a sufficient number of people from each group to do the analysis. Clearly, the size of the smallest community becomes important. The actual numbers required in this group will, again, depend on the levels of measurement to be used and on the kind of analysis to be undertaken. If some of the variables are nominal, and three of these are to be used in a three-way cross-tabulation, the size of the group would need to be about ten times the number of cells in this table. For example, if country of birth (coded into three categories) is to be cross-tabulated with political party preference (three categories), and if the first variable is to be controlled by year of migration (coded into three time periods), then a table of twenty-seven cells will be produced requiring a sub-sample of 270. If the smallest ethnic community makes up 10 per cent of the population, then a total sample of 2,700 would be required. Of course, one way to reduce the total sample size would be to use a stratified sample by ethnic community, and different sampling ratios in each stratum, to make all sub-samples of 270. If there were five ethnic communities, the total sample would be exactly half (1,350), thus producing a considerable reduction in the cost of the study. However, if the variables to be analysed are interval or ratio, much smaller numbers can be used. One rule of thumb is to have a minimum of fifty in each sub-group, but, clearly, many things should be considered in making this decision.

Here are some important relationships between sample size, error and accuracy.

- As sample size increases, sampling error decreases and sample reliability increases.
- As population homogeneity decreases, sample error increases and sample reliability decreases.
- As sample error increases, sample reliability decreases, and vice versa.

'Sample size must take into account the degree of diversity in the population on key variables, the level of sampling error that is tolerated and the reliability required of the sample' (de Vaus 2002: 81). To reiterate, a small increase in the size of small samples can lead to a substantial increase in accuracy, but this is not the case for larger samples.

It will be clear from this discussion that a decision on sample size is rather complex. The best a researcher can do is to be aware of the effects of accuracy requirements, population characteristics, levels of measurement, and the types of analysis to be used. The latter consideration reinforces the need to include in any research design decisions about how the data will be analysed. In my experience, researchers resist pushing their design decisions this far. It is easy to think that this can be put off until later, but it cannot. Failure to make the decision is likely to lead to samples that are the wrong size, to data that cannot be sensibly analysed, and, hence, to research questions that cannot be answered properly. In some studies, it is not possible to know in advance how the population is distributed on the characteristics being studied. Even rough estimates may be impossible to make. In this case, the researcher must be conservative and use a sample that will cope with the worst possible situation, which means making it larger.

Having said all this, one other major consideration enters into the equation. It is the practical issue of resources. The ideal sample needed to answer a set of research questions may be beyond the scope of the available resources. *Sample size decisions are always a compromise between the ideal and the practical, between the size needed to meet technical requirements and the size that can be achieved with the available resources.* In the end, the researcher must be able to defend the decision as being appropriate for answering the research questions, given the particular conditions. If resources require that the sample size be reduced beyond minimum practical limits, then the design of the study would need to be radically changed, or the project postponed until sufficient resources are available.

It is always important to discover what conventions are used for your kind of research in your discipline or sub-discipline, in your university or research organization, and what the consumers of the research, including thesis examiners, find acceptable. These conventions do not always fit well with the technical requirements, but, in the end, may be politically more important. I have a few conventions of my own which I used when students asked me about sample size for quantitative surveys. After going through the points just discussed, I may say something like: 'A sample of 1,000 would be ideal, or 2,000 if you can manage it, but 500 might be enough and even 300 might do in some circumstances.' Students are invariably horrified by the idea of having to work with samples of this size. However, if resources are not available to achieve samples of this size, then a different kind of research design will be required, or the research questions may have to be changed.

Non-probability sample size

As it is not possible to estimate population parameters from the data acquired using a non-probability sample, the discussion in the previous section on confidence levels and acceptable errors in estimates is not relevant. If, however, quantitative analysis is to be undertaken, then sample size *will* be influenced by the requirements of the type of analysis to be undertaken.

When a research project involves the use of time-intensive, in-depth methods, particularly when directed towards theory development, the issue of sample size takes on a very different complexion. As we saw in the case of *theoretical sampling*, sampling decisions evolve along with the theory. It is not possible to determine in advance what the size should be. However, time and resource limitations will inevitably put some restrictions on sample size. In this kind of research, it may be more useful to think of selecting cases for intensive study, rather than getting distracted by sampling concerns that are irrelevant. It is to the discussion of case studies that we now turn.

Case Studies

Throughout the history of social research, *case studies* have been regarded in a variety of ways:

- as a type of research design;
- as involving the use of particular kinds of research methods, usually qualitative; and
- as being a method of selecting the source of data.

The first view is frequently represented in textbooks on social research methods where case studies are included alongside surveys, experiments, and ethnography or field research. As we saw in chapter 2, this way of classifying research designs is inappropriate. The second view goes back many decades to debates about the relative merits of survey research and the use of statistical techniques compared to the use of participant observation and field research. Case study was the collective term used for the latter. While the third view is probably the least common, it is the one I want to emphasize here. 'Case study is not a methodological choice but a choice of what is to be studied' (Stake 2005: 443).

The idea of a case study has some relationship to the notions of both clinical studies in medicine and psychology, and to case histories used in the helping professions, such as social work. However, there are some important differences that should become evident as this discussion proceeds.

The case study has a long history. It has been used extensively in social anthropology, and it is now used in political science (e.g. policy and public administration research), sociology (e.g. community studies), management (e.g. organizational studies), and planning (e.g. research on cities, regions and neighbourhoods). Some writers have suggested that case studies are suitable for single-person research on a limited budget, and that the study of one case provides a manageable opportunity for a researcher to study one aspect of a problem in some depth within a limited time-scale (see e.g. Blaxter *et al.* 2002; Bell 2005). It is implied that they are appropriate for student research, particularly for postgraduate theses, and that most researchers are capable of doing a case study.

Case studies have been used for various purposes: in exploratory, descriptive and explanatory research (Yin 2003a), to generate theory (Mitchell 1983; Eckstein 1992; Hammersley *et al.* 2000) and to initiate change (Gummesson 1991). These uses will depend on the research questions asked, and the extent to which the researcher has control over the events being studied (Yin 2003a).

Background

The case study has had a chequered career in the social sciences. We need to go back to the 1920s, to the period prior to the survey becoming the dominant style of social research in the United States, to find the case study being used as an acceptable way of doing research. This occurred mainly in the Chicago tradition of sociology (e.g. Thomas, Znaniecki, Cooley, Park and Burgess, Zorbaugh, and Blumer). There followed a period in which case studies were contrasted with the social survey, as the latter became the dominant social research method. Arguments centred on which of the two 'methods' was the most scientific, i.e. came closest to the methods used in the natural sciences. Hence, the late 1920s and the 1930s saw a period of defence of the case study (e.g. Shaw 1927; Jocher 1928; Queen 1928; Znaniecki 1934; Young 1939) and debates about the relative merits of 'statistical methods' and 'case studies' (e.g. Burgess 1927).

Following the Second World War, debates continued between advocates of 'surveys' (and sometimes 'experiments') and 'participant observation', essentially between supporters of quantitative and qualitative methods. In the eyes of many, the former were scientific, but not the latter (Lundberg 1929; reviewed by Hammersley 1992). By the 1950s, the discussion of case studies had all but disappeared from textbooks on social research methods, although considerable attention was still given to specific techniques, such as participant observation. This decline in interest was no doubt due to the expansion in the use of quantitative and statistical methods, and the increasing availability of computers to speed up this type of analysis (Mitchell 1983).

Thirty years later, as a result of a revival of interest in qualitative methods, particularly in educational, nursing and evaluation research, and in much British sociology, the discussion of case studies re-emerged (e.g. Mitchell 1983; Yin 1984; Platt 1988). They were now identified with methods that had been commonly used in anthropological research, with techniques of data collection such as participant observation, the use of informants, unstructured interviewing, and the study of personal documents and records. The general tenor of the discussion of such qualitative methods was that they were inferior to quantitative methods; that they were only really useful in exploratory stages of research, and that researchers were unfortunate if they had no alternative but to use them as major methods (Goode and Hatt 1952; Platt 1988).

A major deficiency of the early discussions of case studies was that they were confused with techniques of data collection and analysis. Any research using qualitative methods and data was assumed to be a case study. However, *the case study is not one or a number of specific techniques.*

Definitions

The literature abounds with various definitions of case study. It is still common to use the concept as 'an umbrella term for a family of research methods having in common the decision to focus on inquiry around an instance' (Adelman *et al.* 1977). While some methods may be used frequently, such as observation and interviewing, any method is regarded as being legitimate. Even a survey may be used in a case study. What, then, is peculiar about case studies?

Goode and Hatt (1952) focused their definition on the notion of a social unit and the manner in which it is studied. A *social* unit is a 'real' individual, social event or group of people; and the individual, group or event are treated as a whole. What this means in practice is that the case study attempts 'to keep together, as a unit, those characteristics which are relevant to the scientific problem being investigated' (1952: 333). This is in contrast to survey research that deals with individuals, but only as a collection of traits or variables. Goode and Hatt avoided identifying the case study with a particular technique for collecting data. Rather, they regarded it as 'a *mode of organizing data* in terms of some chosen unit, such as the individual life history, the history of a group, or some delimited social process' (1952: 339).

Creswell (1994) has provided a similar definition. A case study is a single bounded entity, studied in detail, with a variety of methods, over an extended period. While being sympathetic with this emphasis on the unitary character of a case, Mitchell (1983) was critical of it on two counts. First, it gives no place for extrapolation from case studies, leaving this activity to studies using statistical analysis. Second, the stress on the whole appears to ignore the context in which the case is located. In other words, Mitchell objected to case studies being limited to social descriptions in social isolation.

The issue of what constitutes the unit of analysis in a case study has been dealt with in some detail by Yin (2003a). He has suggested that the key to resolving the problem is the way research questions are stated. For example, a research question might ask: 'What internal and external changes are related to changes in religious practices and orientation to the world adopted by new religious movements?' (see the Appendix). In this example, the emphasis is on new religious movements, one or more of which could be treated as case studies. If, however, the research question was 'What kinds of religious movements arise in times of rapid social change?', then one or more rapidly changing societies could be selected as case studies.

Yin has distinguished a case study from other types of research design, or what he called research strategies: experiment, survey, archival analysis and a history. More specifically, he has defined a *case study* as an empirical inquiry that:

- investigates a contemporary phenomenon within its real-life context, especially when
- boundaries between phenomenon and context are not clearly evident.

In addition, case studies enquiry:

- copes with the technically distinctive situation in which there will be many more variables of interest than data points, and as one result
- relies on multiple sources of evidence, with data needing to converge in a triangulation fashion, and as another result
- benefits from the prior development of theoretical propositions to guide that data collection and analysis (Yin 2003a: 13–14).

By defining the case study as a research strategy, Yin has been able to argue that there is no connection between case studies and qualitative research: 'case studies can include, and even be limited to, quantitative evidence' (Yin 2003a: 14).

Hammersley (1992) provided a much more limited definition of the case study. Like Yin, he contrasted case studies with experiments and surveys and confined the comparison to the manner in which each one selects its units for study. The case study is viewed as just one method of selection. In the process, Hammersley rejected the view that case studies use certain kinds of methods of data collection, or a particular logic of enquiry. According to Hammersley, what distinguishes case studies from both experiments and surveys is that they use a comparatively small number of units in naturally occurring settings, and these units are investigated in considerable depth (1992: 185; Hammersley and Gomm 2000: 3).

Types and Uses

According to Gluckman (1961), the anthropological notion of the case study has had three main uses: as *apt illustrations*, as *social situations* and as *extended case studies*. The *apt illustration* is a description of an event in which some general principle is in operation. To illustrate mother-in-law and son-in-law avoidance in daily life, Gluckman used the example of the young man who stepped off the path and hid himself as his mother-in-law approached. The analysis of a *social situation* involves a more complex collection of connected events that occur in a limited time span, and which demonstrate the operation of general principles of social organization. Gluckman referred to the situation of the opening of a new bridge in Zulul that brought together representatives of diverse segments of the population. Their behaviour before, during and after the bridge opening were regarded as being characteristic of the wider social structure. An even more complex use can be found in the *extended case study* that follows the same social actors as they move through a series of linked situations and events. Thus it is possible to identify structural features, for example kinship, by describing social processes over time.

While Gluckman's classification was based mainly on differing degrees of complexity, and to a lesser extent on duration of time, Eckstein's (1975, 1992) five-way classification focused on the different uses of case studies in theory development: *configurative-ideographic* studies, *disciplined-comparative* studies, *heuristic* case studies, *plausibility probes*, and *crucial-case* studies. These uses are elaborated later in this chapter.

While some writers (e.g. Eckstein) have distinguished case studies from comparative research on the basis of whether one or a number of cases are used, Yin (2003a: 39–45) included both single and multiple cases within case-study research. He regarded single-case studies as being of three types: *critical*, *extreme* and *revelatory*. The first is analogous to a single experiment, like Eckstein's crucial-case studies. It provides a *critical* test of a theory, to corroborate, challenge or extend it. The second use of the single-case study is as an *extreme* or unique case. This is common in clinical psychology and can also be used in sociology for the study of deviant or unusual groups. The third use, *revelatory* case studies, occurs in a situation where some phenomenon has not been studied before; where an opportunity arises to research something that has been previously inaccessible.

In all three uses, the single-case study will be a complete study. However, Yin divided them into two types: *holistic* and *embedded* case studies. The *holistic* case study has only one unit of analysis while the *embedded* case study may have a sub-unit or a number of sub-units. For example, an organization could be studied as a holistic case if the main research question was concerned with the type of cultural change that could follow from the use of different technology. In an embedded case study, organizational change associated with technological change might be studied at various levels: change in management style, change in work practices and change in organizational structures, as well as change in organizational culture. The embedded study requires research at different levels within the organization, while still treating the organization as a single-case study.

In contrast to single-case studies, Yin argued that the main use of multiple-case designs is analogous to conducting a series of experiments. He claimed that a well-developed theory can be tested by carefully selecting a series of cases in the same way as theories are tested experimentally. This, as we shall see shortly, requires the use of replication rather than sampling logic.

Just how many cases should be included in a multiple-case design will depend on the complexity of the phenomenon and the conditions in which it occurs; the greater the complexity, the greater the number of cases that will be necessary to achieve confidence in the testing of the theory. Notions of sample size used in association with sampling logic are not relevant to multiple-case study research.

The use of multiple-case studies has both advantages and disadvantages compared to the use of single-case studies. According to Yin, all three types of single-case studies – *critical*, *extreme* or *revelatory* – serve useful purposes on their own. While the use of a number of cases may add greater weight to a study, and make its findings more convincing, their use is only appropriate when replication rather than sampling logic is used. In addition, as case studies are expensive to conduct, multiple-case studies should not be undertaken lightly.

Stake (2005) has proposed another three-way classification: *intrinsic*, *instrumental* and *collective*. *Intrinsic* case studies are used to achive a better understanding of a particular case. The case is studied, not because it represents other cases or illustrates some problem, but because of its particular interest. *Instrumental* case studies are selected to provide insight into an issue or to obtain a better understanding of something else, perhaps to support a developing generalization or theory. *Collective* case studies are also instrumental but involve the joint study of a number of cases that represent some phenomenon, population or general condition. The aim is likely to be theory generation, which it is hoped will apply to an even wider collection of such cases.

We can see from these various attempts to categorize case studies that their use ranges from descriptive, which usually involves single cases, to explanatory, which normally requires multiple cases. Hence, the type of research question(s) being investigated, and the purposes of the research, will determine what use could be made of case studies, and, hence, their role in data selection.

Criticism

The issue of whether case studies can be used for anything other than description, i.e. for producing generalizations and for theory development, has been a matter of considerable controversy. Researchers who favour the use of probability samples and/or who are concerned with theory testing, tend to regard the use of case studies as unsatisfactory for these purposes. Add to this an accompanying preference for quantitative methods of data collection and analysis, the use of case studies has sometimes been viewed sceptically.

There have been three major criticisms that have arisen from the comparison of case studies with quantitative methods (Yin 2003a: 10–11). The first and greatest concern is the possibility of sloppy research and biased findings being presented. What this criticism boils down to is a prejudice that quantitative researchers have had against qualitative data, a view based on the mistaken belief that only numbers can be used to describe and explain social life validly and reliably. Part of this prejudice is that qualitative research, unlike quantitative research, cannot be replicated because there is too much scope for the researcher to influence the results. These issues are taken up in chapter 7.[14]

The second concern is that case studies are not useful for generalizing. There are two aspects of this position: that it is not possible to generalize from a single case, and that if a number of cases are used for the purpose, it is extremely difficult to establish their comparability. Each case has too many unique aspects. However, the same criticisms could be raised about a single experiment, or the study of a single population, whether or not a sample has been used to do so. I will return to this issue in a moment.

A third criticism of the case study is not so much methodological as practical. The complaint is that case studies take too long and produce unmanageable amounts of data. This criticism confuses the case study with specific methods of data collection that are time-consuming, for example, participant observation in particular and ethnography in general. Yin has argued that case studies need not take a long time and that they can now be conducted in a manageable way (2003a: 11).[15]

Two Issues

Both critics and advocates have focused on two issues in discussions on the use of case studies in social research. The first concerns the possibility or even the desirability of trying to generalize findings from case study research. The second issue has to do with the use of case studies in theory development and/or testing. As we have seen, Mitchell, Eckstein and Yin have all raised the issue of whether it is possible to generalize or theorize from case studies. Must the findings from a case study remain just interesting description, or can they be used to generalize and to generate and test theory? These issues are now explored in more detail.

Generalizing

The generalizability of research findings has been a preoccupation of researchers who work with samples drawn from larger populations. As we have seen earlier in this chapter, a carefully selected probability sample allows for generalization of sample statistics to population parameters using probability theory. Case studies are rarely if ever drawn by probability methods, and, in any case, only one case, or perhaps a few, is/are selected. Hence, the methods of selection, and the numbers involved, do not meet the requirements for generalizing to populations. How then is it possible to generalize from case studies?

Perhaps there is a prior question to consider. Why do case study researchers want to generalize their findings? Some qualitative researchers have rejected the need to generalize findings, at least when this is understood as aiming to produce universal laws, and are content to provide 'slices from life' that have intrinsic value (see, for example, Stake 1978; Denzin 1983; Lincoln and Guba 1985). However, as the use of qualitative methods and case studies has increased over the past few decades, researchers have become concerned that their findings will have relevance beyond their research site.

A number of strategies have been proposed, all of which require a different conception of generalizability; this involves judgement rather than probability sampling techniques. However, methods of selection are still a key element. These are: selecting 'typical' cases; studying multiple cases at different sites; the use of 'natural generalization'; the use of 'analytic generalization'; and the use of 'thick' description to facilitate 'transferability' or 'relatability'.

Researchers may feel more comfortable generalizing if they work with 'typical' cases, i.e. if the case being studied can be shown to be similar to other cases in terms of relevant characteristics (see, for example, Goetz and LeCompte 1984; Whyte 1984). However, it may be difficult to demonstrate whether a particular case is typical rather than unique. Certainly, this was not the guiding principle when anthropologists selected small-scale societies to study. Some writers, such as Mitchell (1983: 204), have argued against trying to find typical cases. However, we need to note that Mitchell was more concerned with theorizing rather than generalizing from case studies. As we shall see shortly, when generalizing is the primary concern, finding typical cases *may* be useful.

A second possibility is to select a number of cases across different sites (see review by Firestone and Herriott 1984). While such a strategy can certainly strengthen the basis for generalizing, it has some obvious practical disadvantages. It is very expensive with the possible consequence that each site may not be studied in the depth usually associated with case study research (Schofield 1993).

The third possibility – 'natural generalizability' – has been proposed by Stake (1978). He argued that natural generalization is something we routinely do in everyday life. We can recognize similarities between objects and issues and repetitive patterns. Case studies add to existing experience and understanding. Lincoln and Guba ('transferability' or 'fittingness'), Bassey ('relatability'), and Goetz and LeCompte (1984), have taken this idea further.

According to Lincoln and Guba, transferability between contexts is possible if they can be judged to be similar. Fittingness is the degree of congruence between the context in which the research was conducted and the one to which the findings are to be transferred. This requires information about both contexts. Hence, researchers need to provide sufficient information on the context of the research to allow anyone else to judge whether the findings may be relevant to another context about which they have similar information (1985: 124–5).

In the context of educational research, Bassey argued that 'an important criterion for judging the merit of a case study is the extent to which the details are sufficient and appropriate for a teacher working in a similar situation to relate his [*sic*] decision-making to that described in the case study. The relatability of a case is more important than its generalizability' (1981: 85). Hence, if researchers provide sufficiently 'thick descriptions' of their cases it is possible for others to make judgements about whether the findings can be related. The burden of proof is on the user rather than the originator of the research. However, Gomm *et al.* (2000b) have been critical of a number of aspects of this solution, in particular, that case studies will have sufficient intrinsic relevance that concerns about generalizing can be side stepped, and that researchers can transfer their responsibility for the generalizability of their findings to the users of the research.

Yin has argued for the use of 'analytic generalization' as an alternative to 'statistical generalization' in case studies.

A fatal flaw in doing case studies is to conceive of statistical generalization as the method of generalizing the results of the case. This is because cases are not 'sampling units' and should not be chosen for this reason. Rather, individual case studies are to be selected as a laboratory investigator selects the topic of a new experiment. Multiple cases, in this sense, should be considered like multiple experiments. Under these circumstances, the method of generalization is 'analytic generalization,' in which a previously developed theory is used as a template with which to compare the empirical results of the case study. If two or more cases are shown to support the same theory, replication may be claimed. The empirical results may be considered yet more potent if two or more cases support the same theory but do not support an equally plausible, *rival* theory. . . . Analytic generalization can be used whether your case study involves one or several cases. (Yin 2003a: 32–3)

Hence, Yin saw theory providing a possible link between case studies.

Gomm *et al.* (2000b) have adopted a different approach that returns to more traditional ideas on generalizing. They bring us back to the issue of typical cases and have suggested that researchers should collect information about the wider population to which the case study findings might be generalized. This is particularly necessary where the population is heterogeneous. Selecting a case that includes this degree of heterogeneity would be important. Another suggestion is to select a small sample of cases that cover the range of the diversity in the population. Such a selection would be assisted if a survey of the population, or perhaps a probability sample drawn from it, preceded the case selection. This would give an idea of the kind of diversity that needs to be taken into account.

Hence, generalizing is done by making judgements on the basis of knowledge of the characteristics of the case and the target population. This process is no different from the situation where survey researchers want to generalize from a population they may have studied, with or without probability sampling, to wider populations. For example, the findings of a survey of students at one university could be generalized to students at another university only if critical characteristics of students in both universities are similar. This kind of generalization is a matter of judgement based on evidence. I shall come back to this issue in the next chapter in the context of generalizing in qualitative research.

Theorizing

We have already noted that Eckstein (1975, 1992) proposed a five-way classification of case studies according to their role in theory development. These range from developing an understanding through theory building and theory testing.

Configurative-ideographic studies use descriptions to provide understanding. The configurative element depicts the overall gestalt of the unit under investigation. The ideographic element allows either facts to speak for themselves or for intuitive interpretation. The intensity of such studies, and the empathetic feeling that they can produce, is their claim to validity. The major weakness of this type of case study is that understanding or insight produced by each study cannot be used to generate theory. They tend to stand alone and are usually not designed by their authors for this purpose.

Eckstein's second type of case study, the *disciplined-comparative*, requires that each case be viewed in the context of an established or at least a provisional theory. Ideally, the findings of a particular case study should be able to be deduced from such a theory, or could be used to challenge it. These cases are not used to build theory, apart from serendipitous 'discoveries'.

The third type, the *heuristic* case study, is deliberately used to stimulate theoretical thinking.

> Such studies, unlike configurative-ideographic ones, tie directly into theory building, and therefore are less concerned with overall concrete configurations than with potentially generalizable relations between aspects of them: they also tie into theory building less passively and fortuitously than does disciplined-configurative study, because the potentially generalizable relations do not just turn up but are deliberately sought out. (Eckstein 1975: 104)

Heuristic case studies do not usually exist in isolation and are likely to be conducted in a series to facilitate theoretical development. Therefore, the *heuristic* case study does not guarantee a theoretical outcome; comparative studies may be more fruitful.

Plausibility probes, Eckstein's fourth type of case study, are used in the intermediate stage between the development of a theory, whether by heuristic case studies or some other means, and the testing of that theory. A plausibility probe attempts to establish whether a theoretical construct is worth considering at all by, perhaps, finding an empirical instance of it. Finally, *crucial-case* studies are similar to crucial experiments; they are designed to challenge an existing theory. If a theory survives a test that is loaded against it, confidence in it will be increased.

In the context of anthropological research, Mitchell has championed the view that case studies are not simply descriptions of the life of these people; they have a theoretical aim: 'we may characterize a case study as a detailed examination of an event (or series of related events) which the analyst believes exhibits (or exhibit) the operation of some identified general theoretical principle' (Mitchell 1983: 192). Therefore, a case study is not just a narrative account of an event or a series of related events; it must also involve analysis against an appropriate theoretical framework, or in support of theoretical conclusions. A case study documents a particular phenomenon or set of events 'which has been assembled with the explicit end in view of drawing theoretical conclusions from it' (Mitchell 1983: 191). Anthropological theory has been built up from many case studies over many years.

Issues associated with the selection of case studies are different when theorizing rather than generalizing is the concern. Here we need to return to logics of social enquiry. As Mitchell and Yin have argued, the concern about the representativeness of case studies is based on a mistaken view of the logic appropriate for case studies. The critics of the case study have operated from the logic of statistical inference appropriate to sample surveys. Instead, a different kind of logic is required to test a theory. A variety of logics have been proposed: 'logical inference' (Mitchell); 'analytic generalization' (Yin); and 'analytic induction' (Lindesmith).

Before exploring these ideas it is worth noting that whereas typical cases may be useful for generalizing, Eckstein (1975); Mitchell (1983); Platt (1988); and Yin (2003a) have argued for the use of extreme, deviant or least likely cases in theory testing. If a general theoretical principle can be shown to hold in these types of cases, the degree of corroboration is stronger than in cases that might be regarded as typical.

Mitchell proposed that *logical inference* rather than statistical inference be used in case study research. '[L]ogical inference is the process by which the analyst draws conclusions about the essential linkage between two or more character-istics in terms of some systematic explanatory schema – some set of theoretical propositions' (Mitchell 1983: 199–200). He argued that detailed knowledge of the context is an important element in the researcher's capacity to draw conclu-sions from a case study.

As we have already seen, Yin (2003a) adopted a similar approach to Mitchell in his proposal for the use of *analytic generalization* as a way of linking cases. He also saw this as a form of theory testing, although in the form of accumulated support rather than critical testing, i.e. he proposed the use of inductive rather than deductive logic.

Platt (1988) also adopted the view that prior theory is necessary. She argued that a case study needs to be located in the context of relevant knowledge and appropriate theory. To strengthen their theoretical role, case studies need to be specifically designed rather than being chosen as a matter of convenience or by accident. She supported the use of induction, and the pattern model of explana-tion, rather than deductive logic.

It has been argued that the theoretical value of case studies is the possibility they afford in uncovering causal processes. Because case studies allow research-ers to get a close and detailed view of social phenomena, it is possible to study directly the processes that lead to change. Connelly (1998), for example, argued that correlations established by quantitative methods can be explained by documenting social processes, and this can lead to the identification of causal mechanism(s). Hence, he approached the use of case studies from a critical realist point of view (my *social realist* paradigm), which requires the use of retroductive logic. However, Hammersley *et al.* (2000) rejected this view and argued for com-parative analysis rather than the use of single cases.

This leads us to a form of logic that shares much in common with the trial and error process used in the Deductive research strategy and is known as *analytic induction*. It was developed and used by Znaniecki (1934); Lindesmith (1937, 1968); and Cressey (1950). As expounded by Lindesmith (1968), this logic begins with an initial investigation of a few cases, which leads to the formulation of a tentative causal hypothesis to account for the phenomenon. Additional cases are investigated to test this hypothesis, and this may lead to its reformulation. Further cases are examined until revisions of the hypothesis are no longer required. However, the investigation of other cases at a later time, or in other places, may very well lead to further revisions. Burgess has elaborated this logic as follows.

1 Define the phenomenon to be explained.
2 Formulate a hypothetical explanation of the phenomenon.

3 Study one case to see whether the hypothesis relates to the particular case.
4 If the hypothesis does not fit the case, the phenomenon is either reformulated or redefined in order to exclude the particular case.
5 Practical certainty is achieved with a small number of cases, but negative cases disprove the explanation and require a reformulation.
6 The examination of cases, redefinition of the phenomenon and reformulation of hypotheses, is continued until a universal relationship is established. (Burgess 1984: 179)[16]

A major difference between analytic induction and deductive logic is that deductively derived theories have a more tentative status than is implied in the last step above. It is on this point that Robinson (1951) and Turner (1953) have been critical of analytic induction. However, to its credit, it does not rely on the use of single cases to identify causal mechanisms, as proposed by Connelly, but uses the comparison of cases to stimulate theory development.

While supporting the use of the comparative method, Hammersley *et al.* (2000) have been critical of Lindesmith's formulation of it. Amongst other things, they raise the issue of just how hypotheses are tested in Lindesmith's method. There is a danger that additional cases may be selected to provide confirmation rather than severe testing. They also raise some practical difficulties: the problem of selecting cases that provide good tests of a hypothesis; and the large number of cases that may be required. They have suggested that the second point can be ameliorated if researchers work cumulatively by building on each other's work.

Hammersley *et al.* (2000) make an important distinction between case studies that are used to describe and possibly explain features of a case or a set of cases, and those used for theory development and testing. This brings us back to the issue of generalization. Where the focus is only on the case or set of cases themselves, then generalizing is not the issue. However, in theory development and testing, generalizing is involved. The minimum aim is to develop theories that apply to many situations. We should entertain research questions that require us to strive beyond the particulars of single cases to explanations that have some wider application. Hammersley *et al.* appear to concur with this view when they suggested that pragmatic considerations, such as seeking solutions to practical problems, rather than developing coherent theoretical systems, should be given precedence.

Now we are in a position to get to what is usually regarded as the heart of social research, data collection and analysis. However, the choice from among these methods is very dependent on choices made on all the other research design elements discussed so far. It is only in the context of these choices that consideration can be given to the methods of data collection and analysis.

Further Reading

Most social methods texts have a discussion on sampling methods.
Blaikie, N. 2003. *Analyzing Quantitative Data.*
    Chapter 6 has a reasonably technical discussion of sampling and inferential analysis.

Hammersley, M. 1992. *What's Wrong with Ethnography?*
  Chapter 11 provides a readable point of view on case studies.
Kish, L. 1965. *Survey Sampling.*
  A standard and comprehensive text on sampling but is rather technical.
Lewis-Beck, M. S., A. Bryman and T. F. Liao (eds). 2004. *The Sage Encyclopedia of Social Science Research Methods.* Pp. 985–97 in Vol. 3.
  Covers a number of aspects of sampling at an accessible level.
Moser, C. A. and G. Kalton 1971. *Survey Methods in Social Investigation* (2nd edn).
  A classic text with a useful discussion of sampling.
Stake, R. E. 2005. 'Qualitative case studies.'
  A brief and useful overview of the role of case studies in qualitative research.
Yin, R. K. 2003a. *Case Study Research.*
  A classic text on the use of case studies.

7

Methods for Answering Research Questions: Data Gathering and Analysis

Chapter Summary

- The timing of data collection is a fundamental choice in designing social research.
- This leads to social research being classified as *cross-sectional*, *longitudinal* or *historical*.
- The labels 'quantitative' and 'qualitative' should be applied only to data, methods of data collection and analysis, styles of research and researchers; they are inappropriate for classifying research paradigms.
- The distinction between quantitative and qualitative is closely associated with the degree of involvement researchers have with research participants and sites; usually limited in the former and considerable in the latter.
- The most commonly used quantitative methods of data collection are self-administered questionnaires and structured interviews.
- These two methods need to be distinguished as both the format of the instruments and the methods of administration are different.
- The most commonly used qualitative methods include focused and in-depth interviews, and various types of observation (semi-structured, unstructured and participant).
- Data produced by most methods require some manipulation to make them suitable for analysis.
- Depending on the type of data, methods of data reduction include: coding of various kinds; index and scale construction; and other ways of producing categories, factors, clusters and types.
- Quantitative methods of data analysis are of four main types: univariate descriptive, bivariate descriptive, explanatory and inferential.
- When quantitative methods of data collection are used it is necessary to be fully aware of the level(s) of measurement and their consequences for choice of data analysis and type of conclusions that can be drawn.
- Qualitative methods of data analysis include various kinds of description as well as techniques for theory generation.
- Almost all data used in social research begins in the qualitative form and has to be transposed to become quantitative.

- There is no point in perpetuating arguments about the relative merits of quantitative and qualitative research; both types have their uses and limitations.
- The issue of how findings from qualitative research can be generalized to other sites and populations has received considerable attention in recent years.
- While it is possible to generalize quantitative findings from a probability sample to the population from which the sample was drawn, to generalize beyond that population, across time and space, requires the use of similar procedures to those used to generalize qualitative findings, that is, based on evidence of similarities and differences.
- After years of neglect and controversy, the use of mixed methods in social research is gaining popularity.
- Mixed methods research has been classified in various ways, such as: *triangulation* (concurrent use of both quantitative and qualitative methods); *embedded* (one type of method is supplementary to the other); *explanatory* (sequential use with quantitative preceeding qualitative); and *exploratory* (sequential use in the reverse order).
- Care needs to be taken when methods used with incompatible ontological assumptions are to be combined concurrently rather than sequentially.
- Mixed methods research should be seen as a normal and, perhaps, necessary part of knowledge generation rather than as a special type.

Introduction

With research questions in place, one or more research strategies selected, ontological assumptions made explicit, data source and method of selection established, and, if necessary, hypotheses specified, the next step in the development of a research design is to decide how to collect and analyse data to answer the research questions. The kind of data that are considered to be appropriate will depend on a variety of factors. On the one hand, there are methodological considerations that are linked to research strategies, and, on the other hand, there is a range of pragmatic factors that need to be taken into account. These include the nature of the research topic, the research purposes, the kind of research questions being investigated, the context of the research, the expertise and personality of the researcher(s), time and budget considerations, the availability of equipment (including computer hardware and software), and the expectations of funding bodies, clients, colleagues and/or the consumers of the research findings (Smaling 1994).

This chapter covers six main topics.

- The role of timing of data collection in determining the character of a research design.
- Major qualitative and quantitative methods of data collection, reduction and analysis.
- Differences between qualitative and quantitative methods.
- Problems in generalizing from qualitative research.
- The use of mixed methods.
- The relationships between research strategies and research methods.

From simple beginnings about fifty years ago, there is now a vast and complex literature on data gathering and analysis. There is a tendency in some textbooks on research methods to simplify this complexity into a dichotomy of 'quantitative' and 'qualitative' research designs (e.g. Punch 2005; Neuman 2006). However, I believe it is necessary to confine the use of these two concepts to methods of data collection and analysis. This is the approach taken in this chapter.

Timing Data Collection

All social research adopts a position with regard to the timing of data collection (see figure 7.1). In fact, some writers regard time as the critical defining characteristic of all research designs. This appears to stem from classic experimental designs in which variables in experimental and control groups are measured at two points in time, the experimental group having been subjected to some kind of treatment in between. All other designs are seen as variations of this kind of experiment.

There are three basic choices for the social researcher with regard to time. A study may:

- be confined to the present time – *cross-sectional*;
- extend over a period of time – *longitudinal*;
- be confined to the past – *historical*.

Cross-sectional studies

Cross-sectional studies capture a picture of aspects of social life, including: population (demographic) characteristics; individual attitudes, values, beliefs and

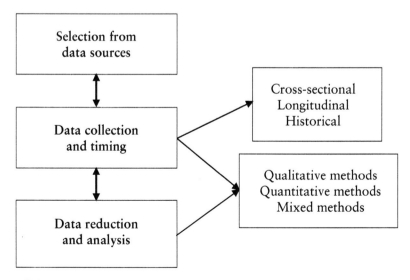

Figure 7.1   Data collection, reduction and analysis

Time Dimension

Cross-sectional
  In the present
Longitudinal
  Before and after
    Impact of an intervention
  Change over time
    Prospective: looking forward
      Time series
      Panel study
      Cohort study
    Retrospective: looking back
Historical
  In the past

behaviour, social interaction; and aspects of social groups, organizations, institutions and structures. However, this type of study is not well suited to research on social processes and social change, as these require the collection of data over time. It also places severe restrictions on achieving the purpose of *explanation*.

Longitudinal studies

Some longitudinal studies involve only two points in time and are referred to as *before-and-after* designs. A common example is the study of social change, which may involve nothing more than two cross-sectional studies at different points in time. Other longitudinal studies involve a number of points in time, or a series of cross-sectional studies on the same or a similar population or group. There are three variations, all of which can be regarded as *prospective* studies as they begin in the present and plan further stages in the future. The first is referred to as *time series* research. For example, a study may be done at different points of time with people who happen to be living in a particular street. The situation remains constant although there may be some changes in the residents. The second, a *panel* study, involves contact with the same people, group or organization over a period of time. A variation of the panel study is *cohort analysis* in which the same categories of people, rather than the same individuals, are studied over time. A cohort is defined in terms of a specific criterion that identifies people who have had similar life experiences due to having had a critical life event in common. Examples of cohorts include people who were born in the same year (birth cohorts), who are in the same year in educational institutions, or who joined or left an organization at around the same time.

Each of these three variations has its advantages and disadvantages. *Panel* studies may be the ideal but are expensive. There is also the constant difficulty of keeping track of the members and dealing with the fact that people will drop out for various reasons. *Cohort* designs are easier to conduct, but their results are less powerful. *Time series* designs are different from the other two. *Panel* studies track the changes in a sample or group of people over time, while a *time series* study may be more concerned with the changing effects over time on people who have some circumstances in common. Therefore, *cohort* and *time series* studies are compromises on *panel* studies; the first two avoid the complex and expensive process of keeping track of people, but have to sacrifice some ability to draw reliable conclusions.

Retrospective studies take the present as a base and seek information about recent history. A common form of this research, oral and life histories, gets people who lived through a particular period to recall those experiences, or uses the traces that such people have left behind, such as diaries. There are clearly some limitations to this kind of research as memory is fallible and its use always involves a possible reconstruction of the past under the influence of subsequent experiences.

Historical studies

By definition, historical studies deal with social events or phenomena in the past. Such studies are very different in character to those that can collect data about and from people in the present. While historical studies may seek information about the past from people who have lived through a particular time period, or who have known people who have, data normally have to come from written records of some kind, or from other traces of past social activity. When a researcher's concerns are essentially in the present, it is usually necessary or desirable to locate the experiences of contemporary individuals, and social events and processes, in some kind of historical context. Hence, depending on the nature of the research topic and research questions, research in the present may need to be linked to the past.

Combinations

Research can be made up of a combination of these approaches to the time dimension. For example, a *cross-sectional* study conducted today can become a *longitudinal* study if it is replicated, say, in five years' time. A *retrospective* or a *prospective* study can be used in combination with a *cross-sectional* study to produce a *longitudinal* study. Also, a *historical* study can be either *cross-sectional* or *longitudinal*.

It follows that research design choices related to the time dimension will be determined largely by the purposes of the study and the type of research questions to be answered. Some purposes and research questions can be pursued successfully using a *cross-sectional* study, whereas others, ideally, require *longitudinal* research. While *exploratory* and *descriptive* studies are likely to be concerned with the present, longitudinal description is certainly a legitimate research activity. Similarly, while the purposes of *explanation* and *understanding* may be more easily achieved in *longitudinal* research, the potential costs involved may lead to the common compromise of trying to do this using *cross-sectional* research. The applied purposes of *change* and *evaluation*, and their associated research questions, might also be better achieved in a *longitudinal* study. However, the tension between achieving the ideal research design to answer the research questions, and the costs involved in doing so, is ever present at the research design stage. *Longitudinal* studies are usually more costly than *cross-sectional* studies. Hence, the time dimension is a critical research design consideration.

A dilemma

A typical dilemma for researchers is how to answer research questions that deal with the passage of time using only a *cross-sectional* study. For example, we may be interested in the effect on students of exposure to a particular three-year educational programme. One method would be to follow a cohort of students over the three years, making measurements of their position on relevant variables at the beginning and end of the programme and, possibly, at intervals in between. However, if the programme has been in operation for at least three years, a compromise would be to measure these variables at one time for each year cohort of students, and see if they differ. This is a compromise as it lacks random assignment to each year cohort. It also lacks controls for the fact that each cohort enters the programme, and passes through the three years, over a different time period, thus making it possible that its members have been subjected to the influence of different social conditions. Nevertheless, versions of this compromise are commonly used, and the passage of time is dealt with statistically.

Qualitative and Quantitative Methods

It has become common practice to divide research methods into two broad types, *quantitative* and *qualitative*. However, the concepts have also been used to contrast five different aspects of the social research enterprise:

- *methods*, that cover the techniques of data collection and analysis;
- *data*, that are produced by particular types of methods;
- *research*, in which particular types of methods are used;
- *researchers*, who use particular methods; and
- *research paradigms* or perspectives that adopt different ontological and epistemological assumptions.

The first four aspects are closely related; a method produces a particular form of data, and research and researchers are related to the use of particular methods. The association of the concepts of qualitative and quantitative with research paradigms is distinctive and different. However, I regard the elevation of a distinction between types of data to the level of a research paradigm as being unhelpful and inappropriate (see also Guba and Lincoln 2005).

As we saw in chapter 6, when the quantitative/qualitative distinction is associated with data, the contrast is usually between data in numbers and words. Data, both at their source, and during and following analysis, can be produced in either form. In studies commonly labelled as quantitative, data are collected in numbers, or are very soon converted into them, and are subsequently analysed and reported in the same form. In qualitative studies, the original data are produced in one of two languages, the technical language of the researcher or the everyday language of the respondents. These languages are used to describe behaviour, social relationships, social processes, social situations, and, in particular, the meanings people give to their activities, the activities of others, and to objects and social contexts. Qualitative analysis, which may occur in conjunction with data collection, and the reporting of results from this analysis, can involve the use of both languages.

Quantitative methods are generally concerned with counting and measuring aspects of social life, while qualitative methods are more concerned with producing discursive descriptions and exploring social actors' meanings and interpretations. While it is convenient to classify research methods as *qualitative* and *quantitative*, and I do this in the first part of this chapter, there is a growing body of literature that has questioned the legitimacy of this dichotomy. These arguments are reviewed later in the chapter.

Data Collection Methods

As there are countless books that describe the nature and use of social research methods, no attempt will be made to provide details. The list in the box below is only intended to be indicative of the common methods used in both quantitative and qualitative research. Many refinements have been made to this classification.

Quantitative data collection methods

The most commonly used quantitative data-gathering methods in the social sciences are undoubtedly the self-administered *questionnaire* and the *structured interview*, both of which keep the researcher at a distance from actual social processes. There is a great deal of confusion, particularly in the popular literature, about the way these two methods are identified. The commonest practice is not to distinguish between them, and, therefore, to assume that they are identical. Sometimes 'survey' will be used to refer to questionnaires, and questionnaires are seen to be used in structured interviews. De Vaus (2002) used 'questionnaire' as the generic term and then distinguished between face-to-face, telephone, postal self-administered and internet as different methods of administration. On the other hand, Oppenheim (1992) made the distinction between 'standardized interview' and 'questionnaire' very clear.

As the processes by which data are collected differ in important ways, I believe that it is necessary to distinguish between these two methods. The formats of the instruments are different and they have their own particular advantages and disadvantages. Questionnaires have to be prepared in such a way that respondents can complete them without any assistance other than built-in and/or separate written instructions. An interview schedule, on the other hand, will usually contain instructions to the interviewer, and the interviewer will provide other instructions to the respondent. Samples of an interview schedule and a questionnaire format can be found in Smith (1981: appendices C and D). There are a number of

Data Collection Methods

Quantitative
  Questionnaire (self-administered)
  Structured interview
  Observation: structured
  Content analysis of documents
Qualitative
  Participant observation
  Observation: semi-structured and unstructured
  Focused interview
  In-depth interview
  Oral/Life histories
  Focus groups/Group interviews
  Content analysis of documents

discussions in the literature on the strengths and weaknesses of both methods (see e.g. Groves and Kahn 1979; Oppenheim 1992; de Vaus 2002).

The use of *structured observation* is much less common and is confined largely to experiments and observational studies in artificial settings. Examples of the former would be observing the response of individuals to periods of social isolation, or their reaction to an authority figure acting in an aggressive manner. Examples of the latter would be observing a group of children at play, or applicants for a leadership position undertaking a problem-solving task. In both cases, video recording may be used, but all this means is that the numerical coding of the behaviour can be delayed and the 'original' data revisited. Structured observation may be combined with other methods of data collection, such as the structured interview.

Quantitative methods of data collection require a choice between four different levels of measurement: *nominal, ordinal, interval* and *ratio*. The most basic level is *nominal* measurement in which objects, events or people are assigned to categories in terms of their shared characteristics. Categories are identified by an arbitrary number or symbol and have no intrinsic order. The next level is *ordinal*. The same conditions as nominal level apply, with the addition that the categories *are* ordered along a continuum. However, the intervals between the categories need not be equal. The third level is *interval* in which the category intervals *are* equal. This allows for much more sophisticated mathematical manipulation than is possible in either nominal or ordinal measurement. Nevertheless, as such measures have an arbitrary zero, as occurs in attitude scales, a few manipulations cannot be undertaken. The highest level of measurement, *ratio*, adds an absolute zero to interval level measurement, and, therefore, allows for any kind of mathematical manipulation. The level of measurement used has an irrevocable influence on the choice of data analysis methods; the lower the level of measurement the less sophisticated the analysis, and *vice versa*. While it is possible to reduce higher levels of measurement to lower levels, the reverse is not possible. (See Blaikie 2003: 22–28) Examples of the levels of measurement can be found in the sample research designs in chapter 8.

Qualitative data collection methods

Some form of *participant observation* is regarded as the qualitative method *par excellence*. It involves a researcher in one or more periods of sustained immersion in the life of the people being studied (see e.g.. Spradley 1980; Jorgensen 1989). This method is commonly referred to as 'field research' (Burgess 1984) or 'ethnography' (Fetterman 1989; Atkinson 1990; Atkinson *et al.* 2001; Bryman 2001; Hammersley and Atkinson 2007). Ethnography literally means producing a picture of the way of life of some group. Field research or ethnography involves a combination of methods of which participant observation may be the main one.

Participant observation can be practised in a variety of ways, ranging from total participation (e.g. Whyte 1943) to mainly observation, and various combinations in between. It is not uncommon for a researcher to use both extremes as well as some combination in the same study (e.g. Gans 1967). Therefore, participant observation is not a single method, and it can combine different styles of observation (Bryman 1988: 47–9).

Contemporary social science is more likely to collect qualitative data by using some form of unstructured or semi-structured *interviewing*, in-depth, focused or group, rather than participant observation (see e.g. Spradley 1979; McCracken 1990; Minichiello *et al.* 2008). Just as with structured interviews, any form of qualitative interview keeps the researcher removed from the natural setting; individual behaviour and social interaction will be reported rather than observed. However, the qualitative interview, particularly the in-depth variety, can get close to the social actors' meanings and interpretations, to their accounts of the social interaction in which they have been involved. Interviewing, in combination with reasonably extensive observation of actual social situations, provides a useful alternative to participant observation.

A special use of unstructured interviewing is *oral history*. One or more individuals are asked to recount aspects of their lives and/or the lives of their contemporaries, and to discuss their perceptions of the processes involved and the changes they have seen (see e.g. Thomas and Znaniecki 1927; Douglas *et al.* 1988; Yow 1994; Ritchie 1995; Perks and Thomson 2006). The personal stories produced by this method can either stand on their own, or can be subjected to some type of qualitative analysis. A related method, but one that works with very different data, is the *life history* (Bertaux 1981; Miller 2000; Plummer 2001a, 2001b; Bornat 2004). In this case, secondary rather than primary data are used to reconstruct the lives of individuals, and, perhaps, to produce an account of a particular historical period from the participant's experience of it. Diaries and autobiographies are the major sources.

Group interviews or discussion, or what is increasingly referred to as *focus groups*, are gaining popularity as a method of data collection (e.g. Krueger 1988; Morgan 1988, 2000; Berg 1995; Kamberelis and Dimitriadis 2005; Stewart *et al.* 2007). Focus groups, which are frequently used in marketing research, have been adapted to more traditional social research, particularly evaluation research. Their purpose is different from that of individual interviews. They allow for group interaction and provide greater insight into why certain opinions are held. Krueger has defined the focus group as 'a carefully planned discussion designed to obtain perceptions on a defined area of interest in a permissive, non-threatening environment' (1988: 18). The assumption is that people become more aware of, and can reflect on, their ideas and assumptions by being confronted with contrary views (Millward 2007).

Documents as a data source can be used differently in conjunction with either quantitative or qualitative methods. Textual material can be treated quantitatively by being coded into categories that are assigned numbers, counted and manipulated statistically. Alternatively, they can be treated qualitatively as identifying phenomena among which connections are established. The ontological assumptions involved, and the end products in these two practices, tend to be different.

Compared with quantitative techniques, and if used diligently, most qualitative methods are relatively time-consuming. This is no doubt a major reason for the attractiveness of quantitative methods, as well as their greater manageability and predictability in terms of outcomes. I have long suspected that each group of methods attracts different kinds of personalities, with level of comfort in being close to people an important factor.

Data Reduction Methods

Data produced by most methods of collection require some manipulation to get them into a suitable form for analysis, using what is commonly referred to as data reduction techniques. This process is most obvious when the analysis is quantitative. Much less work is involved if coding frames are established before the data are collected, such as in questionnaires and structured interview schedules. However, even in these cases, some reorganization of the coding categories, for example, changing the order or combining categories, will usually be required. If the data are recorded in a non-numerical form, such as in open-ended questions, the establishment of a set of coding categories will be necessary after the data are collected (see e.g. Oppenheim 1992; de Vaus 2002: ch. 9).

Data Reduction Methods

Quantitative
  Coding: pre-coding and post-coding
  Index construction
  Scaling: e.g., Likert and Guttman
  Factor analysis
  Cluster analysis
Qualitative
  Coding: open and axial coding
  Developing themes
  Typology construction

It is also possible to combine answers to a number of questions into a composite measure, such as an *index* or a *scale*. The major difference between them is that scales usually involve a demonstration of unidimensionality while an index does not (see e.g. McIver and Carmines 1981; de Vaus 2002: ch. 11).[1] Guttman scaling, factor analysis and cluster analysis are alternative and sophisticated ways of establishing unidimensionality, each one being based on different assumptions (see e.g. Stouffer *et al.* 1950; Lorr 1983; Oppenheim 1992; Lewis-Beck 1994). Simpler methods, such as item analysis, involve an assessment of the degree to which responses to a statement or item in a scale are correlated with the sum of responses to all statements or items (see Cronbach 1990). Factor analysis and cluster analysis are also used in data reduction.

Data reduction techniques are commonly used with qualitative methods, for example, open and axial coding in grounded theory, and typology construction in the Abductive research strategy. However, in these cases, it is impossible to separate data reduction and analysis; in fact, data collection, data reduction and data analysis can blend into one another in a cyclical process (see, e. g. Eckett 1988; Minichiello *et al.* 2008).

Data Analysis Methods

All that will be attempted here is to provide a brief overview of a range of commonly used quantitative and qualitative techniques. Techniques of quantitative analysis are well developed and very diverse. In contrast, however, techniques of qualitative analysis are still evolving.

Quantitative data analysis methods

Quantitative methods of analysis fall into four main categories: univariate descriptive, bivariate descriptive, explanatory, and inferential (see Blaikie 2003). *Univariate descriptive* methods focus on single variables and are used to report the distributions of a sample or population (using all four levels of measurement), and to produce summary measures of the characteristics of such distributions. These summary measures include: frequency counts (which can also be represented graphically); measures of central tendency (such as mode, median and mean, depending on the level of measurement); and measures of the dispersion of a distribution (such as the interquartile range and standard deviation).

Data Analysis Methods

Quantitative
Descriptive (univariate)
  Distribution: numerical and graphical
  Central tendency and dispersion
Descriptive (bivariate)
  Correlation: simple, partial and multiple
  Analysis of variance and covariance
  Regression: simple, partial and multiple
Explanatory
  Factor analysis
  Path analysis
  Regression: simple, partial and multiple
Inferential
  Sample statistic to population parameter
  Sample differences to population differences
Qualitative
Descriptive
Theory generation
  Analytic induction
  Grounded theory: open and axial coding
  Categorizing and connecting
  From everyday typifications to typologies

Bivariate descriptive methods are used to establish the degree to which two variables covary, that is, whether positions on one variable are likely to be consistently associated with positions on another variable. An example is the extent to which people with high levels of education also have high-status occupations and vice versa. The way in which association is established depends on the level or levels of measurement involved and whether there are two or more than two variables being analysed.

In order to answer 'why' questions with cross-sectional quantitative data, it is necessary to establish the influence of one or more independent variables on a dependent variable. There are three popular methods for doing this: factor analysis, path analysis and regression, the latter being the contemporary favourite. The aim in this kind of analysis is to deal with a set or network of relationships in the hope that causation can be demonstrated.

Inferential analysis is used for two purposes: to make estimates of population characteristics (parameters) from sample characteristics (statistics); and to establish whether differences or relationships within a sample (such as an association between education and occupation) can be expected to exist, other than by chance, in the population from which the sample was drawn. It is for these purposes that *tests of significance* are used (see the discussion in chapter 6).

Qualitative data analysis methods

As a result of the growing popularity of qualitative research over recent decades, the literature on methods of qualitative data analysis has expanded considerably (see e.g. Glaser and Strauss 1967; Lofland 1971; Turner 1981, 1994; Martin and Turner 1986; Richards and Richards 1987, 1991, 1994; Dey 1993; Miles and Huberman 1994; Bryman and Burgess 1994; Kelle 1995, 2004; Coffey and Atkinson 1996; Ryan and Bernard 2000; Silverman 2001; Morse and Richards 2002; Northcutt and McCoy 2004; Corbin and Strauss 2008). While there is no one dominant method, various versions of grounded theory have become popular, particularly as software, such as, Ethnograph, NVivo, ATLAS.ti and MAXQDA, is now available to aid the process (see e.g. Seidel and Clark 1984; Richards and Richards 1987, 1991, 1994; Pfaffenberger 1988; Tesch 1990; Fielding and Lee 1991, 1998; Miles and Huberman 1994; Coffey and Atkinson 1996; Weitzman 2000; Fielding 2001; Seale 2002, 2005; Kelle 2004; Lewins and Silver 2007).

We noted in chapter 6 that *analytic induction* has been used in association with case studies as a logic for theory development. While data from such case studies can be either qualitative or quantitative, it is commonly the former. The advocates of grounded theory have argued for the use of the constant comparative method as being superior to analytic induction (Glaser and Strauss 1967: 101–13). Analytic induction refines an initial hypothesis while in grounded theory and its variants, an ongoing process of data collection and data analysis is used to construct new theories from data.

Turner (1981) has systemized grounded theory into a sequence of nine stages, although it is clear that these refer to a developmental process rather than linear steps.

1 After some exposure to the field setting and some collection of data, the researcher starts to develop 'categories' which illuminate and fit the data well.
2 The categories are then 'saturated', meaning that further instances of the categories are gathered until the researcher is confident about the relevance and range of the categories for the research setting. There is recognition in the idea of 'saturation' that further search for appropriate instances may become a superfluous exercise.
3 The researcher then seeks to abstract a more general formulation of the category, as well as specifying the criteria for inclusion in the category.
4 These more general definitions then act as a guide for the researcher, as well as stimulating further theoretical reflection. This stage may prompt the researcher to think of further instances which may be subsumed under the more general definition of the category.
5 The researcher should be sensitive to the connections between the emerging general categories and other milieu in which the categories may be relevant. For example, can categories relating to the dying in hospital (Glaser and Strauss's main research focus) be extended to encapsulate other social settings?
6 The researcher may become increasingly aware of the connections between categories developed in the previous stage, and will seek to develop hypotheses about such links.

7 The researcher should then seek to establish the conditions in which these connections pertain.

8 At this point, the researcher should explore the implications of the emerging theoretical framework for other, pre-existing theoretical schemes which are relevant to the substantive area.

9 The researcher may then seek to test the emerging relationships among categories under extreme conditions to test the validity of the posited connection. (Turner 1981, as summarized by Bryman 1988: 83–4)

The central activity in qualitative data analysis is a special kind of coding. Such coding can facilitate description, but it is also used for analysis and theory generation. Coding in grounded theory involves the use of concepts (labels placed on discrete happenings, events, and other instances of phenomena) and categories (a more abstract notion under which concepts are grouped together). The coding process involves two stages. The first, known as *open coding*, involves breaking the data down into categories and sub-categories; 'Breaking data apart and delineating concepts to stand for blocks of raw data' (Corbin and Strauss 2008: 195). Axial coding is done by using a 'coding paradigm' that involves thinking about possible causal conditions, contexts, intervening conditions, action/interaction strategies used to respond to a phenomenon in its context, and the possible consequences of action/interaction not occurring. A core category is then selected and a descriptive narrative constructed about it (Corbin and Strauss 2008).

Dey (1993) has formulated this type of coding as a circular or spiral process involving three activities: describing, classifying and connecting. The first step is to produce 'thick' or 'thorough' *descriptions* of the phenomenon being studied (Geertz 1973; Denzin 1978). 'Thin' description merely states 'facts', while 'thick' description includes the context of the action, the intentions of the social actors, and the processes through which social action and interaction are sustained and/or changed. The next part of the process, *classifying*, refers to open and axial coding of grounded theory. In the same way, he has argued that classifying data is an integral part of the analysis and without this there is no way of knowing what is being analysed. Classification is achieved by creating categories, assigning categories to the data, and splitting and splicing categories.

Classification is a conceptual process. When we classify, we do two things. We don't just break the data into bits, we also assign these bits to categories or classes which bring these bits together again, if in a novel way. Thus all the bits that 'belong' to a particular category are brought together, and in the process, we begin to discriminate more clearly between the criteria for allocating data to one category or another. Then some categories may be subdivided, and others subsumed under more abstract categories. The boundaries between these categories may be defined more precisely. Logic may require the addition of new categories, not present in the data, to produce a comprehensive classification. Thus the process of classifying the data is already creating a conceptual framework through which the bits of data can be brought together again in an analytically useful way. (Dey 1993: 44–5)

Classification is not a neutral process; the researcher will have a purpose in mind that will provide direction and boundaries.

The third part of the process is making *connections* between categories. The aim is to discover regularities, variations and singularities in the data and thus to begin to construct theories. Following Sayer (1992), Dey has distinguished between formal and substantive relations. Formal relations are concerned with similarities and differences while substantive relations are concerned with how things interact (1993: 152).

Methods of qualitative analysis differ in the extent to which they attempt to 'retain the integrity of the phenomenon'. That is, the extent to which researchers remain close to the language, the concepts and meanings of the social actors rather than imposing their own concepts and categories on lay accounts. There is a choice between a *high* stance, in which the researcher imposes concepts and meanings, and a *low* stance, in which the researcher derives concepts and meanings from lay language. In its purest form, the Abductive research strategy involves a *low* stance because it develops technical concepts and theoretical propositions from accounts provided in lay language (see chapter 4). Technical concepts generated in this way are designed to be more abstract and generalizable than is possible with lay concepts.

Mainstream grounded theory, on the other hand, is much more a process of a researcher 'inventing' and imposing concepts on the data; it adopts a *high* stance. The various forms of coding are a search for technical concepts that will organize and make sense of the data. While these concepts can be either those that are already in use, or can be developed by a researcher for a particular purpose, there appears to be little attempt to derive them from lay concepts, to make use of lay meanings associated with the concepts, or to tie them to lay concepts. For this reason, grounded theory uses inductive rather than abductive logic.

Another major variation in qualitative analysis is whether the researcher is satisfied with description, or whether the goal is the development of theory. There is, however, no clear divide between these two activities. Some would argue that description is all that a researcher can legitimately do; others would argue that description, particularly 'thick' description, already provides understanding and possibly explanation, and that nothing more is needed, while others seek to develop 'bottom-up' theories consisting of testable propositions (Hammersley 1985). For grounded theorists, the testing of these theoretical propositions is tied intimately to the process of their generation. Others may be willing to subject their theories to independent post-testing, although this may consist of examining the relevance of the theory in other contexts, still using 'bottom-up' techniques rather than the formal testing that is advocated by the Deductive research strategy. Researchers interested in combining research strategies, and qualitative and quantitative methods, may develop their theory by some kind of grounded method and then test it deductively using quantitative methods. Clearly there is a range of possibilities here, and if qualitative methods are used, a decision has to be made as to what will constitute *understanding* or *explanation*, and how these will be developed and tested.

There is as yet no clearly articulated method for using the pure version of the Abductive research strategy as advocated by Schütz and Giddens. I began working on this in the 1970s (Blaikie 1974) and committed some preliminary ideas to paper about ten years later (Blaikie and Stacy 1982; 1984). Over the years, a number of my postgraduate students have successfully used versions of it in a variety of studies (Kelsen 1981; Stacy 1983; Drysdale 1985; Balnaves 1990; Smith 1995; Priest 1997; Ong 2005) and other students and colleagues have worked with it (e.g. Drysdale 1996; Priest 2000).

Differences between Quantitative and Qualitative Methods

For decades now, there has been considerable debate about the relative merits of quantitative and qualitative methods, with the protagonists invariably adopting tactics to bolster their own position and denigrate that of the 'opposition'. Quantitative researchers have adopted the methodological high ground and qualitative researchers have been seen by them as the troublesome but largely irrelevant sect. Qualitative researchers have tended to struggle under the shadow of this dominant orthodoxy and have had to be content with much lower levels of funding for their research.[2]

These debates have been conducted in terms of various contrasts in purpose and style, and have produced a slate of pejorative terms used to defend preferred methods and to abuse other methods. Fortunately, in recent years these prejudices have receded to disciplines such as economics and mainstream psychology, and no longer dominate sociology. Social researchers have become more eclectic in their choice of methods.[3]

Almost all data used by social researchers begins in a qualitative form. It is only after work has been done on it, to transpose words into numbers, that quantitative data come into being. 'We can regard all of the information which we acquire about the world as qualitative, and then see that under some circumstances we can use this information to create a particular kind of data, quantitative data, to which the properties of number can be applied' (Turner 1994: 195). Halfpenny (1996) has argued that in spite of the surface differences between words and numbers, quantitative and qualitative data are not fundamentally different.

> Quantitative data is usually produced by coding some other data, which is reduced to a number by stripping off the context and removing content from it. Later, after manipulating the numbers, they are interpreted, that is, expanded by adding content and context which enable one to see through the numerical tokens back to the social world. (Halfpenny 1996: 5)

It is the order and power offered by numerical analysis that have made quantified information so attractive and led qualitative information to be treated with suspicion. However, for quantitative data to achieve these apparent advantages, it is necessary to assume that the properties of a number system correspond to some features of the original data.

> A moment's reflection will reveal to us that, even where the use of numerical analysis seems most self-evident, to use it we need to make certain working assumptions.

We may regularly count apples or sheep or pounds sterling. But every apple, every animal, is unique. When we count, we merely agree, tacitly, that for this everyday purpose, we are willing to apply rules which disregard the differences between individual apples or individual sheep, and which stress their similarities for numbering purposes. (Turner 1994: 195)

When quantitative methods are used, a researcher is likely to have very limited or possibly no contact with the people being studied. The use of some quantitative methods, such as mailed questionnaires, structured observation, and unobtrusive methods that involve the use of secondary data, require no face-to-face or verbal contact at all. When there is contact, such as in structured interviewing and experiments, it is formal and of limited duration. However, even in these cases, the researcher may have no contact if assistants are employed to carry out these tasks. This maintenance of distance from the people being studied, and the fanatical resistance to any form of personal disclosure or emotional involvement by the researcher, is largely practised in the belief that it will ensure that objectivity is achieved. What constitutes objectivity, and why it must be achieved, is, of course, related to the epistemological assumptions (probably from either Positivism or Critical Rationalism) which the researcher has explicitly or implicitly adopted.

On the other hand, the use of qualitative methods usually requires an extended and/or intensive period of involvement in some social world. The most extreme form is participant observation in which a researcher can become fully immersed in the social actors' world with all the levels of personal involvement that this entails. Such qualitative methods allow a researcher to become an 'insider' and to discover the social actors' culture and worldviews.

The contact and involvement in in-depth, unstructured interviewing lies somewhere between participant observation and structured interviewing, and will involve varying degrees of personal involvement and disclosure on the part of the researcher. When a series of in-depth interviews is conducted with the same person, the level of involvement is likely to be higher. Rather than attempt to adopt the position of a detached 'scientific' observer, qualitative researchers may deliberately choose to 'go native'; to allow themselves to become part of the world of the researched and be seduced by the social actors' constructed reality. Some would argue that, without a period of immersion in a social world, no adequate understanding of it can be achieved. While it is probably not possible for a researcher to go completely native, a test of whether the social actors' meanings have been 'discovered' is dependent on the researcher being able to interact with the research participants successfully. To achieve this, it is necessary to become as subjective as possible rather than to try to adopt some kind of objective stance, at least at the data collection stage.

An important feature of the use of quantitative methods is their highly structured nature. They are usually located within a research design that includes a set of predetermined stages, and the data gathering will be accomplished by the use of predetermined procedures and pre-tested instruments. In using such methods, a researcher aims for maximum control over the data gathering and the achievement of uniformity in the application of the techniques. Usually, it is only after data are collected that analysis will begin. The main justification for uniformity, control and rigid stages is to achieve some notion of objectivity and replicability. In my experience, quantitative methods tend to be used by researchers who prefer order, predictability and security, and who have a low level of tolerance for uncertainty and ambiguity.

This contrasts with the use of qualitative methods in which the procedures are much more open and flexible. Frequently, qualitative researchers have a very limited idea of where they should start, how they should proceed, and where they expect to end up. They have to accept opportunities when they open up and they will want to follow leads as they occur. They see research as a learning process and themselves as the measuring (data-absorbing) instrument. They will want to allow concepts, ideas and theories to evolve and they will resist imposing both preconceived ideas on everyday reality and closure on the emerging understanding. Qualitative data gathering is messy and unpredictable and seems to require researchers who can tolerate ambiguity, complexity, uncertainty and lack of control.

Bryman (1988) has identified the preoccupations of quantitative and qualitative researchers. Quantitative researchers are preoccupied with:

- measuring concepts;
- establishing causality;
- generalizing;
- replicating; and
- focusing in individuals.

In contrast, qualitative researchers are concerned with:

- using social actors' point of view;
- describing thickly;
- focusing on social processes;
- adopting a flexible approach; and
- developing concepts and theory.

While studies are frequently classified as being either quantitative or qualitative, some use both kinds of data. Quantitative studies may collect some data in words (e.g. open-ended questions in a survey, or text on which content analysis is to be undertaken). By means of some coding process, these data are transformed into a numerical form. Similarly, some qualitative studies may produce simple tables of frequencies and percentages to summarize some features of non-numerical data. Such counting in qualitative research can provide support for the representativeness of certain features within a social group or category.

Researchers who are wedded to quantitative methods may also use qualitative methods. However, the role that is given to the latter is usually different to that adopted by researchers who regard them as their primary or only methods. Qualitative methods may be used by quantitative researchers in an exploratory stage to suggest hypotheses or to facilitate the development of research instruments. Qualitative methods are viewed as being supplementary to quantitative methods. The range of qualitative methods used is likely to be limited to those that come closest to quantitative methods, for example semi-structured interviews or observation. I have come across some quantitative researchers who regard open-ended questions in a mainly structured questionnaire as constituting qualitative data gathering. The fact that the questions are in the researcher's language, and that the method used to code the responses is devised by the researcher, makes it a very different kind of data collection to the more traditional use of qualitative methods.

Quantitative and qualitative researchers have different methods for achieving rigour in their research. Traditionally, the former have focused on establishing the 'validity' and 'reliability' of their measurements; that their instruments measure what they claim to measure and that they do so consistently. An examination of the methods by which validity and reliability are established, reveals that they involve corroboration and replication. However, there are no ultimate standards against which a measuring instrument can be compared; there are only well-used instruments about which communities of researchers have a high degree of confidence. Objectivity is always relative.

The character of qualitative data makes corroboration and replication more difficult, some would say impossible. The qualitative researcher is usually the measuring instrument and no two instruments are the same. If you were to conduct in-depth interviews with twenty people about their working life, you may discover three different types of work orientations. Clearly, it would be difficult for me or others to then interview these same people. However, we could interview samples of people from the same population. Even if you and I have agreed ahead of time to discuss the same topics, your conversations with your sample may be different from those I had with my sample, and similarly for other interviewers. We may end up with a variety of typologies, and, if we happened to agree on the types, there may be differences in their descriptions. However, this is not to suggest that one of us has produced the correct account and the other is wrong. Hopefully, we accurately reported what *we* learnt from *our* sample of people.

Qualitative researchers are rather divided on the need to establish the authenticity of their findings. Some would argue that researchers produce their unique accounts and that corroboration or replication is impossible. They would claim that if they have acted professionally, and have explained how they went about their research, their accounts should be trusted. Other qualitative researchers have argued that the social actors concerned must corroborate any account that a researcher gives of social life. In other words, the researcher's account must correspond closely to social actors' accounts. (See Blaikie 2007 for a discussion of this issue.)

Generalizing in Qualitative Research

Many of the issues raised in the previous chapter about generalizing and theorizing from case studies are echoed in discussions about the possibility of generalizing from studies that use qualitative methods. As indicated earlier, case studies can use any kind of method for data collection and analysis; they are not restricted to qualitative methods. However, the use of qualitative methods in any kind of research poses a similar set of problems; combine case studies and qualitative methods and the problems are exacerbated.

For a start, the kind of generalizing that is available to quantitative researchers is not available to qualitative researchers. As probability sampling is not a usual feature of qualitative research, methods of statistical inference cannot be used. In addition, many qualitative researchers have given generalization low priority, and some have explicitly rejected any form of context-free generalization as a goal (e.g. Guba and Lincoln 1981, 1982; Denzin 1983). Also, the idea of replicating previous studies, a goal of much experimental and survey research, is usually regarded as being inappropriate in qualitative research. The reflexive character of qualitative research means that individual researchers inevitably inject something of themselves into the research process and, hence, into the outcomes. In addition, social situations are never sufficiently similar, across space and time, to make replication possible. Hence, it is argued, replication is inappropriate. Studies conducted by different researchers, in different locations, and at different times, will be unique because of the particular characteristics of the researcher and the researched, their effects on each other, and the hermeneutic processes involved in the production of the researcher's account (see Blaikie 2007). 'The goal is *not* to produce a standardized set of results that any other careful researcher in the same situation or studying the same issues would have produced. Rather it is to produce a coherent and illuminating description of and perspective on a situation that is based on and consistent with detailed study of that situation' (Schofield 1993: 202). In contrast, quantitative researchers generally believe that their methods, and the application of them, can control for any possible researcher influence; they also ignore or try to eliminate the hermeneutic processes; and they tend to assume that time and space do not pose insurmountable limitations.

In recent years, there has been a marked increase in interest in the issue of generalizability among qualitative researchers, particularly in educational research where qualitative methods are now used extensively in evaluation studies. Agencies that fund this type of research are usually interested in its relevance beyond the site in which it was conducted, and ethnographic researchers in education are also likely to want their research to have wider relevance.

How can generalization be achieved in qualitative research? Answers to this question are mainly confined to generalizing from one research site to some other site or population. The aim is to make statements about this other location on the basis of the research results. As we have seen in the previous discussion of generalizing from case studies, a number of answers were offered that are relevant here (see e.g. Stake 1978; Bassey 1981; Guba and Lincoln 1981, 1982; Goetz and LeCompte 1984; Gomm *et al.* 2000b). Some of these suggestions require detailed descriptions of both the site in which a study is conducted and the sites about which generalizations are to be made. Similarities and differences can then be taken into account in any judgement about the relevance of findings obtained from one site for some other sites (Schofield 1993: 207). The aim in such comparisons is to establish whether the research site is typical of other sites. Attempts are made to generalize across time as well as across research sites. Hence, a researcher may wish to make a judgement about whether the findings from a particular site will also hold in the future at the same site as well as at the same or other times at other sites (Hammersley 1992: 87).

Now let us turn this discussion on its head and tie it back to sampling issues discussed in the previous chapter. It is a mistaken belief that problems of generalizing are confined to case-study research and the use of qualitative methods. Rather, statistical generalization is only possible when probability sampling is used, and then only to the population from which the sample was drawn. While some populations may be large, for example in national studies, they can also be very limited in size, for example an organization. Once sample results are statistically generalized to the population, the problem still remains as to whether the findings about this population can be generalized to other populations or to other social contexts, such as other organizations or countries. Therefore, if a researcher wishes to generalize beyond a population, whether or not sampling is used, issues concerning the selection of the population are similar to those in the selection of case studies and of research sites in ethnographic research. There are only limited advantages in using samples and quantitative methods when it comes to wider generalization, as the scope of statistical generalization is limited to the population selected. Beyond that population, the problems and their solutions are the same, regardless of whether quantitative or qualitative methods are used.

Mixed Methods

The use of mixed methods involves the collection, analysis and mixing of both quantitative and qualitative data in a single study or a series of studies (Creswell and Plano Clark 2007: 6, 168). Some writers have gone so far as to suggest that mixed methods constitute a third methodological movement, with quantitative and qualitative research being the other two (Teddlie and Tashakkori 2003; Johnson and Onwuegbuzie 2004).

While there is no general agreement on nomenclature, there seems to be a move towards using 'mixed methods' as the identifying concept. Over the past fifty years other concepts have been used. They are: 'multi-trait/multi-method research' (Campbell and Fiske 1959), although this referred to the use of several quantitative methods; 'triangulation' (Denzin 1970); 'mixed strategies' (Douglas 1976); 'combining methods' (Reichardt and Cook 1979); 'linking data' (Fielding and Fielding 1986); 'combining research' (Bryman 1988); 'multi-method research' (Brewer and Hunter 1989, 2006); 'combined research' (Creswell 1994); and 'mixed methodology' (Tashakkori and Teddlie 1998).

The term 'triangulation' was used initially to refer to the use of combinations of methods. In some fields, such as nursing research, it is still the more commonly used term (see Twinn 2003). Recently, Tashakkori and Teddlie (2003b) have argued for the use of terms that distinguish various types of combinations. The term 'multi-method research' is used to refer to studies that use more than one method but of the same type, i.e. combinations of either qualitative or qualitative methods. 'Mixed methods' is used to refer to studies that combine quantitative and qualitative methods, either in parallel or sequence. 'Mixed model' refers to studies that combine methods that are used within different ontological and epis-temological assumptions.

On the assumption that quantitative and qualitative methods are being com-bined, the following kinds of arguments have been used for the use of mixed methods.

- Strengths of one method offset weaknesses in other methods.
- Provide more comprehensive evidence.
- Help answer research questions that cannot be answered by one method alone.
- Encourage researchers with different views (and skills) to collaborate.
- Encourage the use of multiple paradigms (assumes methods are linked to para-digm, whatever paradigm means).
- Is practical as the researcher is free to use all possible methods (Creswell 2007: 9–10).

The idea of using a combination of methods of data collection goes back to the early years of social research in America and Europe. A variety of methods were used in the pioneering study that was commenced in London in 1886 by Charles Booth and his associates (*The Life and Labour of the People of London*, published in seventeen volumes between 1891 and 1903). His collaborator, Beatrice Webb, claimed that Booth's research showed us 'for the first time how best to combine the quantitative and qualitative examination of social structure' (Webb 1948: 210–12). Interviews, participant observation and statistical data from secondary sources were used. Later, community studies in America, such as, 'Middletown' (Lynd and Lynd 1937, 1956) and 'Yankee City' (Warner and Lunt 1941), and the community study of 'Marienthal' in Austria (Lazarsfeld *et al.* 1933), all used a combination of methods. However, the way these researchers combined methods has been questioned as satisfying the criteria of mixed methods research (see e.g. Creswell and Plano Clark 2007: 169). If you are prepared to regard mixing broadly, I think they do.

Beginning in the 1920s, the issue of the relative merits of 'statistical studies' and 'case studies' began to receive attention in America. This is when the debates about quantitative and qualitative methods started. A few voices at the time argued that the two traditions were complementary rather than being in conflict (see e.g. Burgess 1927). Prior to the Second World War, the style of research prac-tised in the Chicago School of Sociology combined case studies with historical and statistical methods. This appears not to have been a conscious methodologi-cal decision but, rather, a natural way of trying to understand the phenomena being investigated (Cortese 1995; Platt 1996).

These debates re-emerged in the late 1950s as a war between survey researchers and fieldworkers. In the face of the overwhelming dominance of survey research at the time, Becker and Geer (1957) argued that participant observation is the most complete method of data collection. However, given that not all social research is conducted in situations where such a method is possible, others argued that different kinds of information need to be gathered in different ways. The method will be determined by the research topic (see e.g. Trow 1957; Zelditch 1962)

Early Advocates

It was not until the 1960s that ideas began to develop about how this combining could be done. Building on the ideas of Campbell and Fiske (1959), the concept of triangulation was introduced into the social sciences by Webb *et al.* (1966) and was taken up and elaborated soon after by Denzin (1970). The overriding concern of Webb *et al.* was to improve the validity of the measurement of theoretical concepts by the use of independent measures, including some for which there could be no reactivity from respondents. It is important to note here that what they advocated was not the combination of different methods to produce more reliable results, but the testing of a hypothesis using different measures of the same concept.

In taking up this concern, Denzin (1970: 13) argued that 'sociologists must learn to employ multiple methods in the analysis of the same empirical event', on the assumption that each method will reveal different aspects of empirical reality. He advocated the use of multiple *triangulation* that involves the use of a variety of data sources, investigators, theories and methodologies.[4]

At about the same time, Sieber (1973) was largely responsible for defining the use of multi-methods as a new style of research. He moved beyond concerns about validity checking to seeing data collection methods as building upon one another in a staged process. His ideas on how survey research and fieldwork can be usefully combined anticipated many current ideas and are still relevant.

While the use of multiple methods was advocated enthusiastically to exploit their assets and neutralize their liabilities (see e.g. Denzin 1970; Jick 1979; Brewer and Hunter 1989), some recognition was given to the possibility of methods producing both convergent and divergent results. The latter may indicate that further research is required and that caution must be exercised in interpreting the significance of any results. The persuasiveness of convergent findings needs to be tempered by recognizing that measurement deficiencies can both cancel and compound.

Early Developments

As we have seen, much of the early discussion about combining methods focused in the idea of triangulation (e.g. Denzin 1970). As the discussion evolved beyond concerns with measurement validation the concept tended to be retained as the generic term. The triangulation metaphor had its origin in navigation, military strategy and surveying (Jick 1979; Smith 1981; Hammersley and Atkinson 2007).

Elsewhere (Blaikie 1991) I have argued that, as it has been applied to the social sciences, the metaphor grossly misrepresents its use in surveying and is misleading.[5] In surveying, triangulation was used as an economical way of accurately fixing the position of dispersed reference points on the surface of the earth. It was not used as a method for checking the reliability of single measurements, or for reducing error or bias, as was the original concern in social science.

One of the naive aspects of early discussions of triangulation was the focus on combining results from the use of a number of methods of data collection. However, what researchers usually do is to *compare* results. If they are convergent, they will usually be regarded as reliable, although, as we have seen, caution must be exercised. If they are divergent, five main courses of action are possible: trust none of them; treat all the findings with caution; give precedence to one set of data; produce a compromise interpretation; or view the discrepancy as something that requires further investigation. Just what alternative a researcher chooses will depend on such things as background knowledge of the research topic and the social context, relative confidence in the methods themselves, and the aims of the research. The so-called 'combining' of methods is not a mechanical process; it requires a great deal of judgement based on knowledge and experience. It is the comparison of data produced in different ways that is of greatest value.

There is a danger in adopting a simple-minded view of triangulation, i.e. that a combination of different methods and data will provide a more complete picture of some phenomenon, like taking photographs of an object from different points of view. 'One should not, therefore, adopt a naively "optimistic" view that the aggregation of data from different sources will unproblematically add up to produce a more accurate or complete picture' (Hammersley and Atkinson 2007: 184).

In my 1991 article I argued that it is time to stop using the concept of triangulation in the social sciences. The reasons I offered were that:

- lip-service is paid to it but few researchers use it in its original conception as a validity check (mainly because convergence is rare);
- it means so many things to so many people; and
- it encourages a naive view of ontology and epistemology.

I suggested that what is needed is a more systematic understanding of how different research strategies, methods and data can be used creatively within a research project, for example, as a developmental process, or as a way of stimulating theory construction. Neither of these uses is remotely related to multiple 'fixes' on social reality. We need different metaphors to identify these activities. Fortunately, the social research world has moved on since then and the narrow view of mixed methods presented by the early advocates of triangulation has been superseded by much more sophisticated ideas.

Rossman and Wilson (1985) recognized that data produced by different methods will invariably not converge. They used combinations of quantitative and qualitative data for three purposes: *corroboration*, *elaboration* and *initiation*. *Corroboration* is the classic use of triangulation to establish validity, *elaboration* occurs when a variety of data expands understanding of the phenomenon, perhaps by providing different perspectives, and *initiation* refers to the use of non-convergent data in a provocative way to produce new interpretations and conclusions, to suggest further areas of research, or to reformulate research questions. They illustrated these uses in their own research.

Obstacles

A number of writers have recognized that there are obstacles to using a combination of methods: it can be expensive; it takes more time; researchers may not have sufficient training in both qualitative and quantitative methods; and fads in the preferences of funding agencies for one type of method (Reichardt and Cook 1979).

However, we need to ask why social researchers have tended to use only *one* method of data collection. There are a number of possibilities, some of which we have already encountered.

- The paradigm wars of the 1960s and 1970s, between positivism and inter-pretivism, were translated into a war between quantitative and qualitative research.
- Methods were regarded (falsely) as being associated with particular paradigms/approaches.
- The rise and dominance of the social survey following WWII led to a narrow-ing and greater specialization in social research (Sieber 1973; Platt 1996).
- The scale of much research was limited by restricted funding and the publish or perish scourge in academia.
- Individual postgraduate student research is done with limited time and finan-cial resources.

Research in the social sciences has been characterized by individual researchers working on individual research projects with single methods of data collection and analysis. The team research so characteristic of the natural sciences seems to have been largely absent. For example, when a student in the social sciences undertakes a postgraduate degree, they are likely to choose their own project and work on it on their own. In the natural sciences, such students are likely to work on part of their supervisor's research programme, which is also likely to be a team effort.

Recent Developments

Beginning with some seminal texts that began to appear about twenty years ago (e.g. Fielding and Fielding 1986; Bryman 1988; Brewer and Hunter 1989; Brannen 1992; Tashakkori and Teddlie 1998), the discussion of what is now commonly called 'mixed methods' has seen an explosion in the writing of new texts (e.g. Brewer and Hunter 2006; Bryman 2007; Creswell and Plano Clark 2007) and handbooks/readers (e.g. Tashakkori and Teddlie 2003a; Todd *et al.* 2004; Bryman 2006a; Bergman 2008). In 2007, the *Journal of Mixed Methods Research* was established, and other journals have had special issues on the topic (e.g. *Journal of Research in Nursing* 2006, Vol. 11(3); *Research in Schools* 2006, Vol. 18(1)). A book on qualitative and quantitative approaches to research design (Creswell 1994) has added mixed methods approaches in the second and later editions (Creswell 2003, 2009); research methods texts in education have made substantial references to mixed methods (e.g. McMillan and Schumacher 2001; Johnson and Christensen 2008); and some recent general social research methods texts have devoted an entire chapter to mixed methods (e.g. Bryman 2008; Johnson and Christensen 2008).

Creswell and Plano Clark (2007) have divided the development of mixed method research into four somewhat overlapping periods, beginning in the 1950s. The first *formative* period went up until the 1980s and is represented in the work of Campbell and Fiske (1959); Sieber (1973); Jick (1979); and Cook and Reichardt (1979). The second *paradigm debate* period ran from the 1970s to the 1980s and centred on whether or not quantitative and qualitative methods could be combined. Protagonists included Guba and Lincoln (1988) and Smith (1983), while Bryman (1988), Reichardt and Rallis (1994) and Greene and Caracelli (1997) favoured the combination of methods and argued that we move beyond the paradigm debate. Rossman and Wilson (1985) characterized the protagonists as 'purists' (the methods are incompatible), 'situationalists' (adapt their methods to the situation) and 'pragmatists' (believe combination is possible). In the third *procedural development* period, which began in the late 1980s, proposals were made for the design of mixed methods research. Major contributors to this period were Brewer and Hunter (1989); Morse (1991); Creswell (1994); and Tashakkori and Teddlie (1998). The fourth period, *advocacy as a separate design,* covers the last decade, and, in addition to the recent references listed above, included contributions from Johnson and Onwuegbuzie (2004) and Creswell (2009). The move has been towards regarding multi-method research as a special type of design to be placed alongside traditional research designs. For example, Brewer and Hunter (2006) have identified five styles of research: fieldwork, surveys, experiments, non-reactive research, which includes the use of secondary sources, and multi-method research.

The second period identified by Creswell and Plano Clark (2007) has been characterized as a war between two major paradigms or worldviews. The worldviews have invariably been reduced to two, on the one hand, 'positivism', 'logical positivism' or 'postpositivism'. and, on the other hand, 'constructivism', 'interpretivism', 'phenomenology' or 'naturalism' (see, for example, Lincoln and Guba 1985). A reading of my *Approaches to Social Enquiry* (2007) will show how unsatisfactory is this simplistic dichotomy. However, its appeal was that it could be easily glossed into the dichotomy of 'quantitative' and 'qualitative'.

A common theme to arise out of the paradigm wars is that as paradigms are considered to be incommensurable or incompatible in their ontological and epistemological assumptions, as well as their axiology (stance on bias), research strategy (simplified to inductive and deductive) and rhetoric (style of language), and as methods were assumed to be associated with particular paradigms, then using combinations of methods, particularly within a single research project, is just not possible.

Based on observation and experience over forty years, and some involvement in the paradigm wars back in the 1970s (Blaikie 1977, 1978), it is my impression that these conflicts have subsided.

- Quantitative methods are no longer dominant.
- Qualitative methods have been developed and refined.
- Rigid notions of objectivity and subjectivity have been challenged and modified.
- Some of the challenges of postmodernism have been accepted as well as tempered.

- There is a growing sophistication in the understanding of the philosophical underpinnings of social research, of ontology and epistemology.
- More pragmatic attitudes have developed.

The pragmatic alternative has been advocated by Morgan (2007) as a way of supporting the use of mixed methods. His approach places emphasis on gaining knowledge in the pursuit of solving problems. This involves concentrating on the area that connects issues at the abstract level of epistemology (the nature of knowledge) and the mechanical level of actual methods (the generation of knowledge). He rejected the dichotomy between 'objectivity' and 'subjectivity' and replaced it with the 'intersubjectivity' that is necessary for a mutual understanding between the researcher and research participants, as well as with those who read the products of research. By adopting this pragmatic approach, he believed that it is possible to move beyond the technical issues of mixing methods to an integrated methodology.

Types of Mixed Methods Research

Over the past twenty years, various attempts have been made to identify a range of mixed methods research designs (see e.g. Greene *et al.* 1989; Patton 1990; Morse 1991; Steckler *et al.* 1992; Hammersley 1996; Greene and Caracelli 1997; Morgan 1998; Tashakkori and Teddlie 1998; Creswell 1999; Sandelowski 2000; Creswell *et al.* 2003; Tashakkori and Teddlie 2003b; Creswell *et al.* 2004; Bryman 2006b).

Creswell and Plano Clark (2007) have provided an elaboration of Hammersley's classification. They classified mixed research into four major types: *triangulation, embedded, explanatory* and *exploratory*.

Triangulating of both quantitative and qualitative data can be done in a variety of ways:

- comparing quantitative and qualitative data of equal weight within the same time frame (convergence model);
- transforming one type of data into the other form and mixing them during the analysis stage (data transformation model);
- within a survey instrument, including a few open-ended questions to provide interesting quotes (validating quantitative data model); and
- using different methods at different levels within, for example, an organization (multi-level model).

In the *embedded* procedure, one type of data plays a supplementary role in helping to design the study, elaborate the procedures and/or interpret the results. Usually it is the qualitative component that is supplementary, although the reverse is in principle possible. Embedding can occur in both experimental and non-experimental research.

The *explanatory* procedure is the most straightforward kind of mixed methods research and comes in two forms: a quantitative phase produces results that need to be elaborated or explained and this is done by a follow-up qualitative phase; or a preliminary quantitative phase is used to provide the basis for selecting participants for the major qualitative phase.

The *exploratory* procedure usually reverses the order of the phases. An initial qualitative phase can be used to develop new quantitative measures or instruments. Alternatively, this phase can be used to identify unknown variables, develop a classification system or develop propositions to be tested, perhaps from an emergent theory.

A more elaborate classification can be found in Tashakkori and Teddlie (2003b). Bryman (2006b, 2008) has undertaken a study of 232 articles in which mixed methods were used by researchers in five fields: sociology; social psychology; human, social and cultural geography; management and organization behaviour; and media and cultural studies. He concluded that sixteen distinct types of mixed methods research have been practiced. Most of these can be classified into Creswell and Plano Clark's (2007) four types above.

A Neglected Issue

In the current explosion of writing on the use of mixed methods, the issue of ontological assumptions is largely absent. The focus has been on methods of data collection and, sometimes, data analysis. I do not wish to suggest that qualitative and quantitative methods are associated with particular ontological assumptions, although this may frequently occur in practice. Rather, whenever a particular method is used, the researcher will consciously or unconsciously adopt ontological assumptions. Some researchers appear to work with one type of assumption consistently, regardless of what method they are using. However, as methods can be used with different assumptions, it is possible that different ontological assumptions can be used within a research project.

If a researcher does adopt different ontological assumptions with a mixture of methods, the question arises as to how this should be handled. Is it legitimate to compare or combine results that have been produced with different assumptions? Is it possible to move between different assumptions as different methods are used? And how can this be done? The answers to these questions will differ depending on whether methods are being used concurrently or sequentially. And they can become relevant when one type of data is transformed into another type. What is assumed about the nature of reality when each method is being used can become significant when they are mixed in some way.

As we have seen, methods can be combined both concurrently and in sequence. The first alternative allows for the use of qualitative and quantitative methods together, provided both types are used with the same ontological assumptions. It is only under these circumstances that most of what has been written about triangulation is relevant. Different methods *can* be used to explore aspects of the same (assumed) 'objective' reality, regardless of whether they use words or numbers. They might also be used to explore (assumed) single or multiple socially constructed realities, although some methods (qualitative) might be more suitable for this than others. Data from different sources can be translated from one form to another (although usually from qualitative to quantitative) with impunity. However, what cannot be done is to combine data that are produced by methods that each deal with different (assumed) realities. It is not possible to use data related to a single 'absolute' reality to test the validity of data related to multiple 'constructed' realities, regardless of what methods are used in each case.

If different types of methods are used with the same ontological assumptions, the implications of achieving convergence or divergence of results can be handled, either in terms of providing reciprocal support in the case of convergence, or as an explanatory challenge in the case of divergence. When two or more methods are used with different assumptions, convergence and divergence take on different meanings; the results may relate to different realities. In this case, while converging results cannot be used as any kind of test of validity, or for mutual support, comparison *can* be used to stimulate theory development or further research.

The second alternative is to use different methods, possibly with different assumptions, during different stages of a research project. It is not necessary for all stages to adopt a consistent set of ontological and epistemological assumptions. To answer research questions relevant to each stage, the researcher can move back and forth between research strategies during the course of the research. Data collected at one stage can be *interpreted* in the light of data gathered at another stage. For example, statistical results from a survey could be interpreted, that is, be better understood in terms of social actors' meanings and motives that have produced the statistical patterns, using some in-depth interviews with a carefully selected sub-sample of respondents.

Switching between ontological assumptions requires considerable awareness of the various sets of assumptions that are being used and the capacity to keep the various (assumed) realities separate. For example, a researcher may use a questionnaire within the Deductive research strategy, and then in-depth interviewing within the Abductive strategy. However, to then attempt to combine the data produced by these two methods is to fail to recognize the differences in ontological assumptions between the research strategies. What is more common is for a researcher to use a combination of qualitative and quantitative methods within one research strategy, say the Inductive or Deductive strategies. The ontological problems of combining different methods, particularly quantitative and qualitative methods, are not an issue in these two research strategies; all methods are interpreted within a consistent ontology. In this case, qualitative data are likely to be viewed as uncoded quantitative data that the researcher has to translate into variables rather than, say, evidence of the social actors' meanings and interpretations. Where meanings are recognized, they will be conceived differently than they would in the Abductive research strategy (see Halfpenny 1979: 815–16).

Conclusion

It should be clear from this discussion that, while the use of combinations of methods within research projects can be traced back more than a hundred years, and arguments for their explicit use goes back about forty years, there has been a quite recent upsurge in the interest in mixed methods in a number of branches of social research. However, mixed methods are still regarded by many as the poor relation of single methods.

In my view, the use of mixed methods should be seen as normal and usually necessary in many types of research, and particularly when more than one research question is being investigated. This should be clear from the four sample research designs in chapter 8. They represent a series of stages in a research programme that began with quantitative methods and then moved to the use of qualitative methods as knowledge in the area increased and the nature of the research questions changed. Social research should be seen as a process of moving back and forth between stages that may require the use of different research strategies and methods for different purposes at each stage. Incidentally, this process has nothing to do with conventional views of triangulation and its accompanying concern with the improvement of validity.

Mixed methods should not be seen as a special category of research; perhaps single methods should be treated this way. The use of single methods is usually associated with narrow and perhaps one-off research topics. Such research provides limited opportunities for advancing knowledge. The use of a variety of methods, however this is organized, should be seen as the norm.

Research Strategies and Methods

There is no necessary connection between research strategies and methods of data collection and analysis. While some methods may be more commonly associated with a particular research strategy, this is largely a matter of convention rather than a methodological requirement. However, this does not mean that methods can be used without ontological and epistemological assumptions. Rather, if a particular method (e.g. unstructured interviewing) is used in association with the Inductive research strategy, in that context it will be serving that strategy's assumptions. Similarly, if the same method is associated with the Abductive research strategy, the data that it produces will need to be interpreted within that strategy's assumptions. In other words, methods can serve a number of masters, but they need to change their 'colours' to do so, and the data they produce will need to be interpreted within the particular ontological and epistemological assumptions that are adopted.

When the Inductive research strategy is used, any kind of data is appropriate; generalizations can be produced from data in either words or numbers. While numbers may allow for more precise propositions, the relevance, or the possibility of achieving such precision, will be a matter of judgement or circumstances; sometimes using words alone may be all that is possible or necessary. In any case, propositions in words are still necessary in quantitative studies. The issue is how such propositions were arrived at, and that is a matter of choice or opportunity.

The Deductive research strategy is more commonly used in association with quantitative methods and data, but this need not be so. Qualitative researchers may also construct theories in the deductive form and test them using qualitative data. The more important issue is whether researchers are engaged in theory construction or theory testing rather than the type of methods or data they use.

It is clear from research inspired by Harré's constructionist version of the Retroductive research strategy that a combination of methods can be used. Pawson (1995) and Pawson and Tilley (1997) have certainly advocated the use of both quantitative and qualitative methods, very much in a sequence, in terms of establishing and exploring observed patterns, contexts and mechanisms. Both these versions of the Retroductive strategy rely on cognitive mechanisms for their explanations and they incorporate constructionist elements. The question of the ontological status of cognitive mechanisms (in contrast to the structures and mechanisms in Bhaskar's version), that are dependent on the socially constructed reality social actors inhabit, needs further consideration.

In the Abductive strategy, qualitative methods predominate because of the nature of the subject-matter (social actors' meanings, motives, and interpretations) at its core. However, the patterns for which understanding or explanation is sought may have been established using quantitative data.

It should now be clear that the choice of research strategy does not determine the method or methods that should be used in social research. However, careful consideration needs to be given to what a method is supposed to do for a particular research strategy, and the ontological and epistemological assumptions that lie behind its use at a particular time and in a particular place.

Many researchers appear to use particular methods with little or no awareness of the ontological and epistemological assumptions that they have adopted. In my experience, this is common among quantitative researchers who have been socialized in, or have confined themselves to, a narrow research tradition; their assumptions are taken for granted and are unlikely to be seen to involve choices. I started my own research career this way. On the other hand, some researchers have the capacity, and find the need, to move between research paradigms, and to work with a range of research strategies, either for different research projects, or even within a single project. This requires a sophisticated awareness of both the assumptions and the logics of enquiry that are being used at any time.

Further Reading

Blaikie, N. 2003. *Analyzing Quantitative Data.*
   A non-technical introduction to the theory and practice of quantitative analysis.
Bryman, A. 2008. *Social Research Methods.*
   A readable and comprehensive introduction to both quantitative and qualitative methods.
Bryman, A. (ed.) 2006a. *Mixed Methods* (4 vols).
   A comprehensive review of the development and variety of mixed methods research.
Corbin, J. M. and A. Strauss 2008. *Basics of Qualitative Research.*
   A long-standing and well-used discussion of grounded theory.
Creswell, J. W. and V. L. Plano Clark 2007. *Designing and Conducting Mixed Methods Research.*
   One of a new batch of texts on mixed methods.
Denzin, N. K. and Y. S. Lincoln (eds) 2005. *Handbook of Qualitative Research.*
   This and previous editions provide a comprehensive coverage.
de Vaus, D. 2002. *Surveys in Social Research.*
   The standard text on survey research.

Flick, U. 2006. *An Introduction to Qualitative Research.*
  A useful introduction with a European flavour.
Hammersley, M. and P. Atkinson. 2007. *Ethnography.*
  The standard text on ethnography
Hardy, M. and A. Bryman 2004. *Handbook of Data Analysis.*
  A broad, middle-range collection on quantitative and qualitative analysis.
Kaplan, D. (ed.) 2004. *The Sage Handbook of Quantitative Methodology for the Social Sciences.*
  A narrow and advanced collection on quantitative data analysis.
Lewins, A. and C. Silver 2007. *Using Software in Qualitative Research: A Step-by-step Guide.* London: Sage.
  Practical and comprehensive using a variety of software.
Lewis-Beck, M. S., A. Bryman and T. F. Liao (eds) 2004. *The Sage Encyclopedia of Social Research Methods* (3 vols).
  A comprehensive coverage of everything a social researcher needs to know, and more.
Mason, J. 2002. *Qualitative Researching.*
  A practical and methodologically sophisticated introduction.
Minichiello, V., R. Aroni, E. and T. Hays 2008. *In-Depth Interviewing.*
  A very useful coverage of this method.
Neuman, W. L. 2006. *Social Research Methods.*
  A standard and comprehensive discussion of both quantitative and qualitative methods.
Plano Clark, V. L. and J. W. Creswell (eds) 2008. *The Mixed Methods Reader.*
  A useful collection of previously published papers.
Punch, K. K. F. 2005. *Introduction to Social Research.*
  Covers both quantitative and qualitative methods of data collection and analysis.
Seale, C. (ed.). 2004. *Researching Society and Culture.*
  A wide-ranging collection of original papers on most aspects of social research.
Tashakkori, A. and C. Teddlie (eds) 2003a. *Handbook of Mixed Methods in Social and Behavioral Research.*
  An extensive set of especially written papers.
See also the Sage four-volume collections on various aspects of social research.

8

Sample Research Designs

Introduction

Now that the core elements and choices involved in preparing a research design have been explored, I conclude with some examples of what research designs might look like, were you to follow the scheme laid out in the previous chapters. These four examples cover a range of research purposes and illustrate how each of the four research strategies can be used. They are intentionally simple designs of the kind that are common in postgraduate research, and they are presented in outline only. More complex designs, using more sophisticated methods, can easily be developed from these designs by researchers who wish to use them. My aim is to provide basic starting-points.

The four designs follow a research programme in the sociology of the environment. As I worked in this field on and off over a number of years, I am reasonably familiar with the literature and have had experience in doing this kind of research. Publications from this programme can be found in Blaikie (1992, 1993b), Blaikie and Ward (1992), and Blaikie and Drysdale (1994). However, I have modified the original designs somewhat to make them suitable for the present purpose and have assumed that the research programme ran from the early to the middle 1990s. The literature reviews are illustrative only.

The designs follow a progression. The first is a descriptive study that establishes some patterns using the Inductive research strategy. The next two designs take up some of these and other patterns and try to explain them using the Deductive and Retroductive research strategies, respectively. The fourth returns to description, but also tries to develop an understanding of differences in behaviour, by using the Abductive research strategy.

I would not like these research designs to be used as exemplars. Their major purpose is to give some idea of what has to go into a research design, how it might be structured, and, depending on the topic, the kinds of research questions and research strategies that might be adopted, and how these decisions relate to the context, the units to be studied, and the research methods selected. However, they are written in such a way that they review what has been covered in the preceding chapters. Therefore, slavishly following these sample designs may not produce the most appropriate documents. In any case, there is rather more commentary in these examples than might be necessary in an actual design. Every research design has to be based on choices that are appropriate to the investigation of a problem and set of research questions, at a particular time, in a particular place, taking into account the motives and goals of the researcher.

Research Design 1   Environmental Worldviews and Behaviour among Students and Residents

The problem

Environmental issues have received considerable attention in the Australian media in recent years. Problems, such as global warming and the depletion of the ozone layer over the South Polar Region, have dominated, and have been the subject of discussion in public forums. At the same time, environmental issues have featured prominently in both federal and state politics, and in debates about the logging of native forests, mining in national parks and alternatives to the use of non-renewable resources.

While concern about the environment goes back many decades, with the 1970s seeing a wave of interest, the level of public awareness, and the degree to which politicians have been willing to include it in their agendas, appears to be at a higher level now than at previous times. Many events around the world, not the least being the Chernobyl disaster, have brought into stark relief the global nature of environmental problems and the urgency with which they need to be addressed.

For anyone interested in raising environmental awareness and changing behaviour towards the environment, it is necessary to know the current status of environmental worldviews and behaviour. This project, to be conducted in Melbourne, Australia, aims to provide such knowledge.

Motives and goals

The primary motivation for this study is the desire to fill a gap in knowledge about the nature of environmental worldviews and the level of environmentalism in Australia. Extensive research has been conducted in this field in the United States, and in some other parts of the world, but systematic data on Australia are largely absent. Hence, there is no basis for examining differences in environmental worldviews and behaviour in the Australian population. A related motivation is a curiosity about how the situation in Australia compares with that in the United States.

A second major motivation is to give students doing a degree in socio-environmental studies at the RMIT University some practical experience, not only in the use of social research methods, but on a topic of relevance to their programme.

Research questions and purposes

The study will be *descriptive* in two ways: by establishing distributions on the key variables of environmental worldview and behaviour; and by establishing patterns in the relationships between these and commonly used socio-demographic variables.

The following research questions provide the focus and direction for the research.

1 To what extent do students and residents hold different environmental worldviews?
2 To what extent is environmentally responsible behaviour practised?
3 What is the level and type of involvement in environmental movements?
4 To what extent, and in what ways, is environmental behaviour related to environmental worldviews?

Review of the literature

This research will build on a tradition of environmental sociology that goes back to the 1970s in the United States. Various attempts have been made to conceptualize the changes in beliefs and values that appeared to be occurring then, and to measure changes in environmental concern, attitudes and behaviour. One tradition of this activity, centring on the work of Catton and Dunlap and their associates, has developed notions of various worldviews and paradigms (Catton and Dunlap 1978, 1980; Dunlap and van Liere 1978; Dunlap and Catton 1979; van Liere and Dunlap 1980). They argued that the worldview that had dominated American society was being challenged by the 'new environmental paradigm' (NEP).

Dunlap and van Liere (1978) developed a scale of twelve items to measure the NEP. This was constructed as a single dimension, but later replications have suggested that it consists of three dimensions: 'balance of nature', 'limits of growth' and 'man [*sic*] over nature' (Albrecht *et al.* 1982; Geller and Lasley 1985).

While the socio-demographic basis of the NEP appears to have received little or no attention, the basis of 'environmental concern' *has* been explored. Van Liere and Dunlap (1980) reviewed twenty-one studies, conducted between 1968 and 1978, in which some or all of the following variables were used: age, social class (income, education and occupation), place of residence, political partisanship, political ideology and gender. They concluded that 'younger, well-educated, and politically liberal persons tend to be more concerned about environmental quality than their older, less educated, and politically conservative counterparts' (van Liere and Dunlap 1980). The other variables were not systematically correlated with environmental concern.

Age has been found consistently to have the strongest association with environmental concern. This has been supported in subsequent studies by Buttel (1979); Lowe *et al.* (1980); Honnold (1981, 1984); Lowe and Pinhey (1982); Mohai and Twight (1987); and Arcury and Christianson (1990). Studies of the relationship between environmental concern and gender have produced conflicting results (McStay and Dunlap 1983; Blocker and Eckberg 1989; Samdahl and Robertson 1989; Acury and Christianson 1990).

Therefore, the associations of both age and gender with environmental worldviews and environmentally responsible behaviour will be explored. Five other variables will also be examined: marital status, number and ages of children, religious affiliation, religiosity, and political party preference. Apart from being standard variables, the first two may be associated with a concern for future generations, the second two may be a source of related beliefs and values, and the last one may reflect such values.[1]

Research strategies

The study will use the Inductive research strategy. It will collect data related to certain concepts, it will produce limited generalizations, and it will search for patterns in the data. Given the nature of the research questions, a choice must be made between the Inductive and Abductive research strategies. As the previous studies with which the findings of this research will be compared have all used the Inductive strategy and quantitative methods, it is appropriate to use the same.

Concepts

The concepts to be investigated are defined as follows.

Environmental worldview: attitudes towards issues such as the preservation of wilderness environments and natural flora and fauna, the conservation of natural resources, environmental degradation, environmental impacts of economic growth, and the use of science and technology to solve environmental problems.

Environmentally responsible behaviour: individual actions that preserve nature and conserve resources, and involvement in communal actions that confront environmental problems and seek solutions.

The following standard concepts are also included for possible later use. They are not required to answer the research questions.

Age: number of years since birth.

Gender: socially defined categories of male and female based on human biological differences.

Marital status: legal or *de facto* relationship between couples.

Number and ages of children: number of children of all ages for which the respondent is socially regarded as the parent or is the legal guardian. This definition would exclude unrecognized illegitimate children and any that have been given up for adoption.[2]

Religious affiliation: identification with a particular religion or religious denomination.

Religiosity: the degree to which an individual adopts religious beliefs and engages in religious practices.

Political party preference: support of a particular political party through voting at elections.

These concepts will be operationalized as follows:

> *Environmental worldview*: by means of responses to a set of attitude items concerned with the range of environmental issues. The items will be drawn from existing scales: six from the NEP scale, six from the 'dominant social paradigm' scale (Dunlap and van Liere 1984), and eight from the Richmond and Baumgart (1981) scales, two with modifications to their wording. Another four have been added. Five Likert-type response categories will be used: 'strongly agree', 'agree', 'neither agree nor disagree', 'disagree' and 'strongly disagree'. These categories will be assigned values from 1 to 5 in the direction that gives the highest value to responses that are pro-environment. The scale will be pre-tested on a diverse sample of thirty and subjected to item analysis to establish the degree to which responses to each item are consistent with the total score. It will also be post-tested using factor analysis to establish its degree of unidimensionality and the possible presence of sub-scales.

> *Environmentally responsible behaviour*: by three measures. First is the degree to which the use of environmentally dangerous products is avoided. Respondents will be asked how frequently they avoid such products ('regularly', 'occasionally' and 'never'), and then to list them. Second, the extent to which products made of paper, glass (e.g. bottles), metal (e.g. food and drink cans) and plastic are regularly recycled. For each type of product, responses will be made in the categories of 'do not use', 'regularly', 'occasionally' and 'never'.[3] These categories will be scored from 3 to 0 respectively. The responses to each type of product, as well as the total scores for all four types, will be analysed. Third, support given to environmental groups will be measured by two questions: the degree of support ('regularly', 'occasionally' and 'never'); and an open-ended question on the forms of this support (responses to be coded for analysis).

> *Age*: by asking respondents how old they are in years.

> *Gender*: by asking respondents whether they are male or female.

> *Marital status*: by asking respondents to identify with one of the following categories: 'now married', '*de facto* stable relationship', 'never married and not in a stable relationship', 'widowed and not remarried', 'separated and not in a stable relationship', 'divorced and neither remarried nor in a stable relationship'.[4]

> *Number and ages of children*: respondent's reporting of the number and ages of their biological and other children for whom they are responsible and/or regard as theirs.

> *Religious affiliation*: by asking respondents with which religion or religious denomination, if any, they identify. Only the most frequently referred to religions and denominations will be given separate codes.

> *Religiosity*: by asking respondents to what extent they regard themselves as being religious. Four response categories will be used: 'very religious', 'moderately religious', 'somewhat religious' and 'not religious'.[5]

Political party preference: by asking respondents what political party they would vote for if an election were held today. Categories for the major parties, and 'other', will be provided.

As this is a descriptive study, it will not test any theory. In any case, the Inductive research strategy prohibits the use of hypotheses. However, it will examine the patterns of the relationships between environmental worldview and the various measures of environmentally responsible behaviour. These findings will be compared with previous research.

Data sources, types and forms

Data will be obtained from individuals in semi-natural settings. They will be asked to report on their attitudes and behaviour.

Only primary data will be used. With a few exceptions, responses will be recorded in pre-coded categories. After the few open-ended questions have been coded, all the data will be quantitative. The levels of measurement for each of the variables will be as follows:

Environmental worldview: an interval scale of total scores, and sub-scale scores (if they are established), as well as four approximately equal (ordinal) categories ('very high', 'high', 'moderate' and 'low') based on divisions in the distribution of the total scores.

Environmentally responsible behaviour:

(a)   Avoiding environmentally dangerous products: an ordinal measure of the frequency of avoidance, a post-coded (nominal) list of 'types of products', and a ratio scale of the 'number of products avoided'.

(b)   Recycling: ordinal 'frequency of recycling' categories for each of the four products, scores for each product, and a total 'recycling score' for the four products, based on an assumption of equal intervals between the 'frequency of recycling' categories.

(c)   Support for environmental groups: ordinal categories for 'level of support', scores based on the 'level of support' categories, nominal categories for the 'forms of support' and scores for the 'number of types of support'.

Age: ratio scale in years and five (ordinal) age categories to produce a rectangular distribution.

Gender: dichotomous nominal categories.

Religious affiliation: nominal categories.

Religiosity: ordinal categories and scores based on the assumption of equal intervals between categories.

Political party preference: nominal categories and a 'conservative'–'liberal' dichotomy.

Some variables will be measured at more than one level to facilitate different forms of analysis.

Selection of data sources

As this is a low-budget study, and as it is designed to give students a variety of social research experiences, data will be collected from two main sources. The first will be from students in the university in which the study is being conducted. The second will come from residents in the Melbourne Metropolitan Area (MMA), Australia's second-largest and most ethnically diverse urban area with a population of about four million. It consists of a number of independently administered city councils.

The student component will not only provide a significant proportion of young people, but will also include respondents who are likely to be environmentally aware because of their education and exposure to related student activities and movements. The study will work with two populations: first, university students from the RMIT University; and second, residents in the City of Box Hill[6] which is located in the eastern part of the MMA. This city has been selected as its socio-demographic characteristics closely match those of the MMA. It is important to note that both of these populations have been selected from larger populations on the basis of both judgement and convenience. This constitutes a prior stage in the sampling designs.

The student population is defined as 'students taking undergraduate degree courses at the RMIT University city campus in the second half of the 1990 academic year'. The sample to be drawn from this population will be based on classes in the university-wide general education curriculum.[7] In the semester in which the sample will be drawn, 160 classes will be offered with an average of twenty-five students per class. Therefore, a population of about 4,000 will be taking these courses at this time; this is about half of all undergraduate students at the university. A sample of one in eight of the classes (= 20) will be selected randomly. Assuming an average attendance of twenty students per class, the sample size should be about 400. This is regarded as adequate for the kinds of analysis to be conducted.

The resident population is defined as 'householders who occupy all types of residences in the City of Box Hill in October 1990'. A sample will be selected in three stages. The first stage will be a one in five random sample from the sixty census collectors' districts, i.e. reasonably small areas allocated to a person responsible for distributing and collecting the forms at the time of the census. Within the twelve collectors' districts, interviewers will select one in four residences using systematic sampling. They will select a starting-point at a corner of the district and proceed along the sides of each street until the residences in the district have been covered. The address of each selected residence will be recorded and a letter explaining the study left in the mailbox. A week later, the interviewer will return and seek an interview with a person of at least 18 years of age who has responsibility for the household. Should more than one person present meet this criterion (e.g. a married couple or two or more adults), a selection – the third sampling stage – will be made giving preference to females in residences with even numbers and males in the case of odd numbers. Interviewers will need to stagger the distribution of the explanatory letters to correspond with the pace at which they can conduct the interviews.

While there is some variation in the size of the collectors' districts, they average about 200 residences. Allowing for a non-response rate of 30 per cent, this proce-dure should produce a second sample of about 400.

With this expected response rate, it will be necessary to compare the distribu-tion on key demographic variables in the sample with that in the census for Box Hill. If they are similar, inferential analysis can be used to generalize from the sample to the population. The extent to which these statistics can be general-ized further, to the population of residents in the MMA or other urban areas in Australia, will be a matter of judgement based on a careful comparison of demo-graphic characteristics. It will be possible to apply inferential statistics to general-ize the results from the student sample to the population of students taking classes in the general education programme at the RMIT University in that particular semester. Judgement will be required to generalize to the whole student popula-tion at the University and to Australian university students.

A second study will be conducted in 1995 using similar samples, thus eventu-ally creating a longitudinal study.

Data collection and timing

For the present, this will be a cross-sectional study. A week will be required to collect the data from the student sample, and, immediately after, sampling of the residents will begin. The latter will take three weeks to complete. The actual timing of the data collection is still to be decided.

A self-administered, structured questionnaire will be used with the student sample and a structured interview schedule with the sample of residents. The former is appropriate for administration to 'captive' groups and will ensure a good response rate. The latter will allow the sampling to be combined with interviewing and will facilitate a better response rate than would be possible with a questionnaire. The two instruments will use identical questions but will be structured slightly differently. The questionnaire will be pre-tested with two classes, not included in the sample, a month before its administration, and the interview schedule will be pre-tested with thirty residents in an adjoining part of the MMA.

For the student sample, arrangements will be made with the lecturer respon-sible for the selected classes to have the students complete the questionnaire in class. This should take twenty-five to thirty minutes. The administration of the questionnaire will be organized and supervised by the students from the Research Methods class, operating in pairs. With forty students in the Research Methods class, each pair will be responsible for one class. A brief explanation of the purpose of the study will be given and ethical issues (e.g. anonymity, confidential-ity and voluntary participation) will be explained. Responses will be recorded by ticking in boxes alongside the appropriate category.

The interviewers with the residents will be conducted by the same students from the Research Methods class. Forty students will each conduct ten interviews.

Public transport is available to (train) and through (bus) the research site. Interviews will be conducted in the late afternoon and early evening during the week, and at weekends. Interviewers will be required to make up to two return visits if they fail to find someone at home on the first visit. Again, a brief explanation of the purpose of the study will be given and ethical issues explained. Respondents will be encouraged to participate to ensure the success of the study. They will be asked if they would like a copy of a summary of the report of the study. If the time is unsuitable, arrangements will be made for a return visit. Interviewers will make every effort to conduct the interview in private and in a relaxed atmosphere. Responses will be recorded by circling the coding numbers alongside the appropriate category.

The interviewers will receive thorough training in interview techniques and the use of this particular interview schedule. In the week before the interviewing commences, an article will appear in the local suburban newspaper giving some background to the study. Interviewers will wear identification tags and carry a letter of authority from the university.

Data reduction and analysis

Very limited post-coding will be required. A codebook will be prepared for use with the questionnaire and for the open-ended questions in the interview schedule. An SPSS (PC version) data matrix will be prepared for each sample and the responses entered. This will be done directly from the questionnaires, using the codebook, and from the interview schedules. Following an initial frequency count, it may be necessary to re-code some variables, either reordering and/or collapsing some of the categories. The students in the Research Methods class will be involved in the coding, data entry and data analysis.

Data from the two samples will be analysed separately as well as combined. Comparisons will be made between the two samples and inferential statistics will be used to estimate the population parameters from the sample statistics. To answer the research questions, the following methods of analysis will be undertaken with each sample and the combined sample.

RQ1 Means and standard deviations for the scores from the 'environmental worldview scale' and sub-scales; medians and inter-quartile range for the ordinal category version of the scale.

RQ2 Frequency counts and percentages for the categories in the list of 'products avoided'; frequency counts, percentages, means and standard deviations for the 'number of products avoided'; frequency counts and percentages for the 'frequency of recycling' categories for each product; mean and standard deviation for the 'recycling score'.

RQ3 Frequency counts and percentages for the 'level of support' and 'form of support' categories; frequency counts, percentages and means for the number of 'types of support'.

RQ4 Cross-tabulation and non-parametric tests of significance for environmental worldview scale (ordinal categories) with 'types of products', 'frequency of recycling' for each product, 'level of support' (ordinal categories) and 'forms of support' for environmental groups. Product moment correlation coefficients and a parametric test of significance will be used to correlate 'environmental worldview scale' and the sub-scales with 'number of products avoided', 'recycling score', 'level of support' (scores) and 'number of types of support'.

Problems and limitations

A major strength of the study is that it will explore environmental issues systematically in this way for the first time in Australia. It will also develop a new environmental worldview scale and test it in local conditions. And it will provide students with valuable experience in developing and using research instruments, and in data analysis.

The major limitation derives from the exploratory and descriptive nature of the study. This has made it difficult to attract research funds; only a small seeding grant is available. The participation of the forty students from the Research Methods class will partially compensate, although the need to limit the extent of their involvement, to only those experiences necessary for their course, places another set of limitations.

As a consequence, sampling methods will have to be devised to produce a substantial size, with appropriate diversity, but with the available resources. While the student sample, in combination with residents, ensures a good age spread, university students may not be typical of young people in this age range. In addition, there are some weaknesses in the assumption that students taking the general education classes in a particular semester are typical of all students at the university, and of all university students in Australia. However, such claims will not be made, although readers of the research report may want to make judgements about these matters.

The selection of only one suburb in one city to represent urban Australia clearly has severe limitations. Again, readers of the research report will have to judge for themselves how typical this sample might be. What will be possible with these two samples is to undertake a separate analysis of the attitudes and behaviour of a sample of young educated people and to compare them with a reasonably typical sample of urban residents.

The major advantage in concentrating the study in one area, and using this particular sampling method, is that interviewing can be done efficiently, as little travelling is required. An alternative would have been to select samples from a diverse range of socio-demographic areas in the MMA. This would have involved a great deal of extra travelling for limited gains. A random sample of residents in the MMA would have been impossible with the available resources.

A technical point concerns the use of questionnaires with the student sample and structured interviews with the residents' sample. While the question wording will be the same in each instrument, differences in the methods of administration could produce differences in responses. Conducting interviews with a second sample of, say, 100 students could test this. If time and resources permit, this will be carried out.[8]

Research Design 2   Age and Environmentalism: A Test of Competing Hypotheses

The problem

Research over many decades in the United States has shown that there is a consistently stronger association between age and environmental attitudes and concern than with any other socio-demographic variable; younger people have more positive attitudes and greater concern than older people. However, just why age is associated with environmentalism is not clear.

Motives and goals

The main motive is to advance our knowledge of why some people have more favourable environmental attitudes, and engage in higher levels of environmentally friendly behaviour, than others. This may have some practical benefits for environmental education programmes and for groups and organizations that are committed to improving the quality of the natural and built environments.

Research questions and purposes

The research has two purposes: to *describe* the form of the relationship between age and environmentalism in Australia; and to *explain* this by developing and testing a theory. Three research questions will be explored.

1 To what extent is age related to environmental worldviews and environmentally responsible behaviour?
2 If there are relationships, what are their forms?
3 Why do these relationships exist?

Review of the literature

Research in the United States has explored three hypotheses for the association between age and environmental concern. One suggests that it is due to the sociobiological ageing process (the 'ageing' hypothesis). The second suggests that important historical events have a differential influence on birth cohorts (the 'cohort' hypothesis). The third claims that there are period effects due to changes in social, cultural and economic conditions (the 'period' hypothesis) (Buttel 1979; Honnold 1984; Mohai and Twight 1987). The 'ageing' hypothesis is based on the view that young people have a lower level of commitment to dominant social values and institutions, the 'cohort' hypothesis relates to Mannheim's (1952) theory of generations, or to C. Wright Mills's (1959) notion of the intersection of biography and history, while the 'period' hypothesis requires that both of these processes can be overridden by adaptations to changing circumstances.

There has been some support for the 'cohort' hypothesis (Mohai and Twight 1987; Samdahl and Robertson 1989) and the 'period' hypothesis (Honnold 1984). However, it is possible that all three processes can have an influence. The advocates of the 'cohort' hypothesis point to events of the late 1960s and early 1970s in American society.

An examination of these three hypotheses suggests that the relationship need not be linear, i.e. that the level of environmentalism need not decrease with age. It is possible that a particular birth cohort of young people has been differentially influenced by a particular wave of interest in environmental issues. They may pass through a period of history as a ripple of environmental concern. This can be expressed as the following theoretical argument.

1 In the late 1960s and early 1970s, young people in Australia were influenced by a period of student radicalism and the concern for environmental issues that followed.
2 These experiences have had a lasting impact on this age cohort, even though the intensity may have subsided.
3 Until very recently, no events of similar historical significance have occurred to influence the environmental attitudes of subsequent cohorts of young people.[9]
4 Other 'period' changes, such as economic cycles, have influenced all contemporary generations more or less equally.
5 The youth cohort of the late 1960s and the 1970s, who are now in middle age, will be the most receptive present generation to the new wave of environmental concern.
6 Therefore, the present middle-aged cohort will have the most favourable environmental worldviews and the highest level of environmental concern. The 'ageing' hypothesis would suggest that the present youth cohort would be the most susceptible to the current wave of environmental issues. The question is whether their one exposure matches the two exposures of the middle-aged generation.

The conclusion of this theory will be tested, i.e. that *the present middle-aged cohort has the most favourable environmental worldviews and the highest level of environmentally responsible behaviour.*

Research strategies

The Deductive research strategy will be used. A theory has been proposed, based on some existing hypotheses, and a new hypothesis has been deduced for testing. According to the Deductive research strategy, testing the conclusion of the theory tests the theory.

Concepts

The following concepts will be measured.

Environmental worldview
Environmentally responsible behaviour
Age

(See Research Design 1 for the formal and operational definitions of these concepts.)

Data sources, types and forms

Data will come from the study on 'Environmental Worldviews and Behaviour among Students and Residents' (see Research Design 1). As these data were originally obtained from individuals in semi-natural settings, this study will use secondary quantitative data. (See Research Design 1 for details of the levels of measurement for each variable.)

Selection of data sources

Samples will be taken from two populations, university students at the RMIT University and householders in the City of Box Hill. (See Research Design 1 for the details of the sampling methods used.)

Data collection and timing

The data come from a cross-sectional study conducted in 1990. A self-administered questionnaire was used with the student sample and a structured interview with the sample of residents. (See Research Design 1 for the details of the timing and methods of data collection.)

Data reduction and analysis

The responses to all questions were coded in the previous study; the categories will be interpreted from the codebook supplied with the database. If necessary, some further re-coding will be undertaken. The original database is available on disc, and the same software package will be used. The following analyses will be undertaken to answer the two research questions and test the hypothesis.

RQ1   Cross-tabulation and non-parametric tests of significance for 'environmental worldview' (ordinal categories) with 'age' (ordinal categories). Product moment correlation coefficient and a parametric test of significance will be used for 'environmental worldview' (scores) with 'age' (in years). The same analysis will be undertaken between the 'environmental worldview' sub-scales and 'age'. Similarly, the associations between 'age' and the ordinal and interval/ratio versions of the three 'environmentally responsible behaviour' variables will be analysed, where appropriate, using the same methods of analysis.

RQ2, RQ3 The 'age' distribution will be tabulated and plotted against the 'environmental worldview' scores and the sub-scale scores, and these will be presented in tables and graphs. Similar tables and graphs will be produced for 'age' against the measures of 'environmentally responsible behaviour'. The distribution of scores and ordinal categories against age, and the shape of the distributions and the curves in these graphs, will determine whether the hypothesis about 'age' and 'environmental worldview' is corroborated or needs to be rejected.

Problems and limitations

As secondary data will be used, the strengths and limitations of the previous study will also apply to this one. However, there is a further limitation in that this study has to accept the form and scope of the data provided. Some desirable data, such as respondents' reports of their involvement in the student movement of the 1960s and 1970s, and their level of environmental concern at that time, are just not available. Therefore, the theory can only be tested in a limited way.

Research Design 3   Gender Differences in Environmentalism: Towards an Explanation

The problem

In the many studies on environmental attitudes, concern and behaviour conducted from the 1960s until the 1990s, gender differences in environmentalism received much less attention than other socio-economic variables. When gender has been included, the findings have been inconsistent and often of limited magnitude. More recently, eco-feminists have presented arguments that are based on fundamental differences in environmentalism between males and females. Hence, it is clear that further research is required to help clarify these issues.

This study will examine the gender differences in environmental worldviews and behaviour in an Australian context, and will attempt to explain the differences that are found to exist.

Motives and goals

The major motivation is to extend the understanding of environmental worldviews and behaviour. While gender differences in environmentalism appear to be rather elusive, it may be possible to learn important lessons from gender socialization, experiences and responsibilities. If women are more committed to an environmental worldview and are more likely to practise environmentally responsible behaviour than men, then discovering why this is so may help to understand how men's attitudes and behaviour could be changed.

Research questions and purposes

The project will have both *descriptive* and *explanatory* purposes, and will address three research questions.

1 To what extent do women hold more favourable environmental worldviews than men?
2 To what extent are women more willing then men to engage in environmentally responsible behaviour?
3 If there are gender differences, why do they exist?

Review of the literature

Eco-feminists have argued that environmental problems are the result of male domination, and, that if women had had equality or super-ordination over men, there would be many fewer environmental problems (for reviews, see Salleh 1984, 1988/9, and Hallebone 1989). Nevertheless, research has provided only limited support for the existence of gender differences in environmental concern. In fact, the van Liere and Dunlap review (1980) provided no support, and Acury and Christianson (1990) found males to be more inclined to be environmentally aware than females. However, McStay and Dunlap (1983) found modest support for gender differences, even when controls for age, education, income and residence were introduced, but they argued that women, in contrast to men, are more likely to engage in behaviour concerned with environmental quality that is personal rather than public. Blocker and Eckberg (1989) found that women were no more concerned than men about general environmental issues, but were significantly more concerned about local environmental issues.

Blaikie (1992) found that while gender differences in environmental worldview were consistent, with females holding more caring attitudes towards the environment than males, the magnitude of these differences was relatively small. However, the gender differences were greatest on the issue of confidence in the capacity of science and technology to solve environmental problems: women were much less confident than men.

In terms of environmental behaviour, Blaikie and Ward (1992) found that females were more likely than males to avoid environmentally damaging products, but there were no significant differences in recycling behaviour or in the level of support for environmental groups. While these differences in environmental worldviews and behaviour are consistent with a feminist explanation, the relationship between environmentalism and gender is clearly a complex one. It is only in particular areas that females show stronger pro-environmental attitudes and behaviour, and then the differences are generally limited.

Research strategies

The first two research questions will be explored using the Inductive research strategy. The third research question will use the Retroductive strategy as expounded by Pawson and Tilley (1997). It is assumed that if there are gender differences in environmental worldviews and behaviour they are the result of the operation of different cognitive mechanisms in different social contexts.

Concepts and model

The central concepts for the first two research questions are as follows. (See Research Design 1 for the formal and operational definitions of these concepts.)

Environmentalism

Environmental worldview

Environmentally responsible behaviour

Gender

In order to establish why there are gender differences in environmentalism, the following model of the connection between cognitive mechanisms and social contexts has been constructed.

1 Attitudes towards the environment, and decisions to engage in environmentally responsible behaviour, are produced by a combination of the social contexts within which an individual is located and the particular roles performed in those contexts.

2 Child-bearing and child-rearing roles entail a concern for the welfare of succeeding generations.

3 The particular social contexts in which everyday activities occur produce differences in the scope and level of awareness and concern about human issues. These social contexts range from private (domestic/local community) to public (work/wider community).

4 Persons whose lives are predominantly in the public sphere will have a broad range of (global) concerns while persons whose lives are predominantly in the private sphere will have a narrower (local) range of concerns.

5 Persons who have primary responsibility for child-bearing and/or child-rearing will be concerned about the health and future of the next and succeeding generations.

Therefore, the following can be concluded from this model.

• Women who have been primarily involved in home-making and child-rearing will have a higher level of environmentalism and a greater concern with local environmental issues than men who have been primarily breadwinners and have pursued careers in the public sphere. In other words, differences in environmentalism between men and women will be greatest when both are involved in traditional segregated roles and social contexts.

• Women who have had a significant involvement in the public sphere will be more like 'traditional' men in their level of environmentalism and locus of concern about environmental issues.

• Men who have had and continue to have a significant involvement in the private sphere will be more like 'traditional' women in their level of environmentalism and locus of concern about environmental issues.

• Women who have never had child-rearing responsibilities will have a lower level of environmentalism than women with these responsibilities and who are involved in similar social contexts.

These conclusions will be examined to assess the relevance of the contexts and cognitive mechanisms postulated in the model.

Data sources, types and forms

Data to answer the first two research questions will come from previous research (see Research Design 1) and will entail secondary analysis. The third research question will require qualitative, primary data from individuals in semi-natural settings.

Selection of data sources

For the third research question, two contrasting populations will be used, both defined as 'men and women who are married or living in a stable *de facto* relationship, aged between 25 and 50, and with dependent children'. The first population will include men and women who have 'traditional' marriages or *de facto* relationships, and the second will have 'modern' marriages or stable relationships. In order to achieve some matching in the social contexts, couples will be included.

Quota sampling will be used with the following criteria: couples who meet the definition of a 'traditional' or 'modern' relationship (two categories), who come from a variety of socio-economic backgrounds (three categories – 'high status', 'middle status' and 'low status', based on occupation and education), who live in both urban and rural areas (three categories – city, country town and rural), and who have a range of environmental behaviour (two categories). These criteria produce a matrix of thirty-six cells. Socio-economic background and urban and rural areas have been included as criteria only to ensure a diverse sample; they will not be discussed as contexts in the model.

Initially, thirty-six couples will be selected for intensive case-study research. If necessary, further cases will be added as the study proceeds.

Data collection and timing

Again, for the third research question, data will be collected by a combination of in-depth and 'realist' interviews, the latter using the method of interviewing advocated by Pawson (1995, 1996) and Pawson and Tilley (1997).

'Realist' interviewing is used to involve the research participants in the process of testing the model of their cognitive mechanisms and how these operate in particular social contexts. This process is different from that in which respondents are required to provide answers to the researcher's predetermined questions (as in the use of questionnaires or structured interview schedules), or where the researcher tries to faithfully report social actors' accounts of their worldviews and activities (as in some in-depth interviews). Rather, it

> requires a teacher–learner relationship to be developed between researcher and informant in which the medium of exchange is the CMO [context, mechanism, outcome] theory and the function of that relationship is to refine CMO theories. The research act thus involves 'learning' the stakeholder's theories, formalizing them, 'teaching' them back to the informant, who is then in a position to comment upon, clarify and further refine the key ideas. (Pawson and Tilley 1997: 218)

In short, the researcher has to learn about the research participant's cognitive mechanisms and contexts from *them*, construct a model of the mechanisms and the context, teach the informant about this model, and then seek feedback in order to either confirm or refine it.

The in-depth interviews will be conducted first. They will focus on the

- contexts in which everyday life now occurs, and has occurred in the past;
- roles undertaken in these contexts;
- involvement in child-rearing activities, past and present; and
- perceptions of threats to the welfare of the next and future generations.

Each interview is expected to take up to one and a half hours. Subject to the agreement of the respondent, all interviews will be recorded on audio cassette. The 'realist' interviews will follow the in-depth interviews on a later occasion. Each interview will take about forty-five minutes, will be recorded, and will be conducted by the researcher.

The in-depth interviews will be used to refine the hypothesized model and to fill out the details of the contexts and mechanisms. The 'realist' interviews will then be used to present the model to the informants for confirmation or further refinement.

Data reduction and analysis

The secondary data to be used to answer the first two research questions have already been reduced. Some further re-coding may be undertaken as the analysis proceeds. The data generated to answer the third research question will come from the recorded conversations in the in-depth and 'realist' interviews.

The following analyses will be undertaken to answer the research questions.

RQ1 Cross-tabulation and non-parametric tests of significance for 'environmental worldview' (ordinal categories) with 'gender' (nominal categories). Product moment correlation coefficient and a parametric test of significance for 'environmental worldview' (scores) with 'gender' (as a dichotomous variable). The same analysis will be undertaken between the 'environmental worldview' sub-scales and 'gender'.

RQ2 The associations between 'gender' and the ordinal and interval/ratio versions of the three 'environmentally responsible behaviour' variables will be analysed, where appropriate, using the same methods of analysis.

RQ3 All in-depth interviews will be transcribed and formatted for entry into an NVivo database. The NVivo software will be used to create categories and index the data to assist with the elaboration of the model.

Problems and limitations

While the method of sampling for the in-depth and 'realist' interviews will provide a diversity of respondents, it will not be possible to generalize statistically from it. However, as the aim is to understand how certain cognitive mechanisms operate in particular social contexts, this sample will allow for an exploration in a limited range of contexts.

Subject to what the study reveals, further cognitive processes (e.g. associated with different types of education, or different exposure to information in the media) and social contexts could be explored in further studies to expand our knowledge of gender differences in environmentalism. Similar models could be developed to understand differences in environmentalism associated with factors such as regional, ethnic, and religious differences, should they be found to exist.

Research Design 4   Motivation for Environmentally Responsible Behaviour: The Case of Environmental Activists

The problem

This project addresses the issue of what motivates and sustains environmentally responsible behaviour. As solutions to many local and global environmental problems are dependent on changes in everyday behaviour, it is necessary to understand what motivates this behaviour in order to be able to develop programmes to try to encourage change. Most research in this field has been quantitative and essentially descriptive; it has established levels of attitudes, knowledge, concern and behaviour, and the relationship between these variables, and with standard socio-demographic variables. Some studies have begun to suggest that various forms of environmental behaviour, such as recycling, avoidance of environmentally damaging products, and energy conservation, are motivated by a range of factors. However, motivation has still to be studied intensively. What is therefore required is the development and testing of theories that will explain these forms of behaviour.

Motives and goals

The main motive is to provide a better basis for programmes designed to increase the practice of environmentally responsible behaviour. The continuation of social life as we know it, and survival of many species, including the human race, is at risk if dramatic changes in human behaviour do not occur quickly.

Research questions and purposes

The research will address four questions.

1 In what range and types of behaviour do environmentally responsible individuals engage?
2 Why do these people act responsibly towards the environment?
3 Why do some of these people manage to sustain this behaviour?
4 How can the incidence of this type of behaviour be increased?

While the study will have a *descriptive* foundation, its main emphasis will be on *understanding* this behaviour in order to bring about *change*. While it is hoped that recommendations can be made concerning the fourth research question, the development and evaluation of programmes for this must await another project.

Review of the literature

Beginning with the wave of environmentalism in the 1970s, and continuing into the middle of the 1980s, traditions of research have focused on attitudes towards the environment and environmental issues and problems, and levels of environmental concern and knowledge. More recently, these topics have been supplemented with research on everyday behaviour that either exacerbates environmental problems (e.g. pollution, global warming, depletion of the ozone layer, energy consumption, and the use of non-renewable resources) or contributes to their amelioration, i.e. on the extent to which people practise environmentally responsible behaviour.

Recently, various research projects have established patterns in environmental attitudes and the types and levels of environmentally responsible behaviour in the Australian population (e.g. Blaikie 1992, 1993b; Blaikie and Ward 1992; Castles 1993; Blaikie and Drysdale 1994; Environment Protection Authority of New South Wales 1994). It is now possible to compare the Australian situation with that in twenty-two other countries, using the study conducted by Dunlap *et al.* (1992).

Since the 1970s, environmental attitudes and behaviour in Western societies has been subject to considerable fluctuations. According to opinion polls in Australia, the most recent wave of concern, which began in the late 1980s, has exhibited considerable changes in environmental attitudes. Some of these have been attributed to the effects of an economic recession on the capacity of governments and businesses to cope with the costs involved in acting responsibly towards the environment, and the more immediate pressures on the population in dealing with unemployment and economic insecurity.

The search for ways to motivate and facilitate pro-environment behaviour began to engage researchers in the United States back in the late 1970s. Particular attention has been given to recycling (e.g. Reid *et al.* 1976; Witmer and Geller 1976; Humphrey *et al.* 1977; Luyben and Bailey 1979; Pardini and Katzev 1983/4; De Young 1986, 1988/9). Extrinsic incentives, such as the purchase of recycled materials or the provision of rewards for carrying out recycling, have had mixed success; they tend to produce only short-term results (e.g. Cook and Berrenberg 1981; Pardini and Katzev 1983/4) but not enduring behaviour change (Witmer and Geller 1976). This may be related to the finding that 'non-recyclers' need financial incentives and convenient recycling systems much more than regular 'recyclers' (Vining and Ebreo 1990). In many cases, the cost of the incentives exceeded the revenue from the collections (Jacobs *et al.* 1984). Similar problems in the balance of cost and benefit have been found with energy conservation (Newsom and Makranczy 1978; McClelland and Canter 1981).

Psychologists, mainly in the United States, have applied behavioural (reward and punishment) techniques to environmental problems, beginning with the problem of littering (Burgess *et al.* 1971; Tuso and Geller 1976; Casey and Lloyd

1977; Cone and Hayes 1984; Lahart and Bailey 1984; Levit and Leventhall 1986). Some researchers have argued that the use of behavioural techniques to discourage littering is superior to methods of persuasion and education, and may be more cost-effective than traditional clean-up methods. While it has been argued that the same behavioural techniques can be applied to other problems, such as energy conservation and recycling, this approach has been criticized for providing only short-term solutions. As soon as the rewards are withdrawn the behaviour tends to return to previous levels (Gudgion and Thomas 1991).

The relationship between attitudes and behaviour, and the ability of attitudes to predict behaviour, has concerned social psychologists for at least seventy years (for reviews see Ajzen and Fishbein 1980; McGuire 1968; Fazio 1986; Chaiken and Stangor 1987). Theory and research on this relationship have gone through a number of stages (Zanna and Fazio 1982). Until the mid-1960s, the predominant assumption was that a one-to-one correspondence must exist between attitudes and behaviour. This was followed by a period of questioning of whether there is a relationship and whether it is worth pursuing. By the 1970s the question became: 'When do attitudes guide behaviour?' There was a shift in concern to the conditions under which attitudes might predict behaviour, with the result that many situational and personality variables were identified as moderators of the relationship. In the 1980s the question became: 'How do attitudes guide behaviour?' This has involved recognizing the effects of attitudes on perception, the role of interpretation (definition) of situations, and the intervention of norms (Fazio 1986). However, this extensive tradition has tended to neglect the relationship between agency and structure; it has ignored the alternative tradition that views attitudes as an epiphenomenon of a person's location in the social structure, and has virtually overlooked the effects of social context on behaviour.

The relationship between attitudes and behaviour has also been a central topic of research in environmental sociology and social psychology (e.g. Ehrlich 1969; Vicker 1969; Geller *et al.* 1982; Dunlap *et al.* 1983; Dunlap and van Liere 1984; Heberlein 1989; Gigliotti 1992). The predominant assumption has been that changing people's environmental attitudes will change their environmentally related behaviour. However, as pro-environmental attitudes have become more socially acceptable, and concern for the environment has become better established, the gap in this relationship has become a focus of attention. In some cases, environmental knowledge has been added to produce a two-stage model with causal implications: knowledge is related to attitude and attitude is related to behaviour (e.g. Pettus 1976; Ramsey and Rickson 1976; Borden and Schettino 1979; Hausbeck *et al.* 1990).

There has been a long tradition of research on environmental attitudes and behaviour in the Netherlands (see e.g. Scheepers and Nelissen 1989; Nelissen and Scheepers 1992). Using a variety of measures of environmental behaviour (recycling, consumption of ecological products, energy consumption, and means of transport) with a national sample in 1990, Nelissen and Scheepers (1992) identified patterns of consistency and non-consistency in a typology that related environmental attitudes (ecological consciousness) and behaviour: 'consistent non-ecologists' (low ecological consciousness and no ecological behaviour); 'inconsistent consciousness-ecologists' (moderate ecological consciousness and moderate ecological behaviour); and 'consistent ecologists' (strong ecological consciousness and consistent ecological behaviour). They found that one form of ecological behaviour, buying ecologically sound products and refraining from buying non-ecological products, had the weakest association with both ecological consciousness and other forms of ecological behaviour.

More recently, the role of social context has been given explicit recognition in the link between environmental attitudes and behaviour (Derksen and Gartrell, 1993). These researchers compared two Canadian cities (Edmonton and Calgary) and the remaining small towns and rural areas in the province of Alberta. Only one of the cities, Edmonton, had a well-developed and user-friendly recycling programme. They found a very high level of concern for the environment across the province, with a result that socio-demographic variables, such as age, gender, education and income, showed weak associations. Predictably, the Edmonton residents had a much higher level of recycling than in the rest of the province, particularly in the rural areas.

Changes in environmental attitudes and behaviour in Australia have been investigated between 1989 and 1994 (Blaikie 1992, 1993b; Blaikie and Ward 1992; Blaikie and Drysdale 1994) using samples of residents in the Melbourne Metropolitan Area and university students. These studies found that the strongest commitment to an environmental worldview is to be found in the middle-aged cohort; younger cohorts hold a middle position and older cohorts have the lowest levels of commitment. Compared with people generally, on average, university students did not rate higher on environmental worldview, were no more active in or supportive of environmental groups, and did not exhibit a higher level of environmentally responsible behaviour. This raises some questions about the extent to which a university education produces higher levels of environmental commitment and action.

American research has produced conflicting results on the relationship between environmental concern and gender (van Liere and Dunlap 1980; McStay and Dunlap 1983; Blocker and Eckberg 1989; Samdhal and Robertson 1989; Acury and Christianson 1990). Australian data indicate that women of all ages are only marginally more committed to an environmental worldview than men (Blaikie 1992).

Each type of environmental behaviour appears to have its own form of motivation (Blaikie and Drysdale 1994). While the level of 'avoidance of environmentally dangerous products' is associated as strongly as any other variable with 'environmental worldview', which products are avoided appears to have been influenced by the attention received in the media. In spite of the small increase in the level of 'support for environmental groups', this form of environmental behaviour has remained low; it is very much an activity of those with very favourable 'environmental worldviews'. Dramatic increases in recycling have occurred, but this form of environmental behaviour shows little or no association with environmental attitudes; it is dependent on the availability of convenient, regular and publicly supported collection systems. However, it also appears to be motivated by attitudes, values and practices that have arisen from periods when conservation (i.e. making things last by taking good care of them and maintaining them well) and reuse were a necessity. People who lived through the depression of the 1930s and the Second World War can be keen recyclers without having favourable environmental worldviews.

It is clear from the literature that the relationship between environmental worldviews and behaviour is complex and that such worldviews are not good predictors of behaviour. The explanation for environmentally responsible behaviour must be sought elsewhere. Some useful ideas have emerged about how this type of behaviour can be changed. The following conclusions about changing environmental behaviour have been drawn from the literature.

1 Various forms of environmental behaviour have different types of motivation, thus requiring different strategies for changing environmental behaviour.
2 Changing environmental attitudes, certainly on their own, is not an effective way to change environmental behaviour.
3 Improving environmental knowledge, through education and the media, may change attitudes. Improving knowledge is a necessary condition for change in some forms of behaviour. However, this knowledge needs to be accompanied by both opportunity and meaningful motivation for behaviour to be sustained.
4 Some forms of behaviour can be changed dramatically, and, perhaps, can only be changed with the establishment of effective, convenient and socially acceptable systems.
5 Generating social acceptance and support for different behaviour is an underrated, and, perhaps, a necessary condition for some forms of behaviour change.

While this project will not test these possible hypotheses by the more conventional Deductive strategy, they will provide some ideas about the direction in which to look in the process of theory generation.

Research strategies

It is clear from the literature review that, with the exception perhaps of the Retroductive research strategy, a different strategy than the ones that have been used so far is required to understand environmental behaviour. As there are no clear theoretical leads from the literature, theory generation is required. Therefore, the Abductive research strategy will be adopted in order to explore this understanding in depth.

Concepts

Some concepts will be used in a sensitizing mode to provide initial direction for the study. The aim will be to explore the meaning given to them by the people studied, and to discover other concepts they use that are roughly equivalent, or are different. The main concepts are:

- environment
- nature
- environmental problems
- environmental protection
- conservation
- recycling
- economic growth

No theories or hypotheses are proposed. Models in the form of ideal types will be developed to grasp the variety of motives and behaviour.

Data sources, types and forms

Primary data will be obtained from individuals in semi-natural settings. Apart from a few simple frequency counts and percentages, the data will be qualitative at all stages of the research.

Selection of data sources

The population will include individuals who engage in a range of environmentally responsible behaviour, such as:

- active involvement in environmental groups and movements;
- involvement in local protests on environmental issues;
- minimizing the use of non-renewable resources;
- avoiding the use of environmentally damaging products; and
- recycling 'waste' products.

The intention is to include both public and private activities.

Given the nature of the population, non-probability sampling will be used with a combination of quota sampling, as well as snowball and opportunistic sampling. Interviewers will collectively maintain a gender balance and an age and social class distribution in the selection of respondents. The aim will be to include as diverse a range of people as possible. Some respondents will be contacted through environmental organizations and the interviewers will recruit others, using their own friends and acquaintances. Persons contacted will be asked to suggest other possible respondents. It is expected that a sample of about one hundred will be used.

Data collection and timing

Data will be collected by in-depth interviews over a period of four months. Each interview is expected to take about two hours. In addition to the researcher, five experienced interviewers will be employed. Subject to the agreement of the respondent, all interviews will be recorded on audio cassette. Each respondent will complete a one-page bio-data sheet.

Initially, the following themes will be used:

- meaning of 'environment', 'environmental problems', 'nature', etc.;
- knowledge and awareness of environmental problems;
- understanding of the causes and effects of these problems;
- views on who is responsible for dealing with them and whether individual actions can make a difference;
- actions taken by the respondent;
- motivation for these actions;

- influences of significant others; and
- experience with natural environments and animals as a child and youth.

After fifty interviews have been completed, the transcripts will be analysed. This may lead to some changes in the interview themes. After a further fifty interviews, further analysis will be undertaken. The first fifty respondents will be re-interviewed, using what has been learnt to increase the focus of the interview. Further analysis of these interviews will occur before the second fifty respondents are re-interviewed. Following the analysis of these transcripts, a few respondents may be selected for a third interview if it is felt that theoretical saturation has not been reached. In this way, the data collection and analysis will involve a spiral learning process in which each wave of interviews builds on the understanding gained up to that point. Re-interviewing will allow an in-depth understanding of all respondents.

As it is impossible to anticipate when theoretical saturation will be reached, the size of the sample must remain approximate at this stage. However, for budget purposes, it is assumed that a total of 225 interviews will be required.

Data reduction and analysis

All interviews will be transcribed and formatted for entry into an NVivo data-base. The basic information on the bio-data sheets will be included in the file for each respondent. The NVivo software will be used to create categories and index the data. The methods of open and axial coding (grounded theory) will be used to generate typologies and, hopefully, theory.

Alongside this method of analysis, interviewers will be asked to write a brief summary of their impressions of each interview, and, from time to time, their impressions of what they see developing from the interviews. The researcher will listen to all the cassettes and also record impressions and ideas from the record-ings. Interviewers' impressions of each interview will be added to the transcript of the relevant interview. Overall impressions will be entered into separate inter-viewer files and will constitute additional data.

Problems and limitations

The major problem with a study of this kind is the uncertainty about how it will develop. A balance must be struck between the order of a planned programme and the flexibility required to allow the learning process to evolve. Another problem is the time required to collect and analyse the data. Given limited resources, and the developmental nature of the research strategy, the sample size must be limited.

The sample will not allow for generalization to a population. However, this is not the intention of this project. Its aim is to generate a theoretical understand-ing that can be used as the basis for an intervention programme. Any theory that emerges can be tested in other contexts to establish its range of application, as will the evaluation of any intervention programmes based on it.

Postscript

I hope that these sample research designs will provide not only some guidance as to what is required, but also encouragement to spend the time attending to the decisions that must be made. In many ways, designing a research project is more difficult than doing it. If a project is well designed, the steps involved in carrying it out should follow reasonably smoothly. Of course, the ability to collect and analyse data successfully requires a great deal of knowledge, skill, persistence and ingenuity. It is also fraught with difficulties and barriers that have to be overcome, before and during the research process.

Even in the most carefully planned research projects, there is always the possibility that something will go wrong. We may have overlooked something, or factors outside our control may upset our plans. Published reports of research rarely mention these. They present us with a 'reconstructed logic'. I have been guilty of this myself, and would therefore like to give an example of a problem I experienced and how it was overcome.

In the late 1960s I directed a class in social research methods to undertake a study of values and occupational choice among university students (Blaikie 1971). The research design included a combined stratified and systematic sampling method with students from three different degree programmes, arts (including most of the social sciences), law and science at Monash University in Melbourne. These three categories, as well as year at university (1, 2 and 3+), were used as strata. Systematic sampling, with different sampling ratios, was to be used to produce roughly the same number in each stratum. Lists of students in these programmes, and their addresses, were available from the university's administration and data were to be collected by a mailed questionnaire.

Precisely at the time that we were about to draw the sample, the university put an embargo on access to such student records. It was the time of the Vietnam War, and young Australians were being conscripted by ballot to go and fight. Some university students were trying to dodge the draft. Being the most radical campus in the country at the time, the very powerful student body had persuaded the university authorities not to release any information about students to anyone, without the individual student's written permission. Therefore, we were unable to get the anticipated access to the information required to draw the sample.

Clearly, there were some options. Abandon the study, get the students' permission, or modify the design. We couldn't really exercise the first option because the completion of the study was an integral part of the course. We considered the second, but it was impractical. How do you contact members of a sample without first drawing the sample? The university was not prepared to do this for us, and, in any case, as we had no research funds, this, and the cost incurred by the university in writing to all the students, could not be covered. In addition, this process would have taken some time, and we were operating within the limits of one semester. Time had already been lost in dealing with the problem. We had no alternative but to modify the research design.

Instead of the rather complex two-stage sampling plan, and collecting the data using mailed questionnaires, we used a quota sample with structured interviewing. Because this method of data collecting was more labour-intensive, and time was limited, we decided to restrict the sample to arts students. These changes clearly limited our ability to deal with some of the original research questions and to test the theoretical model (see the section on 'Theoretical Models' in chapter 5). Nevertheless, some useful and publishable results were obtained (see Blaikie 1971).

The core theme of this book has been that all social research needs to be planned thoroughly in order to ensure a successful outcome, and that inevitable setbacks will not be fatal. At the same time, it is recognized that research design is always a compromise between the ideal way of answering research questions and what is practical in the light of financial, time and other constraints. In short, good research designs are creative and professionally acceptable solutions to the problems and limitations that are encountered at the beginning and during the course of the research.

The time and care taken to prepare a detailed and comprehensive research design is bound to be worth the effort. It only remains for me to wish you well in your research activities and to hope that meticulous and creative planning will lead to successful and fruitful outcomes.

Afterword

When these sample research designs were originally prepared for the first edition of this book, the level of political, media and public awareness and knowledge of the significance and consequences of global warming (now called climate change) was very much lower than they are at the time of writing this second edition. What I find disappointing is the fact that what have now become issues of great concern, such as global warming, were already well articulated in the environmental science literature twenty years ago. While there has been a big shift in public and political knowledge in the intervening period, the battle to persuade the sceptics continues. So much time has been wasted and we may come to regret this.

Appendix

Examples of Research Topics, Problems and Questions

Research Topics

Topic 1   'Absenteeism in the Public Sector: A Case Study of Nurses in the Public Hospital in Kota Lama'

Topic 2   'Job Satisfaction among Administrative Staff at the University of Stewart Island'

Topic 3   'Student Plagiarism at the University of Alice Springs'

Topic 4   'Industrialization, Urbanization and Juvenile Delinquency in Ping Kong, Andanasia'

Topic 5   'Changing Religious Practices and Orientations to the World in New Religious Movements: The Case of the New Light Sect in Brownsville'

The statement of the research topic should locate the research. However, these topics have been given fictional locations.

Most topics can be stated at various levels of precision. For example, topic 4 could have been stated as 'Juvenile Delinquency in Andanasia', but this would be rather general. It could be stated precisely in terms of both the key concepts to be investigated, and the location of the study, as 'Juvenile Delinquency and the Breakdown of Family and Religious Values in the Context of Industrialization and Urbanization in Ping Kong, Andanasia. This version has the advantage of being very informative, and it also illustrates how the scope of a research project can be focused and narrowed. However, it is rather long; too long for the spine of a thesis! Hence, it is useful to use a double-barrelled title. The general and long versions could be combined as 'Juvenile Delinquency in Andanasia: The Breakdown of Family and Religious Values in the Context of Industrialization and Urbanization in Ping Kong. Alternatively, the title above is a reasonable compromise.

Research Problems

The first four topics deal with social problems, and the last one with a sociological problem.

Topic 1   Stems from difficulties in maintaining adequate staffing levels at a particular hospital and the possible adverse effects of this on patient care and hospital management.

Topic 2   Was prompted by a perceived lack of efficiency in the university's administration, as well as the overt behaviour of the staff, such as complaints to supervisors and disruptive actions.

Topic 3   Emerged from anecdotal evidence reported by lecturers at the university about the incidence of this practice in students' essays and papers, and a concern that this is a serious academic offence with possible educational consequences.

Topic 4   Arose from evidence of rising rates of juvenile crime that seem to accompany industrialization and urbanization associated with economic development. The specific problem is how to prevent young people becoming involved in such activities.

Topic 5   Based on curiosity about new religious movements in general, and about the beliefs and practices of a particular religious sect. Just why a researcher has this interest is another matter.

Research Questions

Topic 1: Absenteeism

Absenteeism here refers to absences from work on other than approved leave.

1 What is the rate of absenteeism among nurses?
2 What kinds of nurses are most frequently absent from work unofficially?
3 What effects does absenteeism have on patient care and hospital management?
4 Why does absenteeism occur?
5 How can absenteeism be reduced?

The first two questions are seeking *descriptions* of the frequency of the behaviour and the types of nurses involved. Question 4 seeks an *explanation* for these patterns, and Question 5 looks for an *intervention* strategy. Question 3 is about the consequences of this behaviour for the organization; it could be regarded as being concerned with *impact assessment*, and it expresses this by asking a 'what' question. This example clearly illustrates a sequence of 'what', 'why' and 'how' questions.

Topic 2: Job Satisfaction

This topic has a rather more complex set of research questions.

1 What is the level and range of job satisfaction among the administrative staff?
2 To what extent can the level and range of job satisfaction be regarded as satisfactory?
3 Under what circumstances do staff experience job satisfaction and dissatisfaction?
4 Why do some staff experience job satisfaction and others dissatisfaction in these circumstances?
5 What consequences does level of job satisfaction have for work performance?
6 How can the level of job satisfaction be improved?

Again, the first three questions require *descriptions*, Question 4 an *explanation*, Question 5 refers to the *impact* of job satisfaction on relevant behaviour, and Question 6 seeks strategies for *change*. It is worth noting that Question 3, a 'what' question, verges on a 'why' question. This illustrates the point that answers to some 'why' questions can be achieved by asking a number of 'what' questions.

Topic 3: Student Plagiarism

This project has a similar sequence of questions.

1 What has been the extent of detected student plagiarism over the past five years?
2 In what types of plagiarism have students engaged?
3 What types of students have been caught plagiarizing?
4 What attitudes do lecturers and university administrators have towards plagiarism?
5 What consequences does plagiarism have for students' intellectual development?
6 Why do students plagiarize?
7 How can student plagiarism be eliminated?

Again, most of the research questions are 'what' questions (Questions 1 to 4), including one (Question 5) which is about *impact assessment*. This would be a very large, complex and difficult project as it would require a number of separate studies to complete it: secondary sources (Question 1–3); attitude surveys of both lecturers and administrators (Question 4); a longitudinal comparative study of plagiarizers and non-plagiarizers (Question 5); an in-depth study of the plagiarizers (Question 6); and a policy development study (Question 7). Question 5 would be the most challenging in this set of research questions.

Topic 4: Juvenile Delinquency

1 What is the incidence of the main types of juvenile delinquency in Ping Kong, Andansaia?
2 Why do young people engage in these types of criminal activities?
3 To what extent has the incidence changed in the past ten years?
4 (If the incidence has increased): Why has there been an increase?
5 What is the role of industrialization and urbanization in this increase?
6 How can the incidence of juvenile delinquency be reduced?

This is a more complex set of questions. Questions 1 and 2 are concerned with the *description* and *explanation* of the present situation, while Questions 3 and 4 are concerned with the *description* and *explanation* of change. Question 4 has a subsidiary question which is proposing a possible answer, a broad hypothesis, that 'the increase in juvenile delinquency is a result of industrialization and urbanization'. However, this doesn't explain very much. What is needed is an understanding of how these social and economic changes affect family, community and religious life. This would require the development of a theory from which hypotheses could be deduced for testing. Finally, the study seeks solutions to what is regarded as a social problem. It may be difficult to answer such a 'how' question within this study. Further policy-oriented research to develop intervention programmes, and then evaluation studies of these programmes, would be required.

Topic 5: New Religious Movements

This study provides an example of how a research project might address only one research question.

> What internal and external social changes are related to changes in the religious practices and orientation to the world adopted by the New Light Sect in Brownsville?

The question is also an example of how the descriptive answer to a 'what' question constitutes a possible answer to a 'why' question. For example, changes in membership or leadership, and social and economic changes in the wider society that result in the emergence of different individual needs, might be related to changes in beliefs and practices. Such a description could be an answer to the question, 'Why do new religious movements change their orientations to the world?' Both the internal and external changes may be regarded as a set of necessary and sufficient conditions, or as causal mechanisms operating in a particular context.

Notes

1 Preparing Research Designs

1 North American readers will need to substitute 'graduate' for 'postgraduate' whenever it occurs.
2 This list comes from the British Economic and Social Research Council application form for research funds. Similar lists will be found in other such documents.
3 This may be included in the 'Aims and significance' section as it follows logically from its specifications.
4 I mention this point out of exasperation at the number of occasions, in spite of clear instructions, in which I have seen this confusion occur.

2 Designing Social Research

1 'Strategy' is given a somewhat different meaning in this book.
2 This distinction between inductive and deductive forms of enquiry is elaborated in chapter 4. An alternative to 'inductive' is also proposed for the processes to which Lincoln and Guba refer.
3 The question of whether causation can be established in such non-experimental designs has been a matter of considerable debate.
4 'Research purposes' replaces 'research objectives' in the first edition as terms such as Aims and Objectives, which are commonly included in research proposals, have different meanings to what is intended here.
5 'Social' problems are frequently referred to incorrectly as 'sociological' problems. 'Social' has to do with social life; 'sociological' has to do with the discipline that studies social life.
6 See Maxwell (2005) for a similar discussion.
7 Refinements have been made to this dichotomy (e.g. pure basic, oriented basic, applied strategic and applied specific). However, this dichotomy is adequate for the present purposes.

3 Research Questions and Purposes

1 Hedrick et al. (1993) have suggested a similar division between 'primary' and 'subordinate' research questions and Creswell (2009) refers to 'central' and 'subquestions'.

2   See also, Mathison (2004); Shaw *et al.* (2006); and Stufflebeam and Shinkfield (2007).
3   While the research purpose of *understand* and *explain* use the same kind of research question, it is necessary to keep them separate as they answer 'why' questions in different ways.

4 Strategies for Answering Research Questions

1   The research strategies discussed here are not the classical versions found in the literature but are my revisions of them designed to overcome their major deficiencies (see Blaikie 2007, ch. 3).
2   In the first edition of this book, a similar set of questions took Malaysia as the context. As I wrote the book there, I was very aware of the concern being expressed at the rise in the rate of juvenile delinquency as the country urbanized and industrialized. Such changes are typical of developing nations.
3   An earlier version of this (Blaikie 2000, 2007) was intended as an account of how the Retroductive research strategy is used in the natural sciences. This adaptation draws heavily on the work of Pawson.
4   These reviews are based on the end of section summaries in Blaikie (2007, chs 4 and 5).

5 Concepts, Theories, Hypotheses and Models

1   Writers in this tradition differ in terms of whether they regard sensitizing concepts as an alternative to the operationalizing tradition or as complementing it.
2   While he has followed Schütz's idea that these typifications must be descriptive of the everyday social worlds of people to whom they relate, he appears to have moved these concepts further away from these social worlds than Schütz and, certainly, some of his followers would allow.
3   This would not be so for the classical version of the Inductive research strategy the founders of which considered that concepts were somehow revealed in the process of making observations. The world was regarded as being already divided into discrete categories of things and events. As these categories were revealed through observation, it was assumed that the concepts that applied to them would be self-evident and would not need to be defined by the observer.
4   Some versions of this classification subdivide the interpretive perspective, for example, into symbolic interactionism and ethnomethodology.
5   He would have regarded Weber's work on the Protestant Ethic, and Durkheim's work on suicide and his concept of anomie as good examples of middle-range theory.
6   Failure to distinguish theoretical and statistical hypotheses is common in the literature. For example, see Neuman (2006: 165).
7   Some time ago, I attempted to apply Willer's scheme to a study on the occupational choices of university students (Blaikie 1971).

6 Sources and Selection of Data

1   These categories closely resemble Layder's (1993) stratified model of society.
2   In using such distinctions as *micro*, *meso* and *macro*, as well as primary and secondary social groups, we encounter problems of definition and boundaries. It is not the intention here to try to be definitive about such distinctions, but, rather, to distinguish broadly between a range of social phenomena.

3 The concept of 'society' is not included here as a social phenomenon, partly because of the diversity of its uses and the vagueness of its meaning, but also because it adds nothing to the range of concepts being discussed, i.e. organizations, communities, social movements and nations. Differences between 'society' and 'nation' hinge on both political and geographical criteria. However, the details of these differences need not concern us here. Some writers, perhaps economists, use 'economy' instead of 'nation'. While an 'economy' may be a large social unit with relatively autonomous political and legal institutions, globalization and regional trading blocks are reducing this autonomy. As I write, the 2008–2009 world economic 'crisis' is much in evidence.

4 See Campbell and Stanley (1963a) and Cook and Campbell (1979) for classic discussions of experiments in social research, and Kidder and Judd (1986: chs 4 and 5) and Neuman (2006: ch. 9) for useful reviews.

5 Even although sampling is widely discussed in research methods and statistical texts, I have devoted considerable space to data selection here because I believe many discussions of the topic are inadequate, even badly flawed, and, from my experience of working with novice researchers, is frequently very badly done. In other words, understanding sampling 'properly' is one of my hobby horses. Elsewhere I have provided a more statistical treatment of the topic (see ch. 6 in Blaikie 2003).

6 In addition to Kish (1965) and Scheaffer *et al.* (1996), Moser and Kalton (1971: chs 3–7) provide a comprehensive discussion, and Hoinville and Jowell (1977), Kalton (1983), Henry (1990), and de Vaus (2002) have brief, readable overviews.

7 Textbooks on social research methods often include a table of random numbers. See, for example, de Vaus (2002) for instructions on how to use such tables and Neuman (2006: 535–6) for a large table.

8 For useful discussions of the use of sampling in qualitative research, see Burgess (1982b), Honigmann (1982), Mason (2002), Gobo (2004), and Flick (2006).

9 I have used a similar set of categories, but such a large number can create difficulties for interviewers. A simpler set could be based on gender and age (say, four categories) which would create only eight quota categories.

10 See Moser and Kalton (1971: 63–9) or Kish (1965: chs 1 and 13) for more details.

11 I once managed an 87 per cent response rate in a survey using mailed questionnaires, a method renowned for low rates. This high response rate was achieved by the use of very elaborate and time-consuming follow-up procedures with a very particular population. As a population was studied, the problem of having to estimate its characteristics from sample data was eliminated, thus further improving the precision of the data.

12 I have no idea why 10 per cent is regarded as some magical figure to determine sample size. It has been quoted to me *ad nauseam* by colleagues and students.

13 Formulae are available for calculating these intervals. They can vary depending on the sampling method used and the type of data, for example, means or percentages (see Kish 1965).

14 See Eckstein (1992) for a critical review of use of case studies and comparative studies in political science, with particular reference to their role in theory building.

15 See de Vaus (2001, ch. 14) for a more detailed discussion of critical issues in case study research.

16 Denzin (1978: 192) has produced a similar set of six steps.

7 Methods for Answering Research Questions: Data Gathering and Analysis

1 Scaling is a relatively ancient art in social science and the classic references are still useful. See, for example, Thurstone and Chave (1929); Likert (1970); Bogardus

(1933); Stouffer *et al.* (1950); Goode and Hatt (1952); Eysenck (1954); and Edwards (1957). The last reference provides a useful review of the state of the art at the time and Maranell (1974/2007) a more extensive coverage.

2 The dominance of quantitative methods has been most evident in decision-making associated with research grant allocations. You only have to ask any qualitative researcher how difficult it is to compete for research funds, and examine the statistics on the distribution of grant allocations within the broad range of the social and behavioural sciences. For example, economics and psychology consistently fare much better than sociology, anthropology and history in grants allocated by the Australian Research Council. My experience suggests that this is probably due to the prejudices of at least some members of such funding agencies.

3 My position is that all methods have their place in social research and that the choice should be determined by the nature of the problem, the purpose of the research and the type of research questions being investigated. A few years ago I wrote a text on quantitative data analysis (Blaikie 2003), having been socialized as a quantitative researcher. Some of my former students, who had been championing the cause of qualitative methods for many years, were appalled at this because they thought I was on their side. I certainly had been (see Blaikie 1977, 1978), but I have become more ecumenical with age!

4 Denzin has used the concepts of 'method', 'methodology' and 'methodological' interchangeably. My discussion will concentrate on methods and data and will not include investigators and theories. Combining investigators can be useful, but combining theories is difficult to put into practice, unless by theories are meant perspectives or paradigms.

5 I can speak with some authority on this matter as my first career was in surveying.

8 Sample Research Designs

1 The standard practice of including such variables is usually based on some implicit theories about their explanatory relevance to particular types of attitude and behaviour. Because these theories are not spelt out, it is difficult to judge whether these variables should be used. Not too much harm is done including them in exploratory and descriptive research, but it is bad practice to expect that a selection of such variables will be any use in explanatory research, without first articulating the theory to which they might be related.

2 The 'number of children' is another example of a superficially simple but in fact complex concept to define, particularly in this era of step-families.

3 This research was planned before local authorities had established schemes for collecting recyclables.

4 Due to the changing forms of different-sex and same-sex relationships, and the relatively limited duration of many such relationships in most contemporary societies, this variable is no longer easy to operationalize.

5 A more elaborate and perhaps more meaningful way to measure this variable would be to ask questions about attendance at public services of worship, type and frequency of private devotional practices, and participation in religious organizations.

6 The City of Box Hill no longer exists due to an amalgamation with an adjoining city and a name change. It still exists as a suburb and regional shopping centre.

7 All undergraduate students were required to take four of the twenty general education courses offered in this programme. These courses were designed to expose students to a range of intellectual discourses and to address issues of relevance to a student's future role as a responsible citizen.

8 In the original study (Blaikie 1992), two student samples were used. One of about

200 used the method described here, and another quota sample of the same size (with selection criteria of field of degree and gender) was interviewed. In spite of the radically different sampling methods, and the different method of administration, the distributions on the main variables were almost identical.

9 It is necessary to keep in mind that this research design was for a study to be conducted in the early 1990s. The situation at the time of publication is different.

References

Ackoff, R. 1953. *The Design of Social Research*. Chicago, IL: University of Chicago Press.

Acury, T. A. and E. H. Christianson 1990. 'Environmental worldview in response to environmental problems: Kentucky 1984 and 1988 compared.' *Environment and Behavior* 22: 387–407.

Adelman, C., D. Jenkins and S. Kemmis 1977. 'Rethinking case study: notes from the second Cambridge conference.' *Cambridge Journal of Education* 6: 139–50.

Ajzen, I. and M. Fishbein 1980. *Understanding Attitudes and Predicting Social Behavior*. Englewood Cliffs, NJ: Prentice-Hall.

Albrecht, D., G. Bultena, E. Hoiberg and P. Novak 1982. 'The new environmental scale.' *Journal of Environmental Education* 13: 39–43.

Alexander, J. C. 1982. *Theoretical Logic in Sociology*, vol. 1: *Positivism, Presuppositions, and Current Controversies*. London: Routledge and Kegan Paul.

Anderson, R. E. 1992. 'Computer applications in the social sciences.' In E. F. Borgatta and M. L. Borgatta (eds), *Encyclopedia of Sociology*, vol. 1. New York: Macmillan. Pp. 282–8.

Andrews, R. 2003. *Research Questions*. London: Continuum.

Appelrouth, S. and L. D. Edles 2008. *Classical and Contemporary Sociological Theory*. Los Angeles, CA: Pine Forge.

Aron, R. 1965. *Main Currents in Sociological Thought 1*. London: Weidenfeld and Nicolson.

—— 1968. *Main Currents in Sociological Thought 2*. London: Weidenfeld and Nicolson.

Aronson, E. and J. M. Carlsmith 1968. 'Experimentation in social psychology.' In G. Lindzey and E. Aronson (eds), *The Handbook of Social Psychology*, vol. 2: *Research Methods*. Reading, MA: Addison-Wesley. Pp. 1–78.

Atkinson, P. 1990. *The Ethnographic Imagination: Textual Constructions of Reality*. London: Routledge.

Atkinson, P., A. Coffey, S. Delmont, J. Lofland and L. Lofland (eds) 2001. *Handbook of Ethnography*. London: Sage.

Babbie, E. R. 2004. *The Practice of Social Research* (10th edn). Belmont, CA: Wadsworth.

Bailey, K. D. 1994. *Methods of Social Research* (4th edn). New York: Free Press.

Balnaves, M. 1990. 'Communication and information: an analysis of concepts.' PhD thesis, Royal Melbourne Institute of Technology, Melbourne.

Barnes, H. E. 1948. *An Introduction to the History of Sociology*. Chicago, IL: University of Chicago Press.

Barnes, H. E. and H. Becker 1938. *Social Thought from Lore to Science*. Boston: Heath.

Bassey, M. 1981. 'Pedagogic research: on the relative merits of search for generalization and study of single events.' *Oxford Review of Education* 7 (1): 73–93.

Becker, H. and H. E. Barnes 1961. *Social Thought from Lore to Science*, (3rd edn). New York: Dover.

Becker, H. A. 1997. *Social Impact Assessment: Method and Experience in Europe, North America and the Developing World*. London: UCL Press.

Becker, H. S. and B. Geer 1957. 'Participant observation and interviewing.' *Human Organization* 16: 28–32.

Beilharz, P. (ed.) 1991. *Social Theory: A Guide to Central Thinkers*. St Leonards, NSW: Allen and Unwin.

Bell, J. 2005. *Doing Your Research Project: A Guide for First-time Researchers in Education and Social Science* (4th edn). Maidenhead: Open University Press.

Berg, B. L. 1995. *Qualitative Research Methods for the Social Sciences* (2nd edn). Boston, MA: Allyn and Bacon.

Bergman, M. M. (ed.) 2008. *Advances in Mixed Methods Research: Theories and Applications*. London: Sage.

Bertaux, D. (ed.) 1981. *Biography and Society: The Life History Approach in the Social Sciences*. Beverly Hills, CA: Sage.

Bhaskar, R. 1978. *A Realist Theory of Science* (2nd edn). Hassocks: Harvester.

—— 1979. *The Possibility of Naturalism: A Philosophical Critique of the Contemporary Human Sciences*. Brighton: Harvester.

—— 1986. *Scientific Realism and Human Emancipation*. London: Verso.

Biddle, B. J. 1979. *Role Theory: Expectations, Identities, and Behaviors*. New York: Academic Press.

Black, M. 1962. *Models and Metaphors: Studies in Language and Philosophy*. Ithaca, NY: Cornell University Press.

Blaikie, N. W. H. 1968. 'An analysis of religious affiliation, activity and attitudes in St Albans, Christchurch.' MA thesis, University of Canterbury, New Zealand.

—— 1969. 'Religion, social status, and community involvement: a study in Christchurch.' *The Australian and New Zealand Journal of Sociology* 5 (1): 14–31.

—— 1971. 'Towards a theoretical model for the study of occupational choice.' *Sociology* 5 (3): 313–33.

—— 1972. 'What motivates church participation? Review, replication, and theoretical reorientation in New Zealand.' *The Sociological Review* 20 (1): 39–58.

—— 1974. 'The dialectics of social research, or where should I begin?' In J. S. Williams and W. C. West (eds), *Sociological Research Symposium IV*. Richmond, VA: Virginia Commonwealth University.

—— 1977. 'The meaning and measurement of occupational prestige.' *The Australian and New Zealand Journal of Sociology* 13 (2): 102–15.

—— 1978. 'Towards an alternative methodology for the study of occupational prestige: a reply to my reviewers.' *The Australian and New Zealand Journal of Sociology* 14(1): 87–95.

—— 1991. 'A critique of the use of triangulation in social research.' *Quality and Quantity* 25: 115–36.

—— 1992. 'The nature and origins of ecological world views: an Australian study.' *Social Science Quarterly* 73: 144–65.

—— 1993a. *Approaches to Social Enquiry*. Cambridge: Polity.

—— 1993b. 'Education and environmentalism: ecological world views and environmentally responsible behaviour.' *Australian Journal of Environmental Education* 9: 1–20.

—— 1994. 'Models and ideal types: the relationship between Harré's realism and Weber's interpretivism.' Paper presented at the XIII World Congress of Sociology, Bielefeld, Germany, July.

—— 2000. *Designing Social Research: The Logic of Anticipation*. Cambridge: Polity.

—— 2003. *Analyzing Quantitative Data: From Description to Explanation*. London: Sage.

—— 2007. *Approaches to Social Enquiry: Advancing Knowledge* (2nd edn). Cambridge: Polity.

Blaikie, N. W. H. and M. Drysdale 1994. 'Changes in ecological world views and environmentally responsible behaviour between 1989 and 1994: an Australian study.' Paper presented at the XIII World Congress of Sociology, Bielefeld, Germany, July.

Blaikie, N. W. H. and S. J. G. Stacy 1982. 'The dialogical generation of typologies in the study of the care of the aged.' Paper presented at the X World Congress of Sociology, Mexico City, August.

—— 1984. 'The generation of grounded concepts: a critical appraisal of the literature and a case study.' Paper presented at the European Symposium on Concept and Theory Formation, Rome.

Blaikie, N. W. H. and R. Ward 1992. 'Ecological world views and environmentally responsible behaviour.' *Sociale Wetenschappen* 25: 40–63.

Blalock, H. M. 1968. 'The measurement problem: a gap between the languages of theory and research.' In H. M. Blalock and A. B. Blalock (eds), *Methodology in Social Research*. New York: McGraw-Hill. Pp. 5–27.

—— 1969. *Theory Construction: From Verbal to Mathematical Formulations*. Englewood Cliffs, NJ: Prentice-Hall.

Blaxter, L., C. Hughes and M. Tight 2002. *How to Research* (2nd edn). Buckingham: Open University Press.

Blocker, T. J. and D. L. Eckberg 1989. 'Environmental issues and women's issues: general concern and local hazards.' *Social Science Quarterly* 70: 586–93.

Blumer, H. 1969. *Symbolic Interactionism: Perspective and Method*. Englewood Cliffs, NJ: Prentice-Hall.

Bogardus, E. S. 1933. 'A social distance scale.' *Sociology and Social Research* 17: 265–71.

—— 1940. *The Development of Social Thought*. New York: David McKay.

Borden, R. J. and A. P. Schettino 1979. 'Determinants of environmentally responsible behavior.' *Journal of Environmental Education* 10: 35–9.

Bornat, J. 2004. 'Oral History.' In Seale, C. *et al.* (eds), *Qualitative Research Practice*. London: Sage. Pp. 34–47.

Brannen, J. (ed.) 1992. *Mixing Methods: Qualitative and Quantitative Research*. Aldershot: Avebury.

Brent, E. and R. E. Anderson 1990. *Computer Applications in the Social Sciences*. New York: McGraw-Hill.

Brewer, J. and A. Hunter 1989. *Multimethod Research: A Synthesis of Styles*. Newbury Park, CA: Sage.

—— 2006. *Foundations of Multimethod Research: Synthezising Styles*. Thousand Oaks, CA: Sage.

Brodbeck, M. 1968. *Readings in the Philosophy of the Social Sciences*. NewYork: Macmillan.

Bruyn, S. 1966. *The Human Perspective in Sociology*. Englewood Cliffs, NJ: Prentice-Hall.

Bryant, C. G. A. and D. Jary (eds) 1991. *Giddens' Theory of Structuration: A Critical Appreciation*. London: Routledge.

Bryman, A. 1988. *Quality and Quantity in Social Research*. London: Unwin Hyman.

—— (ed.) 2001. *Ethnography*. 4 Vols. London: Sage.

—— (ed.) 2006a. *Mixed Methods*. 4 Vols. London: Sage.

—— 2006b. 'Integrating quantitative and qualitative research. How is it done?' *Qualitative Research* 6 (1): 97–113.

—— 2007. *Mixed Methods Research*. London: Sage.

—— 2008. *Social Research Methods*, (3nd edn). Oxford: Oxford University Press.

Bryman, A. and R. G. Burgess (eds) 1994. *Analyzing Qualitative Data*. London: Routledge.

Bulmer, M. 1982. *The Uses of Social Research*. London: Allen and Unwin.

—— 1986. *Social Science and Social Policy*. London: Allen and Unwin.

Burdge, R. J. and F. Vanclay 1995. 'Social impact assessment.' In F. Vanclay and D. A. Bronstein (eds), *Environmental and Social Impact Assessment*. New York: Wiley. Pp. 31–65.

Burgess, E. W. 1927. 'Statistics and case studies as methods of sociological research.' *Sociology and Social Research* 12: 103–20.

Burgess, R. G. (ed.) 1982a. *Field Research: A Sourcebook and Field Manual*. London: Allen and Unwin.

—— 1982b. 'Elements of sampling in field research.' In R. G. Burgess (ed.), *Field Research: A Sourcebook and Field Manual*. London: Allen and Unwin. Pp. 75–8.

—— 1984. *In the Field*. London: Allen and Unwin.

Burgess, R. L., R. N. Clark and J. L. Hendee 1971. 'An experimental analysis of anti-litter procedures.' *Journal of Applied Behavior Analysis* 4: 71–5.

Buttel, F. H. 1979. 'Age and environmental concern: a multivariate analysis.' *Youth and Society* 10: 237–56.

Campbell, D. T. and D. W. Fiske 1959. 'Convergent and discriminant validation by the multitrait-multimethod matrix.' *Psychological Bulletin* 56: 81–105.

Campbell, D. T. and J. C. Stanley 1963a. *Experimental and Quasi-Experimental Evaluations in Social Research*. Chicago, IL: Rand McNally.

—— 1963b. 'Experimental and quasi-experimental designs for research in teaching.' In N. L. Gage (ed.), *Handbook of Research on Teaching*. Chicago, IL: Rand McNally. Pp. 171–246.

Campbell, J. P., R. L. Daft and C. L. Hulin 1982. *What to Study: Generating and Developing Research Questions*. Beverly Hills, CA: Sage.

Casey, L. and M. Lloyd 1977. 'Cost effectiveness of litter removal procedures in an amusement park.' *Environment and Behavior* 9: 535–46.

Castles, I. 1993. *Environmental Issues: People's Views and Practices*. Canberra: Australian Bureau of Statistics.

Catton, W. R. and R. E. Dunlap 1978. 'Paradigms, theories, and the primacy of the HEP–NEP distinction.' *American Sociologist* 13: 256–9.

——1980. 'A new ecological paradigm for post-exuberant sociology.' *American Behavioral Scientist* 24: 15–47.

Chadwick, B. A., H. M. Bahr and S. L. Albrecht 1984. *Social Science Research Methods*. Englewood Cliffs, NJ: Prentice-Hall.

Chafetz, J. S. 1978. *A Primer on the Construction and Testing of Theories in Sociology*. Itasca, IL: Peacock.

Chaiken, S. and C. Stangor 1987. 'Attitudes and attitude change.' *Annual Review of Psychology*, 575–630.

Chalmers, A. F. 1982. *What Is This Thing Called Science?* St Lucia, QLD: University of Queensland Press.

Charmaz, K. 2005. 'Grounded theory in the 21st Century.' In N. K. Denzin and Y. S. Lincoln (eds), *The Sage Handbook of Qualitative Research* (3rd edn). Thousand Oaks, CA: Sage. Pp. 507–35.

—— 2006. *Constructing Grounded Theory: A Practical Guide Through Qualitative Analysis*. London: Sage,

Charmaz, K. and R. G. Mitchell 2001. 'Grounded theory in ethnography.' In P. Atkinson, A. Coffey, S. Delamont, J. Lofland and L. H. Lofland (eds), *Handbook of Ethnography*. London: Sage. Pp. 160–74.

Christensen, L. B. 1988. *Experimental Methodology* (4th edn). Boston, MA: Allyn and Bacon.

Clarke, A. E. 2005. *Situational Analysis: Grounded Theory After the Postmodern Turn*. Thousand Oaks, CA: Sage.

Coffey, A. and P. Atkinson 1996. *Making Sense of Qualitative Data: Complementary Research Strategies*. London: Sage.

Cohen, I. J. 1989. *Structuration Theory: Anthony Giddens and the Constitution of Social Life*. London: Macmillan.

Cone, J. and S. Hayes 1984. *Environmental Problems/Behavioral Solutions*. Cambridge: Cambridge University Press.

Connelly, P. 1998. '"Dancing to the wrong tune": ethnography, generalization, and research on racism in schools.' In P. Connelly and B. Troyna (eds), *Researching Racism in Education*. Buckingham: Open University Press.

Cook, S. W. and J. L. Berrenberg 1981. 'Approaches to encouraging conservation behavior: a review and conceptual framework.' *Journal of Social Issues* 37: 73–107.

Cook, T. D. and D. T. Campbell 1979. *Quasi-Experimentation: Design and Analysis Issues in Field Settings*. Chicago, IL: Rand McNally.

Cook, T. D. and C. S. Reichardt 1979. *Qualitative and Quantitative Methods in Evaluation Research*. Beverly Hills, CA: Sage.

Cooke, B. and J. W. Cox (eds) 2005. *Fundamentals of Action Research*, 4 Vols. London: Sage.

Corbin, J. M. and A. Strauss 2008. *Basics of Qualitative Research: Techniques and Procedures for Developing Grounded Theory* (3rd edn). Thousand Oaks, CA: Sage.

Cortese, A. J. 1995. 'The rise, hegemony, and decline of the Chicago School of Sociology, 1892–1945.' *Social Science Journal* 32: 235–54.

Costello, P. J. M. 2003. *Action Research*. London: Continuum.

Coser, L. A. 1971. *Masters of Sociological Thought: Ideas in Historical and Social Context*. New York: Harcourt Brace Jovanovich.

—— 1975. 'Presidential address: two methods in search of a substance.' *American Sociological Review* 40 (6): 691–701.

Craib, I. 1992. *Modern Social Theory* (2nd edn). New York: Harvester Wheatsheaf.

—— 1997. *Classical Social Theory: An Introduction to the Thought of Marx, Weber, Durkheim and Simmel*. Oxford: Oxford University Press.

Cressey, D. 1950. 'Criminal violation of financial trust.' *American Sociological Review* 15: 738–43.

Creswell, J. W. 1994. *Research Design: Qualitative and Quantitative Approaches*. Thousand Oaks, CA: Sage.

—— 1999. 'Mixed method research: introduction and application.' In G. J. Cizek (ed.), *Handbook of Educational Policy*. San Diego, CA: Academic Press. Pp. 455–72.

—— 2003. *Research Design: Qualitative, Quantitative, and Mixed Methods Approaches* (2nd edn). Thousand Oaks, CA: Sage.

—— 2007. *Qualitative Inquiry and Research Design: Choosing Among Five Traditions* (2nd edn). Thousand Oaks, CA: Sage.

—— 2009. *Research Design: Qualitative, Quantitative, and Mixed Methods Approaches* (3rd edn). Thousand Oaks, CA: Sage.

Creswell, J. W., M. D. Fetters and N. V. Ivankova 2004. 'Designing a mixed methods study in primary care.' *Annals of Family Medicine* 2 (1): 7–12.

Creswell, J. W. and V. L. Plano Clark 2007. *Designing and Conducting Mixed Methods Research*. Thousand Oaks, CA: Sage.

Creswell, J. W., V. L. Plano Clark, M. Gutmann and W. Hanson 2003. 'Advanced mixed methods designs.' In A. Tashakkori and C. Teddlie (eds), *Handbook of Mixed Methods in Social and Behavioral Research*. Thousand Oaks, CA: Sage. Pp. 209–40.

Cronbach, L. 1963. 'Course improvement through evaluation.' *Teachers College Record* 64: 672–83.

—— 1982. *Designing Evaluations of Educational and Social Programs*. San Francisco, CA: Jossey-Bass.

—— 1990. *Essentials of Psychological Testing* (5th edn). New York: Harper and Row.

Cuff, E. C. and G. C. F. Payne (eds) 1979. *Perspectives in Sociology*. London: Allen and Unwin.

Cuff, E. C., W. W. Sharrock and D. W. Francis 2006. *Perspectives in Sociology* (5th edn). London: Routledge.

David, M. (ed.) 2006. *Case Study Research*, 4 vols. London: Sage.

Davis, A. and G. Bremner 2006. 'The experimental method in psychology.' In G. M. Breakwell, S. Hammond, C. Fife-Schaw and J. A. Smith (eds), *Research Methods in Psychology* (3rd edn). London: Sage. Pp. 64–87.

de Leeuw, E. D., J. J. Hox and D. A. Dilman (eds) 2008. *International Handbook of Survey Methodology*. New York: Lawrence Erlbaum.

de Vaus, D. A. 2001. *Research Design in Social Research*. London: Sage.

—— 2002. *Surveys in Social Research* (5th edn). London: Routledge.

—— (ed.) 2006. *Research Design*. 4 vols. London: Sage.

De Young, R. 1986. 'Some psychological aspects of recycling: the structure of conservation satisfactions.' *Environment and Behavior* 18: 435–49.

—— 1988/9. 'Exploring the difference between recyclers and non-recyclers: the role of information.' *Journal of Environmental Systems* 18: 341–51.

Denzin, N. K. 1970. *The Research Act in Sociology*. London: Butterworth.

—— 1971. 'The logic of naturalistic inquiry.' *Social Forces* 50: 166–82.

—— 1978. *The Research Act in Sociology* (2nd edn). New York: McGraw-Hill.

—— 1983. 'Interpretive interactionism.' In G. Morgan (ed.), *Beyond Method: Strategies for Social Research*. Beverly Hills, CA: Sage. Pp. 129–46.

Denzin, N. K. and Y. S. Lincoln 2005. *The Sage Handbook of Qualitative Research* (3rd edn). Thousand Oaks, CA: Sage.

Derksen, L. and J. Gartrell 1993. 'The social context of recycling.' *American Sociological Review* 58: 434–42.

Dey, I. 1993. *Qualitative Data Analysis: A User Friendly Guide for Social Scientists*. London: Routledge.

Douglas, J. D. 1971. *Understanding Everyday Life*. London: Routledge and Kegan Paul.

—— 1976. *Investigative Social Research*. Beverly Hills, CA: Sage.

Douglas, L., A. Roberts and R. Thompson 1988. *Oral History Handbook*. Sydney: Allen and Unwin.

Drysdale, M. S. 1985. 'Beliefs and behaviours of the community with regard to social justice: an application of dialogical method.' MA thesis, Royal Melbourne Institute of Technology, Melbourne.

—— 1996. 'Environment, culture and the experience of nature among Australian visual artists.' PhD thesis, RMIT University, Melbourne

Dubin, R. 1969. *Theory Building: A Practical Guide to the Construction and Testing of Theoretical Models*. New York: Free Press.

—— 1978. *Theory Building: A Practical Guide to the Construction and Testing of Theoretical Models* (2nd edn). New York: Free Press.

Dunlap, R. E. and W. R. Catton 1979. 'Environmental sociology.' *Annual Review of Sociology* 5: 243–73.

Dunlap, R. E., G. H. Gallup and A. M. Gallup 1992. 'Health of the planet survey.' Paper presented at the International Conference on Current Developments in Environmental Sociology, Woudschoten, The Netherlands, June.

Dunlap, R. E., J. K. Grienecks and M. Rokeach 1983. 'Human values and pro-environmental behavior.' In W. D. Conn (ed.), *Energy and Material Resources: Attitudes, Values and Public Policy*. Boulder, CO: Westview Press.

Dunlap, R. E. and K. D. van Liere 1978. 'The "New Environmental Paradigm": a proposed measuring instrument and preliminary results.' *Journal of Environmental Education* 9: 10–19.

—— 1984. 'Commitment to the dominant social paradigm and concern for environmental quality.' *Social Science Quarterly* 65: 1013–28.

Durkheim, E. 1951. *Suicide.* New York: Free Press.

Eckett, J. 1988. 'Ethnographic research on ageing.' In S. Reinharz and G. Rowles (eds), *Qualitative Gerontology.* New York: Springer.

Eckstein, H. 1975. 'Case study and theory in political science.' In F. E. Greenstein and N. W. Polsby (eds), *Handbook of Political Science*, vol. 7: *Strategies of Inquiry.* Reading, MA: Addison-Wesley. Pp. 79–137.

—— 1992. *Regarding Politics: Essays on Political Theory, Stability and Change.* Berkeley, CA: University of California Press.

Edwards, A. L. 1957. *Techniques of Attitude Scale Construction.* New York: Appleton-Century-Crofts.

Ehrlich, H. J. 1969. 'Attitudes, behavior, and the intervening variables.' *American Sociologist* 4: 29–34.

Ellis, L. 1994. *Research Methods in the Social Sciences.* Madison, WI: Brown and Benchmark.

Elmes, D. G., B. H. Kantowitz and H. L. Roediger 2006. *Research Methods in Psychology* (8th edn). Belmont, CA: Thomson Wadsworth.

Environment Protection Authority of New South Wales 1994. *Benchmark Study on Environmental Knowledge, Attitudes, Skills and Behaviour in New South Wales.* Chatswood, NSW: Environment Protection Authority.

Etzioni, A. 1961. *The Comparative Analysis of Complex Organizations.* New York: Free Press.

Eysenck, H. J. 1954. *The Psychology of Politics.* London: Routledge and Kegan Paul.

Fay, B. 1975. *Social Theory and Political Practice.* London: Allen and Unwin.

—— 1987. *Critical Social Science: Liberation and its Limits.* Ithaca, NY: Cornell University Press.

Fazio, R. H. 1986. 'How do attitudes guide behavior?' In R. M. Sorrentino and E. T. Higgins (eds), *Handbook of Motivation and Cognition.* New York: Guilford Press. Pp 204–43.

Featherman, D. L. 1976. 'Coser's . . . "In search of substance".' *The American Sociologist* 11: 21–7.

Fetterman, D. M. 1989. *Ethnography: Step by Step.* Newbury Park, CA: Sage.

Fielding, N. 2001. 'Computer applications in qualitative research.' In P. Atkinson, A. Coffey, S. Delamont, J. Lofland and L. Lofland (eds), *Handbook of Ethnography.* London: Sage. Pp. 453–67.

Fielding, N. G. and J. L. Fielding 1986. *Linking Data.* London: Sage.

Fielding, N. G. and R. M. Lee. (eds) 1991. *Using Computers in Qualitative Research.* London: Sage.

—— 1998. *Computer Analysis and Qualitative Research.* London: Sage.

Fink, A. 2005. *Conducting Research Literature Reviews: From the Internet to Paper* (2nd edn). Thousand Oaks, CA: Sage.

Finsterbusch, K. 1983. *Social Impact Assessment Methods.* Beverly Hills, CA: Sage.

—— 1985. 'State of the art in social impact assessment.' *Environment and Behavior* 17 (2): 193–221.

Firestone, W. A. and R. E. Herriott 1984. 'Multisite qualitative policy research: some design and implementation issues.' In D. M. Fetterman (ed.), *Ethnography on Educational Evaluation.* Beverly Hills, CA: Sage.

Flick, U. 2006. *An Introduction to Qualitative Research* (3nd edn). London: Sage.

—— 2007. *Designing Qualitative Research.* London: Sage.

Foddy, W. H. 1988. *Elementary Applied Statistics for Social Sciences.* Sydney: Harper and Row.

—— 1993. *Constructing Questions for Interviews and Questionnaires: Theory and Practice in Social Research*. Cambridge: Cambridge University Press.

Fontana, A. 1994. 'Ethnographic trends in the postmodern era.' In D. R. Dickens and A. Fontana (eds), *Postmodernism and Social Enquiry*. London: UCL Press. Pp. 203–23.

Fowler, F. J. 2009. *Survey Research Methods* (4th edn). Los Angeles, CA: Sage.

Freire, P. 1970. *Pedagogy of the Oppressed*. New York: Seabury Press.

Friedrichs, R. W. 1970. *A Sociology of Sociology*. New York: Free Press.

Gadamer, H.-G. 1989. *Truth and Method* (2nd edn). New York: Crossroad.

Gans, H. J. 1967. *The Levittowners: Ways of Life and Politics in a New Suburban Community*. London: Allen Lane.

Garfinkel, H. 1952. 'The perception of the other: A study in social order.' PhD dissertation, Harvard University.

—— 1967. *Studies in Ethnomethodology*. Englewood Cliffs, NJ: Prentice-Hall.

Garson, D. D. 1990. 'Expert systems: an overview for social scientists.' *Social Science Computer Review* 8: 387–410.

Geertz, C. 1973. 'Thick description: toward an interpretive theory of culture.' In C. Geertz (ed.), *The Interpretation of Cultures: Selected Essays*. New York: Basic Books. Pp. 1–32.

—— 1988. *Works and Lives: The Anthropologist as Author*. Stanford, CA: Stanford University Press.

Geller, E. S., R. A. Winett and P. B. Everett 1982. *Preserving the Environment: New Strategies for Behavior Change*. New York: Pergamon Press.

Geller, J. M. and P. Lasley 1985. 'The new environmental paradigm scale: a reexamination.' *Journal of Environmental Education* 17: 9–12.

Giddens, A. 1971. *Capitalism and Modern Social Theory*. Cambridge: Cambridge University Press.

—— 1976. *New Rules of Sociological Method*. London: Hutchinson.

—— 1979. *Central Problems in Social Theory: Action, Structure and Contradiction in Social Analysis*. London: Macmillan.

—— 1984. *The Constitution of Society: Outline of the Theory of Structuration*. Cambridge: Polity.

Giddens, A. and J. Turner (eds) 1987. *Social Theory Today*. Cambridge: Polity.

Giddens, A., M. Duneier and R. P. Appelbaum 2003. *Introduction to Sociology* (4th edn). New York: Norton.

Gigliotti, L. M. 1992. 'Environmental attitudes: 20 years of change?' *Journal of Environmental Education* 24: 15–26.

Gilbert, G. H. and J. Doran (eds) 1993. *Simulating Societies: The Computer Simulation of Social Processes*. London: UCL Press.

Gilbert, N. 1995. 'Using computer simulation to study social phenomena.' *Bulletin de Méthodologie Sociologique* 47 (June): 99–111.

—— 2008. 'Research, theory and method.' In N. Gilbert (ed.), *Researching Social Life* (3rd edn) London: Sage. Pp. 21–40.

Glaser, B. G. 1978. *Theoretical Sensitivity*. Mill Valley, CA: The Sociology Press.

—— 1992. *Basics of Grounded Theory Analysis: Emergence vs. Forcing*. Mill Valley, CA: The Sociology Press.

—— 2001. *The Grounded Theory Perspective: Conceptualization Contrasted with Description*. Mill Valley, CA: The Sociology Press.

Glaser, B. G. and A. L. Strauss 1965. *Awareness of Dying*. Chicago, IL: Aldine.

—— 1967. *The Discovery of Grounded Theory*. Chicago, IL: Aldine.

Gluckman, M. 1961. 'Ethnographic data in British social anthropology.' *Sociological Review* 9: 5–17.

Gobo, G. 2004. 'Sampling, representativeness and generalizability.' In Seale, C., G. Gobo, J. F. Gubrium and D. Silverman (eds), *Qualitative Research Practice*. London: Sage.

Goetz, J. P. and M. D. LeCompte 1984. *Ethnography and Qualitative Design in Educational Research*. Orlando, Fl: Academic Press.

Gomm, R., M. Hammersley and P. Foster (eds). 2000a. *Case Study Method: Key Issues, Key Texts*. London: Sage.

—— 2000b. 'Case study and generalization.' In R. Gomm, M. Hammersley and P. Foster (eds), *Case Study Method*. London: Sage. Pp. 98–115.

Goode, E. 1992. *Collective Behavior*. Fort Worth: Harcourt Brace Jovanovich.

Goode, W. J. and P. K. Hatt 1952. *Methods in Social Research*. New York: McGraw-Hill.

Goodwin, C. J. 2008. *Research in Psychology: Methods and Design* (5th edn). Hokoken, NJ: Wiley.

Green, N. 2008. 'Formulating and refining a research question.' In N. Gilbert (ed.), *Researching Social Life* (3rd edn). London: Sage. Pp. 43–62.

Greene, J. C. and V. J. Caracelli (eds), 1997. *Advances in Mixed Method Evaluation: The Challenges and Benefits of Integrating Diverse Paradigms: New Directions for Evaluation, 74*. San Francisco: Jossey-Bass.

Greene, J. C., V. J. Caracelli and W. F. Graham 1989. 'Toward a conceptual framework for mixed-method evaluation designs.' *Educational Evaluation and Policy Analysis* 11 (3): 255–74.

Groves, R. M. and R. L. Kahn 1979. *Surveys by Telephone: A National Comparison with Personal Interviews*. New York: Academic Press.

Guba, E. G. 1978. *Toward a Methodology of Naturalistic Inquiry in Educational Evaluation*. Los Angeles, CA: Centre for the Study of Education, UCLA Graduate School of Education.

Guba, E. G. and Y. S. Lincoln 1981. *Effective Evaluation: Improving the Usefulness of Evaluation Results through Responsive and Naturalistic Approaches*. San Francisco. CA: Jossey-Bass.

—— 1982. 'Epistemological and methodological bases of naturalistic inquiry.' *Educational Communication and Technology Journal* 30: 233–52.

—— 1988. 'Do inquiry paradigms imply inquiry methodologies?' In D. M. Fetterman (ed.), *Qualitative Approaches to Evaluation in Education*. New York: Praeger. Pp. 89–115.

—— 1989. *Fourth Generation Evaluation*. Newbury Park, CA: Sage.

—— 2005. 'Paradigmatic controversies, contradictions, and emerging confluences.' In N. K. Denzin and Y. S. Lincoln 2005. *The Sage Handbook of Qualitative Research* (3rd edn). Thousand Oaks, CA: Sage. Pp. 191–215.

Gudgion, T. J. and M. P. Thomas 1991. 'Changing environmentally relevant behaviour.' *International Journal of Environmental Education and Information* 10: 101–12.

Gullahorn, J. T. and J. E. Gullahorn 1963. 'A computer model of elementary social behavior.' *Behavioral Science* 8 (4): 354–92.

Gummesson, E. 1991. *Qualitative Methods in Management Research*. Newbury Park, CA: Sage.

Habermas, J. 1970. 'Knowledge and interest.' In D. Emmet and A. MacIntyre (eds), *Sociological Theory and Philosophical Analysis*. London: Macmillan. Pp. 36–54.

—— 1971. *Towards a Rational Society*. London: Heinemann.

—— 1972. *Knowledge and Human Interests*. London: Heinemann.

——1987. *The Theory of Communicative Action*, vol. 2: *Lifeworld and System: The Critique of Functionalist Reason*. Cambridge: Polity.

Hage, J. 1972. *Techniques and Problems of Theory Construction in Sociology*. New York: Wiley.

Hakim, C. 2000. *Research Design* (2nd edn). London: Routledge.

Halfpenny, P. 1979. 'The analysis of qualitative data.' *Sociological Review* 27 (4): 799–825.

—— 1996. 'The relation between social theory and the practice of quantitative and qualitative social research.' Paper presented at the Fourth International Social Science Methodology Conference, University of Essex, UK, July.

Hallebone, E. 1989. 'Environmental attitudes and gender.' Paper presented at the conference of the Australian and New Zealand Sociological Association, Melbourne.

Hammersley, M. 1985. 'From ethnography to theory: a programme and paradigm in the sociology of education.' *Sociology* 19 (2): 244–59.

—— 1992. *What's Wrong with Ethnography?* London: Routledge.

—— 1996. 'The relationship between qualitative and quantitative research: paradigm loyalty versus methodological eclecticism.' In J. E. T. Richardson (ed.), *Handbook of Qualitative Research Methods for Psychology and the Social Sciences*. Leicester: British Psychological Society. Pp. 159–72.

Hammersley, M. and P. Atkinson 2007. *Ethnography: Principles in Practice* (3nd edn). London: Routledge.

Hammersley, M. and R. Gomm 2000. 'Introduction.' In R. Gomm, M. Hammersley and P. Foster (eds). *Case Study Method*. London: Sage.

Hammersley, M., R. Gomm and P. Foster 2000. 'Case study and theory.' In R. Gomm. M. Hammersley and P. Foster (eds), *Case Study Method*. London: Sage.

Hanneman, R. A. 1988. *Computer-Assisted Theory Building: Modeling Dynamic Social Systems*. Newbury Park, CA: Sage.

Haralambos, M. and M. Holborn 2004. *Sociology: Themes and Perspectives* (6th edn). London: Collins.

Haraway, D. 1988. 'Situated knowledges: the science question in feminism and the privilege of partial perspective.' *Feminist Studies* 14 (3): 575–99.

Harding, S. 1993. 'Rethinking standpoint epistemology: what is "strong objectivity"?' In L. Alcoff and E. Potter (eds), *Feminist Epistemologies*. New York: Routledge. Pp. 48–92.

Hardy, M. and A. Bryman 2004. *Handbook of Data Analysis*. London: Sage.

Harré, R. 1961. *Theories and Things*. London: Sheed and Ward.

—— 1974. 'Blueprint for a new science.' In N. Armistead (ed.), *Restructuring Social Psychology*. Harmondsworth: Penguin. Pp. 240–49.

—— 1977. 'The ethogenic approach: theory and practice.' *Advances in Experimental Social Psychology* 10: 283–314.

Harré, R. and P. F. Secord 1972. *The Explanation of Social Behaviour*. Oxford: Blackwell.

Hart, C. 1998. *Doing a Literature Review: Releasing the Social Science Research Imagination*. London: Sage.

Hartley, J. 2008. *Academic Writing and Publishing: A Practical Handbook*. London: Routledge.

Hausbeck, K. W., L. W. Milbrath and S. M. Enright 1990. 'Environmental knowledge, awareness and concern among 11th grade students: New York State.' *Journal of Environmental Education* 24: 27–34.

Heberlein, T. A. 1989. 'Attitudes and environmental management.' *Journal of Social Issues* 45: 37–57.

Hedrick, T. E., L. Bickman and D. J. Rog 1993. *Applied Research Design*. Newbury Park, CA: Sage.

Hempel, C. E. 1966. *Philosophy of Natural Science*. Englewood Cliffs, NJ: Prentice-Hall.

Henry, G. T. 1990. *Practical Sampling*. Newbury Park, CA: Sage.

Hoinville, G. and R. Jowell 1977. *Survey Research Practice*. London: Heinemann.

Homans, G. C. 1964. 'Contemporary theory in sociology.' In R. E. L. Faris (ed.), *Handbook of Modern Sociology*. Chicago, IL: Rand McNally. Pp. 951–77.

—— 1974. *Social Behavior: Its Elementary Forms*. New York: Harcourt Brace Jovanovich.

Honigmann, J. J. 1982. 'Sampling in ethnographic fieldwork.' In R. G. Burgess (ed.), *Field Research: A Sourcebook and Field Manual*. London: Allen and Unwin. Pp. 79–90.

Honnold, J. A. 1981. 'Predictors of public environmental concern in the 1990s.' In D. Mann (ed.), *Environmental Policy Formation*, vol. 1. Lexington, MA: Lexington Books. Pp. 63–75.

—— 1984. 'Age and environmental concern: some specification of effects.' *Journal of Environmental Education* 16: 4–9.

Hughes, J. A. and W. W. Sharrock 1997. *The Philosophy of Social Research* (3rd edn). London: Longman.

Humphrey, C. R., R. J. Bord, M. M. Hammond and S. H. Mann 1977. 'Attitudes and conditions for cooperation in a paper recycling program.' *Environment and Behavior* 9: 107–23.

Hutheesing, O. K. 1990. *Emerging Sexual Inequality among the Lisu of Northern Thailand*. Leiden: E. J. Brill.

Inbar, M. and C. S. Stoll 1972. *Simulation and Gaming in Social Science*. New York: Free Press.

Inkeles, A. 1964. *What is Sociology?* Englewood Cliffs, NJ: Prentice-Hall.

Inter-organizational Committee on Guidelines and Principles 1994. *Guidelines and Principles for Social Impact Assessment*. Washington, DC: Department of Commerce.

Jacobs, H. E., J. S. Bailey and J. I. Crews 1984. 'Development and analysis of a community based resource recovery program.' *Journal of Applied Behavior Analysis* 17 (2): 127–45.

Jick, J. D. 1979. 'Mixing qualitative and quantitative methods: triangulation in action.' *Administrative Science Quarterly* 24: 602–11.

Jocher, K. 1928. 'The case study method in social research.' *Social Forces* 7: 512–15.

Johnson, R. B. and L. B. Christensen 2008. *Educational Research: Quantitative, Qualitative and Mixed Approaches* (3rd edn). Thousand Oaks, CA: Sage.

Johnson, R. B. and A. J. Onwuegbuzie 2004. 'Mixed methods research: a research paradigm whose time has come.' *Educational Researcher* 33 (7): 14–26.

Johnson, T., C. Dandecker and C. Ashworth 1984. *The Structure of Social Theory: Dilemmas and Strategies*. London: Macmillan.

Jones, P. 1985. *Theory and Method in Sociology: A Guide for the Beginner*. London: Bell and Hyman.

Jorgensen, D. L. 1989. *Participant Observation: A Methodology for Human Studies*. Newbury Park, CA: Sage.

Kalton, G. 1983. *Introduction to Survey Sampling*. Beverly Hills, CA: Sage.

Kamberelis, G. and G. Dimitriadis 2005. 'Focus groups: strategic articulations of pedagogy, politics, and inquiry.' In N. K. Denzin and Y. S. Lincoln (eds), *The Sage Handbook of Qualitative Research* (3rd edn). Thousand Oaks, CA: Sage. Pp. 887–907.

Kamler, B. and P. Thomson 2006. *Helping Doctoral Students Write: Pedagogies for Supervision*. London: Routledge.

Kaplan, A. 1964. *The Conduct of Inquiry: Methodology for Behavioral Science*. San Francisco, CA: Chandler.

Kaplan, D. (ed.) 2004. *The Sage Handbook of Quantitative Methodology for the Social Sciences*. Thousand Oaks, CA: Sage.

Keat, R. and J. Urry 1975. *Social Theory as Science*. London: Routledge and Kegan Paul.

—— 1982. *Social Theory as Science* (2nd edn). London: Routledge and Kegan Paul.

Kelle, U. (ed.) 1995. *Computer-aided Qualitative Data Analysis: Theory, Methods and Practice*. London: Sage.

—— 2004. 'Computer assisted qualitative data analysis.' In C. Seale, G. Gobo, J. F. Gubrium and D. Silverman (eds), *Qualitative Research Practice*. London: Sage. Pp. 473–89.

Keller, E. F. 1985. *Reflections on Gender and Science*. New Haven, CON: Yale University Press.

Kelly, M. 2004. 'Research design and proposals.' In C. Seale (ed.), *Researching Society and Culture* (2nd edn). London: Sage. Pp. 129–42.

Kelsen, G. P. 1981. 'The process of radical self-change or conversion: a study in world view and the maintenance of reality, with particular regard to minority religious sects.' PhD thesis, Monash University, Melbourne.

Kemmis, S. and R. McTaggart 2005. 'Participatory action research: communicative action and the public sphere.' In N. K. Denzin and Y. S. Lincoln (eds), *The Sage Handbook of Qualitative Research* (3rd edn). Thousand Oaks, CA: Sage. Pp. 559–603.

Kerlinger, F. N. and E. J. Pedhazur 1973. *Multiple Regression in Behavioral Research*. New York: Holt, Rinehart and Winston.

Kidder, L. H. and C. M. Judd 1986. *Research Methods in Social Relations* (5th edn). New York: CBS Publishing.

Kish, L. 1965. *Survey Sampling*. New York: Wiley.

Krausz, E. and S. Miller 1974. *Social Research Design*. London: Longman.

Krueger, R. A. 1988. *Focus Groups: A Practical Guide for Applied Research*. Newbury Park, CA: Sage.

Kuhn, T. S. 1970. *The Structure of Scientific Revolutions* (2nd edn). Chicago, IL: Chicago University Press.

Kumar, R. 2005. *Research Methodology: A Step-by-Step Guide for Beginners* (2nd edn). London: Sage.

Labovitz, S. and R. Hagedorn 1976. *Introduction to Social Research*. New York: McGraw-Hill.

Lahart, D. E. and J. S. Bailey 1984. 'The analysis and reduction of children's littering on a nature trail.' In J. Cone and S. Hayes (eds), *Environmental Problems/Behavioral Solutions*. Cambridge: Cambridge University Press.

Lave, C. A. and J. G. March 1975. *An Introduction to Models in the Social Sciences*. New York: Harper and Row.

Layder, D. 1993. *New Strategies in Social Research*. Cambridge: Polity.

—— 1994. *Understanding Social Theory*. London: Sage.

—— 1998. *Sociological Practice: Linking Theory and Social Research*. London: Sage.

Lazarsfeld, P. F., M. Jahoda and H. Zeisel 1933. *Die Arbeitslosen von Marienthal*. Leipsig: Hirzel.

Lazarsfeld, P. F. and N. W. Henry 1966. *Readings in Mathematical Social Science*. Cambridge, MA: MIT Press.

Lee, R. M. (ed.) 1995. *Information Technology for the Socialist Scientist*. London: UCL Press.

Leik, R. K. and B. F. Meeker 1975. *Mathematical Sociology*. Englewood Cliffs, NJ: Prentice-Hall.

Lenski, G. E. 1961. *The Religious Factor*. Garden City, NY: Doubleday.

Levit, L. and G. Leventhall 1986. 'Litter reduction: how effective is the New York State Bottle Bill?' *Environment and Behavior* 18: 467–79.

Lewins, A. and C. Silver 2007. *Using Software in Qualitative Research: A Step-by-step Guide*. London: Sage.

Lewis-Beck, M. S. (ed.) 1994. *Factor Analysis and Related Techniques*. Thousand Oaks, CA: Sage.

Lewis-Beck, M. S., A. Bryman and T. F. Liao (eds) 2004. *The Sage Encyclopedia of Social Research Methods* (3 vols). Thousand Oaks, CA: Sage.

Likert, R. 1970. 'A technique for the measurement of attitudes.' In G. Summers (ed.), *Attitude Measurement*. Chicago, IL: Rand McNally. Pp. 149–58.

Lin, N. 1976. *Foundations of Social Research*. New York: McGraw-Hill.

Lincoln, Y. S. and E. G. Guba 1985. *Naturalistic Inquiry*. Beverly Hills, CA: Sage.

—— 2000. 'Paradigmatic controversies, contradictions, and emerging confluences.' In N. K. Denzin and Y.S. Lincoln (eds), *Handbook of Qualitative Research* (2nd edn). Thousand Oaks, CA: Sage. Pp. 163–88.

Lindesmith, A. R. 1937. *The Nature of Opiate Addiction*. Chicago: University of Chicago Press.

—— 1968. *Addiction and Opiates*. Chicago: Aldine

Lofland, J. 1967. 'Notes on naturalism.' *Kansas Journal of Sociology* 3: 45–61.

——1971. *Analyzing Social Settings: A Guide to Qualitative Observation and Analysis*. Belmont, CA: Wadsworth.

Lorr, M. 1983. *Cluster Analysis for Social Scientists*. San Francisco, CA: Jossey-Bass.

Lowe, G. D. and T. K. Pinhey 1982. 'Rural–urban differences in support for environmental protection.' *Rural Sociology* 47: 114–28.

Lowe, G. D., T. K. Pinhey and M. D. Grimes 1980. 'Public support for environmental protection: new evidence from national surveys.' *Pacific Sociological Review* 23: 423–45.

Lundberg, G. A. 1929. *Social Research*. New York: Longman, Green.

—— 1942. *Social Research: A Study in Methods of Gathering Data* (2nd edn). New York: Longman, Green.

Luyben, P. D. and J. S. Bailey 1979. 'Newspaper recycling: the effects of rewards and proximity of containers.' *Environment and Behavior* 11: 539–57.

Lynd, R. S. and H. M. Lynd 1937. *Middletown in Transition: A Study in Cultural Conflicts*. New York: Harcourt, Brace and Co.

—— 1956. *Middletown: A Study of American Culture*. New York: Harvest Books.

Mannheim, K. 1952. 'The problem of generations.' In *Essays on the Sociology of Knowledge*. New York: Oxford University Press. Pp. 276–320.

Maranell, G. M. (ed.) 1974/2007. *Scaling: A Sourcebook for Behavioral Scientists*. New Brunswick, NJ: Transaction.

Markley, O. W. 1964. 'A simulation of the SIVA model of organizational behavior.' *American Journal of Sociology* 73: 339–47.

Marsh, C. 1982. *The Survey Method: The Contribution of Surveys to Sociological Explanation*. London: Allen and Unwin.

Marshall, C. and G. B. Rossman 2006. *Designing Qualitative Research* (4th edn). Thousand Oaks, CA: Sage.

Martin, P. Y. and B. A. Turner 1986. 'Grounded theory and organizational research.' *Journal of Applied Behavioral Science* 22: 141–57.

Martindale, D. 1960. *The Nature and Types of Sociological Theory*. Boston, MA: Houghton Mifflin.

Marx, G. T. and D. McAdam 1994. *Collective Behavior and Social Movements*. Englewood Cliffs, NJ: Prentice-Hall.

Mason, J. 1996. *Qualitative Researching*. London: Sage.

—— 2002. *Qualitative Researching* (2nd edn). London: Sage.

Mathison, S. 2004. *Encyclopedia of Evaluation*. London: Sage.

Matza, D. 1969. *Becoming Deviant*. Englewood Cliffs, NJ: Prentice-Hall.

Maxwell, J. A. 2005. *Qualitative Research Design: An Interactive Approach*. (2nd edn). Thousand Oaks, CA: Sage.

Maynard, M. and J. Purvis (eds) 1994. *Researching Women's Lives from a Feminist Perspective*. London: Taylor and Francis.

McClelland, L. and R. J. Canter 1981. 'Psychological research on energy conservation: context, approaches, methods.' In A. Baum and J. E. Singer (eds), *Advances in Environmental Psychology*, vol. 3: *Energy Conservation: Psychological Perspectives*. Hillsdale, NJ: Lawrence Erlbaum.

McCracken, G. 1990. *The Long Interview*. Beverly Hills, CA: Sage.

McGuire, W. J. 1968. 'The nature of attitudes and attitude change.' In G. Lindzey and E. Aronson (eds), *The Handbook of Social Psychology*, vol. 3 (2nd edn). Reading MA: Addison-Wesley. Pp. 136–314.

McIntyre, A. 2008. *Participatory Action Research*. Los Angeles, CA: Sage.

McIver, J. P. and E. G. Carmines 1981. *Unidimensional Scaling*. Beverly Hills, CA: Sage.

McMillan, J. H. and S. Schumacher 2001. *Research in Education: A Conceptual Introduction* (5th edn). New York: Longman.

McNiff, J. and J. Whitehead 2006. *All You Need to Know About Action Research*. London: Sage.

McStay, J. R. and R. E. Dunlap 1983. 'Male–female differences in concern for environmental quality.' *International Journal of Women's Studies* 6: 291–301.

Menzies, K. 1982. *Sociological Theory in Use*. London: Routledge and Kegan Paul.

Merton, R. K. 1967. *On Theoretical Sociology*. New York: Free Press.

Mies, M. 1983. 'Towards a methodology for feminist research.' In G. Bowles and R. D. Klein (eds), *Theories of Women's Studies*. London: Routledge and Kegan Paul. Pp. 117–39.

Miles, M. B. and A. M. Huberman 1994. *Qualitative Data Analysis: An Expanded Sourcebook* (2nd edn). Thousand Oaks, CA: Sage.

Miller, R. L. 2000. *Researching Life Stories and Family Histories*. London: Sage.

Mills, C. W. 1959. *The Sociological Imagination*. New York: Oxford University Press.

Millward, L. J. 2007. 'Focus groups.' In G. M. Breakwell, S. Hammond, C. Fife-Schaw and J. A. Smith (eds), *Research Methods in Psychology* (3rd edn). London: Sage. Pp. 274–98.

Minichiello, V., R. Aroni and T. Hays 2008. *In-Depth Interviewing: Principles, Techniques, Analysis* (3rd edn). Sydney: Pearson.

Mitchell, J. C. 1983. 'Case and situation analysis.' *Sociological Review* 31(2): 187–211.

Mitchell, M. and J. Jolley 1992. *Research Design Explained* (2nd edn). New York: Harcourt Brace Jovanovich.

—— 2007. *Research Design Explained* (6th edn). New York: Harcourt Brace Jovanovich.

Mohai, P. and B. W. Twight 1987. 'Age and environmentalism: an elaboration of the Buttel model using national survey evidence.' *Social Science Quarterly* 68: 798–815.

Morgan, D. L. 1988. *Focus Groups as Qualitative Research*. Newbury Park, CA: Sage.

—— 1998. 'Practical strategies for combining qualitative and quantitative methods: Applications to Health Research.' *Qualitative Health Research* 8 (3): 362–76.

—— 2000. 'Focus group interviewing.' In J. Gubrium and J. Holstein (eds), *Handbook of Interview Research*. Thousand Oaks, CA: Sage. Pp. 141–60.

—— 2007. 'Paradigms lost and pragmatism regained: methodological implication of combining qualitative and quantitative methods.' *Journal of Mixed Methods Research* 1 (1): 48–76.

Morse, J. M. 1991. 'Approaches to qualitative-quantitative methodological triangulation.' *Nursing Research* 40: 120–3.

Morse, J. M. and L. Richards 2002. *Readme First for a User's Guide to Qualitative Methods*. Thousand Oaks, CA: Sage.

Moser, C. A. and G. Kalton 1971. *Survey Methods in Social Investigation* (2nd edn). London: Heinemann.

Murray, R. 2002. *How to Write a Thesis*. Maidenhead: Open University Press.

Nelissen, N. and P. Scheepers 1992. 'Ecological consciousness and behaviour examined: an empirical study in the Netherlands.' *Sociale Wetenschappen* 35 (4): 64–81.

Neuman, W. L. 1997. *Social Research Methods: Qualitative and Quantitative Approaches* (3rd edn). Boston, MA: Allyn and Bacon.

—— 2006. *Social Research Methods: Qualitative and Quantitative Approaches* (6th edn). Boston, MA: Allyn and Bacon.

—— 2007. *Basics of Social Research: Qualitative and Quantitative Approaches* (2nd edn). Boston, MA: Allyn and Bacon.

Newsom, T. J. and U. J. Makranczy 1978. 'Reducing electricity consumption of residents living in mass metered dormitory complexes.' *Journal of Environmental Systems* 1: 215–36.

Northcutt, N. and D. McCoy 2004. *Interactive Qualitative Analysis: A Systems Method for Qualitative Research*. Thousand Oaks, CA: Sage.

O'Hear, A. 1989. *An Introduction to the Philosophy of Science*. Oxford: Clarendon Press.

Ong, B. K. 2005. 'The experience of work: a case study of Chinese sales workers in an electronics company and a life insurance company.' PhD thesis, University of Science, Malaysia.

Oppenheim, A. N. 1992. *Questionnaire Design, Interviewing and Attitude Measurement*. London: Pinter.

Outhwaite, W. 1975. *Understanding Social Life: The Method Called Verstehen*. London: Allen and Unwin.

—— 1987. *New Philosophies of Social Science: Realism, Hermeneutics and Critical Theory*. London: Macmillan.

Pardini, A. U. and R. D. Katzev 1983/4. 'The effects of strength of commitment on newspaper recycling.' *Journal of Environmental Systems* 13: 245–54.

Parsons, T. and E. A. Shils 1951. 'Introduction' to Part 2, 'Values, motives, and systems of action.' In T. Parsons and A. E. Shils (eds), *Toward a General Theory of Action*. Cambridge, MA: Harvard University Press. Pp. 47–52.

Patton, M. Q. 1990. *Qualitative Evaluation and Research Methods*. (2nd edn). Newbury Park, CA: Sage.

Pawson, R. 1989. *A Measure for Measures: A Manifesto for Empirical Sociology*. London: Routledge.

—— 1995. 'Quality and quantity, agency and structure, mechanism and context, dons and cons.' *Bulletin de Méthodologie Sociologique* 47 (June): 5–48.

—— 1996. 'Theorizing the interview.' *British Journal of Sociology* 47 (2): 295–314.

—— 2000. 'Middle-range realism.' *Archives Européennes de Sociologie* 41: 283–325.

—— 2006. *Evidence-Based Policy: A Realist Perspective*. London: Sage.

Pawson, R. and N. Tilley 1994. 'What works in evaluation research?' *British Journal of Criminology* 36: 291–306.

——1997. *Realistic Evaluation*. London: Sage.

Perks, R. and A. Thomson (eds). 2006. *The Oral History Reader*, 2nd edn. London: Routledge.

Pettus, A. 1976. 'Environmental education and environmental attitudes.' *Journal of Environmental Education* 8: 48–51.

Pfaffenberger, B. 1988. *Microcomputer Applications in Qualitative Research*. Beverly Hills, CA: Sage.

Plano Clark, V. L. and J. W. Creswell (eds) 2008. *The Mixed Methods Reader*. Thousand Oaks, CA: Sage.

Platt, J. 1988. 'What can case studies do?' *Studies in Qualitative Methodology* 1: 1–23.

—— 1996. *A History of Sociological Research Methods in America 1920–1960*. Cambridge: Cambridge University Press.

Plummer, K. 2001a. *Documents of Life 2: An Invitation to a Critical Humanism*. London: Sage.

—— 2001b. 'The call of life histories in ethnographic research.' In P. Atkinson *et al.* (eds), *Handbook of Ethnography*. London: Sage. Pp. 395–406.

Popper, K. R. 1959. *The Logic of Scientific Discovery*. London: Hutchinson.

—— 1961. *The Poverty of Historicism*. London: Routledge and Kegan Paul.

Priest, J. G. 1997. 'A framework to manage delivery of information systems.' M. Eng. Thesis, RMIT University, Melbourne.

—— 2000. 'Managing investments in information systems: Exploring effective practice.' DBA thesis, RMIT University, Melbourne.

Punch, K. F. 2005. *Introduction to Social Research* (2nd edn). London: Sage.

—— 2006. *Developing Effective Research Proposals* (2nd edn). London: Sage.

Queen, S. 1928. 'Round table on the case study in sociological research.' *Publications of the American Sociological Society* 22.

Ragin, C. C. and H. S. Becker 1989. 'How the microcomputer is changing our analytic habits.' In E. Brent and J. L. McCartney (eds), *New Technology in Sociology*. New Brunswick, NJ: Transaction Press.

Raison, T. (ed.) 1969. *The Founding Fathers of Social Science*. Harmondsworth: Penguin.

Ramazanoğlu, C. and J. Holland 2002. *Feminist Methodology: Challenges and Critiques*. London: Sage.

Ramsey, C. E. and R. E. Rickson 1976. 'Environmental knowledge and attitudes.' *Journal of Environmental Education* 8: 10–18.

Reason, P. and H. Bradbury (eds). 2008. *The Sage Handbook of Action Research: Participatory Inquiry and Practice*. London: Sage.

Reichardt, C. S. and T. D. Cook 1979. 'Beyond qualitative *versus* quantitative methods.' In T. D. Cook and C. S. Reichardt (eds.), *Qualitative and Quantitative Methods in Evaluation Research*. Beverly Hills, CA: Sage. Pp. 7–32.

Reichardt, C. S. and S. F. Rallis (eds). 1994. *The Qualitative–Quantitative Debate: New Perspectives*. San Francisco: Jossey-Bass.

Reid, D. H., P. D. Luyben, R. J. Rawers and J. S. Bailey 1976. 'Newspaper recycling behavior: the effects of prompting and proximity of containers.' *Environment and Behavior* 8: 471–81.

Reynolds, P. D. 1971. *A Primer in Theory Construction*. Indianapolis, IN: Bobbs-Merrill.

Richards, L. and T. Richards 1987. 'Qualitative data analysis: can computers do it?' *The Australian and New Zealand Journal of Sociology* 23: 23–36.

—— 1991. 'The transformation of qualitative method: computational paradigms and research processes.' In N. Fielding and R. Lee (eds), *Using Computers in Qualitative Research*. London: Sage. Pp. 38–53.

—— 1994. 'From filing cabinet to computer.' In A. Bryman and R. G. Burgess (eds), *Analyzing Qualitative Data*. London: Routledge. Pp. 146–72.

Richmond, J. M. and N. Baumgart 1981. 'A hierarchical analysis of environmental attitudes.' *Journal of Environmental Education* 13: 31–7.

Ricoeur, P. 1981. 'What is a text? Explanation and Understanding.' In J. B. Thompson (ed.), *Paul Ricoeur, Hermeneutics and the Social Sciences*. Cambridge: Cambridge University Press. Pp. 145–64.

Riggs, P. L. 1992. *Whys and Ways of Science: Introducing Philosophical and Sociological Theories of Science*. Melbourne: University of Melbourne Press.

Ritchie, D. 1995. *Doing Oral History*. New York: Twayne.

Ritzer, G. 1980. *Sociology: A Multiple Paradigm Science* (rev. edn). Boston, MA: Allyn and Bacon.

—— (ed.) 2003. *The Blackwell Companion to Major Classical Theorists*. Malden, MA: Blackwell.

—— (ed.) 2005. *Encyclopedia of Social Theory*. Thousand Oaks, CA: Sage.

Ritzer, G. and D. J. Goodman 2007a. *Classical Social Theory* (5th edn). New York: McGraw-Hill.

—— 2007b. *Modern Sociological Theory* (7th edn). New York: McGraw-Hill.

Robinson, W. S. 1951. 'The logical structure of analytic induction.' *American Sociological Review* 16: 812–18.

Rosenberg, M. 1968. *The Logic of Survey Analysis*. New York: Basic Books.

Rossi, P. H. and H. E. Freeman 1985. *Evaluation: A Systematic Approach* (3rd edn). Beverly Hills, CA: Sage.

Rossman, G. B. and B. L. Wilson 1985. 'Numbers and words: combining quantitative and qualitative methods in a single large-scale evaluation study.' *Evaluation Research* 9 (5): 627–43.

Ryan, G. W. and H. R. Bernard 2000. 'Data management and analysis methods.' In N. K. Denzin and Y. S. Lincoln (eds), *Handbook of Qualitative Research* (2nd edn). Thousand Oaks, CA: Sage. Pp. 769–802.

Salleh, A. K. 1984. 'From feminism to ecology.' *Social Alternatives* 4: 8–12.

—— 1988/9. 'Environmental consciousness and action: an Australian study.' *Journal of Environmental Education* 20: 26–31.

Samdahl, D. M. and R. Robertson 1989. 'Social determinants of environmental concern: specification and test of the model.' *Environment and Behavior* 21: 57–81.

Sandelowski, M. 2000. 'Combining qualitative and quantitative sampling, data collection, and analysis techniques in mixed-method studies.' *Research in Nursing and Health* 23: 246–55.

Sarantakos, S. 2005. *Social Research* (3rd edn). New York: Palgrave Macmillan.

Sayer, A. 1992. *Method in Social Science: A Realist Approach* (2nd edn). London: Routledge.

—— 2000. *Realism and Social Science*. London: Sage.

Scheaffer, R. L., W. Mendenhall and L. Ott 1996. *Elementary Survey Sampling* (5th edn). Belmont, CA: Duxbury Press.

Scheepers, P. and N. Nelissen 1989. 'Environmental consciousness in The Netherlands.' *Netherlands Journal of Housing and Environmental Research* 4 (3): 199–216.

Schmuck, R. A. (ed.). 2009. *Practical Action Research* (2nd edn). Thousand Oaks, CA: Sage.

Schofield, J. W. 1993. 'Increasing the generalizability of qualitative research.' In M. Hammersley (ed.), *Social Research: Philosophy, Politics and Practice*. London: Sage. Pp. 200–25.

Schütz, A. 1945. 'On multiple realities.' *Philosophy and Phenomenological Research* 5: 533–76.

—— 1963a. 'Concept and theory formation in the social sciences.' In M. A. Natanson (ed.), *Philosophy of the Social Sciences*. New York: Random House. Pp. 231–49.

—— 1963b. 'Common-sense and scientific interpretation of human action.' In M. A. Natanson (ed.), *Philosophy of the Social Sciences*. New York: Random House. Pp. 302–46.

Scott, J. 1995. *Sociological Theory: Contemporary Debates*. Aldershot: Edward Elgar.

Seale, C. 1999. *The Quality of Qualitative Research*. London: Sage.

—— 2002. 'Computer-assisted analysis of qualitative interview data.' In J. Gubrium and J. Holstein (eds), *Handbook of Interview Research*. Thousand Oaks, CA: Sage. Pp. 651–70.

—— (ed.) 2004. *Researching Society and Culture* (2nd edn). London: Sage.

—— 2005. 'Using computers to analyse qualitative data.' In D. Silverman (ed.), *Doing Qualitative Research: A Practical Handbook* (2nd edn). London: Sage. Pp. 188–208.

Sedlack, R. G. and J. Stanley 1992. *Social Research: Theory and Methods*. Boston, MA: Allyn and Bacon.

Seidel, J. V. and J. A. Clark 1984. 'The ethnograph: A computer program for the analysis of qualitative data.' *Qualitative Sociology* 7: 110–25.

Seltiz, C., L. S. Wrightsman and S. W. Cook 1976. *Research Methods in Social Relations* (3rd edn). New York: Holt, Rinehart and Winston.

Shaughnessy, J. J., E. B. Zechmeister and J. S. Zechmeister 2006. *Research Methods in Psychology* (7th edn). Boston, MA: McGraw-Hill.

Shaw, C. 1927. 'Case study method.' *Publications of the American Sociological Society* 21: 149–57.

Shaw, I. F., J. C. Greene and M. M. Mark (eds.) 2006. *Handbook of Evaluation: Policy, Programs and Practices*. London: Sage.

Sieber, S. D. 1973. 'The integration of fieldwork and survey methods.' *American Sociological Review* 78 (6): 1335–59.

Silverman, D. 2001. *Interpreting Qualitative Data: Methods for Analysing Talk, Text and Interaction*, 2nd edn. London: Sage.

—— (ed.). 2005. *Doing Qualitative Research: A Practical Handbook* (2nd edn). London: Sage.

Smaling, A. 1994. 'The pragmatic dimension: paradigmatic and pragmatic aspects of choosing a qualitative or quantitative method.' *Quality and Quantity* 28: 233–49.

Smith, H. M. 1981. *Strategies of Social Research: The Methodological Imagination* (2nd edn). Englewood Cliffs, NJ: Prentice-Hall.

Smith, J. K. 1983. 'Quantitative versus qualitative research: an attempt to clarify the issue.' *Educational Researcher* 12 (3): 6–13.

Smith, M. J. 1998. *Social Science in Question*. London: Sage.

Smith, P. B. 1995. 'Industry transition and sustainable development: management perspectives in the urban water industry.' PhD thesis, Royal Melbourne Institute of Technology, Melbourne.

Somekh, B. 2006. *Action Research: A Methodology for Change and Development*. Maidenhead: Open University Press.

Sorensen, A. B. 1978. 'Mathematical models in sociology.' *Annual Review of Sociology* 4: 345–71.

Spencer, H. 1891. *The Study of Sociology*. New York: Appleton.

Spradley, J. P. 1979. *The Ethnographic Interview*. New York: Holt, Rinehart and Winston.

—— 1980. *Participant Observation*. New York: Holt, Rinehart and Winston.

Stacy, S. J. G. 1983. 'Limitations of ageing: old people and caring professions.' PhD thesis, Monash University, Melbourne.

Stake, R. E. 1978. 'The case-study method in social inquiry.' *Educational Researcher* 7: 5–8.

—— 2005. 'Qualitative case studies.' In N. K. Denzin and Y. S. Lincoln (eds), *The Sage Handbook of Qualitative Research* (3rd edn). Thousand Oaks, CA: Sage. Pp. 443–66.

Stanley, L. and S. Wise 1993. *Breaking Out Again: Feminist Ontology and Epistemology* (new edn). London: Routledge.

Steckler, A., K. R. McLeroy, R. M. Goodman, S. T. Bird and L. McCormick 1992. 'Toward integrating qualitative and quantitative methods: an introduction.' *Health Education Quarterly* 19 (1): 1–8.

Stern, E. (ed.) 2005. *Evaluation Research Methods*, 4 vols. London: Sage.

Stewart, D. W., P. N. Shamdasani and D. W. Cook 2007. *Focus Groups: Theory and Practice* (2nd edn). Thousand Oaks, CA: Sage.

Stinchcombe, A. 1968. *Construction of Social Theories*. New York: Harcourt BraceWorld.

Stouffer, S. A., L. Guttman, E. A. Suchman, P. F. Lazarsfeld, S. A. Star and J. A. Clausen 1950. *Measurement and Prediction*. Princeton, NJ: Princeton University Press.

Strauss, A. L. 1987. *Qualitative Analysis for Social Scientists*. Cambridge: Cambridge University Press.

Strauss, A. and J. Corbin 1990. *Basics of Qualitative Research: Grounded Theory Procedures and Techniques*. Newbury Park, CA: Sage.

——1998. *Basics of Qualitative Research: Techniques and Procedures for Developing Grounded Theory* (2nd edn). Thousand Oaks, CA: Sage.

Stringer, E. T. 2007. *Action Research* (3rd edn). Thousand Oaks, CA: Sage.

Stuart, A. 1984. *The Ideas of Sampling*. New York: Oxford University Press.

Stufflebeam, D. L. and A. J. Shinkfield 2007. *Evaluation Theory, Models and Applications*. San Francisco, CA: Wiley.

Tashakkori, A. and C. Teddlie 1998. *Mixed Methodology: Combining Qualitative and Quantitative Approaches*. Thousand Oaks, CA: Sage.

—— (eds), 2003a. *Handbook of Mixed Methods in Social and Behavioral Research*. Thousand Oaks, CA: Sage.

—— 2003b. 'The past and future of mixed methods research: From data triangulation to mixed model designs.' In A. Tashakkori and C. Teddlie (eds), *Handbook of Mixed Methods in Social and Behavioral Science*. Thousand Oaks, CA: Sage. Pp. 671–701.

Taylor, C. 1964. *The Explanation of Behaviour*. London; Routledge and Kegan Paul.

Teddlie, C. and A. Tashakkori 2003. 'Major issues and controversies in the use of mixed methods in social and behavioural sciences. In A. Tashakkori and C. Teddlie (eds), *Handbook of Mixed Methods in Social and Behavioral Science*. Thousand Oaks, CA: Sage. Pp. 3–50.

Tesch, R. 1990. *Qualitative Research: Analysis Types and Software Tools*. New York: Falmer.

Thomas, W. I. and F. Znaniecki 1927. *The Polish Peasant in Europe and America*. New York: Alfred A. Knopf.

Thompson, J. B. 1981. *Critical Hermeneutics: A Study in the Thought of Paul Ricoeur and Jürgen Habermas*. Cambridge: Cambridge University Press.

Thurstone, L. L. and E. J. Chave 1929. *The Measurement of Attitudes*. Chicago, IL: University of Chicago Press.

Todd, Z., B. Nerlich, S. McKeowen and D.C. Clarke (eds), 2004. *Mixing Methods in Psychology: The Integration of Quantitative and Qualitative Methods in Theory and Practice*. London: Psychology Press.

Treiman, D. J. 1976. 'A comment on Professor Lewis Coser's Presidential Address.' *The American Sociologist* 11: 27–33.

Trow, M. 1957. 'Comment on participation observation and interviewing: A comparison.' *Human Organization* 16: 3–5.

Turner, B. A. 1981. 'Some practical aspects of qualitative data analysis: one way of organising the cognitive processes associated with the generation of grounded theory.' *Quality and Quantity* 15: 225–47.

—— 1994. 'Patterns of crisis behaviour: a qualitative inquiry.' In A. Bryman and R. G. Burgess (eds), *Analyzing Qualitative Data*. London: Routledge. Pp. 195–215.

Turner, J. H. 1987. 'Analytical theorizing.' In A. Giddens and J. H. Turner (eds), *Social Theory Today*. Cambridge: Polity; Stanford, CA: Stanford University Press. Pp. 156–94.

—— 1991. *The Structure of Sociological Theory* (5th edn). Belmont, CA: Wadsworth.

Turner, R. H. 1953. 'The quest for universals in sociological research.' *American Sociological Review* 18(6): 604–11.

Turner, R. H. and L. M. Killian 1972. *Collective Behavior* (2nd edn). Englewood Cliffs, NJ: Prentice-Hall.

Tuso, M. W. and E. S. Geller 1976. 'Behavior analysis applied to environmental/ecological problems: a review.' *Journal of Applied Behavior Analysis* 9: 526.

Twinn, S. 2003. 'Status of mixed methods research in nursing.' In A. Tashakkori and C. Teddlie (eds), *Handbook of Mixed Methods in Social and Behavioral Science*. Thousand Oaks, CA: Sage. Pp. 541–6.

van Krieken, R., P. Smith, D. Habibis, K. McDonald, M. Haralambos and M. Holborn 2000. *Sociology: Themes and Perspectives* (2nd edn). Frenchs Forest, NSW: Pearson.

van Liere, K. D. and R. E. Dunlap 1980. 'Social bases of environmental concern: a review of hypotheses, explanations and empirical evidence.' *Public Opinion Quarterly* 44: 181–97.

Vanclay, F. and D. A. Bronstein (eds) 1995. *Environmental and Social Impact Assessment*. Chichester: John Wiley.

Vicker, A. W. 1969. 'Attitudes vs. action: the relationship of verbal and overt behavior responses to attitudinal objects.' *Journal of Social Issues* 25: 41–78.

Vining, J. and A. Ebreo 1990. 'What makes a recycler? A comparison of recyclers and nonrecyclers.' *Environment and Behavior* 22: 55–73.

von Wright, G. H. 1971. *Explanation and Understanding*. London: Routledge and Kegan Paul.

Wallace, R. A. and A. Wolf 2006. *Contemporary Sociological Theory: Expanding the Classical Tradition* (6th edn). Upper Saddle River, NJ: Prentice-Hall.

Wallace, W. L. 1971. *The Logic of Science in Sociology*. Chicago, IL: Aldine-Atherton.
—— 1983. *Principles of Scientific Sociology*. Chicago, IL: Aldine.
Warner, W. L. and P. S Lunt 1941. *The Social Life of a Modern Community*. New Haven: Yale University Press.
Waters, M. 1994. *Modern Sociological Theory*. London: Sage.
Wathern, P (ed.). 1988. *Environmental Impact Assessment: Theory and Practice*. London: Unwin Hyman.
Webb, B. 1948. *My Apprenticeship*. London: Longman, Green and Co.
Webb, E. J., D. T. Campbell, R. D. Schwartz and L. Sechrest 1966. *Unobtrusive Measures: Nonreactive Research in the Social Sciences*. Chicago IL: Rand McNally.
Weber, M. 1958. *The Protestant Ethic and the Spirit of Capitalism*. New York: Scribner.
—— 1964. *The Theory of Social and Economic Organization*, trans. A. M. Henderson and T. Parsons. New York: Free Press.
Weiss, C. H. 1972. *Evaluation Research: Methods for Assessing Program Effectiveness*. Englewood Cliffs, NJ: Prentice-Hall.
—— 1976. 'Using research in the policy process: potential and constraints.' *Policy Studies Journal* 4: 224–8.
Weiss, C. H. and M. Bucuvalas 1980. *Social Science Research and Decision-Making*. New York: Columbia University Press.
Weitzman, E. A. 2000. 'Software and qualitative research.' In N. K. Denzin and Y. S. Lincoln (eds), *Handbook of Qualitative Research* (2nd edn). Thousand Oaks, CA: Sage. Pp. 803–20.
Whitehead, J. and J. McNiff 2006. *Action Research: Living Theory*. London: Sage.
Whyte, W. F. 1943. *Street Corner Society*. Chicago, IL: University of Chicago Press.
—— 1984. *Learning from the Field: A Guide from Experience*. Beverly Hills, CA: Sage.
—— (ed.) 1991. *Participatory Action Research*. Newbury Park, CA: Sage.
Willer, D. 1967. *Scientific Sociology: Theory and Method*. Englewood Cliffs, NJ: Prentice-Hall.
Williams, M. and T. May 1996. *Introduction to the Philosophy of Social Research*. London: UCL Press.
Winch, P. 1958. *The Idea of Social Science*. London: Routledge and Kegan Paul.
Winter, R. 1987. *Action Research and the Nature of Social Inquiry*. Aldershot: Avebury.
—— 1989. *Learning from Experience: Principles and Practice in Action Research*. London: Falmer.
Witmer, J. F. and E. S. Geller 1976. 'Facilitating paper recycling: effects of prompts, raffles, and contexts.' *Journal of Applied Behavior Analysis* 9: 315–22.
Yin, R. K. 1984. *Case Study Research: Design and Methods*. Newbury Park, CA: Sage.
—— 2003a. *Case Study Research: Design and Methods* (3rd edn). Thousand Oaks, CA: Sage.
—— 2003b. *Applications of Case Study Research* (2nd edn). Thousand Oaks, CA: Sage.
Young, P. 1939. *Scientific Social Surveys and Research*. New York: Prentice-Hall.
Yow, V. R. 1994. *Recording Oral Histories: A Practical Guide for Social Scientists*. Newbury Park, CA: Sage.
Zanna, M. P. and R. H. Fazio 1982. 'The attitude–behavior relation: moving toward a third generation of research.' In M. P. Zanna, E. T. Higgins and C. P. Herman (eds), *Consistency in Social Behavior: The Ontario Symposium*, vol. 2. Hillsdale, NJ: Erlbaum. Pp. 283–301.
Zelditch, M. 1962. 'Some methodological problems of field studies.' *American Journal of Sociology* 67: 566–76.
Znaniecki, F. 1934. *The Method of Sociology*. New York: Farrar and Rinehart.
Zuber-Skerrit, O. (ed.) 1996. *New Directions in Action Research*. London: Falmer.

Index